3/98

~~INVENTIONS~~

~~OF THE~~

~~MARCH HARE~~

By T. S. Eliot

THE COMPLETE POEMS AND PLAYS OF T. S. ELIOT

poetry

COLLECTED POEMS 1909–1962

FOUR QUARTETS

THE WASTE LAND AND OTHER POEMS

THE WASTE LAND
A Facsimile and Transcript of the Original Drafts
Including the Annotations of Ezra Pound
Edited by Valerie Eliot

SELECTED POEMS

OLD POSSUM'S BOOK OF PRACTICAL CATS

GROWLTIGER'S LAST STAND AND OTHER POEMS

ANABASIS, BY ST.-JOHN PERSE
Translated by T. S. Eliot

plays

THE COMPLETE PLAYS OF T. S. ELIOT

MURDER IN THE CATHEDRAL

THE FAMILY REUNION

THE COCKTAIL PARTY

THE CONFIDENTIAL CLERK

THE ELDER STATESMAN

literary criticism

SELECTED ESSAYS

THE USE OF POETRY AND THE USE OF CRITICISM

TO CRITICIZE THE CRITIC

ON POETRY AND POETS

ESSAYS ON ELIZABETHAN DRAMA

FOR LANCELOT ANDREWES

SELECTED PROSE OF T. S. ELIOT
Edited by Frank Kermode

THE VARIETIES OF METAPHYSICAL POETRY
Edited by Ronald Schuchard

social criticism

THE IDEA OF A CHRISTIAN SOCIETY
Edited by David Edwards

NOTES TOWARDS THE DEFINITION OF CULTURE

correspondence

THE LETTERS OF T. S. ELIOT, VOLUME I: 1898–1922
Edited by Valerie Eliot

T. S. ELIOT

INVENTIONS OF THE MARCH HARE

POEMS 1909–1917

edited by
Christopher Ricks

HARCOURT BRACE & COMPANY
New York   San Diego   London

Library of Congress Cataloging-in-Publication Data
Eliot, T. S. (Thomas Stearns), 1888–1965.
Inventions of the March Hare: poems 1909–1917/by T. S. Eliot;
edited by Christopher Ricks.
p.   cm.
Includes index.
ISBN 0-15-100274-6
I. Ricks, Christopher B.   II. Title.
PS3509.L43I58   1997
821'.912—dc21   96-45399

Text set in Sabon

Printed in the United States of America

First U. S. edition

A C E F D B

Illustration on page i (reduced 50%)

[Inventions of the March Hare]
This title, in black ink, crossed through by TSE,
is on the blank flyleaf at the front of the Notebook. For
TSE's title on the front free endpaper, *Complete Poems
of T. S. Eliot,* and for the preference here given to
Inventions of the March Hare, see pp. 3–5.

Contents

APPENDIX A

APPENDIX B

APPENDIX C

APPENDIX D

Preface

The Manuscripts

On 21 August 1922, T. S. Eliot wrote from London to John Quinn in New York. Quinn, lawyer and patron, had been generous to Eliot, who was writing to him now about giving him the manuscript of *The Waste Land*. (The poem was to appear in *The Criterion* in October 1922, in *The Dial* in November, and as a volume from Boni and Liveright in December.) Quinn had insisted: 'I shall be glad to have it, but you must agree to the condition that I send you a draft for what I think it is worth'. Eliot counter-insisted:

I certainly cannot accept your proposal to purchase the manuscript at your own price, and if you will not accept it in recognition of what you have done for me lately and in the past, it will not be any pleasure to me to sell it to you. I therefore hope that you will accept it. But as I feel that perhaps you like some of my early poems best I should be glad, for example, to send you the manuscript of "Prufrock" instead, and I hope you will let me do this.

Quinn did not demur, but accepted *The Waste Land* manuscript as a gift on condition that he might buy the manuscript of the early poems. His letter to Eliot said:

We won't quarrel about the MS. of The Waste Land. I'll accept it from you, not "for what I have lately done for you and in the past", but as a mark of friendship, but on this condition: That you will let me purchase of you the MS. of the Early Poems that you referred to. If you have the Prufrock only, then I'll purchase that. But if you have the MS. of the whole volume of your poems, including the Prufrock, I should *greatly value* that, and then I'll have two complete manuscripts of yours.[1]

Quinn paid $140, £29.14.10.

Eliot described the Notebook to Quinn on 21 September 1922:

The leather bound notebook is one which I started in 1909 and in which I entered all my work of that time as I wrote it, so that it is the only original manuscript barring of

---

1 *The Waste Land: A Facsimile and Transcript of the Original Drafts*, ed. Valerie Eliot (1971), pp.xxiii–iv, xxvi. *The Letters of T. S. Eliot*, volume i: *1898–1922*, ed. Valerie Eliot (1988), pp.563–4.

course rough scraps and notes, which were destroyed at the time, in existence. You will find a great many sets of verse which have never been printed and which I am sure you will agree never ought to be printed, and in putting them in your hands, I beg you fervently to keep them to yourself and see that they never are printed.[2]

More than once, Eliot deprecated these early poems. There is a letter to B. L. Reid, 23 July 1963, which refers to the poems in the Notebook (its whereabouts then unknown to Eliot), as 'unpublished and unpublishable'.[3] And there is his letter to Daniel Woodward, 3 April 1964: 'I cannot feel altogether sorry that this [typescript] and the notebook have disappeared. The unpublished poems in the notebook were not worth publishing'.[4]

Quinn died in 1924. When in 1965 Eliot died, he had never learned what had become of these early manuscripts.

The earliest poems in the Notebook are dated, by Eliot, Nov. 1909. There is in the Notebook only one poem – *Humouresque (After J. Laforgue)* – of the seven which, between 24 May 1907 and 24 June 1910, he published in the *Harvard Advocate*.[5]

For all the continuity, then, with the Laforguean elements in some of the *Harvard Advocate* poems – strongest in the one that Eliot has in the Notebook, *Humouresque (After J. Laforgue)* – it is clear that the Notebook promised a fresh start, one which was to issue, in 1917, in *Prufrock and Other Observations*. For the Notebook, which opens with a poem which went into *Prufrock and Other Observations* (*Conversation Galante*), contains *The Love Song of J. Alfred Prufrock*, *Portrait of a Lady*, *Preludes* (IV being on a separate leaf laid in), and *Morning at the Window*. *Rhapsody on a Windy Night* and *Mr. Apollinax* are among the loose leaves now with the Notebook; so, of the poems in *Prufrock and Other Observations*, only five are unrepresented: *The 'Boston Evening Transcript', Aunt Helen, Cousin Nancy, Hysteria* and *La Figlia Che Piange*.

2 *Letters* i 572.
3 B. L. Reid, *The Man from New York: John Quinn and His Friends* (1968), p.540.
4 Daniel H. Woodward, *Notes on the Publishing History and Text of The Waste Land* (*Papers of the Bibliographical Society of America*, lviii, 1964, 268).
5 For these, see *Poems Written in Early Youth* (1967): *Song. When we came home across the hill* (24 May 1907); *Before Morning* (13 Nov. 1908); *Circe's Palace* (25 Nov. 1908); *Song: The moonflower opens to the moth* (26 Jan. 1909); *On a Portrait* (26 Jan. 1909); *Nocturne* (12 Nov. 1909); *Humouresque (After J. Laforgue)* (12 Jan. 1910); *Spleen* (26 Jan. 1910); and [*Harvard Class*] *Ode* (24 June 1910).

The Notebook has in addition twenty-seven poems (four on separate leaves laid in), plus *Prufrock's Pervigilium* within *The Love Song of J. Alfred Prufrock*. To these are added, first, the bawdy verses which survive on leaves (now at Yale) excised from the Notebook; and second, from loose papers with the Notebook, a further seventeen poems, two of them in French. The whole runs from 1909 to 1917, the year of *Prufrock and Other Observations*.

These early unpublished poems include five sequences: *Mandarins* (*1–4*); *Easter: Sensations of April* (*i–ii*); *Goldfish* (*i–iv*); *Suite Clownesque* (*i–iv*); and *The Engine* (*i–ii*). Eliot was asked in 1959, 'You seem often to have written poems in sections. Did they begin as separate poems?' He replied: 'That's one way in which my mind does seem to have worked throughout the years poetically – doing things separately and then seeing the possibility of fusing them together, altering them, and making a kind of whole of them.'[6]

The Notebook of Eliot's which contains the poems now published as *Inventions of the March Hare* is in the Berg Collection of the New York Public Library. Together with the long-lost manuscript of *The Waste Land*, it was bought by the Library in 1958 (the year of Eliot's seventieth birthday), but – because of the favouring of B. L. Reid's biography of Quinn – no announcement was made until 25 October 1968, three years after Eliot's death.

Both *The Waste Land* manuscript and the Notebook were described in detail by the great bibliographer of Eliot, Donald Gallup, in the *Times Literary Supplement*, 7 November 1968: *The 'Lost' Manuscripts of T. S. Eliot*. This account (slightly revised) subsequently appeared in the *Bulletin of the New York Public Library* (lxxii, Dec. 1968, 641–52).[7]

6 *Paris Review* 21 (Spring/Summer 1959), p.58. Interview with Donald Hall.
7 See also James Torrens, S.J., *The Hidden Years of the Waste Land Manuscript* (*Santa Clara Review*, lxxvi, 1989, 36–42; reprinted in *Critical Essays on T. S. Eliot's The Waste Land*, ed. Lois A. Cuddy and David H. Hirsch, 1991). He quotes Dr Thomas F. Conroy: 'At no time, so far as my wife [Quinn's niece, who inherited the manuscripts from Quinn's sister] and I know, did T. S. Eliot ever attempt to find out where *The Waste Land* manuscript was. He knew that Quinn had left only one heir, and that all he needed was to make inquiries to find her, and he never did.' In two interviews late in life, Eliot misremembered the financial transaction, the wrong way round: 'I sold it [*The Waste Land* MS] to John Quinn. I also gave him a notebook of unpublished poems, because he had been kind to me in various affairs. That's the last I heard of them. Then he died and they didn't turn up at the sale' (*Paris Review* 21, Spring/Summer 1959, p.53). Quinn 'bought the [*Waste Land*] manuscript from me [. . .] I gave him out of gratitude for

In 1971 there appeared *The Waste Land: A Facsimile and Transcript of the Original Drafts Including the Annotations of Ezra Pound*, edited by Valerie Eliot. This appended, as 'The Miscellaneous Poems', ten poems from certain leaves which did not form part either of *The Waste Land* manuscript itself or of the (earlier) Notebook. These leaves had been judged by Mrs Eliot, in concurrence with Dr Gallup, to belong with, and sometimes to contain draft lines for, *The Waste Land*. 'The Miscellaneous Poems' published in 1971 are: (i) *The Death of Saint Narcissus* (which was 'set up in type apparently for publication in *Poetry*', Oct. 1915, Gallup reported, and was included in *Poems Written in Early Youth*, 1950, 1967); (ii) *Song: The golden foot I may not kiss or clutch* (published as *Song to the Opherian*, in *The Tyro*, April 1921); (iii) *Exequy: Persistent lovers will repair*; (iv) *The Death of the Duchess*; (v) *After the turning of the inspired days*; (vi) *I am the Resurrection and the Life*; (vii) *So through the evening, through the violet air*; (viii) *Elegy: Our prayers dismiss the parting shade*; (ix) *Dirge: Full fathom five your Bleistein lies*; (x) *Those are pearls that were his eyes. See!*

The authoritative account of the Notebook was given by Dr Gallup. It is quoted now, with his kind permission, from the *Bulletin of the New York Public Library*.

Bound in quarter brown leather, with marbled-paper sides, the notebook measures approximately 20.5 × 17 cm. A ticket in the upper-left corner of the inside front cover indicates that it was purchased at Procter Brothers Co., Old Corner Bookstore, Gloucester, Mass. (The Eliots used to spend their summers at a cottage on Eastern Point, Gloucester.) The price seems to have been 25¢. Originally it must have contained 72 leaves of ruled white paper, of which 12 have been excised, 10 leaving traces of stubs. Eight leaves contain manuscript on rectos only, two on versos only, 22 on both rectos and versos, and 28 are blank. The leaves or pages actually written upon (with the exception of the last two) are numbered from 1 to 52, possibly by T. S. Eliot at a later date. (Two leaves at the end of the book have been used by T. S. Eliot with the volume reversed, and the writing therefore appears on their versos, upside-down in relation to the rest of the notebook.) In addition there are five leaves laid in the first part of the notebook, four of them with blank versos, and two leaves are laid in at the end, also both with versos blank. (One of the first group of leaves laid in, that

---

other things he'd done for me another manuscript – a manuscript book of early poems of mine, certain few of which have been printed but most of which remain unprinted' (*Kenyon Review*, xxvii, 1965, p.21; the interview was conducted in 1958). But it was *The Waste Land* manuscript that he gave, and the Notebook that he sold.

containing an untitled poem beginning "Of these ideas in his head", was transferred from the loose leaves (miscellaneous) after The New York Public Library's press release [in October 1968].)

The front free end paper bears the (early) signature of T. S. Eliot in blue ink, underlined, with title above, "Complete Poems of," and dedication below (as in the *Prufrock* volume, but with slightly enlarged epigraph) added in black ink not before 1915. An otherwise blank flyleaf at the front has the title in black ink, cancelled, "Inventions of the March Hare." Two blank forms for reporting "Fortnightly Marks and Order" (at the Highgate School? [where Eliot taught in early 1916]) are stuck to the inside back cover.

The notebook was apparently used by Eliot, beginning after January and before April 1910, writing at first only on the rectos but subsequently filling in most of the blanks with later poems.

Dr Gallup followed his account of the Notebook with a list of the poems, briefly described as to their titles, their being in ink or pencil, their length, and their having been published or not.

The poems in the Notebook are dated by Eliot, mostly in pencil and mostly (it would seem from the hand) at about the same time. A letter from Eliot to Eudo C. Mason, 21 Feb. 1936, is informative about the dates for the related poems in *Prufrock and Other Observations*:

J. Alfred Prufrock was written in 1911, but parts of it date from the preceding year. Most of it was written in the summer of 1911 when I was in Munich. The text of 1917, which remains unchanged, does not differ from the original version in any way. I did at one time write a good bit more of it, but these additions I destroyed without their ever being printed. It is by no means true that all of the other poems in the 1917 volume were written after Prufrock. *Conversation Gallante*, for instance, was written in 1909, and all of the more important poems in the volume are earlier than Prufrock, except *La Figlia che Piange*, 1912, and two or three short pieces written in 1914 or '15.[8]

Excised leaves from the Notebook have come to light since 1968 among the Ezra Pound papers now in the Beinecke Rare Book and Manuscript Library at Yale University. In the catalogue of a 1975 exhibition in honour of Pound, Dr Gallup wrote:

On various occasions, over many years, Ezra Pound expressed his admiration for a series of vigorously scatological poems that Eliot had begun while at Harvard, dealing with two redoubtable characters, King Bolo and his Queen. In 1922, when Eliot sold to John Quinn (for $140) a notebook containing manuscript copies of all his early

8 Harry Ransom Humanities Research Center, Austin.

poems, published and unpublished, he took the precaution of excising those leaves containing parts of the Bolo series. He seems to have given them, along with scraps of other versions (probably laid into the same notebook), to Pound.[9]

On the envelope which accompanies these excised leaves and others with similar verses, Pound wrote in pencil: 'T.S.E. Chançons ithyphallique'.

None of these excised pages is without scatological verses, which corroborates Eliot's motive, but the excision brought about the mutilation of poems thereby left incomplete in the Notebook, lacking lines that had been written on the recto or verso of the torn-out pages.

The present edition supplies, from Yale, verses which, not recovered at that date, could not be listed in Dr Gallup's 1968 article but which he has kindly made known: of *Goldfish IV*, the closing twenty lines; of *Suite Clownesque*, the closing line of *III* and the whole of *IV*; and the closing lines of *Portrait of a Lady* I plus an epigraph from Laforgue, not adopted, for 'III'.

The ithyphallic songs, including Columbo and Bolo verses, are to be found here in Appendix A, separated from the other poems in accordance with their excision from the Notebook. On balance, it was judged right to include the ribald verses, despite Eliot's having excised their leaves and their therefore not having formed part of the work sent to, and seen by, Quinn. The editor is aware that such scabrous exuberances may lend themselves to either the wrong kind or the wrong amount of attention. But the case for including them is a combination of the following considerations: that the excised leaves cannot be simply set aside, since on recto or verso they supply missing lines of the poems proper, and even one whole poem; that the ribald verses constitute part of the story of the poet's transition from the Laforguean velleities of 1917 to the Corbièresque bluntnesses, such as *Sweeney Erect*, of 1920; that some details in these verses furnish valuable cross-references for the poems proper; that such verses are rightly being included by Mrs Eliot, in her edition of the letters, whenever they figure within such; and finally that, as Mrs Eliot has made clear, nothing of Eliot's is to be suppressed or censored.

With the Notebook there are loose leaves, described in 1968 by Dr Gallup:

These leaves were divided apparently by John Quinn or one of his clerks into two groups: those for poems included in *Poems* (1920), and miscellaneous poems mostly unpublished. The first group contained 28 leaves, the second, 29, when the manuscripts were received, but since the Library's press release [October 1968] two

9 *The Yale University Library Gazette*, January 1976, item 69.

leaves have been transferred from the second to the first group, and one leaf from the second group has been laid in the notebook. The poems are in various states and versions, with corrections, and are written on a variety of papers, most of them showing traces of having been folded and some much worn at the folds.

The present edition follows Dr Gallup in these respects: in its use of the terms 'page' and 'leaf' in relation to the Notebook (a leaf being numbered on the recto only – see p.xiv above for this numbering); in its division of the loose leaves into 'published' and 'miscellaneous'; and in the sequence given to the poems from the loose leaves in accordance with Dr Gallup's numbering.

The Notebook poems are here presented in the order in which they stand there. Two other possible orderings, both chronological, suggest themselves: order of the poems' composition, and order of their being written in or copied into the Notebook. Though each of these would repay study and would usher certain aspects into the light, neither is – in the present editor's judgement – to be preferred to the straight reproduction of the order as it stands in the Notebook.

For any chronological ordering will at some points cut across Eliot's ordering of the poems into sequences (*Mandarins 1–4, Goldfish I–IV . . .*). Moreover, the order in which the poems were written in or copied into the Notebook cannot be confidently or entirely established. The present edition follows Dr Gallup in recording that some poems are in blue ink, others in black ink, others in pencil. The blue ink antedates the black ink, and there is the evidence of changes in Eliot's hand. Agreed, further, there are anomalies when one reproduces the Notebook order as it stands; *Fourth Caprice in Montparnasse* ([page] 5), which is in black ink, stands between *First Caprice in North Cambridge* and *Second Caprice in North Cambridge*, both in blue ink. But, were one to move *Fourth Caprice in Montparnasse*, or *Interlude in London* (likewise in black ink, and following *Second Caprice in North Cambridge*), where exactly would one move them to, and upon what principle of location?

Granted, it is not entirely satisfactory to leave them (and a few others such) where Eliot entered them, since they are not altogether orderly there, but it would be very unsatisfactory to feel obliged to exercise editorial authority in order to place them elsewhere, especially upon such insufficient evidence of authorial intentions or wishes.

Dr Gallup's original article in the *Times Literary Supplement* in 1968 said:

The Notebook was apparently used by Eliot, beginning after January and before April, 1910, writing at first only on the rectos but subsequently filling in many of the blanks with later poems; no attempt can be made, however, to establish any such order for this account of the manuscripts in the time and space available.

In revising slightly this article for the *Bulletin of the New York Public Library*, Dr Gallup changed 'establish any such order' to 'establish the probable order'. The most that could be established, then, is a probable order for Eliot's writing in, or copying in, the poems; and even a *probable* order for all the poems might be thought on occasion beyond our ascertaining. Dr Gallup valuably urges that this order should be borne in mind, even if sometimes the most one can do is guess at it, but with regret he has acknowledged, in a letter to the present editor, that it is probably not possible to try to print the poems in such an order.

This Edition

From both the Notebook and the loose leaves, this edition prints, as the body of the book, and annotates textually and contextually, all the poems which were not published either by Eliot or within Mrs Eliot's edition of *The Waste Land MS*. Plus, at the end, one poem from the McKeldin Library, University of Maryland.

Of these poems, five only have previously been published, all in volume i of *The Letters of T. S. Eliot*, edited by Valerie Eliot. Four of these accompany letters: *Afternoon, Suppressed Complex, The Love Song of St. Sebastian*, and *Oh little voices of the throats of men*. Of the fifth, *Easter: Sensations of April [1]*, a facsimile of the manuscript page from the Notebook was tipped into the limited edition (1989) of volume i of the *Letters*, with a facing transcription of the poem.

Scholars of Eliot have since 1968 been permitted to study and to describe these manuscripts, though not to quote other than to identify the poems by their titles or their opening words. Frequent reference was made to them in Lyndall Gordon, *Eliot's Early Years* (1977); in Marianne Thormählen, *The Waste Land: A Fragmentary Wholeness* (1978), and *Eliot's Animals* (1984); in John T. Mayer, *T. S. Eliot's Silent Voices* (1989); and in Manju Jain, *T. S. Eliot and American Philosophy: The Harvard Years* (1992), which should be consulted as to Eliot's philosophy courses, and his teachers, when he studied at Harvard.

An editor of Eliot has to acknowledge the force not only of the poet's feelings but of his arguments. He wrote to the Master of Magdalene College, Cambridge, on 9 November 1962:

With the publication of my own verse I have always been firm on three points. First, I will not allow any artist to illustrate my poems. Second, I will not allow any academic critic (and there are plenty of these in America only too willing) to provide notes of explanation to be published with [any of *deleted*] my poems. Third, I will not allow any of my poems to be set to music unless they seem to me to be lyrics in the proper sense of being suitable for singing. My objection to all three of these methods of employing my works is the same, that I should be allowing interpretation of the poem to be interposed between me and my readers. An artist is providing the illustrations which should be left to the imagination of the reader, the commentator is providing information which stands between the reader and any immediate response of his sensibility, and the music also is a particular interpretation which is interposed between the reader and the author. I want my readers to get their impressions from the words alone and from nothing else.[10]

Mrs Eliot, who commissioned the present edition, is the best judge of what her husband would have wished in changed cultural circumstances and in the case of these particular early poems. But some reply to Eliot's points may be put. One, that Eliot himself sometimes applauded an annotated edition. Two, that he did himself provide Notes for the most allusive of his poems, *The Waste Land*. Three, that there can now be little confidence that his readers, however immediately responsive, will be able to bring to their reading a sufficient acquaintance with works once generally known. Four, that the poet – if we may apply a later comment of his about a poem of this period and its line borrowed from Meredith – judged that 'the whole point was that the reader should recognize where it came from and contrast it with the spirit and meaning of my own poem'.[11] Five, that an editor can try to abstain from what Eliot calls notes *of explanation*, that is, from notes which are not primarily the supplying of information.

'Good commentaries can be very helpful', Eliot conceded, and moved at once to *but*: 'but to study even the best commentary on a work of literary art is likely to be a waste of time unless we have first read and been excited by the text commented upon even without understanding it'.[12]

10 The Library of Magdalene College, Cambridge. Eliot must have considered *Old Possum's Book of Practical Cats* a special case, when, after deciding not to illustrate it himself after all, he had Nicolas Bentley do so. But the artwork for his Ariel Poems, by E. McKnight Kauffer, Gertrude Hermes and David Jones, was achieved by mitigating this self-imposed rule.
11 See p.xxiv.
12 Introduction to David Jones, *In Parenthesis* (1961 edn), p.viii.

As to textual decisions: poems in the body of this edition are presented in the final form in which the poet left them, with a record, at the foot of the page, of earlier readings. So, for instance, lines that were deleted are reduced to variants.

In the case, though, of the poems in Appendix B and C (but not of *The Love Song of J. Alfred Prufrock*, moved to the body of the book), poems published by Eliot and known to all his readers, the text presented is – except where noted – the earliest one, since here the prime interest attaches to the distance between the earliest form of the poem and the published one. So for these poems it is not the first readings, but the subsequent readings as they approach the published text, which are recorded as variants (and the textual apparatus therefore records, as the later version, *revision*). Three caveats: there is, inevitably, uncertainty sometimes as to what precisely was the earliest state of the text, since a revision – say, of punctuation – may not be manifest; sometimes a deleted reading might not have been *en route* for the wording which follows; and sometimes the earliest reading proved a false start and so cannot provide a consecutive intelligibility, in which case the revision is adopted. For instance, *Gerontion* 43–4, published as 'Think / Neither fear nor courage saves us', had previously begun 'Think / How courage', these last two words then being deleted; here, since the sequence of words would otherwise be broken, the published text is followed and the first reading recorded as a variant.

In cases where Eliot wrote in alternative readings (sometimes bracing them with the earlier readings) without deleting his earlier reading, the editorial practice has been to retain the earlier reading and to note the alternative. So *alternative* means that this wording was not deleted, and *1st reading* (*2nd reading*, *3rd reading*) that it was deleted. But there are a few exceptions to the practice of choosing the earlier of the alternative readings, for instance in *First Debate between the Body and Soul* 11, where an original undeleted reading fails to cohere with its much-revised context and so the alternative has been preferred. A caret ∧ indicates the position of the variant given:

4. *their* ∧ *uncertainties*] certain *1st reading*.

That is, the word 'certain' followed 'their' and was then deleted.

In the manuscripts, Eliot put a full stop after the titles and the title-numbers within sequences; but this convention was not his practice on publication and is not followed here.

Appendix A prints the ribald verses which are on the leaves excised by Eliot.

Appendix B gives the text – as it first stood in the Notebook or the loose leaves – of *Humouresque* (*Harvard Advocate*, 12 Jan. 1910) and of the poems (here in the order of the volume) in *Prufrock and Other Observations* (1917):

Humouresque (After J. Laforgue)
Portrait of a Lady
Preludes
Rhapsody on a Windy Night
Morning at the Window
Mr. Apollinax
Conversation Galante

These are annotated only as to textual variants.

The Love Song of J. Alfred Prufrock, though one of the poems published in *Prufrock and Other Observations*, is here treated differently. Its text as it stood within the Notebook is found, not like the other published poems of 1917 in Appendix B, but in the body of the book, preceding and following *Prufrock's Pervigilium*. For *Prufrock's Pervigilium* is not an unpublished poem but an unpublished passage from within *The Love Song of J. Alfred Prufrock*, and so it constitutes a different case. Sense can best be made of *Prufrock's Pervigilium* when it is not separated off but granted the context of *The Love Song of J. Alfred Prufrock*.

Appendix C gives the text – as it first stood in the loose leaves – of the poems in *Poems* (The Hogarth Press, 1919), *Ara Vos Prec* (The Ovid Press, 1920), and *Poems* (Alfred A. Knopf, 1920):

Gerontion
Burbank with a Baedeker: Bleistein with a Cigar
Sweeney Erect
A Cooking Egg
Mélange Adultère de Tout
Lune de Miel
Dans le Restaurant
Whispers of Immortality
Mr. Eliot's Sunday Morning Service
Sweeney Among the Nightingales
Ode [in *Ara Vos Prec*, 1920, but not then in *Poems*, 1920]

These are annotated only as to textual variants.

Appendix D, on Influence and Influences, consists of Eliot's own state-ments, and is described in the next section of this Preface.

Annotation

The poet's mind is in fact a receptacle for seizing and storing up numberless feelings, phrases, images, which remain there until all the particles which can unite to form a new compound are present together.

(Tradition and the Individual Talent, 1919)[13]

— and for 'interpretation' the chief task is the presentation of relevant historical facts which the reader is not assumed to know.

(TSE, Hamlet, 1919)[14]

— You've got to know what you want to ask them
— You've got to know what you want to know
— It's no use asking them too much
— It's no use asking more than once
— Sometimes they're no use at all.

(Sweeney Agonistes: Fragment of a Prologue, about the tarot cards)

This edition is based on the conviction that, subordinate to the establishing of the text and of textual variants (which are given at the foot of a poem's page), the important thing is evidence of where the poems came from, and of where they went to in Eliot's other work.

That these early poems were later to contribute to new compounds owes something to Eliot's not having kept the manuscripts. He said in an interview in 1959:

As a rule, with me an unfinished thing is a thing that might as well be rubbed out. It's better, if there's something good in it that I might make use of elsewhere, to leave it at the back of my mind than on paper in a drawer. If I leave it in a drawer it remains the same thing but if it's in the memory it becomes transformed into something else.[15]

Better than leaving it on paper in a drawer might be to send the papers out of the country.

The sources of these early poems are fascinating, and so is their being so often a source or quarry. Though there are included in the present edition

13 *Selected Essays* (1932, 1951 edn), p.19.
14 *SE,* p.142.
15 *Paris Review* 21 (Spring/Summer 1959), p.57.

other kinds of information (such as *Oxford English Dictionary* entries, topical references, and on occasion personal and biographical material), parallel passages – within and without Eliot – are of the essence.

Eliot said as much – and more, in that he then moved to a caveat: 'We cannot, as a matter of fact, understand the *Vita Nuova* without some saturation in the poetry of Dante's Italian contemporaries, or even in the poetry of his Provençal predecessors. Literary parallels are most important, but we must be on guard not to take them in a purely literary and literal way.' Of the content in Dante, he wrote: 'It is often expressed with such a force of compression that the elucidation of three lines needs a paragraph, and their allusions a page of commentary.'[16] One page of commentary by Eliot is addressed to the point of principle:

Readers of my *Waste Land* will perhaps remember that the vision of my city clerks trooping over London Bridge from the railway station to their offices evoked the reflection 'I had not thought death had undone so many'; and that in another place I deliberately modified a line of Dante by altering it – 'sighs, short and infrequent, were exhaled.' And I gave the references in my notes, in order to make the reader who recognized the allusion, know that I meant him to recognize it, and know that he would have missed the point if he did not recognize it.[17]

That it was only for *The Waste Land* that Eliot supplied Notes as to his meaning (including 'that I meant him to recognize it') in no way implies that the question of such recognition is a matter only for the art of *The Waste Land*.

As to borrowings, which may or may not constitute allusions, three of Eliot's insistences need to be borne in mind. They show the facets of the one concern, with the first stressing the 'utterly different', the second stressing 'something like the feeling', and the third the 'contrast'. First, his famous comments in *Philip Massinger* (1920):

One of the surest of tests is the way in which a poet borrows. Immature poets imitate; mature poets steal; bad poets deface what they take, and good poets make it into something better, or at least something different. The good poet welds his theft into a whole of feeling which is unique, utterly different from that from which it was torn; the bad poet throws it into something which has no cohesion. A good poet will usually borrow from authors remote in time, or alien in language, or diverse in interest.[18]

16 *Dante* (1929), *SE*, pp.275, 238.
17 *What Dante Means to Me* (1950), *To Criticize the Critic* (1965), p.128.
18 *SE*, p.206.

Second, his address on *The Bible as Scripture and as Literature*, given in Boston, December 1932:

You cannot effectively 'borrow' an image, unless you borrow also, or have spontaneously, something like the feeling which prompted the original image. An 'image', in itself, is like dream symbolism, is only vigorous in relation to the feelings out of which it issues, in the relation of word to flesh. You are entitled to take it for your own purposes in so far as your fundamental purposes are akin to those of the one who is, for you, the author of the phrase, the inventor of the image; or if you take it for other purposes then your purposes must be consciously and *pointedly* diverse from those of the author, and the contrast is very much to the point; you may not take it merely because it is a good phrase or a lovely image. I confess that I never felt assured that Henry James was justified in naming a novel *The Golden Bowl*, though my scruples may only show that I have not understood the novel.[19]

Third, taking up the 'consciously and *pointedly* diverse', Eliot's comment in an interview in August 1961:

In one of my early poems [*Cousin Nancy*] I used, without quotation marks, the line 'the army of unalterable law . . .' from a poem by George Meredith, and this critic accused me of having shamelessly plagiarised, pinched, pilfered that line. Whereas, of course, the whole point was that the reader should recognise where it came from and contrast it with the spirit and meaning of my own poem.[20]

Eliot, in the matter of influences, saw that there may be safety in numbers:

A poet cannot help being influenced, therefore he should subject himself to as many influences as possible, in order to escape from any one influence. He may have original talent: but originality has also to be cultivated; it takes time to mature, and maturing consists largely of the taking in and digesting various influences.[21]

A poem is more than, and other than, matured materials; but the *materia poetica* may be of interest, and no less so when distinguished from what the poem comes to say and to realize.

No parallel passage has here been proposed which the editor judges a coincidence (though coincidences can be very interesting). As Grover Smith has said: 'The critic should not traffic in imaginary parallels, though he may

19 Houghton Library; bMS Am 1691 (26), pp.11–12.
20 *Yorkshire Post*; *The Bed Post* (1962), ed. Kenneth Young, pp.43–4.
21 A lecture in Dublin (1936), published in *Southern Review* (Autumn 1985), and then in *T. S. Eliot: Essays from the Southern Review* (ed. James Olney, 1988), as *Tradition and the Practice of Poetry*, p.13.

often find it beneficial to cite parallels about which he is uncertain, in which case his prudent course is to admit to being of two minds.'[22] There is a spectrum in these matters, from the diction, or furniture, or topoi, of a particular period or of a particular poet (marionettes; omnibuses; the word 'indifferent' as frequent in these poems, and very 1890s, and *very* Arthur Symons); through unconscious reminiscence; to allusion, the calling into play of the words or phrases of another writer. A source may not be an allusion. An allusion always predicates a source.

There is borrowing, and there is the question of the interest. In 1919, Eliot wrote to Mary Hutchinson about Ezra Pound: 'I daresay he seems to you derivative. But I can show you in the thing I enclose how I have borrowed from half a dozen sources just as boldly as Shakespeare borrowed from North. But I am as traditionalist as a Chinaman, or a Yankee.'[23]

An editor's task is not to try to settle, or even to comment upon, where in the spectrum a particular relationship of one poem to another is to be located, since this can be done only by patient precise exposition, both particular and general, of a sort and on a scale incompatible with an editor's contingencies and format. It is for others to decide – if they accept that such-and-such is indeed a *source* for Eliot's lines – whether it is also more than a source, being part not only of the making of the poem but of its *meaning*. So the notes try to put down only the parallels (though in the awareness that interpretation, selection and judgement are inseparable from annotating), and to leave it to the reader to decide what to make of what the poet made of this matter.

Eliot himself, exercising the rights and duties of the poet, was not much concerned to philosophize about the distinctions – as to borrowing, parallels, sources, allusions, echoes – that are judged here to fall within a critic's, not an editor's, enterprise. The poet's own terms permit of a certain play, and make allowance for the merely probable. As when he wrote to Philip Mairet about the line which opens *Burnt Norton* II:

It might amuse your Swiss friend to know that the line: 'Garlic and sapphires in the mud' is an echo of a line in a sonnet by Mallarmé ('Tonnerre et rubis aux moyeux') with probable recollection also of Charles Péguy's description of the Battle of Waterloo ('de la boue jusqu'aux essieux').[24]

22 *The Waste Land* (1983), p.130.
23 9? July? 1919; *Letters* i 311–12.
24 31 October 1956; Harry Ransom Humanities Research Center, Austin.

For such reasons, the neutral editorial injunction 'Compare' has been preferred, since to vary it would be to suggest distinctions that would demand critical elaboration and substantiation. 'Compare' declines to direct a reader as to what to deduce from the comparison. But some flexibility of phrasing has proved necessary in the matter of how confident the claim should be as to there truly being something up for comparison. So the editor permits himself such degrees of the tentative as: may have, possibly, perhaps. Bless per'apsez.

An effort has therefore been made not to use the notes for exegesis, *critical* elucidation, explication or judgement. The frontiers are uncertain, but the principle has been to provide only notes which always constitute or proceed from a point of information.

Sometimes a particular reader may not need the particular information, but then – as William Empson said – 'it does not require much fortitude to endure seeing what you already know in a note'.[25]

Eliot issued an acknowledgement, a distinction, and a warning. He wrote to I. A. Richards, 11 November 1931, about *Ash-Wednesday*:

As for the allusions you mention, that is perfectly deliberate, and it was my intention that the reader should recognize them. As for the question why I made the allusions at all, that seems to me definitely a matter which should not concern the reader [*amended from* author]. That, as you know, is a theory of mine, that very often it is possible to increase the effect for the reader by letting him know [half *deleted*] a reference or a meaning; but if the reader knew more, the poetic effect would actually be diminished; that if the reader knows too much about the crude material in the author's mind, his own reaction may tend to become at best merely a kind of feeble image of the author's feelings, whereas a good poem should have a potentiality of evoking feelings and associations in the reader of which the author is wholly ignorant. I am rather inclined to believe, for myself, that my best poems are possibly those which evoke the greatest number and variety of interpretations surprising to myself. What do you think about this?[26]

An editor is sure to think about this differently from a poet, though the editorial principles would do well to be sensitive to the creative principles of a particular poet. There is a difference between the kind of 'crude material in the author's mind' which is a matter of 'feelings' and the kind which is knowledge, whether common knowledge or arcane knowledge, and particularly knowledge of previous literature.

25 1935; *Collected Poems* (1955), p.93.
26 The Library of Magdalene College, Cambridge.

And any book, any essay, any note in *Notes and Queries*, which produces a fact even of the lowest order about a work of art is a better piece of work than nine-tenths of the most pretentious critical journalism, in journals or in books. We assume, of course, that we are masters and not servants of facts, and that we know that the discovery of Shakespeare's laundry bills would not be of much use to us; but we must always reserve final judgment as to the futility of the research which has discovered them, in the possibility that some genius will appear who will know of a use to which to put them. Scholarship, even in its humblest forms, has its rights; we assume that we know how to use it, and how to neglect it.[27]

One might apply to Eliot what he said of William Blake: 'His early poems show what the poems of a boy of genius ought to show, immense power of assimilation'.[28] Saturated in his reading, Eliot always had an amazing range of susceptibilities. 'I know that a poem, or a passage of a poem, may tend to realize itself first as a particular rhythm before it reaches expression in words, and that this rhythm may bring to birth the idea and the image.'[29] Sometimes (the notes here suggest) a rhythm, or the sound of a word, or the bizarre punning possibilities of a quite other sense, prompted a surprising creation.[30] Some of these suggestions are bound to seem far-fetched. Nevertheless, 'If their conceits were far-fetched, they were often worth the carriage': these words of Dr Johnson on the Metaphysical poets were quoted by Eliot in the Note with which he concluded his Introduction to *The Sacred Wood*.

Eliot wrote of Spinoza: 'The fact that he could receive stimulation from such various sources and remain so independent of the thought of his own time indicates both the robustness and the sensitiveness of genius.'[31] Again, we may apply to Eliot what he said not only of Shakespeare but of one good effect of editorial scholarship:

the evidence that Shakespeare read with the most prodigious memory for words that has ever existed is almost indisputable, and is consonant with everything that we do know of Shakespeare. And in bringing more clearly to light this *verbal* influence Mr. Taylor supplies a corrective to the invariable human impulse to look for mystery and excitement.

27 *The Function of Criticism* (1923), *SE*, p.33.
28 *William Blake* (1920), *SE*, p.318.
29 *The Music of Poetry* (1942), *On Poetry and Poets* (1957), p.38.
30 Grover Smith: 'With this kind of verbal transformation may be compared one that changes meaning and words but keeps from its model an auditory pattern in which the earlier phrasing is indistinctly heard' (*The Waste Land*, p.113).
31 *The Monist*, Oct. 1916; reprinted as Appendix II of *Knowledge and Experience in the Philosophy of F. H. Bradley* (1964), p.199.

'For what the poet looks for in his reading is not a philosophy', Eliot insisted, 'but a point of departure.'[32]

As so often in literary – including editorial – matters, the case is altered incrementally. Any particular instance, say, of a likeness to Symons may seem or be uncogent, but the pattern and the frequency start to strain coincidence and to indicate convergence. Eliot himself formulated the principle. 'Miss Jeffery has not quite as clear a case as Dr. Schoell had in tracing the borrowings of Chapman', Eliot wrote in a review in 1929, 'but her accumulation of probabilities, powerful and concurrent, leads to conviction.'[33] Similarly, there is his praise of Percy Allen, who demonstrated poets' borrowing from themselves. Such genius in re-creation is very germane to these poems that Eliot left unpublished, to their lines and cadences, and to Eliot's visions and revisions. Mr Allen (Eliot wrote) had mustered 'many other parallels, each slight in itself, but having a cumulative plausibility'. If we have 'some knowledge of the way in which other poets have handled and rehandled the same material, and if we weigh all of the parallel passages which Mr. Allen quotes, we are very strongly inclined to believe that Mr. Allen is right.'[34]

Appendix D, on influence and influences, includes Eliot's accounts of the situation of poetry circa 1910 and of his early formation as a poet. His comments are given within a grouped sequence. To gather such material into an Appendix can somewhat reduce the individual annotations to the poems (and avoid repetition), as well as give a conspectus. But the conspectus does not aim to survey all the influences upon Eliot. The Appendix does not deal with such discrete cases of influence as, say, Shakespeare, Milton, Tennyson or Kipling (on all of whom Eliot wrote indispensable criticism), but with those writers whom Eliot himself specifically acknowledged and to whom he gave salience in his accounts of his early development. Much of this commentary of his (for instance, on Dante and on Corbière) is at least as pertinent to his other poems, the *Poems Written in Early Youth* and those published in 1917 and 1920, as to those annotated here. Appendix D is subdivided:

---

32 *TLS*, 24 Dec. 1925, reviewing George Coffin Taylor, *Shakespeare's Debt to Montaigne*; one of several *TLS* reviews which David Bradshaw added to the Gallup TSE canon in 1993 (*Notes and Queries*, June 1995: *Eleven Reviews by T. S. Eliot, Hitherto Unnoted, from the Times Literary Supplement: A Conspectus*).
33 *TLS*, 25 July 1929, reviewing Violet M. Jeffery, *John Lyly and the Italian Renaissance*.
34 *TLS*, 5 April 1928.

As to Eliot's life during these years: Valerie Eliot has supplied an invaluably detailed 'Biographical Commentary 1888–1922' at the front of *Letters* i. It should be noted, though, that the volume has no letters by him between August 1904 and 23 December 1910, and very few from 1911 to 1913. (One in 1910; three in 1911; none in 1912; one in 1913; and only from July 1914 a good many.) Mrs Eliot reports: 'On the deaths of his mother and brother, in 1929 and 1947, TSE recovered his correspondence with them and burnt a good part of it, together with their side, thus removing the family record of his final school year, his student days at Harvard and the period in Paris' (*Letters* i p.xv).

A letter from the fertile month, July 1914, remains comically pertinent to the enterprise of editing; after a bawdy King Bolo stanza of his own invention, Eliot keeps up the good work:

The bracketed portions we owe to the restorations of the editor, Prof. Dr. Hasenpfeffer (Halle), with the assistance of his two inseparable friends, Dr. Hans Frigger (the celebrated poet) and Herr Schnitzel (aus Wien). How much we owe to the hardwon intuition of this truly great scholar! The editor also justly observes: "There seems to be a *double entendre* about the last two lines, but the fine flavour of the jest has not survived the centuries". – Yet we hope that such genius as his may penetrate even this enigma.

(*Letters* i 42)

Dr Hasenpfeffer: Dr Jugged Hare. An editor, or jugger, of *Inventions of the March Hare* must expect some such mockery, but may take some comfort from Eliot's later words about learnèd doctors:

Our only complaint against both editors [Dr Wood and Dr Harrison] is that they have conscientiously limited themselves, in their notes, to what is verifiable, and have deprived themselves and their readers of that delight in aside and conjecture which the born annotator exploits.[35]

35 *John Marston* (1934), *SE*, p.222.

Editorial Conventions

Eliot's poems are cited from the last edition published in his lifetime, *Collected Poems 1909–1962* (Faber and Faber, 1963), with the correction of *Whispers of Immortality* 26, from 'aboreal' to 'arboreal', and of *Gerontion* 40, from 'is still believed' to 'if still believed'. The two volumes not included there, *Old Possum's Book of Practical Cats* and *Poems Written in Early Youth*, are cited, as are his plays, from *The Complete Poems and Plays of T. S. Eliot* (Faber and Faber, 1969). Eliot's prose, from the English editions.

References to *The Waste Land: A Facsimile and Transcript of the Original Drafts* (1971), abbreviated to *The Waste Land MS*, are given in two forms. For *The Waste Land* itself, reference is to that identification first; thus, *The Waste Land MS*, p.5, *The Burial of the Dead* 51. For the appended 'Miscellaneous Poems', reference is first to the poem itself: thus, *So through the evening* 24–5 (*The Waste Land MS*, p.113).

For Eliot's previously published poems of 1917 and 1920, line-numbering within square brackets – [25] – is that of the published version, this in addition to the numbering, given without square brackets, for the version here published; this applies to Appendix B and Appendix C, as well as to *The Love Song of J. Alfred Prufrock* in the body of the book.

Within references to poems, square brackets indicate that the line-numbering does not recommence with each section of the poem but that there is one continuous line-numbering. For instance, *The Waste Land* [II] 90 indicates that the line is in section II but that the lines of the poem are continuously numbered (by Eliot, in this case). Similarly, Tennyson, *Maud* I [xiv] 489, identifies Part I of the poem, section xiv, and indicates that the line-number, 489, is that which is continuous throughout Part I. Byron, *Don Juan* II [cvii] 849 = Canto II, stanza cvii, line 849 of the Canto. Conversely, *Portrait of a Lady* II 35–8 indicates that the line-numbering begins again with Part II of the poem.

Works adduced in the notes are dated when later than, say, Tennyson and Browning. Dates are ordinarily of publication in a volume (not of periodical publication except, for instance, in the few cases when a work may have been known to Eliot although not yet in a volume, such as a poem of Apollinaire). Often a date will assist recognition of how very recent to Eliot many of these writings were (those of Henry James and of Wilde, for example).

Except when something plainly turns on it (as is sometimes the case with the text of Laforgue), no attempt has been made, when quoting, to identify the particular editions owned by or read by Eliot. An excellent start on such identifications has been made by Ronald Schuchard in his masterly edition of

Eliot's Clark Lectures and Turnbull Lectures, *The Varieties of Metaphysical Poetry* (Faber and Faber, 1993). Schuchard's index will prove invaluable in this matter, and his edition should be consulted too for a record of the discrepancies between British and US editions of Eliot's works, for instance *Selected Essays*. But Eliot's library does not survive *in toto*, though Mrs Eliot possesses many of his books and kindly answers particular queries. Some sense of his personal library in 1920 may be gained from a list of books accompanying a letter from his mother (*Letters* i 398–9), and in 1934 from an inventory in an album which belonged to Vivien Eliot (now in the Bodleian Library).

Titles, not only of volumes but of single works, poems, essays, chapters, etc., are given throughout in italics, to distinguish them promptly from quoted words and phrases.

Editorial, as against authorial, ellipses are indicated thus: [. . .], except for editorial ellipses within quotations from poems when given in the notes and not liable to be mistaken: as

4, 6–7 immense . . . an audience . . . suspense: compare *Suite Clownesque I* 14, 17–18: 'immense . . . the audience / Who still continue in suspense'.

There is no entirely satisfactory way of dealing with punctuation for the end of an indented verse-quotation (say, from Tennyson) when what is quoted did not end with a full stop. To replace a comma or a semicolon with simply a blank is itself blank; with a full stop, can be misleading; with an ellipsis, can be equally misleading, especially for a poet such as Laforgue who often ends so. . . And to put an ellipsis within square brackets, [. . .], at the end of every abbreviated indented quotation, would be cumbrous and ugly. On balance, therefore, and despite the slight ungainliness, it has been judged best to preserve the punctuation, or lack of it, which brought a phrase or clause to an end. So:

Compare *The Waste Land* [v] 420–2:

       your heart would have responded
  Gaily, when invited, beating obedient
  To controlling hands

Again:

Compare W. G. Tinckom-Fernandez, *The Street Organ* 1–3 (the *Harvard Advocate*, 25 June 1908):

  Spring shyly taps the window-pane,
  And all the winds of heaven sigh
  With hope for June-sun-scented days –

But the reader should bear in mind that modernized texts are mostly being quoted, except for special cases such as Spenser.

Notes which invoke the *Oxford English Dictionary* (*OED*) mostly bring forward a sense of a word which might escape a present-day reader; they do not attempt to record all the possibly pertinent senses. So *Inventions* is glossed for its musical sense, with the others unmentioned. But sometimes the *OED* is adduced because of the recency of a word or a usage, or its being then slangy, or some such historical context.

Page-references are supplied only for long articles; so for the *Times Literary Supplement* or *New Statesman*, only the date of issue is noted, as against *The Criterion* (where page-references are given).

As to French titles, conventions change, but here the practice has mostly been to capitalize only the first noun in a title; thus *L'Evolution créatrice*. But there are special cases, Laforgue being one. Conventions vary, too, as to accents on French capitals; here, accents are limited to lower-case.

Acknowledgements

The great debt, owed both by the editor of these poems and by all readers of them, is to Mrs Valerie Eliot, who commissioned this volume, making it possible, and who then helped to make it actual.

Warm thanks are owed to many libraries for their help and for their permission to quote. First, the library that owns the Notebook and loose leaves: the Henry W. and Albert A. Berg Collection of English and American Literature, the New York Public Library, Astor, Lenox and Tilden Foundations, its former curator Francis O. Mattson and its curator Rodney Phillips. Next, the library which owns the leaves that Eliot excised from the Notebook: from the Ezra Pound papers in the Yale Collection of American Literature, Beinecke Rare Book and Manuscript Library at Yale University, and the curator of the collection, Patricia C. Willis. Similarly, for the poem *In silent corridors of death*, and for variants in *Oh little voices* and *The Love Song of St. Sebastian*, to the Special Collections, University of Maryland at College Park Libraries, and the curator of literary manuscripts, Beth Alvarez.

For permission to cite other Eliot manuscripts and material, to the Harry Ransom Humanities Research Center, the University of Texas at Austin, and its research librarian Cathy Henderson; to the Board of the British Library, and its manuscripts librarian, T. A. J. Burnett; to the Houghton Library, Harvard University, and its curator of manuscripts, Leslie A. Morris; to the Huntington Library, and its curator of literary manuscripts, Sara S. Hodson;

to King's College Library, Cambridge (the Hayward Bequest), and its Modern Archivist, Jacqueline Cox; to the Library of Magdalene College, Cambridge, and the Pepys Librarian, Richard Luckett; to the Brotherton Collection, Leeds University Library, and its Sub-Librarian, Christopher Sheppard; to the Bodleian Library, University of Oxford; and to Princeton University Libraries and the Reference Librarian/Archivist, Margaret M. Sherry (for typed signed letters in the Paul Elmer More Papers, Box 3, Folder 3, Manuscripts Division).

For permission to quote from comments by Ezra Pound in poems by T. S. Eliot in the Berg Collection, to Faber and Faber Ltd and New Directions Publishing Corporation. All quoted material by Ezra Pound © 1996 by the Trustees of the Ezra Pound Literary Property Trust.

For an editor, a particular challenge attaches to the annotating of hitherto unpublished work. There is no accrual of findings out there, for one to cite, summarize and synthesize. Dr Johnson, thanking Thomas Warton for some notes upon Shakespeare, remarked: 'A commentary must arise from the fortuitous discoveries of many men, in devious walks of literature' (14 April 1758). So I am the more grateful to those who have helped me: William Arrowsmith, W. H. Bizley, David Bradshaw, Laurence Breiner, Carol Clark, David Coleman, Eleanor Cook, Bonnie Costello, Martin Dodsworth, Anne Ferry, David Ferry, Philip Finkelpearl, Carol Fitzgerald, Donald Gallup, James Griffin, Eric Griffiths, John Gross, Kenneth Haynes, Anne Holmes, Philip Horne, Richard Kaye, Hermione Lee, A. Walton Litz, William Logan, James Longenbach, Oliver Lyne, Jeremy Maule, Jim McCue, Adrienne Miesmer, Lee Oser, Adrian Poole, Michael Prince, Lawrence Rainey, Jonathan Ribner, John Paul Riquelme, Wallace Robson, Lisa Rodensky, Peter Sacks, Ronald Schuchard, Sanford Schwartz, Abner Shimony, Roger Shattuck, Eric Sigg, Grover Smith, Peter Swaab, William L. Vance, Louise Watts, and E. S. C. Weiner.

My thanks, too, to John Bodley at Faber and Faber. To the National Endowment for the Humanities, for a grant to undertake research. And, not only for sabbatical leave but for encouragement and stimulus, to Boston University, including the Trustees; the Chancellor, Dr John R. Silber; the President, Mr Jon Westling; and the Provost of the College of Arts and Sciences, Dr Dennis Berkey.

Abbreviations

AVP   *Ara Vos Prec*. London: The Ovid Press, 1920.

KEPB   *Knowledge and Experience in the Philosophy of F. H. Bradley*. London: Faber and Faber, 1964. New York: Farrar, Straus and Company, 1964.

Letters i *The Letters of T. S. Eliot*, volume i: *1898–1922*, edited by Valerie Eliot. Faber and Faber, 1988. New York: Harcourt Brace, 1988.

OED   *The Oxford English Dictionary*. Second edition. Prepared by J. A. Simpson and E. S. C. Weiner. Oxford: Clarendon Press, 1989.

OPP   *On Poetry and Poets*. London: Faber and Faber, 1957. New York: Farrar, Straus & Cudahy, 1957.

SE   *Selected Essays*. London: Faber and Faber, 1932. New edition, New York: Harcourt Brace, 1950. References are to the third edition, London: Faber and Faber, 1951.

SW   *The Sacred Wood*. London: Methuen & Co., 1920. New York: Alfred A. Knopf, 1921. References are to the second edition, London: Methuen & Co., 1928.

TCTC *To Criticize the Critic*. London: Faber and Faber, 1965. New York: Farrar, Straus & Giroux, 1965.

TLS   *Times Literary Supplement*.

UPUC *The Use of Poetry and the Use of Criticism*. London: Faber and Faber, 1933. Cambridge, Massachusetts: Harvard University Press, 1933.

VMP   *The Varieties of Metaphysical Poetry*, ed. Ronald Schuchard. London: Faber and Faber, 1993. New York: Harcourt Brace, 1994.

The Waste Land MS
  The Waste Land: A Facsimile and Transcript of the Original Drafts, ed. Valerie Eliot. London: Faber and Faber, 1971. New York: Harcourt Brace Jovanovich, 1971.

Chronology of T. S. Eliot's Poems 1905–1920

TSE, BORN 26 SEPTEMBER 1888

This chronology is indebted to Valerie Eliot's 'Biographical Commentary 1888–1922' in *Letters* i, supplemented by Donald Gallup's bibliography of TSE, and by Pierre Leyris' translation of TSE, *Poèmes 1910–1930* (1947), where the poems were dated (and given notes by John Hayward).

The left-hand column indicates when a poem was written, and the right-hand, when published. Dates in square brackets are of publication in a volume by Eliot, as follows:

1917 *Prufrock and Other Observations* (The Egoist Ltd., London)
1919 *Poems* (The Hogarth Press, Richmond)
1920 *Ara Vos Prec* (The Ovid Press, London)
    Poems (Alfred A. Knopf, New York)
1950 *Poems Written in Early Youth* (privately printed by John Hayward, Stockholm, 1950, and then published by Faber and Faber, London, 1967)
1971 *The Waste Land: A Facsimile and Transcript of the Original Drafts* (edited by Valerie Eliot), 'The Miscellaneous Poems'

Titles in CAPITALS are poems hitherto unpublished. Titles marked with an asterisk* are of certain poems published by TSE; the asterisks (noted within the right-hand column, headed 'Poems Published') mean that texts of these poems – from the Notebook or loose leaves – are given in Appendix B (1917) and Appendix C (1920). But note that the early text of one such poem, *The Love Song of J. Alfred Prufrock*, is given within the body of the book since there appears within it PRUFROCK'S PERVIGILIUM.

In 1966, Valerie Eliot supplied a Note for TSE's *Poems Written in Early Youth*:

These appear to be the only juvenilia of my husband that survive. At the age of nine or ten, he told me, he wrote 'a few little verses about the sadness of having to start school again every Monday morning'. He gave them to his Mother and hoped they had not been preserved. At about fourteen he wrote 'some very gloomy quatrains in the form of the *Rubáiyát*', which had 'captured my imagination'. These he showed to no one and presumed he destroyed.

Two incidents connected with 'A Lyric' [. . .] remained in the poet's mind. These stanzas in imitation of Ben Jonson were done as a school exercise when he was sixteen. 'My English master, who had set his class the task of producing some verse, was much impressed and asked whether I had had any help from some elder person. Surprised, I assured him that they were wholly unaided'. They were printed in the school paper, *Smith Academy Record*, but he did not mention them to his family. 'Some time later the issue was shown to my Mother, and she remarked (we were walking along Beaumont Street in St. Louis) that she thought them better than anything in verse she had ever written. I knew what her verse meant to her. We did not discuss the matter further'.[36]

POEMS WRITTEN		POEMS PUBLISHED
	1905	
	Jan.	*A Lyric* [1950]
	Feb.	*A Fable for Feasters* [1950]
	June	*At Graduation 1905* (recited) [1950]
	1907	
	May	*Song: When we came home across the hill* [1950]
	June	*If time and space, as Sages say* [rev. *A Lyric*; 1950]
	1908	
	Nov.	*Before Morning* [1950]
		Circe's Palace [1950]
	1909	
	Jan.	*Song: The moonflower opens to the moth* [1950]
		On a Portrait [1950]
Ballade of the Fox Dinner (recited by TSE, 15 May 1909, and privately printed for the Fox Club in 1949)	May	

36 *Poems Written in Early Youth* (1967), pp. 7–8; these poems were subsequently included in *The Complete Poems and Plays of T. S. Eliot* (Faber and Faber, 1969). On TSE and FitzGerald, see also pp. 309–10.

Portrait of a Lady III   Nov.
  and completed
Preludes IV (Cambridge, Mass.,
  1911, Leyris)
La Figlia Che Piange (Cambridge,
  Mass., 1911, Leyris)

PRUFROCK'S PERVIGILIUM   1912(?)

The Ballade of the Outlook   1913
  (seen by Conrad Aiken
  about 1913)[37]

                                     1914
THE BURNT DANCER   June
OH LITTLE VOICES OF   July
  THE THROATS OF MEN
THE LOVE SONG OF ST.
  SEBASTIAN
Morning at the Window   Sept. [?]
  (Oxford, 1915, Leyris)

PAYSAGE TRISTE (1914?)
SUPPRESSED COMPLEX (1914?
  By 2 Feb. 1915)
AFTERNOON (1914?
  By 25 Feb. 1915)
So through the evening
After the turning
I am the Resurrection
  [1971, the three] ('It would
  seem from the handwriting'
  that they 'were written about
  1914 or even earlier', Valerie
  Eliot; The Waste Land MS,
  p.130.)

                    1915
                    June   *The Love Song of J. Alfred Prufrock
                              [1917]
                    July   *Preludes [1917]
                            *Rhapsody on a Windy Night [1917]

37 Grover Smith, T. S. Eliot's Poetry and Plays (1956), p.30. (Ballade pour la grosse Lulu; revised perhaps.)

	Sept.	*Portrait of a Lady* [1917]
	Oct.	The *'Boston Evening Transcript'* [1917]
		Aunt Helen [1917]
		Cousin Nancy [1917]
		The Death of Saint Narcissus (set in type 1915) [1950]
	Nov.	*Hysteria* [1917]

IN THE DEPARTMENT STORE
(1915?)

1916

	Sept.	*Conversation Galante* [1917]
		La Figlia Che Piange [1917]
		Mr. Apollinax [1917]
		Morning at the Window [1917]

1917

	June	*Prufrock and Other Observations*
	July	*Le Directeur* [1919]
		Mélange Adultère de Tout [1919]
		Lune de Miel [1919]
		The Hippopotamus [1919]

Dans le Restaurant
  (London, 1917, Leyris)
AIRS OF PALESTINE, NO. 2 (1917?)
PETIT EPÎTRE (1917?)
TRISTAN CORBIÈRE (1917?)

1918
July

Ode (Ode on Independence
  Day, July 4th 1918)

	Sept.	*Sweeney Among the Nightingales* [1919]
		Whispers of Immortality [1919]
		Dans le Restaurant [1920]
		Mr. Eliot's Sunday Morning Service [1919]

1919

	May	*Poems*
		A Cooking Egg [1920]
	summer	*Sweeney Erect* [1920]

xli

Geronion   July

                                        summer *Burbank with a Baedeker:
                                                  Bleistein with a Cigar* [1920]

The Death of the Duchess [1971]
Dirge [1971]
    (both mentioned in a letter to
    TSE in 1919, Valerie Eliot
    reports)
Elegy [1971] (written by 1919?)

                                        1920
                                        Feb.   *Ara Vos Prec* (includes first printing
                                                  of *Geronion*; and of *Ode* (*Ode
                                                  on Independence Day, July 4th
                                                  1918*), not reprinted)
                                                Poems

Of the hitherto unpublished poems, the following cannot be dated by the
present editor with any confidence, and so are not included in the Chrono-
logy:

THE LITTLE PASSION: FROM "AN AGONY IN THE GARRET"

INTROSPECTION

WHILE YOU WERE ABSENT IN THE LAVATORY

INSIDE THE GLOOM

DO I KNOW HOW I FEEL? DO I KNOW WHAT I THINK?

O LORD, HAVE PATIENCE

HIDDEN UNDER THE HERON'S WING

THE ENGINE I—II

IN SILENT CORRIDORS OF DEATH

From Appendix A:

FRAGMENTS: THERE WAS A JOLLY TINKER CAME ACROSS THE SEA

COLUMBO AND BOLO VERSES

INVENTIONS OF THE
MARCH HARE

With TSE's signature in blue ink, and the rest in black ink, the front free endpaper of the Notebook has:

COMPLETE POEMS OF
T. S. Eliot

FOR
JEAN VERDENAL
1889–1915,
MORT AUX DARDANELLES

. . . TU SE' OMBRA ED OMBRA VEDI.

. . . PUOI, LA QUANTITATE
COMPRENDER DEL AMOR CH' A TE MI SCALDA,
QUANDO DISMENTO NOSTRA VANITATE
TRATTANDO L'OMBRE COME COSA SALDA.
PURG. XXI.

The sardonic 'Complete Poems of T. S. Eliot' suggests an early date for this teasing title-page (prior to *Prufrock and Other Observations*, 1917, and *a fortiori* prior to 1919 since the Notebook contains no poems of 1919–20). Yet the wording of the dedication, and the supplying of the epigraph, pull the other way and suggest a later date.

For *Prufrock and Other Observations* (1917) has a dedication 'To Jean Verdenal 1889–1915', with no epigraph. *Poems* (1919), which includes no 1917 poems, has neither dedication nor epigraph. *Ara Vos Prec* (1920) has at the head of the book the epigraph from Dante (*Purgatorio* XXI 132–6, beginning 'Or puoi'), but with no dedication, either there or preceding the 1917 poems which constitute, following a half-title (a page with PRUFROCK on it), the second half of the book. *Poems* (1920), which likewise has first the 1920 poems and then the 1917 ones (these without an interleaf or half-title), has 'To Jean Verdenal 1889–1915', with no epigraph. So it is

3

not until *Poems 1909–1925* (1925, dedicated 'To Henry Ware Eliot 1843–1919') that there appear, on the half-title for the pages constituting *Prufrock and Other Observations 1917*, the Verdenal dedication and the epigraph. (The epigraph in 1925 differs from that in the Notebook in beginning: 'la quantitate / Puote veder del amor che . . .', and in lacking 'Purg. XXI'.) The dedication in 1925 is worded as in the Notebook, sharing with it 'For' instead of the earlier 'To', and the added 'Mort aux Dardanelles'.

So, unlike 'Complete Poems of T. S. Eliot', the history of the dedication and epigraph suggests that it was between 1920 and 1925 that TSE wrote out what constitutes this title-page of the Notebook, probably when he sold it to Quinn in 1922.

In his *Dante* (1929; *SE*, p. 255, misprinted *veda, saldi*), TSE wrote:

The meeting with Sordello *a guisa di leon quando si posa*, like a couchant lion, is no more affecting than that with the poet Statius, in Canto XXI. Statius, when he recognizes his master Virgil, stoops to clasp his feet, but Virgil answers – the lost soul speaking to the saved:

> 'Frate,
> *non far, chè tu se' ombra, ed ombra vedi.'*
> *Ed ei surgendo: 'Or puoi la quantitate*
> *comprender dell' amor ch'a te mi scalda,*
> *quando dismento nostra vanitate,*
> *trattando l'ombre come cosa salda.'*

'Brother! refrain, for you are but a shadow, and a shadow is but what you see.' Then the other, rising: 'Now can you understand the quantity of love that warms me towards you, so that I forget our vanity, and treat the shadows like the solid thing.'

In the Temple Classics translation (this, reprinted 1909, was TSE's edition when he was young, and his copy is in the Houghton Library): '"Brother, do not so, for thou art a shade and a shade thou seest." And he, rising: "Now canst thou comprehend the measure of the love which warms me toward thee, when I forget our nothingness, and treat shades as a solid thing."' TSE again quoted this passage in his Clark Lectures (1926), *The Varieties of Metaphysical Poetry* (ed. Ronald Schuchard, 1993, p. 88).

Inventions of the March Hare: this title, in capitals, in black ink, crossed through by TSE, is on the blank flyleaf at the front of the Notebook.

Despite TSE's cancelling it, the title is retained in the present edition, as likely to be less inappropriate than any other, as memorable, and as figuring in TSE's correspondence. He wrote to Conrad Aiken, 30 Sept. 1914: 'Do you think it possible, if I brought out the "Inventions of the March Hare", and gave a few lectures, at 5 P.M. with wax candles, that I could become a sentimental Tommy' (*Letters* i 59; punning, as Valerie Eliot notes, on J. M. Barrie's novel of that name and on TSE's name).

Two months earlier, on 25 July 1914, he had written to Aiken: 'I enclose some *stuff* – the *thing* I showed you some time ago, and some of the themes for the "Descent from the Cross" or whatever I may call it' (*Letters* i 44). That title, which does not appear anywhere in the Notebook, would more pertain to certain of the poems, than to the collection.

There is many a notable *Descent from the Cross*, pre-eminently perhaps that by Rubens. One of TSE's poems here, *The Little Passion* (i) 7, speaks of 'one inevitable cross', and there is *He said: this universe is very clever* 9: 'He said: "this crucifixion was dramatic"'. But TSE, writing to Aiken from Germany, may have remembered too the chapter (v) entitled *Berlin* in Henry Adams, *The Education of Henry Adams*:

Even in art, one can hardly begin with Antwerp Cathedral and the Descent from the Cross. He merely got drunk on his emotions, and had then to get sober as he best could. He was terribly sober when he saw Antwerp half a century afterwards. One lesson he did learn without suspecting that he must immediately lose it. He felt his middle ages and the sixteenth century alive. He was young enough, and the towns were dirty enough – unimproved, unrestored, untouristed – to retain the sense of reality. As a taste or a smell, it was education, especially because it lasted barely ten years longer; but it was education only sensual. He never dreamed of trying to educate himself to the Descent from the Cross. He was only too happy to feel himself kneeling at the foot of the Cross; he learned only to loathe the sordid necessity of getting up again, and going about his stupid business.

TSE wrote to his mother, 4 May 1919: 'I am writing now about a cousin of ours, who has written a very interesting book which you would like to read: *The Education of Henry Adams*' (*Letters* i 290). TSE reviewed it in the *Athenaeum*, 23 May 1919; it was first published in 1918, but had been privately issued in 1907 and was known at Harvard.

Inventions: OED 11, 'invention': '*Mus.* A short piece of music in which a single idea is worked out in a simple manner'. On TSE's musical titles, see the note to *First Caprice in North Cambridge*. TSE wrote to John Hayward, 3 Sept. 1942:

How great is the resistance to "quartets"? I am aware of general objections to these musical analogies: there was a period when people were writing long poems and calling them, with no excuse, "symphonies" (J. Gould Fletcher even did a "Symphony in Blue" I think, thus achieving a greater confusion des genres). But I should like to indicate that these poems are all in a particular set form which I have elaborated, and the word "quartet" does seem to me to start people on the right tack for understanding them. ("Sonata" in any case is *too* musical).

(Quoted by Valerie Eliot in a letter to the *TLS*, 16 July 1971; on the implications of TSE's title *Rhapsody on a Windy Night*, see Anne Ferry, *The Title to the Poem*, 1996.)

Inventions of the March Hare may recall Kipling's title *Many Inventions* (1893). In that volume there is a story particularly admired by TSE, *The Finest Story in the World* (it includes: 'and I must even piece out what he had told me with my own poor inventions while Charlie wrote of the ways of bank-clerks'); this story is mentioned together with *Alice's Adventures in Wonderland* in a footnote in TSE's introduction to *A Choice of Kipling's Verse* (1941, *On Poetry and Poets*, 1957, p. 239). On other respects in which this Kipling story mattered to TSE, see Robert Crawford, *The Savage and the City in the Work of T. S. Eliot* (1987), pp. 132–6.

The March Hare is of ancient stock (*The Two Noble Kinsmen*, III v 73, has a woman 'as mad as a March hare'), but he owes his fame to Lewis Carroll, *Alice's Adventures in Wonderland*, ch. VII, *A Mad Tea-Party*. The March Hare reappears as Haigha (as is clear from Tenniel's illustrations) in *Through the Looking-Glass* (again ch. VII, where he is accompanied by Hatta, an avatar of the Mad Hatter); the next chapter is called '*It's My Own Invention*', and it returns repeatedly to the White Knight's claim ('It's my own invention', 'It's an invention of my own', 'It's a plan of my own invention', 'and the tune's my own invention' – ' "But the tune *isn't* his own invention", she said to herself'). So TSE may have intended by his title *Inventions of the March Hare*, a stress amounting to this: *Inventions – not, as you might suppose, of the White Knight, but – of the March Hare.*

TSE's *While you were absent in the lavatory* has a suggestion of *Alice*: 'a white rabbit hopped beneath the table'; the Yale manuscript of this poem has 'around the corner', which is closer to the White Rabbit ('as it turned a corner') and which suggests *Burnt Norton* I 22 ('Round the corner'), for TSE acknowledged in an interview (*New York Times Book Review*, 29 Nov. 1953) the influence of *Alice* – Alice seeking to follow the White Rabbit – upon *Burnt Norton* I 12–14.

> Down the passage which we did not take
> Towards the door we never opened
> Into the rose-garden.

There is more than a touch of *Alice* in a reminiscence by TSE of his childhood:

There was at the front of our house a sort of picket fence which divided our front yard from the schoolyard. This picket fence merged a little later as it passed the wall of the house into a high brick wall which concealed our back garden from the schoolyard and also concealed the schoolyard from our back garden. There was a door in this wall and there was a key to this door. Now, when the young ladies had left the school in the afternoon and at the end of the week, I had access to and used it for my own purposes of play. [. . .] Well, you know, either in spite of or perhaps because of this propinquity it's interesting that I remained extremely shy with girls. And, of course, when they were in the schoolyard I was always on the other side of the wall; and on one occasion I remember, when I ventured into the schoolyard a little too early when there were still a few on the premises and I saw them staring at me through a window, I took flight at once. (Recalling in Nov. 1959 the Mary Institute; *From Mary to You*, Centennial Issue, Dec. 1959, pp. 134–5.)

There is something *Alice*-like about the door, the key, and the girls, and 'extremely shy with girls' has affinities with the Laforguean spirit of the poems in *Inventions of the March Hare*, where *In the Department Store* 4 has a striking conjunction of staring and taking flight:

> But behind her sharpened eyes take flight
> The summer evenings in the park

Like many philosophers, TSE alludes to Carroll, for instance in his paper on T. H. Green:

In this light then, Green's theory is simply utilitarian jabberwocky, and indeed it is possible that by holding Green up to the looking glass, we may get a better utilitarianism than is found in any utilitarian treatises. (Houghton Library; bMS Am 1691.14 (31), p. 10)

The Notebook joins a title from Carroll to an epigraph from Dante, as does TSE's *Dante* (1929):

One ought, indeed, to study the development of the art of love from the Provençal poets onwards, paying just attention to both resemblances and differences in spirit; as well as the development of verse form and stanza form and vocabulary. But such study is vain unless we have first made the conscious attempt, as difficult and hard as re-birth, to pass through the looking-glass into a world which is just as reasonable as our own. (*SE*, p. 276.)

On *Lewis Carroll and T. S. Eliot as Nonsense Poets*, see Elizabeth Sewell, in *T. S. Eliot: A Symposium for his Seventieth Birthday* (1958), ed. Neville Braybrooke; she remarks 'the endless tea-party, interminable as the Hatter's', in *The Love Song of J. Alfred Prufrock*, *Portrait of a Lady*, *Mr. Apollinax*, *Hysteria*, *A Cooking Egg*, *The Waste Land* 'where the typist comes home at tea-time, the first scene of *The Family Reunion*, Skimbleshanks in *Old Possum*, till only the tea-leaves are left in *The Dry Salvages*' (pp. 52–3).

TSE's title may owe something to a moment in Jerome K. Jerome's *Fanny and the Servant Problem* (1908), a play in which TSE played Lord Bantock in the Cambridge Social Dramatic Club's production during the 1912–13 season (*Letters* i 76). In Act III, Fanny exclaims: 'It's Judy's inspiration, this [. . .] She always was as mad as a March hare.'

Alice muses, in ch. vi of *Alice's Adventures in Wonderland*: ' "I've seen hatters before", she said to herself: "the March Hare will be much the most interesting, and perhaps, as this is May, it won't be raving mad – at least not so mad as it was in March".'

OED, 'as mad as a March hare'. 'During March (the breeding season) hares are wilder than at other times'. This would comment ironically upon these love-poems fastidious and not, poems which (on the occasion recorded in *Letters* i when he used this Notebook title) TSE led into as follows, immediately following a ribald Columbo stanza and TSE's comments on it:

I should find it very stimulating to have several women fall in love with me – several, because that makes the practical side less evident. And I should be very sorry for them, too. Do you think it possible, if I brought out the "Inventions of the March Hare", and gave a few lectures, at 5 P.M. with wax candles, that I could become a sentimental Tommy. (To Aiken, 30 Sept. 1914; *Letters* i 59)

As to the hare in heat, TSE may have remembered an author who meant a great deal to him in these years, Remy de Gourmont, and his *Physique de l'amour: essai sur l'instinct sexuel* (1904, ch. xv).

Le lièvre, qui ne passe point pour brave, est un mâle ardent et convaincu; il se bat furieusement avec ses pareils pour la possession d'une femelle. Ce sont des animaux fort bien outillés pour l'amour, pénis très développé, clitoris presque aussi gros. Les mâles font de véritables voyages, courent des nuits entières, à la recherche des hases, qui sont sédentaires: de même que les lapines, elles ne se refusent jamais, mêmes déjà pleines.

On 28 July 1922, TSE enquired of Pound for a copy of his translation, *The Natural Philosophy of Love* (*Letters* i 553).

'Pénis très développé': compare TSE's bawdy verses on a leaf excised from the Notebook, *There was a jolly tinker* (Appendix A):

> It was a sunny summer day the tinker was in heat
> With his eight and forty inches hanging to his feet –

Given how often Hamlet is suggested in or by these poems, compare the line in *Rejected Addresses* (1812), the very popular volume of parodies by James and Horace Smith: 'For what is Hamlet, but a hare in March?'

With madness in mind, there is poignancy in its later being Vivien Eliot who wrote to Mary Hutchinson, 29 Oct. 1919: 'I played the Dormouse to Pasha Schiff's and his concubine's March Hare and Mad Hatter' (*Letters* i 342).

Yet the hare, free from March, is associated too ('starting a hare') with the prompting of inventive thoughts; Henry James relished 'the speculative hare', 'This irrepressible animal' (*The American Scene*, 1907, p. 202).

For an argument as to the shape that TSE gave, or might have given, to the sequence as a whole, see John T. Mayer, *T. S. Eliot's Silent Voices* (1989), and his article *The Waste Land and Eliot's Poetry Notebook* (in *T. S. Eliot: The Modernist in History*, ed. Ronald Bush, 1991).

[Notebook [Leaf] 1: *Conversation Galante*, dated Nov. 1909; Appendix B.]

Convictions (Curtain Raiser)

Among my marionettes I find
The enthusiasm is intense!
They see the outlines of their stage
Conceived upon a scale immense
And even in this later age   5
Await an audience open-mouthed
At climax and suspense.

Two, in a garden scene
Go picking tissue paper roses;
Hero and heroine, alone,   10
The monotone
Of promises and compliments
And guesses and supposes.

And over there my Paladins
Are talking of effect and cause,   15
With "learn to live by nature's laws!"
And "strive for social happiness
And contact with your fellow-men
In Reason: nothing to excess!"
As one leaves off the next begins.   20

And one, a lady with a fan
Cries to her waiting-maid discreet
"Where shall I ever find the man!
One who appreciates my soul;
I'd throw my heart beneath his feet.   25
I'd give my life to his control."
(With more that I shall not repeat.)

My marionettes (or so they say)
Have these keen moments every day.

[Pages] 2–3. Manuscript in blue ink.

2. !] *in pencil*; : *1st reading*.

11] And *added in pencil before the line and then deleted*.

24. *One who*] Who shall *alternative above in pencil and braced, but without the consequential emendation* appreciate.

First Caprice in North Cambridge

A street-piano, garrulous and frail;
The yellow evening flung against the panes
Of dirty windows: and the distant strains
Of children's voices, ended in a wail.

Bottles and broken glass,   5
Trampled mud and grass;
A heap of broken barrows;
And a crowd of tattered sparrows
Delve in the gutter with sordid patience.

Oh, these minor considerations!   10

[Page] 4. Manuscript in blue ink.

Fourth Caprice in Montparnasse

We turn the corner of the street
  And again
Here is a landscape grey with rain
On black umbrellas, waterproofs,
And dashing from the slated roofs   5
Into a mass of mud and sand.
Behind a row of blackened trees
The dripping plastered houses stand
Like mendicants without regrets
For unpaid debts   10
Hand in pocket, undecided,
Indifferent if derided.

Among such scattered thoughts as these
We turn the corner of the street;
But why are we so hard to please?   15

[Page] 5. Manuscript in black ink.

Title. *Montparnasse*] *in pencil*; North Cambridge *1st reading*.

6. *mass*] mess *perhaps*.

10. *unpaid*] *in pencil*; all their *1st reading*.

12. *derided*] derided, chided *1st reading, deletion by pencil*.

13] *added in pencil*.

15. *But*] *added in pencil. Following 15, two lines deleted by pencil*:
    The world is full of journalists,
  And full of universities.
And full] *1st and 3rd (pencil) reading*; Full *2nd (pencil) reading*.

Second Caprice in North Cambridge

This charm of vacant lots!
The helpless fields that lie
Sinister, sterile and blind –
Entreat the eye and rack the mind,
Demand your pity.   5
With ashes and tins in piles,
Shattered bricks and tiles
And the débris of a city.

Far from our definitions
And our aesthetic laws   10
Let us pause
With these fields that hold and rack the brain
(What: again?)
With an unexpected charm
And an unexplained repose   15
On an evening in December
Under a sunset yellow and rose.

[Page] 6. Manuscript in blue ink.

4. *rack*] haunt *1st reading.*

8. *débris*] *accent added in pencil.*

12. *fields*] *in pencil*; lots *1st reading.*

15. *an unexplained*] a quite unknown *1st reading.*

Interlude in London

We hibernate among the bricks
And live across the window panes
With marmalade and tea at six
Indifferent to what the wind does
Indifferent to sudden rains   5
Softening last year's garden plots

And apathetic, with cigars
Careless, while down the street the spring goes
Inspiring mouldy flowerpots,
And broken flutes at garret windows.   10

[Page] 7. Manuscript in black ink.

6. *year's*] years MS.

10. *broken*] timid / furtive *guesses at the further readings, in ink above and below, braced, and deleted in pencil.*

Opera

Tristan and Isolde
And the fatalistic horns
The passionate violins
And ominous clarinet;
And love torturing itself   5
To emotion for all there is in it,
Writhing in and out
Contorted in paroxysms,
Flinging itself at the last
Limits of self-expression.   10

We have the tragic? oh no!
Life departs with a feeble smile
Into the indifferent.
These emotional experiences
Do not hold good at all,   15
And I feel like the ghost of youth
At the undertakers' ball.

[Page] 8. Manuscript in blue ink.

5. love] *probable reading*; life [?] (*there is what may be a dot above, but no ascender or descender for an* f).

Silence

Along the city streets
It is still high tide,
Yet the garrulous waves of life
Shrink and divide
With a thousand incidents   5
Vexed and debated:–
This is the hour for which we waited –

This is the ultimate hour
When life is justified.
The seas of experience   10
That were so broad and deep,
So immediate and steep,
Are suddenly still.
You may say what you will,
At such peace I am terrified.   15
There is nothing else beside.

[Page] 9. Manuscript in blue ink.

6. *Vexed*] *unclear reading at first sight but the* ex *is that of TSE's hand in* next
(*Convictions* 20); *see also the note below, page 125.*

Mandarins

I

Stands there, complete,
Stiffly addressed with sword and fan:
What of the crowds that ran,
Pushed, stared, and huddled, at his feet,
Keen to appropriate the man?   5

Indifferent to all these baits
Of popular benignity
He merely stands and waits
Upon his own intrepid dignity;
With fixed regardless eyes —   10
Looking neither out nor in —
The centre of formalities.

A hero! and how much it means;
How much —
The rest is merely shifting scenes.   15

[Page] 10. Manuscript in blue ink.

7. Of] *in pencil*; For *1st reading*.

2

Two ladies of uncertain age
Sit by a window drinking tea
(No persiflage!)
With assured tranquillity
                    Regard   5
A distant prospect of the sea.
The outlines delicate and hard
Of gowns that fall from neck and knee;
Grey and yellow patterns move
From the shoulder to the floor.   10

   By attitude
It would seem that they approve
The abstract sunset (rich, not crude).

And while one lifts her hand to pour
You have the other raise   15
A thin translucent porcelain,
Murmurs a word of praise.

[Page] 11. Manuscript in blue ink.

3

The eldest of the mandarins,
A stoic in obese repose,
With intellectual double chins,
Regards the corner of his nose;

The cranes that fly across a screen   5
Pert, alert,
Observe him with a frivolous mien –
Indifferent idealist,
    World in fist,
        Screen and cranes.   10

And what of all that one has missed!
And how life goes on different planes!

[Page] 12. Manuscript in blue ink.

4. ;] *in pencil;* – *1st reading.*

8] *Further readings added in pencil, then deleted:* intellectualist *above* idealist; Attentive intuitionist *following* idealist. *TSE has boldly bracketed* ( ) *the line in pencil, probably not as punctuation but for reconsideration.*

Still one more thought for pen and ink!
  (Though not indicative of spleen):
How very few there are, I think
Who see their outlines on the screen.
And so, I say, I find it good   5
(Even if misunderstood)
That demoiselles and gentlemen
Walk out beneath the cherry trees,
The goldwire dragons on their gowns
Expanded by the breeze.   10
The conversation dignified
Nor intellectual nor mean,
And graceful, not too gay . . .

       And so I say
How life goes well in pink and green!   15

[Page] 13. Manuscript in blue ink.

2. *Though*] But *1st reading.*

3] *in pencil*; How [*revised to* But] few (of even those who think) *1st reading.*

4] *in pencil*; Are conscient of what they mean. *1st reading*; Arrange and comprehend the scene. *2nd (pencil) reading*; Arrange their outlines on the screen. *3rd (pencil) reading.*

5. *find*] *in pencil*; think *1st reading.*

7. *demoiselles*] *in pencil*; stately dames *1st reading*; all our *2nd (pencil) reading, presumably governing* dames *deleted.*

Easter: Sensations of April

[1]

The little negro girl who lives across the alley
Brings back a red geranium from church;
She repeats her little formulae of God.

Geraniums, geraniums
On a third-floor window sill.   5
Their perfume comes
With the smell of heat
From the asphalt street.
Geraniums geraniums
Withered and dry   10
Long laid by
In the sweepings of the memory.

The little negro girl across the alley
Brings a geranium from Sunday school

[Page] 14. The title and first three lines are in blue ink; then there are twelve lines in pencil, the final one deleted. It is unclear whether (a) the poem was to begin and end with lines about 'The little negro girl'; or (b) TSE, when he took up his pencil, started the poem again, with 'Geraniums', and concluded by adapting what had been the opening; or (c) whether at the end he was starting the poem again, in revision. The move from ink to pencil is germane. In favour of (b), beginning with 'Geraniums' and the heat, is the parallel then with *Easter: Sensations of April II*, which begins with 'Daffodils' and the heat. In favour though of (a), beginning with 'The little negro girl who . . .', and weighing with the present editor, is the fact that TSE did not delete the opening three lines about her, or delete – as possibility (c) would have asked – the first twelve lines.

7. *With*] *written over the beginning of a word.*

14] *deleted following 14*: She is very sure of God.

II

Daffodils
Long yellow sunlight fills
The cool secluded room
Swept and set in order –
Smelling of earth and rain.   5
And again
The insistent sweet perfume
And the impressions it preserves
Irritate the imagination
Or the nerves.   10

Separate leaf laid in; manuscript in pencil.

4. *Swept*] *written over the beginning of a word.*

[Notebook [pages] 15–17: *Preludes I–III*, dated Oct. 1910, Oct. 1910, July 1911; and, separate leaf laid in, *Preludes IV* [1911]; Appendix B.]

Goldfish
(Essence of Summer Magazines)

I

Always the August evenings come
With preparation for the waltz
The hot verandah making room
For all the reminiscent tunes
– The *Merry Widow* and the rest –   5

That call, recall
So many nights and afternoons –
August, with all its faults!

And the waltzes turn, return;
The *Chocolate Soldier* assaults   10
The tired Sphinx of the physical.
What answer? We cannot discern.

And the waltzes turn, return,
Float and fall,
Like the cigarettes   15
Of our marionettes
Inconsequent, intolerable.

[Page] 18. Manuscript in black ink, with the title and the first three words in pencil.

7. *nights and*] *added in pencil but with a caret in ink.*

12] *in pencil*; For meanings that we not discern. *1st reading*; For meanings we cannot discern. *2nd reading.*

Embarquement pour Cythère

Ladies, the moon is on its way!
Is everybody here?
And the sandwiches and ginger beer?
If so, let us embark –
The night is anything but dark,   5
Almost as clear as day.

It's utterly illogical
Our making such a start, indeed
And thinking that we must return.

Oh no! why should we not proceed   10
(As long as a cigarette will burn
When you light it at the evening star)
To porcelain land, what avatar
Where blue-delft-romance is the law.

Philosophy through a paper straw!   15

[Page] 19. Manuscript in black ink.

1. *its*] *in pencil*; his *1st reading.*

9. *must*] *in pencil*; should *1st reading.*

10. *should*] *in pencil*; do *1st reading.*

III

On every sultry afternoon
Verandah customs have the call
White flannel ceremonial
With cakes and tea
And guesses at eternal truths   5
Sounding the depths with a silver spoon
And dusty roses, crickets, sunlight on the sea
    And all.

And should you ever hesitate
Among such charming scenes –   10
Essence of summer magazines –
Hesitate, and estimate
How much is simple accident
How much one knows
How much one means   15
Well! among many apophthegms
Here's one that goes –
Play to your conscience, through the maze
Of means and ways
And wear the crown of your ideal   20
    Bays
    And rose.

[Pages] 20–1. Manuscript in pencil, cancelled in pencil.

5. *eternal*] immortal *1st reading.*

21–2] *originally one line*: Bays and rose. 22 *in ink.*

IV

Among the débris of the year
Of which the autumn takes its toll:−
Old letters, programmes, unpaid bills
Photographs, tennis shoes, and more,
Ties, postal cards, the mass that fills   5
The limbo of a bureau drawer −
Of which October takes its toll
Among the débris of the year
I find this headed "Barcarolle".

"Along the wet paths of the sea   10
A crowd of barking waves pursue
Bearing what consequence to you
And me.
The neuropathic winds renew
Like marionettes who leave their graves   15
Walking the waves
Bringing the news from either Pole
Or knowledge of the fourth dimension:
"We beg to call to your attention
"Some minor problems of the soul."   20

− Your seamanship is very neat
You scan the clouds, as if you knew,
Your language nautical, complete;
There's nothing left for me to do.
And while you give the wheel a twist   25
I gladly leave the rest to fate
And contemplate
The aged sybil in your eyes
At the four crossroads of the world
Whose oracle replies: −   30
"These problems seem importunate
But after all do not exist."

Between the theoretic seas
And your assuring certainties
I have my fears: 35
– I am off for some Hesperides
Of street pianos and small beers!

[Page] 21. Manuscript in pencil, cancelled in pencil. Lines 18–37 are supplied from the leaf (where they are cancelled) excised from the Notebook (now among the Pound papers in the Beinecke Library at Yale).

7. *which October*] all the [*indecipherable word*: senses?] *1st reading.*

9. *headed*] labelled *1st reading.*

10. *"Along*] *these opening quotation marks are apparently not closed. Along*] Among *doubtful 1st reading.*

14] *added. winds*] waves *1st reading.*

19. *"We ∧ beg*] humbly *deleted.*

32 ∧ 33] *space in MS (coinciding with page-division in this edition).*

36. *– I am off*] And lay my course *1st reading.*

[Following Notebook [page] 21: three leaves excised, two of which are now at Yale, one completing *Goldfish* IV, with Bolo verses on the verso, and the other having *The Triumph of Bullshit*; Appendix A.

[Pages] 22–3: *Portrait of a Lady* I, dated Nov. 1910; Appendix B. Two leaves excised, of which one, now at Yale, has the end of *Portrait of a Lady* I, with Bolo verses on the verso; Appendix A.]

Suite Clownesque

I

Across the painted colonnades
Among the terra cotta fawns
Among the potted palms, the lawns,
The cigarettes and serenades

Here's the comedian again   5
With broad dogmatic vest, and nose
Nose that interrogates the stars,
Impressive, sceptic, scarlet nose;
The most expressive, real of men,
A jellyfish impertinent,   10
A jellyfish without repose.

Leaning across the orchestra
Just while he ponders, legs apart,
His belly sparkling and immense:
It's all philosophy and art.   15
Nose that interrogates the stars
Interrogates the audience
Who still continue in suspense

Who are so many entities
Inside a ring of lights!   20
Here's one who has the world at rights
Here's one who gets away with it
By simple spreading of the toes,
A self-embodied rôle, his soul
Concentred in his vest and nose.   25

[Pages] 24–7, the sequence. Manuscript in black ink, with *Clownesque* added to the title in pencil. A leaf excised from the Notebook (now among the Pound papers in the Beinecke Library at Yale) supplies the closing line of III and the whole of IV.

8. *Impressive*] Infinite *written above in pencil; both readings deleted, apparently, but it is unlikely that TSE who did not consequentially capitalize* sceptic *wanted the lopped line, so* Impressive *is retained here.*

9. *The*] added.   expressive, real] *ringed in pencil.*

9–10] *final commas faintly added in pencil.*

11. *without*] that lacks *1st reading.*

13. *Just while he*] The while the *1st reading.*

18. *still continue*] are always *1st reading.*

Each with a skirt just down to the ancle
Everybody is under age
Three on a side and one in the centre
(Who would venture to be a dissenter)
Hello people!   5
People, hello!
Just while they linger shaking a finger
Perched on stools in the middle of the stage:–

"We've started out to take a walk
Each in a simple hat and gown,   10
Seven little girls run away from school
Now for a peek about the town.
Here's a street car – let's jump in
Oh see the soldiers – let's descend.
When you're out for an afternoon   15
Find somebody with money to spend.

But we're perplexed.
Hello people!
Yes indeed we're fearfully vexed;
People, hello!   20
In trying to construe this text:
'Where shall we go to next?'"

4] ( ) *added in pencil.*

8. *stools*] a stool *1st reading.*

15. *When*] *written over* And [?].

If you're walking down the avenue,
Five o'clock in the afternoon,
I may meet you
Very likely greet you
Show you that I know you   5

If you're walking up Broadway
Under the light of the silvery moon,
You may find me
All the girls behind me,
Euphorion of the modern time   10
Improved and up to date – sublime
Quite at home in the universe
Shaking cocktails on a hearse.
It's Broadway after dark!
                    Here let a clownesque be sounded
                    on the sandboard and bones.

If you're walking on the beach   15
You hear everyone remark
Look at him!
You will find me looking them over
When the girls are ready for a swim
Just out of reach   20
First born child of the absolute
Neat, complete,
In the quintessential flannel suit.
I guess there's nothing the matter with us!
                    – But say, just be serious,   25
Do you think that I'm all right?

The closing line is supplied from the leaf excised from the Notebook, now among the Pound papers in the Beinecke Library at Yale.

10. *time*] world *1st reading.*

11] Improvement on the high sublime *1st reading.*

12. *in*] at *1st reading.*

12 ∧ 13] Seen from the depths of a New York Street, *added and then deleted.*

14. *It's*] Its MS.

19. *the* ∧ *girls*] little *deleted in pencil.*

19–20] *marked to be moved from their original place,* 16 ∧ 17, *to precede* 21, *apparently to follow the line in parentheses* (I'm such a rover) *which was added and then deleted.*

21] '?' *added in pencil off to the right of the line.*

[Following Notebook [page] 27: two leaves excised, one of which is now in the Pound papers in the Beinecke Library at Yale, having the last line of *Suite Clownesque III* with *Suite Clownesque IV*, and, on the verso, *Fragments: There was a jolly tinker*; Appendix A.]

In the last contortions of the dance
The milkmaids and the village girls incline
To the smiling boys with rattan canes
Withdraw, advance;
The hero captures the Columbine   5
The audience rises hat in hand
And disdains
To watch the final saraband
The discovered masquerades
And the cigarettes and compliments   10

But through the painted colonnades
There falls a shadow dense, immense

It's the comedian again
Explodes in laughter, spreads his toes
(The most expressive, real of men)   15
Concentred into vest and nose.

Supplied from the leaf excised from the Notebook, now among the Pound papers in the Beinecke Library at Yale.

3. *smiling*] *in pencil*; Broadway *1st reading.   with* ∧ *rattan*] *the deleted in pencil.*

9] *added in ink.*

10. *And the*] The *1st reading.*

10 ∧ 11] And *deleted.*

12. *falls*] *in pencil*; leans *1st reading.*

15] ( ) *added in pencil.*

The Love Song of J. Alfred Prufrock
(Prufrock among the Women)

"Sovegna vos al temps de mon dolor" –
   Poi s'ascose nel foco che gli affina.

. . . Let us go then, you and I
When the evening is spread out against the sky
Like a patient etherized upon a table
Let us go, through certain half-deserted streets
The muttering retreats   [5]
Of restless nights in one night cheap hotels
And sawdust restaurants with oyster shells:
Streets that join like a tedious argument
Of insidious intent
To lead you to an overwhelming question . . .   [10]

Oh do not ask "what is it?"
Let us go and make our visit.

In the room the women come and go
Talking of Michelangelo.

The yellow fog that rubs its back upon the window panes [15]
The yellow smoke that rubs its muzzle on the window panes
Licked its tongue into the corners of the evening
Lingered upon the pools that stand in drains
Let fall upon its back the soot that falls from chimneys;
Slipped by the terrace, made a sudden leap,   [20]
And seeing that it was a soft October night
Curled once about the house, and fell asleep.

And indeed there will be time
For the yellow smoke that slides along the street
Rubbing its back upon the window panes;   [25]
There will be time, there will be time
To prepare a face to meet the faces that you meet;
There will be time to murder and create,
And time for all the works and days of hands

That lift and drop a question on your plate: [30]
Time for you and time for me,
And time yet for a hundred indecisions
And for a hundred visions and revisions
Between the taking of a toast and tea.

In the room the women come and go   [35]
Talking of Michelangelo.

And indeed there will be time
To wonder "Do I dare?" and "Do I dare?"
Time to turn back and descend the stair
With a bald spot in the middle of my hair   [40]
(They will say "How his hair is growing thin!")
My morning coat, my collar mounting firmly to the chin
My necktie rich and modest, but asserted by a simple pin –
(They will say "But how his arms and legs are thin")
Do I dare . .   [45]
Disturb the universe?
In a minute there is time
For decisions and revisions which a minute will reverse . . .

For
    I have known them all already, known them all
Have known the evenings, mornings, afternoons   [50]
I have measured out my life with coffee spoons;
I know the voices dying with a dying fall
Among the music from a farther room.
    So how should I presume?

And I have known the eyes, I have known them all   [55]
The eyes that fix you in a formulated phrase
And when I am formulated sprawling on a pin
When I am pinned and wriggling on the wall,
Then how should I begin?
– To spit out all the butt ends of my days and ways?   [60]
    But how should I presume?

And I have known the arms, I have known them all
Arms that are braceleted, and white, and bare
(But, in the lamplight, downed with light brown hair)
— Is it the skin, or perfume from a dress   [65]
    That makes me so digress? —
Arms that lie along a cushion, or wrap about a shawl.
    And should I then presume? . .
    And how should I begin? . . .

[Pages] 28–31. The Notebook has:

The Love Song of J. Alfred Prufrock
    (Prufrock among the Women)

"Sovegna vos al temps de mon dolor" –
    Poi s'ascose nel foco che gli affina.

(Temple Classics *a temps de ma.*) This epigraph, added, is the last two lines (147–8) of
Purgatorio XXVI. Compare TSE's parenthesized subtitle with *Sweeney Among the
Nightingales*, itself indebted to Elizabeth Barrett Browning's *Bianca Among the
Nightingales*.

    There follow the first sixty-nine lines of *The Love Song of J. Alfred Prufrock*
(printed above). Then there is a title, in capitals, cancelled, PRUFROCK'S PERVIGI-
LIUM, written over words now illegible and followed by an erased and scratched-out
heading (apparently ending '[. . .] of J. A. Prufrock').

    The title *Prufrock's Pervigilium* is followed by ll.70–2 of *The Love Song of J.
Alfred Prufrock* (variants noted below), uncancelled, and then by a further twenty-
nine lines of *Prufrock's Pervigilium*. These twenty-nine lines are cancelled. Then
come (uncancelled, apparently) *Prufrock's Pervigilium* 33–4, surviving as ll.73–4 of
The Love Song of J. Alfred Prufrock:

I should have been a pair of ragged claws
Scuttling across the floors of silent seas.

— and then the further four (cancelled) lines which conclude *Prufrock's Pervigilium*.
Prufrock's Pervigilium is in a later hand than *The Love Song of J. Alfred Prufrock*.

    The text of *The Love Song of J. Alfred Prufrock* (dated July–Aug. 1911 at the end),
as it appears within the Notebook, [pages] 28–31, 35–8, is here printed in the body of
the present edition, preceding and succeeding *Prufrock's Pervigilium*, this being –
since it involves not an unpublished poem but an unpublished passage within a
published poem – a different case from that of the published poems whose text is
given in Appendix B. Note that though the final line-count is the same as in the

published poem, this accommodates the extra line in the Notebook (104 ∧ 5 of the published poem), which then happens to be compensated for by the compacting in the Notebook into one line of the published lines 108–9. Indenting is uncertain throughout.

The Love Song of J. Alfred Prufrock was published in *Poetry* (June 1915). The 1915 text does not differ in wording from 1917 except where noted.

3] *marked #   # at beginning and end.*

8. *join*] follow *1917.*

10 ∧ 11] *no space 1917.*

19. *soot*] spot *1915 (slip).*

34. *Between*] *1st reading;* Before *(in pencil), 1917.*

49. *For*] *underlined.   all*] MS, *1917; not 1915.*

50–3] *indented below the* I *of the previous line, but the indenting here and elsewhere is uncertain.*

53. *Among*] Beneath *1917.*

55. *eyes, I have*] eyes already, *1917.*

57. *formulated sprawling on a pin*] *the ink is messy here, and there may be commas as in 1917:* formulated, sprawling on a pin,

58. *wriggling*] squirming *1st reading.*

61. *But*] And *1917.*

61 ∧ 62] *space in MS (coinciding with page-division in this edition).*

62. *arms, I have*] arms already, *1917.*

65. *the skin, or*] *not 1917.*

67. *cushion*] table *1st reading, 1917.*

Prufrock's Pervigilium

Shall I say, I have gone at dusk through narrow streets [70]
    And seen the smoke which rises from the pipes [71]
    Of lonely men in shirtsleeves, leaning out of windows. [72]
And when the evening woke and stared into its blindness
I heard the children whimpering in corners   5
Where women took the air, standing in entries –
Women, spilling out of corsets, stood in entries
    Where the draughty gas-jet flickered
    And the oil cloth curled up stairs.

    And when the evening fought itself awake   10
And the world was peeling oranges and reading evening papers
And boys were smoking cigarettes, drifted helplessly together
    In the fan of light spread out by the drugstore on the corner
    Then I have gone at night through narrow streets,
        Where evil houses leaning all together   15
Pointed a ribald finger at me in the darkness
    Whispering all together, chuckled at me in the darkness.

And when the midnight turned and writhed in fever
I tossed the blankets back, to watch the darkness
Crawling among the papers on the table   20
It leapt to the floor and made a sudden hiss
And darted stealthily across the wall
Flattened itself upon the ceiling overhead
Stretched out its tentacles, prepared to leap

And when the dawn at length had realized itself   25
And turned with a sense of nausea, to see what it had stirred:
The eyes and feet of men –
I fumbled to the window to experience the world
And to hear my Madness singing, sitting on the kerbstone
[A blind old drunken man who sings and mutters,   30
With broken boot heels stained in many gutters]
And as he sang the world began to fall apart . . .

I should have been a pair of ragged claws   [73]
Scuttling across the floors of silent seas . . .   [74]

— I have seen the darkness creep along the wall   35
I have heard my Madness chatter before day
I have seen the world roll up into a ball
Then suddenly dissolve and fall away.

[Pages] 32–3 and [leaf] 34. Manuscript in black ink.

1. *Shall I say*] *underlined.*   *gone*] walked *1st reading.*

2. *seen*] watched *1917.*   *which*] that *1917.*

14. *narrow*] vacant *1st reading.*

15. *all together*] altogether *1st reading.*

17 ∧ 18] *probably a space; turn of the page.*

30–1] *the enclosing within* [ ] *is not a later addition, given the alignment of 30.*

32 ∧ 33] *space in MS (coinciding with page-division in this edition).*

[Following Notebook [leaf] 34: one leaf excised, without stub.]

[The Love Song of J. Alfred Prufrock, resumed]

And the afternoon, the evening, sleeps so peacefully! [75]
Smoothed by long fingers;
Asleep . . . tired . . . or it malingers,
Stretched on the floor, here between you and me.
Should I, after so many cakes and ices
Have the strength to force the moment to its crisis? [80]
But though I have wept and fasted, wept and prayed;
Though I have seen my head (grown slightly bald) brought in upon a
   platter,
I am no prophet – and that's no great matter:
I have seen the moment of my greatness flicker
And I have seen the eternal FOOTMAN hold my coat, and snicker – [85]
   And in short, I was afraid.

And would it have been worth it, after all,
After the cups, the marmalade, the tea,
Among the porcelain, among some talk of you and me,
Would it have been worth while [90]
To have bitten off the matter with a smile
To have squeezed the universe into a ball
To roll it toward some overwhelming question –
To say "I am Lazarus, come from the dead
Come back to tell you all, I shall tell you all;" [95]
– If one, settling a pillow by her head
   Should say, "That is not what I meant, at all.
      That is not it, at all."

And would it have been worth it, after all,
Would it have been worth while [100]
After the sunsets and the dooryards and the sprinkled streets
After the novels, after the teacups, and the skirts that trail along the floor,
And this, and so much more
– It is impossible to say just what I mean!
Perhaps it will make you wonder and smile: [105]
But as if a magic lantern threw the nerves in patterns on a screen:
Would it have been worth while
If one, settling a pillow or throwing off a shawl

And turning toward the window, should say "That is not it, at all;
"That is not what I meant, at all."   [110]

No! I am not Hamlet, nor am meant to be.
Am an attendant lord – one that will do
To swell a progress, start a scene or two,
Advise the prince: withal, an easy tool;
Deferential, glad to be of use,   [115]
Politic, cautious, and meticulous,
Full of high sentence, but a bit obtuse;
At times, indeed, appear ridiculous;
     Almost, at times, the Fool.

I grow old . . . I grow old . . .   [120]
I shall wear the bottoms of my trowsers rolled.

     Shall I part my hair behind? Do I dare to eat a peach?
I will wear white flannel trowsers, and walk upon the beach.
I have heard the mermaids singing, each to each.

I do not think that they will sing to me.   [125]

I have seen them riding seaward on the waves,
Combing the white hair of the waves blown back
When the wind blows the water white and black.

We have lingered in the chambers of the sea
By seamaids wreathed with seaweed red and brown,   [130]
Till human voices wake us, and we drown.

78. *here between*] stretched *written in pencil above* here *and braced*; here *beside*
1917.

79. *so many*] tea *and 1917*.

83. *that's*] here's *1917*.

85. *I have seen*] seen *1st reading.* FOOTMAN] Footman *1917*.

93. *toward*] *1917*; towards *1963*.

102. *and the skirts*] after the skirts *1917*.

105] *not 1917*.

109] *one line in 1915; two lines in 1917*: say: / "That

111. *Hamlet*] Prince Hamlet *1917*.　　*am*] was *1917*.

114. *withal*] *1915*; no doubt *1917*.

118. *appear*] almost *1917*.

121. *shall*] *1st and (pencil) 3rd reading, 1917*; will *2nd reading*.

123. *will*] shall *1917*.

124. *each.*] each, *possibly, but what looks like a comma is probably miswritten or misread, given the following space.*

130. *seamaids*] sea-girls *1917*.

131. *us*] up *1st reading (slip)*.

Entretien dans un parc

[Was it a morning or an afternoon
That has such things to answer for!]
We walked along, under the April trees,
With their uncertainties
Struggling intention that becomes intense.   5
I wonder if it is too late or soon
For the resolution that our lives demand.
With a sudden vision of incompetence
I seize her hand
In silence and we walk on as before.   10

And apparently the world has not been changed;
Nothing has happened that demands revision.
She smiles, as if, perhaps, surprised to see
So little her composure disarranged:
It is not that life has taken a new decision –   15
It has simply happened so to her and me.

And yet this while we have not spoken a word
It becomes at last a bit ridiculous
And irritating. All the scene's absurd!
She and myself and what has come to us   20
And what we feel, or not;
And my exasperation. Round and round, as in a bubbling pot
That will not cool
Simmering upon the fire, piping hot
Upon the fire of ridicule.   25

– Up a blind alley, stopped with broken walls
Papered with posters, chalked with childish scrawls! –

But if we could have given ourselves the slip
What explanations might have been escaped –
No stumbling over ends unshaped.   30
We are helpless. Still . . . it was unaccountable . . . odd . . .
Could not one keep ahead, like ants or moles?
Some day, if God –
But then, what opening out of dusty souls!

[Pages] 39–40. Manuscript in black ink. Cancelled title: *Situation*.

4. *their* ∧ *uncertainties*] certain *1st reading*.

13. *as if, perhaps,*] perhaps as if *1st reading*.

26. *broken*] tumbling [?] *very doubtful 1st reading*.

27 ∧ 28] *space in MS (coinciding with page-division in this edition)*.

34. *opening out*] laying out / laying open *alternatives, braced below*.

[Notebook [pages] 41–4 and [leaf] 45: *Portrait of a Lady* II–III, dated Feb. 1910, Nov. 1911; Appendix B.

[Pages] 46–7: *Humouresque (After J. Laforgue)*, dated Nov. 1909; Appendix B.]

Interlude: in a Bar

Across the room the shifting smoke
Settles around the forms that pass
Pass through or clog the brain;
Across the floors that soak
The dregs from broken glass   5

The walls fling back the scattered streams
Of life that seems
Visionary, and yet hard;
Immediate, and far;
But hard . . .   10
Broken and scarred
Like dirty broken finger nails
Tapping the bar.

[Leaf] 48. Manuscript in pencil.

6. *walls*] *written over* f   .

13. *Tapping*] *written over the start of a word.*

[Notebook: one leaf excised, without stub.]

Paysage Triste

The girl who mounted in the omnibus
The rainy day, and paid a penny fare
Who answered my appreciative stare
With that averted look without surprise
Which only the experienced can wear   5
A girl with reddish hair and faint blue eyes

An almost denizen of Leicester Square.
We could not have had her in the box with us
She would not have known how to sit, or what to wear
Yet if I close my eyes I see her moving   10
With loosened hair about her chamber
With naked feet passing across the skies

She would have been most crudely ill at ease
She would not have known how to sit, or what to wear
Nor, when the lights went out and the horn began   15
Have leaned as you did, your elbow on my knees
To prod impetuously with your fan
The smiling stripling with the pink soaped face
Who had your opera-glasses in his care.

Separate leaf laid in; original typescript.

2. *a*] the *1st reading.*

3. *Who*] The girl who *1st reading.*

16. *my*] *in ink*; your *1st reading.*

Afternoon

The ladies who are interested in Assyrian art
Gather in the hall of the British Museum.
The faint perfume of last year's tailor suits
And the steam from drying rubber overshoes
And the green and purple feathers on their hats   5
Vanish in the sombre Sunday afternoon

As they fade beyond the Roman statuary
Like amateur comedians across a lawn
Towards the unconscious, the ineffable, the absolute

[Leaf] 49. Manuscript in black ink.

2. *Museum.*] MS, *typescript made by Aiken*; Museum *typescript of Aiken MS made by Jane Quinby.*

4. *overshoes*] MS, *typescript made by Aiken*; shoes *typescript of Aiken MS made by Quinby.*

7. *statuary*] MS, *typescript of Aiken MS made by Quinby*; statuary, *typescript made by Aiken.*

8. *lawn*] lawn, *typescript made by Aiken, typescript of Aiken MS made by Quinby.*

9. *absolute*] absolute. *typescript made by Aiken, typescript of Aiken MS made by Quinby.*

Suppressed Complex

She lay very still in bed with stubborn eyes
Holding her breath lest she begin to think
I was a shadow upright in the corner
Dancing joyously in the firelight.

She stirred in her sleep and clutched the blanket with her fingers 5
She was very pale and breathed hard.
When morning shook the long nasturtium creeper in the tawny bowl
I passed joyously out through the window.

[Leaf] 50. Manuscript in black ink.

2. *think*] MS, *typescript of Aiken MS made by Jane Quinby;* think. *typescript sent to Pound, typescript made by Aiken.*

7. *shook*] MS, *typescript sent to Pound;* stirred *typescript made by Aiken, typescript of Aiken MS made by Quinby.*

8. *out*] MS, *added with a caret in typescript sent to Pound.*

[Notebook [leaf] 51: *Morning at the Window*; Appendix B.]

In the Department Store

The lady of the porcelain department
Smiles at the world through a set of false teeth.
She is business-like and keeps a pencil in her hair

But behind her sharpened eyes take flight
The summer evenings in the park   5
And heated nights in second story dance halls.

Man's life is powerless and brief and dark
It is not possible for me to make her happy.

Separate leaf laid in; original typescript.

The Little Passion
From "An Agony in the Garret"

Upon those stifling August nights
  I know he used to walk the streets
Now following the lines of lights
  Or diving into dark retreats

Or following the lines of lights   5
And knowing well to what they lead:
To one inevitable cross
Whereon our souls are pinned, and bleed.

[*Another draft including these lines*]

Of those ideas in his head
Which found me always interested
Though they were seldom well digested –
I recollect one thing he said
After those hours of streets and streets   5
That spun around him like a wheel
He finally remarked: "I feel
As if I'd been a long time dead."

Upon those stifling August nights
I know he used to walk the streets   10
Now diving into dark retreats –
Or following the lines of lights

Or following the lines of lights,
And knowing well to what they lead
To some inevitable cross   15
Whereon our souls are spread, and bleed.

And when he leaned across the bar
Twisting a hopeless cigarette
I noticed on his withered face
A smile which I cannot forget   20
A washed-out, unperceived disgrace.

Two drafts are given here. The first (i) is Notebook [leaf] 52, in black ink; the second
(ii), which is untitled, is in pencil on a separate leaf laid in, with lines 17–21 on the
verso.

(ii)

1. *those*] *uncertain reading*; these *Gallup*.

4. *recollect*] remember *1st reading*.

12. *the lines*] a line *1st reading*.

14. *And*] *added.* *they lead*] it leads *1st reading*.

16] Whereon his soul is spread, and bleeds. *1st reading.* *souls*] soul *MS which*
neglected the consequential emendation to the plural here.

16 ∧ 17] *space in MS (coinciding with page-division in this edition).*

21] A thin, unconscious half-disgrace *alternative braced below.* *unperceived*]
infinite *1st reading*; not *written and deleted before* unperceived [*presumably*
intending not perceived]; hardly [?] *or* barely [?] *written and deleted above* infinite.

[The Notebook follows [leaf] 52 with 28 blank leaves and three stubs. In the words of Dr Gallup: 'Then come (on versos of unnumbered leaves and upside-down in relation to the front of the volume) copies by T. S. Eliot in black ink of two of the "Rondels pour après" from *Les amours jaunes* of Tristan Corbière, the first beginning "Buona vespre! Dors: Ton bout de cierge," the second, "Il fait noir, enfant, voleur d'étincelles!" (the first has the initials "T.C." at the end, the second has "Corbière"). On separate leaves laid in at the back are pencil copies of two more of the "Rondels," the first entitled "Mirliton," the second, "Petit Mort Pour Rire," neither with indication of authorship and the second with the name and address of (the publisher) Albert Messein in Paris added in Eliot's hand.' *Bulletin of the New York Public Library*, December 1968, p.649.]

[Loose leaves follow.]

Introspection

The mind was six feet deep in a
cistern and a brown snake with a tri-
angular head having swallowed his
tail was struggling like two fists
interlocked. His head slipped along   5
the brick wall, scraping at the
cracks.

Miscellaneous leaves [4]. Manuscript in black ink, prose poem, written in only the left half of the page with lineation (including the hyphen) so.

While you were absent in the lavatory
There came a negro with broad flat eyes
Bringing a dish with oranges and bananas
And another brought coffee and cigars.
I was restless, my dear, and a little unhappy   5
Needing your wide mouth opposite me.
I hung suspended on the finger-bowl
Until a white rabbit hopped beneath the table
Twitching his nose toward the crumbs

Miscellaneous leaves [4]. Manuscript in black ink, below *Introspection* on the same page. The Beinecke Library (Yale) has among the Pound papers another draft, titled *To Helen*.

3. *bananas*] bananas, *Yale*.

5. *restless*] impatient *Yale*.

6. *wide*] large *Yale*.

7. *finger-bowl*] finger bowl *Yale*.

8. *Until*] Till *Yale*.   *beneath the table*] around the corner *Yale*.

9. *Twitching*] And twitched *Yale* (Tw *deleted*).   *crumbs*] crumbs. *Yale*.

The Burnt Dancer

sotta la pioggia dell' aspro martiro

Within the yellow ring of flame
A black moth through the night
Caught in the circle of desire
Expiates his heedless flight
With beat of wings that do not tire   5
Distracted from more vital values
To golden values of the flame
What is the virtue that he shall use
In a world too strange for pride or shame?
A world too strange for praise or blame   10
Too strange for good or evil:
How drawn here from a distant star
For mirthless dance and silent revel

O danse mon papillon noir!

The tropic odours of your name   15
From Mozambique or Nicobar
Fall on the ragged teeth of flame
Like perfumed oil upon the waters
What is the secret you have brought us
Children's voices in little corners   20
Whimper whimper through the night
Of what disaster do you warn us
Agony nearest to delight?
Dance fast dance faster
There is no mortal disaster   25
The destiny that may be leaning
Toward us from your hidden star
Is grave, but not with human meaning

O danse mon papillon noir!

Within the circle of my brain   30
The twisted dance continues.

The patient acolyte of pain,
The strong beyond our human sinews,
The singèd reveller of the fire,
Caught on those horns that toss and toss,   35
Losing the end of his desire
Desires completion of his loss.
O strayed from whiter flames that burn not
O vagrant from a distant star
O broken guest that may return not   40

O danse danse mon papillon noir!

Miscellaneous leaves [5]. Original typescript, with the French refrain typed in red.

4. *heedless*] little *1st reading.*

14. *mon*] *added in pencil as in 29 (but already there in 41).*

19. *us*] *added in pencil.*

20. *Children's*] Childrens' *typescript.* (A similar misplacing occurs in *The Death of Saint Narcissus* (*The Waste Land MS*, pp.91, 95): Mens' for Men's, twice.)   *little*] hidden *1st reading.*

23. *?*] *added in pencil.*

28. *not with*] with *1st reading.*

32–4] *the terminal commas added in pencil.*

35. *those*] these *1st reading.*   *toss,*] *comma apparently added in pencil.*

First Debate between the Body and Soul

The August wind is shambling down the street

A blind old man who coughs and spits sputters
Stumbling among the alleys and the gutters.

He pokes and prods
With senile patience   5
The withered leaves
Of our sensations –

And yet devoted to the pure idea
One sits delaying in the vacant square
Forced to endure the blind inconscient stare   10
Of twenty leering houses that exude
The odour of their turpitude
And a street piano through the dusty trees
Insisting: "Make the best of your position" –
The pure Idea dies of inanition   15
The street pianos through the trees
Whine and wheeze.

Imaginations
Masturbations
The withered leaves   20
Of our sensations

The eye retains the images,
The sluggish brain will not react
Nor distils
The dull precipitates of fact   25
The emphatic mud of physical sense
The cosmic smudge of an enormous thumb
Posting bills
On the soul. And always come
The whine and wheeze   30
Of street pianos through the trees

Imagination's
Poor Relations
The withered leaves
Of our sensations.   35

Absolute! complete idealist
A supersubtle peasant
(Conception most unpleasant)
A supersubtle peasant in a shabby square
Assist me to the pure idea –   40
Regarding nature without love or fear
For a little while, a little while
Standing our ground –
Till life evaporates into a smile
Simple and profound.   45

Street pianos through the trees
Whine and wheeze

Imagination's
Defecations
The withered leaves   50
Of our sensations –

Miscellaneous leaves [6]. The manuscript, in pencil, is hard to decipher, and there are doubtful readings, especially of deletions, as well as readings left by TSE as alternatives. Title: *Reflections in a Square* was added and cancelled.

1. *down*] up *1st reading.*

2. *man who coughs and spits sputters*] man [*followed by a space left for a word or two*] groans and mutters *1st reading.*

6. *The*] In the *1st reading.*

9. *One sits*] Sits one *1st reading.*

10. *the blind inconscient*] their every leering *1st reading*; their disconcerting *2nd reading.*

11] A score of houses that exude *original reading undeleted. (Not printed above, though an exception to the usual principle, because this undeleted reading does not quite cohere with TSE's revisions, including deletions, in these much-altered lines.) leering]* battered *1st reading. houses]* housefronts *alternative, below.*

12. *their* ∧ *turpitude]* conscious *1st reading;* conscient *2nd reading. Written above* conscious *is* leering *but ringed to move to 11 to replace* battered.

14] That are hinting: "Accept this position" – *1st reading. But since TSE deleted only* That are *and* this *the variant line ought perhaps to be described as partly 1st reading (deleted) and partly alternative (undeleted). TSE apparently intended the quotation marks to be retained after cancelling the 1st reading.*

18. *Imaginations]* Imagination's *would bring this into line with 32, 48, but TSE may well have intended the difference.*

22. *eye]* brain *1st reading.*

23. *brain]* intellect *1st reading.*

24. *Nor distils]* Will not distil *1st reading.*

25. *precipitates]* precipitate *perhaps.*

26] The muddy emphasis of sense! *alternative below, braced.*

27] *Retaining TSE's original line; he proliferated alternatives, none clearly or finally superseding the original. cosmic]* deleted; indifferent *written above, followed by* careless *both deleted;* callous *written below, undeleted and ringed to move to replace* enormous *(deleted) but without the consequential change of* an *to* a. *In the left margin:*

Eternal   Here's
Cosmic,   immense

28] *following 25 there had been a version of this line, erased: [indecipherable]* goes on posting bills.

29. *the* ∧ *soul]* sanctuary of the *1st reading. soul]* brain *written above and deleted. And always come] originally as the next line but marked to be taken back.*

30–1] The street pianos through the trees / Whine and wheeze. *1st reading. (The* deleted, *replaced by* Of. And *deleted.)*

31 ∧ 32] *space in MS (coinciding with page-division in this edition).*

36. *Absolute! complete] a line looped under these two words. idealist]* assist *below* idealist *('Assist me', 40).*

37. *supersubtle]* supersensitive *1st reading.*

38] (No conception [*intending* more?] unpleasant) *1st reading.*

40. *the*] thy *1st reading.*

44] And life evaporating in a smile *1st reading.*

49. *Defecations*] or desquamations *added to the right in a lighter pencil. Probably an alternative, though TSE does not elsewhere use 'or' so.*

Bacchus and Ariadne
2nd Debate between the Body and Soul

I saw their lives curl upward like a wave
And break. And after all it had not broken —
It might have broken even across the grave
Of tendencies unknown and questions never spoken.
The drums of life were beating on their skulls   5
The floods of life were swaying in their brains

A ring of silence closes round me and annuls
These sudden insights that have marched across
Like railway-engines over desert plains.

The world of contact sprang up like a blow   10
The winds beyond the world had passed without a trace
I saw that Time began again its slow
Attrition on a hard resistant face.

Yet to burst out at last, ingenuous and pure
Surprised, but knowing – it is triumph not endurable to miss! 15
Not to set free the purity that clings
To the cautious midnight of its chrysalis
Lies in its cell and meditates its wings
Nourished in earth and stimulated by manure.
– I am sure it is like this   20
I am sure it is this
I am sure.

Miscellaneous leaves [7]. The manuscript, in pencil, is hard to decipher, and there are doubtful readings.

3. *might have broken*] might have happened / should have broken! *alternatives.*

4. *unknown*] suppressed *1st reading.*

5. *drums*] floods *1st reading.*

7. *me*] *written over* the [?].

8. *insights*] incidents *1st reading*; intuitions *alternative.*   *marched*] moved [?] *1st reading.*

11] The wind [*revised from* The life] that breathed across had left no trace *1st reading.* *beyond the world*] *in ink.*

12] The world began again its even [even *deleted*] slow *1st reading*; I saw the world begin again its slow *2nd reading*; And I saw that Time began again its slow *3rd reading.* And / that Time / *the* a *in* began *all in ink.*

13. *Attrition*] Rasping [?] *1st reading.*

14. *burst*] spring *added and deleted.*   *pure*] fresh and pure *1st reading.*

15. *triumph*] *added above an indecipherable word.*   *not endurable*] unendurable *perhaps.*

15 ∧ 16] For purity is not *deleted.*

16] To have found free the purity that springs *1st reading.*

18. *meditates*] *underlined with ? off to the right.*

18, 19] *originally in reverse order; transposed with an arrow.*

20. *sure* ∧ *it*] that *added and deleted.*   *like*] *added.*

The smoke that gathers blue and sinks
The torpid smoke of rich cigars
The torpid after-dinner drinks
The overpowering immense
After dinner insolence   5
Of matter "going by itself"
Existence just about to die
Stifled with glutinous liqueurs
Till hardly a sensation stirs
The overoiled machinery . . .   10

What, you want action?
Some attraction?
Now begins
The piano and the flute and two violins
Someone sings   15
A lady of almost any age
But chiefly breast and rings
"Throw your arms around me – Aint you glad you found me"
Still that's hardly strong enough –
Here's a negro (teeth and smile)   20
Has a dance that's quite worth while
That's the stuff!
(Here's your gin
Now begin!)

Miscellaneous leaves [8]. Manuscript in pencil.

7. *die*] stop *1st reading.*

7 ∧ 8] Machinery *deleted.*

8. *Stifled*] Choaked up *1st reading.* (TSE wrote 'choaked', corrected to 'choked', in a letter to Robert Waller, 21 Sept. 1942, British Library.)

12. *Some attraction?*] Here's the attraction *1st reading.*

21. *'s quite*] ought to be *1st reading.*

He said: this universe is very clever
  The scientists have laid it out on paper
Each atom goes on working out its law, and never
Can cut an unintentioned caper.

He said: it is a geometric net   5
And in the middle, like a syphilitic spider
The Absolute sits waiting, till we get
All tangled up and end ourselves inside her.

He said: "this crucifixion was dramatic
He had not passed his life on officechairs   10
They did not crucify him in an attic
Up six abysmal flights of broken stairs."

He said I am put together with a pot and scissors
Out of old clippings
No one took the trouble to make an article.   15

Miscellaneous leaves [9]. Manuscript in pencil.

3. *goes on working out its law*] has its Place in Life *alternative.*

5. *it is*] it's *1st reading.*

6. *syphilitic*] spongy [?] *1st reading*; bloated *2nd reading*; flattened *undeleted above*
like *possibly as alternative to* syphilitic *possibly for* flattened like.

8. *ourselves*] *in ink over indecipherable 1st reading.*

8 ∧ 9] *line drawn across the page.*

9. *"this*] they *1st reading*; "that *alternative above.*

10. *on officechairs*] *in ink*; upon [*indecipherable*] chairs *1st reading*; in wearing out of
chairs *added above in pencil, and deleted in ink.*

12. *six abysmal*] three unending *2nd reading deleted.*

1
Inside the gloom
Of a garret room

2
The constellations
Took up their stations

3
Menagerie   5
Of the August sky

4
The Scorpion
All alone

5
With his tail on fire
Danced on a wire   10

6
And Cassiopea
Explained the Pure Idea

7
The Major Bear
Balanced a chair

8
To show the direction   15
Of intellection

9
And Pegasus the winged horse
Explained the scheme of Vital Force

10
And Cetus too, by way of a satire
Explained the relation of life to matter   20

11
And the Pole Star while the debate was rife
Explained the use of a Place in Life

12
Then Bootes, unsettled
And visibly nettled

13
Said Are not all these questions   25
Brought up by indigestions?

14
So they cried and chattered
As if it mattered.

Miscellaneous leaves [9], verso. Manuscript in pencil. Couplets are scattered down and across the page, and then numbered for reordering.

1. *gloom*] tomb *1st reading.*

2. *garret*] furnished *1st reading.*

4. *Took up*] Assumed *alternative below, braced.*

5–6] *before 3–4, then transposed.*

7. *Scorpion*] scorpion *1st reading.*

11–12] *added.*

13. *Major Bear*] dancing bear *1st reading. TSE may have intended to delete* The *when making the revision.*

14. *Balanced*] Stood on *1st reading.*

15–16] *added.*

15. *direction*] effect *alternative above, braced.*

16. *intellection*] intellect *alternative below, braced.*

18. *scheme*] notion [nature *perhaps*] *1st reading.*

19. *too*] then *1st reading.*

21. *while the debate was rife*] with a fork and knife *alternative above.*

25. *Said*] Cried *1st reading.*   all] *deleted and then rewritten.*

27. *So*] *added.*

Oh little voices of the throats of men
That come between the singer and the song;
Oh twisted little hands of men held up
To rend the beautiful and curse the strong.
Impatient tireless undirected feet!   5
So confident on wrinkled ways of wrong.
On what remote frontier of heaven and hell
Shall time allow our divers paths to meet?

Yet you do well to run the roads you run,
Yes you do well to keep the ways you keep;   10
And we who seek to balance pleasure and pain
We blow against the wind and spit against the rain:
For what could be more real than sweat and dust and sun?
And what more sure than night and death and sleep?

Appearances appearances he said,   15
I have searched the world through dialectic ways;
I have questioned restless nights and torpid days,
And followed every by-way where it lead;
And always find the same unvaried
Intolerable interminable maze.   20
Contradiction is the debt you would collect
And still with contradiction are you paid,
And while you do not know what else you seek
You shall have nothing other to expect.
Appearances, appearances, he said,   25
And nowise real; unreal, and yet true;
Untrue, yet real; – of what are you afraid?
Hopeful of what? whether you keep thanksgiving,
Or pray for earth on tired body and head,
This word is true on all the paths you tread   30
As true as truth need be, when all is said:
That if you find no truth among the living
You will not find much truth among the dead.
No other time but now, no other place than here, he said.

He drew the shawl about him as he spoke   35
And dozed in his arm-chair till the morning broke.

Across the window panes the plumes of lilac swept
Stirred by the morning air.
Across the floor the shadows crawled and crept
And as the thin light shivered through the trees   40
Around the muffled form they danced and leapt.
They crawled about his shoulders and his knees;
They rested for a moment on his hair
Until the morning drove them to their lair.
And then sprang up a little damp dead breeze   45
That rattled at the window while he slept,
And had those been human voices in the chimneys
And at the shutters, and along the stair,
You had not known whether they laughed or wept.

Miscellaneous leaves [10]. Original typescript, with line 6 added in pencil. Variants from the typescript in the McKeldin Library, which further differs in having no terminal punctuation in the following lines: 2, 9, 10, 12, 13, 15, 16, 17, 18, 22, 25, 28, 29, 31, 38, 41, 42, 44, 46, 48.

6] *added in pencil in margin; not McKeldin.*

8. *paths*] ways *1st reading; McKeldin.*

8 ∧ 9] *no space McKeldin.*

9. *roads*] ways *McKeldin.*

11. *balance pleasure*] measure joy *McKeldin.*

19. *unvaried*] unvarièd *McKeldin.*

20. *Intolerable interminable*] Interminable intolerable *McKeldin.*

25. *Appearances, appearances,*] Appearances appearances *McKeldin.*

27. *yet*] but *McKeldin.*

28. *whether*] Whether *McKeldin.*

30. *word*] truth *1st reading, McKeldin 1st reading (changed in ink).   paths you tread*] ways you keep *McKeldin 1st reading.*

31. *true*] truth *McKeldin.   , when all is said:*] (when all is said) *McKeldin.*

34. *but*] than *McKeldin.   than*] *McKeldin 1st reading*; but *McKeldin.*

34 ∧ 35] *space in MS (coinciding with page-division in this edition).*

36. *arm-chair*] armchair *McKeldin.*

37. *of*] the *McKeldin 1st reading (mistyped?).*

40. *light*] *added in ink.*

43. *They*] The *McKeldin (mistyped?).   on*] in *1st reading*; *McKeldin.*

44. *morning*] daylight *McKeldin.*

47. *in*] at *McKeldin 1st reading.*

49. *known*] *added in ink.*

The Love Song of St. Sebastian

I would come in a shirt of hair
I would come with a lamp in the night
And sit at the foot of your stair;
I would flog myself until I bled,
And after hour on hour of prayer   5
And torture and delight
Until my blood should ring the lamp
And glisten in the light;
I should arise your neophyte
And then put out the light   10
To follow where you lead,
To follow where your feet are white
In the darkness toward your bed
And where your gown is white
And against your gown your braided hair.   15
Then you would take me in
Because I was hideous in your sight
You would take me in without shame
Because I should be dead
And when the morning came   20
Between your breasts should lie my head.

I would come with a towel in my hand
And bend your head beneath my knees;
Your ears curl back in a certain way
Like no one's else in all the world.   25
When all the world shall melt in the sun,
Melt or freeze,
I shall remember how your ears were curled.
I should for a moment linger
And follow the curve with my finger   30
And your head beneath my knees –
I think that at last you would understand.
There would be nothing more to say.
You would love me because I should have strangled you
And because of my infamy;   35
And I should love you the more because I had mangled you

And because you were no longer beautiful
To anyone but me.

Miscellaneous leaves [11]. Original typescript. Title supplied from the typescript sent to Conrad Aiken (McKeldin Library). Variants from the McKeldin typescript, which further differs in having no terminal punctuation in the following lines: 3, 4, 8, 11, 15, 25, 26, 27, 31, 32, 33.

2. *a* ∧ *lamp*] little *McKeldin*.

4. *bled*] bleed *McKeldin 1st reading*.

7. *lamp*] light *1st reading*, *McKeldin 1st reading (changed in ink)*.

9. *arise your neophyte*] arise, your neophyte, *McKeldin (commas added in ink)*.

11. *To*] And *McKeldin 1st reading (changed in ink)*.

18. *in*] in to your bed *McKeldin*.

23. *beneath*] between *McKeldin 1st reading*; below *McKeldin (changed in ink)*. *knees;*] knees. [?] *McKeldin*.

25. *one's*] ones *McKeldin*.

28. *shall*] should *McKeldin 1st reading (changed in ink)*.

29. *should*] shall *1st reading*, *McKeldin 1st reading (changed in ink)*.

31. *beneath*] between *McKeldin*.

32, 33. *would*] will *1st reading*.

33. *be nothing more*] not be one word *McKeldin*.

34. *would . . . should*] will . . . shall *1st reading*.

35. *infamy;*] infammy. *McKeldin 1st reading*. (Deleting the extra m, TSE wrote in the margin: 'N*ot* to rhyme with "mammy" '.)

36. *should . . . had*] shall . . . have *1st reading*.

Do I know how I feel? Do I know what I think?
Let me take ink and paper, let me take pen and ink . . .
Or with my hat and gloves, as if to take the air
Walk softly down the hall, stop at the foot of the stair
Take my letters from the porter — ask him for a drink   5
If I questioned him with care, would he tell me what I think and feel
— Or only "You are the gentleman who has lived on the second floor
    For a year or more" —
Yet I dread what a flash of madness might reveal
If he said "Sir we have seen so much beauty spilled on the open
    street   10
Or wasted in stately marriages or stained in railway carriages
Or left untasted in villages or stifled in darkened chambers
That if we are restless on winter nights, who can blame us?"

Do I know how I feel? Do I know how I think?
There is something which should be firm but slips, just at my finger
    tips.   15
There will be a smell of creolin and the sound of something that drips
A black bag with a pointed beard and tobacco on his breath
With chemicals and a knife
Will investigate the cause of death that was also the cause of the life —
Would there be a little whisper in the brain   20
A new assertion of the ancient pain
Or would this other touch the secret which I cannot find?

My brain is twisted in a tangled skein
There will be a blinding light and a little laughter
And the sinking blackness of ether   25
I do not know what, after, and I do not care either

Miscellaneous leaves [12]. Manuscript in pencil, with final six lines on the upper half
of the verso.

6. *would he tell me*] he would know *1st reading.* *and feel*] *probably added when TSE revised 9.*

8. *or*] of *1st reading.* *more"*] more *MS.*

9] And yet I dread what I know he will not say *1st reading.*

10. *we*] I *1st reading.*

12. *or stifled in*] in neurasthetic *1st reading.*

13. *can*] has the heart to *alternative above, braced.*

15. *There is*] *written over* I have [?].

16. *something*] water *1st reading.*

17. *his*] the *1st reading.*

18] Will investigate *1st reading (anticipating the next line).*

20. *Would*] As he pulls back the skin, would *1st reading.*

23. *in*] like *1st reading.*

25. *ether*] *indecipherable 1st reading.*

Hidden under the heron's wing
Or the song before daybreak that the lotos-birds sing
Evening whisper of stars together
Oh my beloved what do you bring –

With evening feet walking across the grass   5
And fragile arms dividing the evening mist.

I lie on the floor a bottle's broken glass
To be swept away by the housemaid's crimson fist.

Miscellaneous leaves [12], verso. Manuscript in pencil, bottom half of the leaf, following the concluding six lines of *Do I know how I feel?*

1. *wing*] wings *1st reading.*

2. *-birds sing*] -bird sings *1st reading.*

8. *housemaid's*] maid with *1st reading.*   *crimson*] scarlet *added above and then deleted.*

Justitia mosse il mio alto fattore

Mi fece la divina potestate

La somma sapienza e il primo amore
O lord, have patience
Pardon these derelictions –
I shall convince these romantic irritations
By my classical convictions.

Miscellaneous leaves [13]. Manuscript in pencil. The top two-thirds of the page are given to the three widely spaced lines of Dante, each underlined, with TSE's quatrain immediately following the third one. TSE may have intended to supply verses to follow each of the three lines.

Airs of Palestine, No. 2

God from a Cloud to Spender spoke
And breathed command: "Take thou this Rod,
And smite therewith the living Rock";
And Spender hearkened unto God.

God shook the Cloud from East to West,   5
Riding the swart tempestuous blast;
And Spender, like a man possess'd,
Stood quaking, tremulous, aghast.

And Spender struck the living Rock,
And lo! the living Rock was wet,   10
From which henceforth at twelve o'clock
Issues the Westminster Gazette.

Swift at the stroke of Spender's pen
The viscid torrents crawl and writhe
Down the long lanes of dogs and men   15
To Canning Town and Rotherhithe,

To Bermondsey and Wapping Stair,
To Clapham Junction and to Sheen,
To Leicester and to Grosvenor Square
Bubble those floods of bilious green.   20

To Old Bond Street, the street of gems,
To Hammersmith and Stamford's rill;
Troubling the sources of the Thames
Mounting the crest of Highgate Hill.

And higher still the torrent flows   25
And circles Zion's pearly wall,
Wherein, by Mary's garden close,
There sit Saint Peter and Saint Paul.

84

For there the risen souls flock in
And there they innocently strip,　　　30
And purge themselves of all their sin
Up to the navel or the hip.

And such as have the skill to swim
Attain at length the farther shore
Cleansed and rejoiced in every limb,　　35
And hate the Germans more and more.

They are redeemed from heresies
And all their frowardness forget;
The scales are fallen from their eyes
Thanks to the Westminster Gazette.　　40

Miscellaneous leaves [19–20]. Original typescript, with markings and variants in pencil by TSE and by Pound; and carbon of this typescript.

5–8] *braced on the left by Pound.*

11. *henceforth*] thenceforth *1st reading.*

14. *crawl and writhe*] writhe and crawl *alternative by TSE in the margin.*

16] To Cannon St. and London Wall. *alternative by TSE in the margin, with* London Bridge *braced below* Cannon St.

20. *Bubble*] *in pencil*; They flow, *1st reading.*

21–4] *braced on the left by Pound.*

23. *Troubling*] They stir *1st reading.*

24. *Mounting*] They mount *1st reading.*

39–40] instead of scales to shade [cloud *1st reading*] their eyes,
　　They use Spender's gazette. *Pound*

Petit Epître

Ce n'est pas pour qu'on se dégoute
Ou gout d'égout de mon Ego
Qu'ai fait des vers de faits divers
Qui sentent un peu trop la choucroute.
Mais qu'est-ce que j'ai fait, nom d'un nom,   5
Pour faire ressortir les chacals?
J'ai dit qu'il y a une odeur mâle
Et aussi une odeur fémelle
Et que ces deux sont pas la même.
(L'autre jour, à mi-carême,   10
Je l'ai constaté, chez une telle).
Ce que dit autrement le prêtre.
Surtout à la saison de rut.
Alors, on a fait chahue
Et enfoncé mes deux fenêtres.   15

Qu'est-ce que j'ai fait, nom d'un nom,
Pour agiter les morpions?
Ce que j'ai fait, je te le dis,
Je conçevais un Paradis
Ou l'on partagerait ses biens;   20
(J'aurais également les tiens).
Monsieur le préfet de police
Il en a assez, de ses vices,
Il marmotte, lunettes sur le nez:
"C'est de la promiscuité."   25
Alors, il faut que je lui rende
Cinq cents balles, qui sert d'amende.

Messieurs les rédacteurs
Et tous les autres maîtres-chanteurs
Et tous les gens étiquetés   30
M'ont dressé tous, leur questionnaires.
"Il se moque de l'égalité?"
— "Mais c'est un vrai réactionnaire".
"Il dit du mal de nos ministres?"
— "Mais c'est un saboteur, le cuistre".   35

"Ici il cite un allemand?"
– "Mais c'est un suppôt de Satan!"
"Est-ce qu'il doute la vie future?"
– "Certes, c'est un homme de moeurs impures".
"Ne nie pas l'existence de Dieu?"   40
– "Comme il est superstitueux!"
"Est-ce qu'il n'a pas d'enfants?"
– "Il est eunuque, ça s'entend".
"Pour les dames
Ne réclame   45
pas la vote? Pédéraste, sans doute".

"Quant à son livre, qu'on s'en foute!"
Ces baragouins
De sagouins
Je les entends le long de la route.   50

Miscellaneous leaves [21]. Original typescript. No attempt is made here to correct TSE's French.

4. *Qui*] qui *typescript.*

6–7. *chacals . . . mâle*] *braced, with the query in TSE's hand:* 'rhyme?'

21. *aurais*] aurai *1st reading.*

25. *promiscuité."*] promiscuité)." *typescript which lacks an opening bracket.*

27. *qui sert*] *in ink (in TSE's hand);* par voie *1st reading.*

31. *tous,*] tous *1st reading.*

44. *dames*] *in ink (not in TSE's hand, perhaps Dulac's);* femmes *1st reading.* femmes / réclame *braced, with the query in TSE's hand:* 'rhyme?' *(this then deleted, after the revision).*

50. *entends*] entend *1st reading.*

Tristan Corbière

"Il devint pour un instant parisien"

Marin! je te connais, rentier du cinquième
Qui veillait dans la nuit comme un vieil hibou;
Râclant sa gorge, toi qu'on nomme *an Ankou*,
Sur un grabat accroupi, barbe pointue, gueule blême.

Dans la chambre voisine s'entretiennent des scandales   5
Un commis portugais et une dame à cent sous:
Entre les chuchotements à travers quelques trous
– Bat sur les côtes brétonnes la mer en rafales.

Des rayons de soleil, par une chaude après-midi
Nous montrent, au Luxembourg, des messieurs barbus gris   10
Redingotés, clignant des dames à la poudre de riz.

Et Lieutenant Loti, très bien dans sa tenue,
Se promène dans les pages des complaisantes Revues
Comme au coin du boulevard une vielle ancienne grue.

Miscellaneous leaves [22–3]. Original typescript; plus carbon with markings and variants by Pound and pinned to it a scrap of paper with a different version, in TSE's hand, of the final three lines. It is not certain that this supersedes the three lines as typed; TSE did not delete the typed version, and the scrap has two failures of agreement (neither in the typescript), so here the typed text is given, with the other as variants. No attempt is made here to correct TSE's French.

1. *cinquième*] Pound wrote: 'cinquième on the côte or in Paris?? or the mer in his d[   ]'.

3. *sa*] la *alternative* (l *written above the* s).

5. *des*] de *correction by Pound.*

7. *quelques trous*] *deleted by Pound;* le verrou *alternative braced, typed above.*

10. *au Luxembourg*] aux jardins *alternative braced, typed above, deleted by Pound.*

Pound ringed 'Luxembourg', and wrote: 'Avenue Champs Elysèe, ou a L'Etoile – before the clubs in the C.E. next door to Pres. Fallieres back yard'.

11. *clignant*] lorgnant *alternative in pencil by TSE*. Pound wrote (below the previous marginal comment): 'or Cafè de la Paix if they are going to clign/ very heavily'.

12–14] Telle sur le boulevard une ancienne grue
      Le Lieutenant Loti, très bien dans sa tenue
      Fait le trottoirs dans les pages des complaisants revues
TSE, scrap of paper

13–14. Pound wrote '? promène au coin', and ringed 14 with an arrow to move it before 12.

The Engine

I

The engine hammered and hummed. Flat faces of American business men lay along the tiers of chairs in one plane, broken only by the salient of a brown cigar and the red angle of a six-penny magazine. The machine was hard, deliberate, and alert; having chosen with motives and ends unknown to cut through the fog it pursued its course; the life of the deck stirred and was silent like a restless scale on the smooth surface. The machine was certain and sufficient as a rose bush, indifferently justifying the aimless parasite.

II

After the engine stopped, I lay in bed listening while the wash subsided and the scuffle of feet died out. The music ceased, but a mouth organ from the steerage picked up the tune. I switched on the light, only to see on the wall a spider taut as a drumhead, the life of endless geological periods concentrated into a small spot of intense apathy at my feet. "And if the ship goes down" I thought drowsily "he is prepared and will somehow persist, for he is very old. But the flat faces . . ." I tried to assemble these nebulae into one pattern. Failing, I roused myself to hear the machine recommence, and then the music, and the feet upon the deck.

Miscellaneous leaves [24–5]. First drafts: *I. The Engine*: pencil, on the fourth page of a piece of double notepaper.
II. Machinery: Dancers [*Dancers* revised from *Confetti*]: pencil, on the second page of the piece of double notepaper. Fair copy, in ink, titled as above. First drafts *A*; fair copy *B*.

I

hummed] leapt *A 1st reading*.

Flat] The flat *A 1st reading*.

lay ∧ *along*] in tiers *A 1st reading*; in one plane *A, B 1st reading*.

chairs] *A, B 1st and final reading*; deck-chairs *B 2nd reading*.

; *having . . . fog*] , cutting through the fog *A 1st reading*; having chosen to cut through the fog with motives and ends unknown *A, added between* machine *and* was. *with . . . unknown*] for motives and ends of its own *B 1st reading*.

stirred . . . surface] *indecipherable readings in A.*

certain] *A 1st reading indecipherable.*

sufficient as] more eternal than *A 1st reading.*

as] like *A 2nd reading.*

indifferently . . . parasite] justifying and accounting for the parasitic aphis *A.*

aimless] *added in B.*

II

while] as *A.*

scuffle] shuffle [?] *A 1st reading.*

The] *A 1st reading*; And the *A.*

ceased] stopped *A 1st reading.*

from the steerage] *following* tune *A 1st reading.*

only to see] and saw *A 1st reading*; to see *A.*

on the wall] *added in A.*

spider taut] spider *A*; taut spider *B 1st reading.*

as a drumhead] *not A.*

endless] all the *A 1st reading.*

a small] one small black *A.*

at my feet] *added and deleted in A where it follows* wall.

drowsily] confusedly *A.*

But] And [?] *deleted in B.*

faces . . ."] *A*; faces . . . *B.*

then] *added in A.*

and ∧ *the feet*] then *A.*

[End of Berg Notebook and loose leaves. The poem printed on the following page is from the Special Collections, University of Maryland at College Park Libraries.]

In silent corridors of death
Short sighs and stifled breath,
Short breath and silent sighing;
Somewhere the soul crying.
And I wander alone   5
Without haste without hope without fear
Without pressure or touch –
There is no moan
Of Souls dying
Nothing here   10
But the warm
Dry airless sweet scent
Of the alleys of death
Of the corridors of death

Manuscript in pencil, on 8″ by 10″ ruled paper. McKeldin Library. Date unknown.

7] *added.*

8–9] *underlined, perhaps to invite reconsideration.*

14] *Below the end of the poem, written at an angle up from the left-hand corner of the page:*
> Suffused light – light from where?
> Stifled scent – scent of what?

A pencil-line is drawn across, below them, and then there is:
> Stifled sighs and sighing breath
> In vacant ⎱ corridors of death
> stifling ⎰

TWO FACSIMILES

[First Caprice in North Cambridge]
Notebook, [page] 4, in blue ink; see p.13.

First Caprice in North Cambridge.

A street-piano, garrulous and frail;
The yellow evening flung against the panes
Of dirty windows: and the distant strains
Of children's voices, ended in a wail.

Bottles and broken glass,
Trampled mud and grass;
A heap of broken barrows;
And a crowd of tattered sparrows
Delve in the gutter with sordid patience.

Oh, these minor considerations!.....

[Interlude in London]
Notebook, [page] 7, in black ink and in TSE's later spiky hand; see p.16, where there are guesses at the further readings.

Interlude in London.

We hibernate among the bricks
And live across the window panes
With marmalade and tea at six
Indifferent to what the wind does.
Indifferent to sudden rains
Softening last years garden plots

And apathetic, with cigars
Careless, while down the street the spring goes
Inspiring mouldy flowerpots
And flotten flies at garret windows.

il 1911.

NOTES

Convictions (Curtain Raiser)

Dated Jan. 1910, changed from Nov. 1909. Subtitle: (**Curtain Raiser**): originally slang, and first cited in O E D, 1886, as 'The slight opening pieces, or "curtain raisers" as they are profanely styled'. Laforgue has Hamlet brood: 'Un héros! et que tout le reste fût des levers de rideau!' (curtain-raisers; *Moralités légendaires*, 1887; 1992 edn, p.12); see the notes to 9 and 28–9.

1 **Among my marionettes**: compare *Humouresque (After J. Laforgue)* 1: 'One of my marionettes is dead'. In *The Symbolist Movement in Literature* (1899, revised 1908), which was a revelation to TSE in Dec. 1908, Arthur Symons wrote of Maeterlinck: he 'has invented a drama so precise, so curt, so arbitrary in its limits, that it can safely be confided to the masks and feigned voices of marionettes' (p.154). Again: 'Are we not all puppets, in a theatre of marionettes, in which the parts we play, the dresses we wear, the very emotion whose dominance gives its express form to our faces, have all been chosen for us [. . .]? And as our parts have been chosen for us, our motions controlled from behind the curtain, so the words we seem to speak are but spoken through us, and we do but utter fragments of some elaborate invention'. Symons wrote of Jarry's *Ubu Roi*, in *A Symbolist Farce* (1888): 'a generation which has exhausted every intoxicant, every soluble preparation of the artificial, may well seek a last sensation in the wire-pulled passions, the wooden faces of marionettes, and, by a further illusion, of marionettes who are living people; living people pretending to be those wooden images of life which pretend to be living people' (*Studies in Seven Arts*, 1906, pp.374–5). Also *An Apology for Puppets*, which was moved to the front of the 1909 edition of Symons's *Plays, Acting and Music* (1903): 'The marionette may be relied upon. He will respond to an indication without reserve or revolt; an error on his part (we are all human) will certainly be the fault of the author; he can be trained to perfection'; 'I assure you, you will find it quite easy to fall in love with a marionette'; 'In our marionettes, then, we get personified gesture, and the gesture, like all other forms of emotion, generalised' (pp.3–5, 7–8). In 1923 TSE told Alfred Kreymborg, author of *Puppet Plays*, that he was planning puppet plays of his own (Robert Crawford, *The Savage and the City in the Work of T. S. Eliot*, p.161). 'I do not by any means intend the actor to be an automaton, nor would I admit that the human actor can be replaced by a marionette' (*Four Elizabethan Dramatists*, 1924, SE, p.114). Marionettes are everywhere in German romantic literature, notably in Kleist. See also 14 note.

3 **They see the outlines of their stage**: compare *Mandarins 4* 4: 'Who see their outlines on the screen'.

3, 5 **stage . . . later age**: compare Milton, *Il Penseroso* 99–102: Presenting Thebes, or Pelops' line,

Or the tale of Troy divine,
Or what (though rare) of later age,
Ennobled hath the buskined stage.

Also perhaps compare Wordsworth, who rhymes 'stage' / 'Age', in *Ode: Intimations of Immortality* 104–5, having 'immensity' in 110 (TSE, 4, 'immense'), and with the rhyme 'feet' / 'repeat' in 54–5 (TSE, 25, 27).

4, 6–7 immense . . . an audience . . . suspense: compare *Suite Clownesque I* 14, 17–18: 'immense . . . the audience / Who still continue in suspense'.

9 picking tissue paper roses: in Laforgue's *Hamlet* (*Moralités légendaires*), Hamlet tells Kate to wait a moment, 'le temps de cueillir une fleur, une simple fleur en papier' (1992 edn, p.42). Compare *Rhapsody on a Windy Night* 57: 'Her hand twists a paper rose', where 'alone' ends the next line but one ('She is alone'); here, it ends the next line. Compare Remy de Gourmont, *Litanies de la rose* (1892): 'Rose en papier de soie, simulacre adorable des grâces incréées, rose en papier de soie, n'es-tu pas la vraie rose, fleur hypocrite, fleur du silence?' (This prose poem was in *Poètes d'aujourd'hui*, ed. Adolphe Van Bever and Paul Léautaud, 1900; TSE owned the expanded 2-vol. edition, which appeared in 1908 and was often reprinted.) Compare, again, de Gourmont, *Du Style ou de l'écriture*: 'ce que l'on peut recomposer avec les produits de la distillation d'un style ressemble au style comme une rose en papier parfumé ressemble à la rose' (*La Culture des idées*, 1899).

9, 13 roses . . . supposes: the rhyme in Austin Dobson, *Pot-Pourri* (1873) 3, 6 (a poem about disturbing the dust on a bowl of rose-leaves). Dobson's poems are listed among TSE's books, to be sent to him, *c.* Aug. 1920 (*Letters* i 398).

11 The monotone: compare *Portrait of a Lady* I 34: 'Capricious monotone'. The French romantic and symbolist poets reiterate 'monotone'.

12 promises and compliments: given other affinities ('immense', 4, at the line-end and rhyming), compare the line-end of *Suite Clownesque IV* 10: 'cigarettes and compliments'.

13 supposes: as a noun ('an act of supposing'), archaic, though not apparently obsolete, by 1910; the *OED*'s final two citations, 1875 and 1897, have the word within inverted commas, as archaic or self-conscious. Jonson, *Tale of a Tub* (1633): 'Fatted with Supposes of fine Hopes'.

14 over there my Paladins: compare perhaps W. S. Gilbert's Duke of Plaza-Toro, that 'Overflowing, Easy-going Paladin' (*The Gondoliers*, produced 1889). **Paladins**: *OED*: 'In modern forms of the Charlemagne romances, one of the Twelve Peers or famous warriors of Charlemagne's court, of whom the Count Palatine was the foremost; hence sometimes *transf.* a Knight of the Round Table; also *fig.*

a knightly hero, renowned champion, knight-errant'. Samuel Daniel's *Delia* XLVI, 'Let others sing of Knights and Paladins', is in Quiller-Couch's *Oxford Book of English Verse* (1900). TSE's poem of 1910, with its marionettes (1, 28) and its paladins, may recall W.W. [Watson White] in the *Harvard Advocate*, 25 Nov. 1908 (in which issue TSE published his poem *Circe's Palace*). On *Il Teatro Marionetti* in Boston: 'If you have read the board outside, and are somewhat familiar with Italian, you recognize in this puppet no other than *Orlando* – known as "*Furioso*," and you know that he must be waiting for *Rinaldo* or for his sister *Bradamante* [. . .] Presently *Orlando* may be joined by *Carlamagno*, gorgeously caparisoned as befits the ruler of the Holy Roman Empire.' Rimbaud repeats 'paladins' three lines before 'pantins' (puppets; compare TSE's mario-nettes), in *Bal des pendus* (1891) 2–3, 6. TSE associated the word 'paladins' with talkers of cant: 'One characteristic which increased my suspicion of the scientific paladins of religion is that they are all Englishmen, or at least all Anglo-Saxons' (*Thoughts after Lambeth*, 1931, SE, p.371).

15 **talking of effect and cause**: compare TSE on causality, probably 1914 (Houghton Library; bMS Am 1691.14 (18), p.4): 'we will talk of cause and effect whenever a phenomenon or group of phenomena is thought of as lived through and not as contemplated.' Also p.1: 'I agree thoroughly with Mr Russell when he speaks of cause as a superstition: I only question whether we could live without super-stitions.' Likewise as reported at a seminar on 17 March 1914: TSE, 'Cause, etc., can be explained away and not explained. Can we do without superstition?' *Josiah Royce's Seminar, 1913–1914*, ed. Grover Smith, 1963, p.135. **effect and cause**: given Laforgue in this poem about marionettes, compare *Préludes autobiographiques* (1885) 31, likewise at the line-end: 'en effets et causes'. The transposition is also valued in TSE's philosophical writing: 'A *totality* of causes is of course the effect itself, or freedom. But freedom is subject to the same alteration: complete freedom is identity of effect and cause' (*Report on the Ethics of Kant's Critique of Practical Reason*, Harvard, 25 May 1913, p.6; Hayward Bequest). The transposition would have pleased F. H. Bradley, who called succession in question: 'I may be told that in causation a succession is involved with a direction not reversible'; 'And then, even in our own world, how unsatisfactory the succession laid down in causation!' (*Appearance and Reality*, 1893; 1897 edn, pp.192–3).

15–16 **effect and cause . . . laws**: compare Clough, *Say, will it* (1869) 12–13:
Repose upon effect and cause,
And action of unvarying laws,

16 **"learn to live by nature's laws!"**: Stoic doctrine, quizzed by Horace, *Epistles*, I x 12. In his copy of T. H. Green's *Prolegomena to Ethics* (1906, p.10; Houghton Library), TSE marked the second sentence here: 'They seek to discover what are

the laws – the modes of operation of natural forces – under which we have come to be what we are, in order that they may counsel us how to seek our happiness by living according to those laws. [*new paragraph*] Now it is obvious that to a being who is simply a result of natural forces an injunction to conform to their laws is unmeaning.'

19 **nothing to excess**: proverbial in Greek; written in the temple at Delphi by Cleobulus, and quoted by Plato in *Protagoras*. TSE may banter here, but compare his syllabus for his 1916 tutorial course, on Rousseau's responsibility for Romanticism: 'Romanticism stands for *excess* in any direction' (Modern French Literature, Lecture I; see Ronald Schuchard, *T. S. Eliot as an Extension Lecturer, 1916–1919, Review of English Studies*, n.s. xxv, 1974, 163–73, 292–304; 165 quoted).

25–6 **my heart . . . his control**: compare *The Waste Land* [v] 420–2:
>   your heart would have responded
> Gaily, when invited, beating obedient
> To controlling hands

28–9 **marionettes . . . keen**: compare *Hamlet*, III ii 240–2:
>   HAMLET: I could interpret between you and your love, if I could see the puppets
>   dallying.
>   OPHELIA: You are keen, my lord, you are keen.

Given how much Laforgue there is in the poem, with its marionettes, compare Laforgue's Hamlet (see headnote and 9 note), and his having as an epigraph, in English, to his *Fifre* (1890) this exchange (relevant to TSE's preceding lines too):
>   OPHELIA: You are keen, my lord, you are keen.
>   HAMLET: It would cost you a groaning to take off my edge.
>   OPHELIA: Still better and worse.
>   HAMLET: So you must take your husbands.

First Caprice in North Cambridge

Dated Nov. 1909. Title: perhaps the preposition *in* (**Caprice in North Cambridge**, and another *in Montparnasse*, below) is coloured not only by a setting (the distinctly non-Harvard part of Cambridge, Massachusetts), but by a key (Caprice in C). Compare 'Capricious monotone', *Portrait of a Lady* I 34. TSE's musical titles include – in or alongside these *Inventions – Second* and *Fourth Caprice, Interlude in London, Opera, Suite Clownesque, Interlude: in a Bar, The Little Passion*, and *Airs of Palestine, No.2*; and among his published poems, *Nocturne, Preludes, Rhapsody on a Windy Night, Five-Finger Exercises*, through to *Four Quartets*. Arthur Symons had many such titles for his poems from 1895, including *Caprice* (and *Intermezzo, Madrigal, Air de Ballet*). W. D. Howells's *Caprice* was reprinted in Carolyn Wells's *A Vers de Société Anthology* (1907). Théodore de Banville had a sequence of twenty-four poems, *Les Caprices* (1842), and Verlaine has *Caprices* I–V in *Poèmes saturniens* (1866; see also I note below).

With these cityscapes of TSE's, compare others among *Inventions of the March Hare* and published in *Prufrock and Other Observations* (1917), notably *Preludes* and *Rhapsody on a Windy Night*. TSE later recalled his early life: 'So it was, that for nine months of the year my scenery was almost exclusively urban, and a good deal of it seedily, drably urban at that. My urban imagery was that of St. Louis, upon which that of Paris and London have been superimposed' (*The Influence of Landscape upon the Poet*; *Daedalus*, lxxxix, 1960, p.422). Compare this with the present poem, and with *Fourth Caprice in Montparnasse* and *Interlude in London*.

'Caprice' within Bergson's thinking suggests something of Laforgue's cultivated indecision; compare *L'Evolution créatrice* (1907), ch.I: 'Se conduire par caprice consiste à osciller mécaniquement entre deux ou plusieurs partis *tout faits* et à se fixer pourtant enfin sur l'un d'eux: ce n'est pas avoir mûri une situation intérieure, ce n'est pas avoir évolué.'

Compare two poems by John Gray: his sonnet *Poem* (1893) which has, in a sordid city scene, 'The garrulous sparrows', 'child', and 'grass'; and his *Sonnet: Translated from Paul Verlaine* (1890), which rhymes 'tremulous and frail' with 'wail' (TSE, 1, 4, 'garrulous and frail' / 'wail'), and has 'at eve' and 'childlike' (TSE, 2, 4, 'evening' and 'children'); see I note. There may also be affinities with the third stanza of Hardy, *The Darkling Thrush* (1902, written 1900), with its bird, 'frail' (TSE, 1), 'evensong' (TSE, 2, 'evening'), 'fling' (TSE, 2, 'flung'), and 'voice' (TSE, 4, 'voices').

> 1 **A street-piano, garrulous and frail**: compare *Portrait of a Lady* II 39: 'a street-piano, mechanical and tired'. *First Debate between the Body and Soul* 13: 'And a street piano through the dusty trees'. **piano . . . frail**: Verlaine, *Romances sans paroles* (1874) V, begins: 'Le piano que baise une main frêle'. (In the next line in Verlaine, there is, rather than a 'yellow evening', 'le soir rose et gris'; and Verlaine has, in his closing lines, not 'dirty windows', but 'la fenêtre / Ouverte un peu sur le

petit jardin'.) Compare TSE's 'garrulous and frail' with a line of Laforgue which TSE quoted in the Clark Lectures in 1926: 'Les Jeunes Filles inviolables et frêles' (*Dimanches: C'est l'automne*, 1890, 9; *VMP*, p.214). The sound of bells follows in Laforgue. (There may be a filament from TSE's 'garrulous' to Laforgue's 'inviolables' in TSE's later 'inviolable voice', *The Waste Land* [II] 101.)

OED has 'street piano' from 1857. *Oxford Companion to Music* (1956 edn, p.622): 'a barrel-and-pin operated pianoforte, with no proper claim to the name, however, since no "piano" or gradation of tone-quality is in any way possible [. . .] The application of the colloquial term "Barrel Organ" to this instrument is evidently due to mere association of ideas at the time it became popular.' Laforgue's instruments are other: the barrel-organ, *Complainte de l'orgue de Barbarie* and *Autre complainte de l'orgue de Barbarie*, and the piano proper, heard in the street, in *Complainte des pianos qu'on entend dans les quartiers aisés* (1885). In Britain, John Davidson has *To the Street Piano* (1894); and Symons, *The Barrel-Organ* (1897), with 'voice' four times, and 'Wail' (both TSE, 4). Symons's opening lines can be heard mixing memory and desire:

Enigmatical, tremulous,
Voice of the troubled wires,
What remembering desires
Wail to me,

Behind Symons's poem lies a prose-poem of Mallarmé's, *Plainte d'automne* (1864), which Symons translated as *Autumn Lament* and discussed in *The Symbolist Movement in Literature* (pp.122–4): 'when a barrel-organ began to sing, languishingly and melancholy [. . .] the barrel-organ, in the twilight of memory, has set me despairingly dreaming'. The *Harvard Advocate* (in which, by then, TSE had published two poems) published W. G. Tinckom-Fernandez's poem *The Street Organ* (25 June 1908): 'Spring shyly taps the window-pane' (contrast TSE, 2, 'flung against the panes', and see *Interlude in London* 8–9 note). **garrulous**: the transferred sense ('Of birds and inanimate things: Chattering or babbling') became Victorian poetic diction – but of nature, not of instruments; OED includes Tennyson, of the magpie, and in *The Sisters* 257, Tennyson has 'the mother's garrulous wail' ('wail', 4). TSE may have been prompted too by Laforgue, in whose *Salomé* 'un bulbul dégorgeait des garulements distingués' (*Moralités légendaires*, 1992 edn, p.104). **garrulous and frail**: the phrase stayed with TSE; in a letter (Princeton) to Paul Elmer More, 2 June 1930, he referred to Allen Tate as a 'garrulous and frail stripling'. **frail**: Tennysonian at the line-end. (i) *In Memoriam* LVI 25: 'O life as futile, then, as frail!'; Tennyson's immediately preceding lines, 'in their slime, / Were mellow music', might have contributed to TSE's music here (and to the sound of 'yellow'?), and TSE has 'Oh'; Tennyson continues 'O for thy voice' ('voices', 4, and 'Oh', 10). (ii) *Margaret* 7–10:

Your melancholy sweet and frail

As perfume of the cuckoo-flower?
From the westward-winding flood,
From the evening-lighted wood,

Compare TSE: 'and frail; / The yellow evening'. (Similarly at the line-end, *The Hippopotamus* 5: 'Flesh and blood is weak and frail'.) TSE rhymes 'and frail' with 'in a wail'; for John Gray's rhyming 'and frail' with 'wail', see headnote. James Thomson has 'and frail' rhyming with 'in a veil', *The City of Dreadful Night* (1874) II 2, 4. Eleven lines of Shelley, *The Mask of Anarchy* 94–104, share much with TSE's poem; 'Small at first, and weak, and frail' resembles 2 in its line-end, and Shelley has 'child after child' (TSE, 'children's', 4), 'street' ('street-piano', 1), 'patient' ('patience', 9), and an 'image' (see 7 note for 'images'); TSE, 'Trampled' / Shelley, 'Right before the horses' feet'.

2 **The yellow evening flung against the panes**: compare *The Love Song of J. Alfred Prufrock* 2: 'When the evening is spread out against the sky', where 15 and 16 both have: 'yellow . . . panes'. **yellow evening**: compare *Portrait of a Lady* IV 32: 'evening yellow and rose'; *Second Caprice in North Cambridge* 17: 'a sunset yellow and rose'. **evening flung**: compare *Paradise Lost* VIII 515–9: 'from their wings / Flung rose, flung odours . . . / . . . the evening star', with 'Joyous the birds' (contrast the sparrows, 8). **flung**: given 'windows' in the next line (4), compare *The Waste Land* [II] 92: 'Flung their smoke' (with 'window', 90). *OED*, 'fling' 9: 'To emit, send forth, give out, diffuse (light . . . etc.)'; the first instance is Milton, *Il Penseroso* 131–2:

And when the sun begins to fling
His flaring beams,

against the panes: again a Tennysonian placing at the line-end; *Balin and Balan* 338–41:

                                  leaves
Laid their green faces flat against the panes,
Sprays grated, and the cankered boughs without
Whined in the wood.

Compare *In Memoriam* LXXXVII 8–9: 'The prophet blazoned on the panes; // And caught once more the distant shout'; TSE has 'distant' (3), and his street-piano might be in contrast to Tennyson's musical instruments here, the 'high-built organs' (6) of the Cambridge colleges, TSE's poem being *First Caprice in North Cambridge*, Massachusetts. For another poem of TSE in relation to this section of *In Memoriam*, see *Interlude: in a Bar* 4–5 note.

4 **children's voices**: compare *The Burnt Dancer* 20: 'Children's voices in little corners'. *Landscapes I: New Hampshire* 1: 'Children's voices in the orchard'. *The Waste Land* [III] 202: 'Et O ces voix d'enfants'. Given TSE's fascination with Coriolanus, perhaps touched by Coriolanus's question 'Have I had children's voices?' (*Coriolanus*, III i 30).

5–6 broken glass . . . grass: given 'voices' (4), compare *The Hollow Men* I 5, 8–9: 'Our dried voices';
> As wind in dry grass
> Or rats' feet over broken glass

6 Trampled: given TSE's title (*First Caprice*), compare Shelley, *The Cenci*, III i 235: 'Would trample out, for any slight caprice'.

6–7 grass . . . barrows: given TSE's intermediate word 'heap', compare Tennyson, *Tithonus* 71: 'And grassy barrows of the happier dead'.

7 A heap of broken barrows: compare *The Waste Land* [I] 22: 'A heap of broken images'.

8–9 crowd . . . sordid: Tennyson, *Locksley Hall Sixty Years After* 222–4, describes a grim cityscape, 'sordid attic . . . crowded couch of incest', with, at 218, 'City children' (compare 4). **sparrows . . . gutter with sordid:** compare *Preludes* III 4, 9: 'The thousand sordid images', 'And you heard the sparrows in the gutters'. (For 'images', see 7 note.) Also *Rhapsody on a Windy Night* 35, 38: 'the gutter' (and 'the child'); and, given 'evening' (2), compare *Gerontion* 14: 'at evening, poking the peevish gutter'.

9 Delve: compare Longfellow, *Hiawatha* XIII, where 'crows and blackbirds', 'jays and ravens', are
> Delving deep with beak and talon,
> For the body of Mondamin.

9–10 gutter with sordid patience . . . considerations: compare *First Debate between the Body and Soul* 5–7: 'With senile patience', rhyming with 'sensations', and having 'gutters' two lines earlier. *The Waste Land* [V] 326, 330: 'reverberation' / 'With a little patience'. Similarly, *O lord, have patience* 1, 3: 'patience' / 'irritations'; and *How to Pick a Possum* 17, 19: 'stations' / 'patience' (contributed by TSE to *Noctes Binanianae*, 1939). **with sordid patience:** compare *Paradise Lost* II 569: 'With stubborn patience'.

10 minor considerations: TSE to Aiken, 30 Sept. 1914: 'Sometimes I think – if I could only get back to Paris. But I know I never will, for long. I must learn to talk English. Anyway, I'm in the worry way now. Too many minor considerations. Does anything kill as petty worries do?' (*Letters* i 58). Compare Laforgue, *Complainte d'une convalescence en mai* (1885) 13: 'Je me sens fou d'un tas de petites misères'.

Fourth Caprice in Montparnasse

Dated Dec. 1910. Title: the words *North Cambridge* cancelled from original ink title and *Montparnasse* instead in pencil. Compare the locations, and a change of location, in *Preludes* as they appear within the Notebook: *Preludes I* was *Prelude in Roxbury* (*Houses*), amended from *Dorchester*; *Preludes II* and *III* were each *Prelude in Roxbury*. *Montparnasse*: TSE was much influenced in his early poems by Charles-Louis Philippe's novel *Bubu de Montparnasse* (1901), for a translation of which he later provided a preface (1932). (*Preludes III* has in the Notebook an epigraph from it.) Ch. VII, which mentions Montparnasse, imagines a squalid 'caprice', evoking married men who engage a prostitute and who think to themselves, 'Une petite aventure, un sourire, un caprice pour celle qui passe'. For further French colouring, see the notes below. TSE either did not write or did not preserve a Third Caprice.

1 **We turn the corner of the street**: compare *Preludes I* 11: 'And at the corner of the street'. Compare Apollinaire, *La Chanson du Mal-Aimé* 16 (May 1909): 'Au tournant d'une rue brûlant'; 7 has 'mains dans les poches' (TSE, 11, 'Hand in pocket'). **the street**: at the line-end, very characteristic of TSE, as of Tennyson (and of Symons).

7 **blackened trees**: given 'street' (1, 14), compare *Preludes IV* 8: 'The conscience of a blackened street'.

9 **like mendicants without regrets**: contrast, as to regrets, Baudelaire, *Au Lecteur* (1857) 3–4:
   Et nous alimentons nos aimables remords,
   Comme les mendiants
(The poem ends with the line which TSE adapted to end section I of *The Waste Land*: ' – Hypocrite lecteur, – mon semblable, – mon frère!')

9, 13 **regrets . . . Among such scattered thoughts**: compare *Portrait of a Lady I* 15: 'Among velleities and carefully caught regrets' (which then rhymes with 'cornets' – note 'corner' in 14 below).

11 **Hand in pocket, undecided**: Laforgue's *Locutions des Pierrots* XIV (1886) begins its first stanza, a street-scene (TSE has houses):
   Les mains dans les poches,
   Le long de la route,
and ends the stanza: 'Sans que tu t'en doutes!'

12 **Indifferent if derided**: compare *The Waste Land* [III] 238, 242: 'Which still are unreproved, if undesired'; 'And makes a welcome of indifference'. **if derided**: at the line-end, compare Meredith, *The Vital Choice* (1901) 5: 'Each can torture if derided'. (On TSE and Meredith, see the note to *Entretien dans un parc* 34.)

13–14 scattered . . . corner . . . street: compare Donne, *The Lamentations of Jeremy* 272: 'Scattered in corners of each street do lie'. Three lines later, Donne has 'stand', and then in the next line 'hand' / TSE, 8, 11.

15 **But why are we so hard to please . . . universities**: [two deleted lines, following 15]. Laforgue has, within three lines, 'l'Université' and 'Je m'ennuie, nous nous ennuyons tant! n'est-ce pas, messieurs?' (*Salomé, Moralités légendaires*, 1992 edn, p.116).   **hard to please**: given 'undecided' (11), compare Scott, *Marmion* VI xxx:

O Woman! in our hours of ease,
Uncertain, coy, and hard to please.

hard to please? The world is full of: compare Robert Louis Stevenson, *Happy Thought* (*A Child's Garden of Verses*, 1885), which runs:

The world is so full of a number of things,
I'm sure we should all be as happy as kings.

For his tutorial class on Modern English Literature in 1917, TSE listed: 'Stevenson as a poet. Read: *A Child's Garden of Verses, Collected Poems*' (Ronald Schuchard, *Review of English Studies*, n.s. xxv, 1974, 295). In *A Note on Ezra Pound* (*To-Day*, iv, Sept. 1918, p.4), TSE explicitly contrasted with Stevenson's verses the plight of the poet circa 1910 (writing of Pound but thinking clearly of himself too): Pound 'is well known, exciting various reactions of harmony or irritation; but there is no tradition in English verse which might have prepared for the general acceptance of his work; and England in 1910 could have been no more ready for him than in 1890; and perhaps there is even less to respond to him in 1918 than in 1910 [. . .] But while the mind of man has altered, verse has stood still; and the majority of our poets can only touch us as a "Child's Garden of Verses," a heavy trifling; they have nothing to say to the adult, sophisticated, civilized mind; are quite unaware of its tragedies and ecstasies.'   **The world is . . . full of universities**: as against full of possibilities; compare TSE on William James: 'But James has an exceptional quality of always leaving his reader with the feeling that the world is full of possibilities – in a philosopher, a rare and valuable quality' (*New Statesman*, 8 Sept. 1917).   **The world . . . universities**: TSE to Aiken, from Merton College, Oxford, 16 Nov. 1914, on his unsentimental journey: 'University towns, my dear fellow, are the same all over the world; only they order these matters better in Oxford' (*Letters* i 68). Again to Aiken, 31 Dec. 1914: 'As you know, I hate university towns and university people, who are the same everywhere' (*Letters* i 74).   **journalists . . . universities**: compare TSE, *Mélange Adultère de Tout* 1–2:

En Amérique, professeur;
En Angleterre, journaliste.

Second Caprice in North Cambridge

Dated Nov. 1909.

1 **This charm of**: compare Tennyson, *Merlin and Vivien* 327–8; 'this charm / Of woven paces'. Sinister (like TSE's scene), *Merlin and Vivien* three times has 'this charm', and its line 330 – 'The charm so taught will charm us both to rest' – may have influenced 'charm . . . repose' (14–15). With the sun (TSE, 17, 'sunset'), perhaps recalling *Paradise Lost* IV 651–2 and its play upon 'charm' as bird-song:
  With charm of earliest birds, nor rising sun
  On this delightful land,
OED sb.2 1: 'The blended singing or noise of many birds; the blended voices of school-children, and the like' (compare *First Caprice in North Cambridge*); and *OED* 3: 'A company or flock (of finches, etc.)'. **vacant lots**: so placed at the end of the line – but to close, not open, a poem – in *Preludes* IV 16: 'Gathering fuel in vacant lots'. TSE translated St-J. Perse, 'dans ce quartier aux détritus!', as: 'in this quarter of vacant lots and rubbish' (*Anabasis* IV, 1930, p.35). Compare TSE's (unadopted) revised ending in 1933 for *Sweeney Agonistes: Fragment of an Agon*, which introduces as prologue 'The old gentleman': 'Good evening. My name is Time. I come from the vacant lot in front of the Grand Union Depot' (Hallie Flanagan, *Dynamo*, 1943, pp.82–3). Virginia Woolf reported TSE in her *Diary*, 10 Sept. 1933: 'His father was a brick merchant in St Louis; & they lived in the slums among vacant lots' ('vacant lots' and 'Shattered bricks' in the present poem). TSE's recurrence to 'vacant lots' resembles Laforgue's to 'terrains vagues' (*Pierrots* I; *Complainte sur certains ennuis*; *Cythère*). The poem as a whole is coloured by Henry James's similarly unexpected complex of feeling in three consecutive sentences of *The Bostonians* (1886), ch.xx: 'the red sunsets of winter [. . .] a collective impression of boards and tin and frozen earth, sheds and rotting piles [. . .] loose fences, vacant lots, mounds of refuse, yards bestrewn with iron pipes, telegraph poles, and bare wooden backs of places. Verena thought such a view lovely, and she was by no means without excuse when, as the afternoon closed, the ugly picture was tinted with a clear, cold rosiness.' (Note red sunsets, tin, piles, vacant lots, and rosiness.)

2–4 **helpless fields that lie . . . eye**: compare *Comus* 977–9:
  And those happy climes that lie
  Where day never shuts his eye,
  Up in the broad fields of the sky.
Compare with TSE's cityscape Wordsworth's sonnet *Composed upon Westminster Bridge* ('Earth has not anything to show more fair'), sharing the mimetic line-end at 'lie':
  Ships, towers, domes, theatres, and temples lie

Open unto the fields, and to the sky;
All bright and glittering in the smokeless air.

Wordsworth, 4, 'City' / TSE, 8, 'city'; Wordsworth, 9, 'sun' / TSE, 17, 'sunset'; Wordsworth, 7–8, 'fields . . . smokeless' / TSE, 'helpless fields'. **helpless . . . sterile and blind . . . eye**: given 'repose' (15), compare Shakespeare, *The Rape of Lucrece* 756–8:

'Upon my cheeks what helpless shame I feel'. //
Here she exclaims against repose and rest,
And bids her eyes hereafter still be blind.

3–4 Sinister, sterile . . . Entreat the eye: compare Job 24:21: 'He evil entreateth the barren that beareth not', followed by 'his eyes' (24:24). **Entreat the eye**: compare *Romeo and Juliet*, II ii 15–17:

Two of the fairest stars in all the heaven,
Having some business, do entreat her eyes
To twinkle in their spheres till they return.

TSE remarked 'some artificiality' there: 'For it seems unlikely that a man standing below in the garden, even on a very bright moonlight night, would see the eyes of the lady above flashing so brilliantly as to justify such a comparison' (*Note to "Poetry and Drama"*, *OPP*, p.87, excerpted by TSE from an Edinburgh lecture of 1937). Romeo and Juliet are invoked in TSE's *Nocturne*. **Sinister, sterile and blind**: compare *Samson Agonistes* 366: 'Thy foes' derision, captive, poor, and blind'. (TSE's preceding poem in the Notebook, *Fourth Caprice in Montparnasse* 12, has 'derided'.)

6–7, 9 tins . . . bricks . . . Far from our definitions: tins and bricks challenge our definitions elsewhere in TSE, in his paper on T. H. Green (1913–14; Houghton Library; bMS Am 1691.14 (31), p.8): 'such words as "world" or "self" denote objects which are by no means simple [. . .] Towards objects of this type there are two points of view which seem to me mistaken. One is to hypostasise them, to treat them as more real, or as manifestations of a higher reality, than such objects as bricks and tin cans.'

7 bricks and tiles: given 'charm' (1, 14), compare Verlaine, *Walcourt (Paysages Belges*, 1874) 1–2:

Briques et tuiles,
O les charmants

7–8 Shattered bricks and tiles / And the débris of a city: compare C. F. G. Masterman, *From the Abyss* (1902), p.12: 'broken bottles, and the refuse of the city'. (*From the Abyss* has been proposed by James Kissane as a source for *The Waste Land*; *Yeats Eliot Review*, vi, 1, 1979, 24–8.)

9 definitions: recognizing the etymology. On the title-page of *Notes towards the Definition of Culture* (1948), is the epigraph:

DEFINITION: 1. The setting of bounds;
limitation (rare) – 1483
—*Oxford English Dictionary*

11 **Let us pause:** on 'aesthetic laws' (10) and Nature, compare Wordsworth, *Thoughts Suggested . . . on the Banks of Nith* 37–42:
Proud thoughts that Image overawes,
Before it humbly let us pause,
And ask of Nature from what cause
And by what rules
She trained her Burns to win applause
That shames the Schools.
TSE has 'fields' in the next line; Wordsworth seven lines later.

14, 16–17 **charm . . . evening . . . sunset yellow and rose:** the third stanza of Tennyson, *The Lotos-Eaters*, has 'The charmèd sunset lingered low adown / In the red West', and 'rosy flame'. Compare *Portrait of a Lady* III 32: 'evening yellow and rose'.

15 **repose:** at the line-end, frequent in Wordsworth (see also the notes to 2–4, 11), as in TSE, *Mandarins* 3 2, and concluding *La Figlia Che Piange*.

Interlude in London

Dated April 1911. Title: **Interlude**: its original musical sense was grave, less playful: 'An instrumental piece played between the verses of a psalm or hymn, or in the intervals of a church-service, etc.' (*OED*). Compare W. G. Tinckom-Fernandez, *The Street Organ* 1–3 (the *Harvard Advocate*, 25 June 1908):

> Spring shyly taps the window-pane,
> And all the winds of heaven sigh
> With hope for June-sun-scented days –

TSE, 2, 'And live across the window panes'; TSE, 4, 'the wind'; TSE, 8, 'the spring goes'; note the similarity of metre and syntax between Tinckom-Fernandez and TSE's opening lines, including the sequence of lines: [statement] / And . . . / With . . . (For *The Street Organ* elsewhere, see *First Caprice in North Cambridge* 1 note, and *Do I know how I feel?* 21–2 note.) TSE's April poem, with its 'hibernate', 'live', 'sudden rains', 'garden plots' and 'spring', has affinities with the opening and closing of section 1 of *The Waste Land*.

1 **We hibernate among the bricks**: Valerie Eliot points out TSE's letter of 26 April 1911, from Paris, to Eleanor Hinkley (*Letters* i 17–18): 'I just came back from London last night [his first visit] [. . .] Paris has burst out, during my absence, into full spring; and it is such a revelation that I feel that I ought to make it known. At London, one pretended that it was spring, and tried to coax the spring, and talk of the beautiful weather; but one continued to hibernate amongst the bricks. And one looked through the windows, and the waiter brought in eggs and coffee, and the *Graphic* (which I conscientiously tried to read, to please them).' In Paris, TSE remembered Laforgue, the epigraph to *L'Imitation de Notre-Dame la Lune selon Jules Laforgue* (1886): 'Ah! quel juillet nous avons hiverné'. To this of Laforgue ('. . . we have hibernated'), should be added Apollinaire, whose *La Chanson du Mal-Aimé* has 'J'ai hiverné' (46), and 'briques' (bricks) at the line-end: 'Que tombent ces vagues de briques' (11); also Apollinaire, 59, 'L'année dernière' / TSE, 6, 'last year's'. *La Chanson du Mal-Aimé* (May 1909) is itself an *Interlude in London*; it begins 'Un soir de demi-brune à Londres' (and it probably influenced *Fourth Caprice in Montparnasse*). **hibernate**: to the direct sense ('said esp. of animals that pass the winter in a state of torpor') might be added 'To winter in a milder locality', 1865, *OED*. **hibernate among the bricks**: compare Hawthorne, 'vegetate among the bricks' (and compare TSE, 21 Aug. 1916: 'We are vegetating', *Letters* i 145); Hawthorne, *The Blithedale Romance*, ch.VII: 'she had reminded me of plants that one sometimes observes doing their best to vegetate among the bricks of an enclosed court, where there is scanty soil, and never any sunshine'. (Compare 'the damp souls of housemaids / Sprouting despondently at area gates', *Morning at the Window* 3–4.) **among the bricks**:

compare *Portrait of a Lady* III 9: 'among the bric-à-brac' (and 'Among the windings' in I 29).

I, 3 **bricks . . . six:** a simple rhyme, but compare Tennyson, *Locksley Hall Sixty Years After* 257–60:
> From that casement where the trailer mantles all the mouldering bricks –
> I was then in early boyhood, Edith but a child of six – //
> While I sheltered in this archway from a day of driving showers –
> Peept the winsome face of Edith like a flower among the flowers.

Tennyson, 'mouldering' / TSE, 9, 'mouldy'; Tennyson, 'flower' / TSE, 9, 'flowerpots'; Tennyson, 'a day of driving showers' / TSE, 5, 'sudden rains'; also TSE, I, 'among', and 8, 'while'.

2 **across the window panes:** as in *Oh little voices of the throats of men* 37; and, at the line-end, *Mr. Eliot's Sunday Morning Service* 3: 'Drift across the window-panes'. Compare *The Love Song of J. Alfred Prufrock* 15 (25), 16: 'upon the window-panes' (twice) and 'on the window-panes'. For Tinckom-Fernandez's *The Street Organ*, see the headnote. **across:** contrast what it might be to 'live across the window panes' with the literal, 'who lives across the alley' (*Easter: Sensations of April [1]* 1), and with *Preludes IV* 1: 'His soul stretched tight across the skies'.

3 **With marmalade and tea at six:** compare *The Love Song of J. Alfred Prufrock* 88: 'After the cups, the marmalade, the tea'.

4–5 **Indifferent . . . Indifferent:** compare *Conversation Galante* 16: 'With your air indifferent and imperious'. 'Indifferent' comes again and again in Symons's early poems. TSE has it in many of these Notebook poems, and often later, for instance in *Coriolan I: Triumphal March* 31: 'And the eyes watchful, waiting, perceiving, indifferent'.

5–6 **sudden rains . . . last year's garden plots:** compare *The Waste Land* [I] 71–3:
> 'That corpse you planted last year in your garden,
> 'Has it begun to sprout? Will it bloom this year?
> 'Or has the sudden frost disturbed its bed?

Swinburne had been lavish with *last year's*; for instance, 'last year's rose' (*The Two Dreams*, 1866, the 8th verse-paragraph); 'last year's leaf' (*Thalassius*, 1871, the 18th); 'last year's birds' and 'last year's roses' (*Pastiche*, 1878, 12, 14).

5, 8–10 **sudden rains . . . down the street . . . flowerpots . . . broken:** compare *Preludes I* 9–11:
> The showers beat
> On broken blinds and chimney-pots,
> And at the corner of the street

6 **Softening**: compare the generative dampness of the Creation, *Paradise Lost* VII 279–82:

> with warm
> Prolific humour softening all her globe,
> Fermented the great mother to conceive,
> Satiate with genial moisture;

7 **with cigars**: compare *Burbank with a Baedeker: Bleistein with a Cigar*.

7–8, 10 **cigars . . . street . . . goes . . . windows**: given the time of day ('at six', 3), compare *The Love Song of J. Alfred Prufrock* 70–2:

> I have gone at dusk through narrow streets
> And watched the smoke that rises from the pipes
> Of lonely men in shirt-sleeves, leaning out of windows? . . .

8 **Careless**: including *OED* 1: 'Free from care, anxiety, or apprehension. (Since c.1650, *arch.*, *poetic*, or *nonce-word*)'.

8–9 **down the street the spring goes / Inspiring**: on TSE, Frazer and other anthropologists, and 'the magical rites of spring festivals', see Robert Crawford, *The Savage and the City*, pp.71–2, 94–5.

9 **flowerpots**: given 'garden plots' (6) and 'broken' (10), compare Tennyson, *Mariana* 1: 'With blackest moss the flower-plots'; often misquoted as 'flowerpots'. (Tennyson has 'broken' four lines later.)

10 **broken flutes**: *OED* 4, 'flute': '*Architectural*. A channel or furrow in a pillar'; but the musical sense may be heard (compare *Portrait of a Lady* II 17: 'a broken violin'). Compare André Salmon, *La flûte brisée* (1905) 1–6:

> La flûte s'est brisée sur mes dents,
> La flûte est brisée! La flûte est brisée!
> C'était un tuyau d'ivoire et rien dedans.
> Mais le vent qui passait? . . . Le vent a passé. //
> Mes dents l'ont brisée la flûte d'ivoire
> Et le vent chanteur a fui je ne sais où,

The poem ends:

> Tout ce qui n'a pas fui avec le vent
> Je l'ai brisé avec mes dents.

Compare Salmon with 'Indifferent to what the wind does' (TSE, 4), along with TSE's 'Inspiring' as breathing into. (Also TSE's play upon 'breathless' in *Ash-Wednesday* IV 24: 'Whose flute is breathless'.) TSE listed Salmon among 'The more important men there', poets in France, in a letter to Scofield Thayer (14 Feb. 1920, *Letters* i 362–3). **at garret windows**: compare, at the line-end, *Morning at the Window* 4: 'Sprouting despondently at area gates'.

Opera

Dated Nov. 1909. In *The Birth of Tragedy*, Nietzsche deplored opera while praising *Tristan und Isolde*. Much of his argument is relevant to TSE's *Opera*. In W. A. Haussmann's translation (1909): 'The man incapable of art [. . .] dreams himself into a time when passion suffices to generate songs and poems: as if emotion had ever been able to create anything artistic. The postulate of the opera is a false belief concerning the artistic process, in fact, the idyllic belief that every sentient man is an artist.' 'On close observation, this fatal influence of the opera on music is seen to coincide absolutely with the universal development of modern music.' 'I ask the question of these genuine musicians: whether they can imagine a man capable of hearing the third act of *Tristan und Isolde* without any aid of word or scenery, purely as a vast symphonic period, without expiring by a spasmodic distension of all the wings of the soul? [. . .] the furious desire for existence issuing therefrom' (pp.146–7, 150, 161).

Opera anticipates TSE's critique of Romanticism. First, as in TSE's 1916 tutorial class on Modern French Literature, where the syllabus for Lecture 1 (*The Origins: What is Romanticism?*) says: 'Romanticism stands for *excess* in any direction'; and speaks of 'vague emotionality' and 'Emphasis upon *feeling* rather than *thought*'. (Ronald Schuchard, *Review of English Studies*, n.s. xxv, 1974, 165.) Second, in *After Strange Gods* (1934), pp.54–6. The poem speaks of the 'passionate' (3), of 'torturing itself / To emotion' (5–6), of 'paroxysms' (8), of 'self-expression' (10), and of 'emotional experiences' (14). These are central to TSE's deploring of Hardy's fiction: 'He seems to me to have written as nearly for the sake of "self-expression" as a man well can; and the self which he had to express does not strike me as a particularly wholesome or edifying matter of communication.' Hardy is 'an author who is interested not at all in men's minds, but only in their emotions; and perhaps only in men as vehicles for emotions. It is only, indeed, in their emotional paroxysms that most of Hardy's characters come alive. This extreme emotionalism seems to me a symptom of decadence; it is a cardinal point of faith in a romantic age, to believe that there is something admirable in violent emotion for its own sake, whatever the emotion or whatever its object.' 'But as the majority is capable neither of strong emotion nor of strong resistance, it always inclines to admire passion for its own sake.' 'It is a refined form of torture on the part of the writer, and a refined form of self-torture on the part of the reader.' Relatedly, the reflection 'We have the tragic? oh no!' (11) anticipates *After Strange Gods*, p.43, on Pound: 'It is, in its way, an admirable Hell, "without dignity, without tragedy" ' (quoting Pound, Canto xiv).

1 **Tristan and Isolde:** Peter Ackroyd, *T. S. Eliot* (1984), p.38: the poem 'seems to have been written after he had seen a performance in Boston [. . .] When he was in his sixties he discussed this opera with Stravinsky, and from that conversation Stravinsky inferred that it must have been "one of the most passionate experiences of his life". But there is none of that response in the early poem.'

(Stravinsky, *Esquire*, Aug. 1965.) Jean Verdenal wrote in a letter to TSE, 5 Feb. 1912: 'Tristan et Y., du premier coup vous émeuvent atrocement, et vous laissent aplati d'extase, avec une soif d'y revenir' (*Letters* i 28). *The Waste Land* [I] 31–4 and 42, as TSE's Notes acknowledge, reproduce *Tristan und Isolde* in German (I, verses 5–8; III, verse 24); on Wagner's presence there, see Bernard Harris, in *The Waste Land in Different Voices* (1974), ed. A. D. Moody; Stoddard Martin, *Wagner to The Waste Land* (1982), pp.194–234; and Raymond Grant, *Yeats Eliot Review* ix (1988) 93–105. On the importance of Wagner to Laforgue, see Anne Holmes, *Jules Laforgue and Poetic Innovation* (1993), pp.145–51. TSE said in 1926, of Laforgue: 'It is noticeable how often [. . .] such philosophical terms from the vocabulary of Schopenhauer and Hartmann, the Valkyrie, and such properties from the dramas of Wagner, recur. Laforgue is the nearest verse equivalent to the philosophies of Schopenhauer and Hartmann, the philosophy of the unconscious and of annihilation, just as Wagner is the nearest music equivalent to the same philosophies, though apart from this approximation to a similar philosophic mood, it would be difficult to say what there is in common between Wagner and Laforgue. But in Laforgue there is continuous war between the feelings implied by his ideas, and the ideas implied by his feelings. The system of Schopenhauer collapses, but in a different ruin from that of *Tristan und Isolde*' (*VMP*, p.215). TSE mentioned this opera in *Dante* (1929, *SE*, p.264), and in 1932 he wrote of 'an attraction as fatal as that indicated by the love-potion motif in *Tristan und Isolde*' – compare 'fatalistic' in the poem's next line (*John Ford*, 1932, *SE*, pp.197–8).

2 **And the fatalistic horns**: compare *Rhapsody on a Windy Night* 9: 'Beats like a fatalistic drum'. Laforgue began section III of *Salomé*: 'Sur un mode allègre et fataliste, un orchestre aux instruments d'ivoire improvisait une petite ouverture unanime' (*Moralités légendaires*, 1992 edn, p.109). Again Laforgue: 'cette éternelle valse de Chopin usée comme l'amour – ô délices poignantes, ô bon fatalisme!' (*Mélanges posthumes*, 1903, p.30).

2–4 **the fatalistic horns / The passionate violins / And ominous clarinet**: compare *Portrait of a Lady* I 29–32:
>   Among the windings of the violins
>   And the ariettes
>   Of cracked cornets
>   Inside my brain a dull tom-tom begins

Edward J. H. Greene, *T. S. Eliot et la France* (1951), p.36: 'On retrouve aussi dans "Portrait of a Lady" tout cet appareil musical, depuis les pianos et les violons jusqu'aux orgues de Barbarie, en passant par le cornet à piston, qui a été une des caractéristiques de la poésie symboliste. C'est surtout chez Laforgue qu'Eliot a pris ce symbolisme instrumentaliste; il a pu également s'inspirer de Verlaine.' Verlaine's *Il parle encore* (1888) 18 has, for instance, 'la flûte impure'. Such characterizing of musical instruments recalls not only the French symbolists but also Dryden, *A Song for St. Cecilia's Day* 25, 33, 37–8: 'The trumpet's loud clangour', 'The soft complaining flute':

> Sharp violins proclaim
> Their jealous pangs, and desperation,

(The *Song* is in *The Golden Treasury*, which TSE knew well.)

2–4 horns . . . violins . . . clarinet: 'TSE was perhaps thinking especially of Act II of *Tristan und Isolde* with its paroxysmic love-duet preceded by sequences for six horns (bar 76ff.) and solo clarinet (bar 126ff.), and with its "passionate violins" ' (Eric Griffiths).

3, 5–6 passionate . . . And love torturing itself / To emotion for all there is in it: compare TSE, *The Monist*, xxviii (April 1918), 319–20: 'To be in love with emotion has been our affliction since Rousseau [. . .] Strong passions do not need explanation; but just as a man who is not very much in love excuses the follies which he has committed for the purpose of appearing passionate, so the philosophical Christian apologizes for the religion in which he would like to believe.' (For this second, revised, review of Merz by TSE, see Elizabeth R. Eames and Alan M. Cohn, *Papers of the Bibliographical Society of America*, lxx, 1976, 420–4.) TSE, in a sentence on Donne in the Clark Lectures (1926), speaks of 'emotional infusion' and 'extremities of torturing of language' (*VMP*, p.85). **torturing itself**: likewise of music, Laforgue, *Complainte propitiatoire à l'Inconscient* (1885) 9: 'Dans l'orgue qui par déchirements se châtie'. **itself / To emotion**: compare *The Dry Salvages* II 9: 'emotion takes to itself'.

10 self-expression: in 1909, still a fairly recent compound. *OED* has as its first instance, 1892, *Nation*: 'This doctrine of unbounded self-indulgence – or, as his [Walt Whitman's] admirers would prefer to call it, self-expression.' Compare TSE's lines in the manuscript of *Portrait of a Lady* II (Appendix B):

> Oh, spare these reminiscences!
> How you prolong the pose!
> These emotional concupiscences
> Tinctured attar of rose.
> (The need for self-expression
> Will pardon this digression).

TSE twice conveyed his suspicions in 1926, writing of J. E. Spingarn: 'For Mr. Spingarn the phrase "self-expression" appears to be completely adequate' (*TLS*, 12 August), and of Donne: 'his sermons, one feels, are a "means of self-expression" ' (*Lancelot Andrewes*, SE, p.351).

11 We have the tragic? oh no!: TSE to Aiken, 19 July 1914: 'For when you have all those little things you cease to fret about them, and have room for a sort of divine dissatisfaction and *goût* for the tragic which is quite harmless, *d'ailleurs*, and compatible with a bank account. I think perhaps that only the happy can appreciate the tragic, or that the tragic only exists for the happy' (*Letters* i 43). Again to Aiken, 30 Sept. 1914: 'That, in fact, is I think the great use of suffering, if it's *tragic* suffering – it takes you away from yourself – and petty suffering does exactly the reverse, and kills your inspiration. I think now that all my good stuff was done before I had begun to worry – three years ago' (*Letters* i 58). Compare *Eeldrop and Appleplex*: 'A man is only important as he is classed. Hence there is no tragedy, or no appreciation of tragedy, which is the same thing' (*Little Review*, iv, May 1917, 9). Compare Nietzsche, *The Birth of Tragedy*, on the third act of *Tristan*: 'Here there interpose between our highest musical excitement and the music in question the tragic myth and the tragic hero' (tr. W. A. Haussmann, 1909, pp.161–2).

11–12 **We have the tragic? oh no! / Life departs with a feeble smile**: compare the closing lines of *The Hollow Men*:
> *This is the way the world ends*
> *Not with a bang but a whimper.*

12 **Life departs with a feeble smile**: compare *First Debate between the Body and Soul* 44: 'Till life evaporates into a smile'. *Spleen* 11–13:
> And Life, a little bald and gray,
> Languid, fastidious, and bland,
> Waits, hat and gloves in hand,

16 **I feel like the ghost of youth**: compare Symons on Rimbaud: 'there is a certain irony, which comes into that youthful work as if youth were already reminiscent of itself, so conscious is it that youth is youth, and that youth is passing' (*The Symbolist Movement in Literature*, p.73). Robert Crawford compares James Thomson, *Insomnia* (1884) 270: 'I felt a ghost already' (*The Savage and the City*, p.49). Compare TSE's address at Milton Academy, 17 June 1933: 'it occurred to me that as I had to talk to somebody, I would take more or less a metaphorical figure and make him as real as I could – that is, it occurred to me to say a few words to the ghost of myself at the age of seventeen or thereabouts, whom we may suppose to be skulking somewhere about this hall' (*Milton Graduates Bulletin*, Nov. 1933, p.5).

16–17 **the ghost of youth / At the undertakers' ball**: TSE later mingled with Edward Lear two lines from the Dirge in *Cymbeline*, IV ii:
> Golden lads and girls all must,
> As chimney-sweepers, come to dust.

Five-Finger Exercises II 10–12:
> Pollicle dogs and cats all must
> Jellicle cats and dogs all must
> Like undertakers, come to dust.

Shakespeare's golden lads and girls become the ghost of youth. **the undertakers' ball**: compare also 'the Whore House Ball' in the refrain of *Ballade pour la grosse Lulu* and in one of the Columbo verses (Appendix A). In *Departmental Ditties* (ninth edn, 1897), Kipling followed *The Undertaker's Horse* with *One Viceroy Resigns*, which has 'O Youth, Youth, Youth!' (6) and 'That ghost has haunted me for twenty years' (18). For one of life's little ironies (such as TSE anticipated), compare Wyndham Lewis to Pound, 10 Aug. 1939: 'The "Undertaker" as Lady Ottoline used to call him (you call him "Possum") I have not seen' (*Pound/Lewis*, ed. Timothy Materer, 1985, p.212).

Silence

Dated June 1910. Title: **Silence**, with 'I am terrified', suggests Pascal; see 15 note. In a paper on ethics (1912–13?), TSE wrote: 'For chance is merely absence of explanation, and a gigantic hand organ of atoms, grinding out predictable variations on the same tune, would fill the vast silences which idealism leaves empty' (Houghton Library; bMS Am 1691.14 (30), pp.19–20). *Silence* has some affinity with Tennyson, *In Memoriam* CXXIII 3–4:

> There where the long street roars, hath been
> The stillness of the central sea.

Lyndall Gordon (*Eliot's Early Years*, p.35) and John Mayer (*T. S. Eliot's Silent Voices*, p.56) suggest the influence of Laforgue's *Hamlet* (*Moralités légendaires*, 1992 edn, p.29), Hamlet's invocation: 'Et toi, Silence, pardonne à la Terre; la petite folle ne sait trop ce qu'elle fait', etc. (Symons had quoted this, in translation, in *The Symbolist Movement in Literature*, pp.105–6; relatedly, p.166 quotes Maeterlinck's essay *Silence*.) Closer is the passage in Laforgue's *Mélanges posthumes* (1903, pp.116–7, on Baudelaire): 'La Beauté c'est le Silence éternel. Tout notre tapage de passions, de discussions, d'orages, d'art, c'est pour, par le bruit, nous faire croire que le *Silence n'existe pas*. Mais quand nous retombons las, nous l'écoutons restagner de partout et nous sommes plus tristes, pas assez forts pour un tapage éternel ou pour nous faire au Silence éternel'.

1–2 **Along the city streets**: compare *The Death of Saint Narcissus* 18: 'If he walked in city streets'. Given the title *Silence*, contrast *Aunt Helen* 4–5:
> Now when she died there was silence in heaven
> And silence at her end of the street.

Along the city streets . . . high tide: compare Dr Johnson: 'Why, Sir, Fleet-street has a very animated appearance; but I think the full tide of human existence is at Charing-cross' (Boswell, 2 April 1775).

1, 3 **Along the . . . streets . . . the garrulous waves of life**: compare *Morning at the Window* 2, 5: 'And along the trampled edges of the street' ('street' at the line-end), and 'The brown waves of fog'.

3 **garrulous**: see *First Caprice in North Cambridge* 1 note, adding (of water, as here) 'The stream stayed / Its garrulous tongue' (*OED* 1b, Lewis Morris, 1877).

3–4 **waves . . . Shrink**: of waters, compare *Sweeney Among the Nightingales* 10: 'hushed the shrunken seas' ('hushed' contrasting with 'garrulous waves' here). Compare *Paradise Lost* XI 845–6, after the Flood: 'the fresh wave [. . .] their flowing shrink'. **divide**: as in the miracle at the Red Sea, but also with a suggestion of the creation; *Paradise Lost* VII 262–3, which – like TSE's lines –

has 'divide' at the line-end, the line-division: 'let it divide / The waters from the waters'.

4, 9 divide . . . justified: compare a poem by TSE's mother, Charlotte Eliot, *Saint Barnabas: A Missionary Hymn* 8–10 (undated, in the Hayward Bequest):

No longer shall the law thy tribes divide,
Through faith and love shall all be justified.
Let me go forth, O Lord!

TSE's 'seas of experience' / *Saint Barnabas* 17: 'With Paul to distant lands I sail abroad'.

5 With a thousand incidents: compare Henri Bergson, *L'Evolution créatrice* (1907, ch. 1): 'Il est vrai que notre vie psychologique est pleine d'imprévu. Mille incidents surgissent' (followed in the paragraph by 'la masse fluide', 'un écoulement sans fin' – compare TSE's 'tide', 'waves', and 'seas'). Bergson, *Introduction à la métaphysique* (1903), has 'les milles incidents'; also 'indivisible' (TSE, 4, 'divide'), and 'couler naturellement' (compare TSE, 2–3). Bergson, *Oeuvres*, ed. A. Robinet (1959), p.1394. Compare Shelley, *Prometheus Unbound* IV 247: 'with a thousand motions' (245, 'deep' / TSE, 11). Compare *The Love Song of J. Alfred Prufrock* 32: 'for a hundred indecisions'.

6 Vexed and debated: compare 'vex', *OED* 7: 'To subject (a matter) to prolonged or severe examination or discussion; to debate at excessive length'; the first citation is Donne, *Biathanatos*. Compare TSE's silence and water, throughout, with the one sentence of Donne's Preface, which moves from 'the voyce and sound' to: 'as in the poole of *Bethsaida*, there was no health till the water was troubled, so the best way to finde the truth in this matter, was to debate and vexe it'. **debated**: compare *First Debate between the Body and Soul*; *Bacchus and Ariadne: 2nd Debate between the Body and Soul*; and *Inside the gloom* 21: 'while the debate was rife'.

7–8 the hour . . . the . . . hour: in two consecutive lines, *Ash-Wednesday* I 40–1:

Pray for us sinners now and at the hour of our death
Pray for us now and at the hour of our death.

(This, adapting the 'Hail Mary'.)

9 life is justified: compare Psalm 143:2: 'For in thy sight shall no man living be justified.' Compare Nietzsche, *The Birth of Tragedy*: 'that we have our highest dignity in our significance as works of art – for only as an *aesthetic phenomenon* is existence and the world eternally *justified*' (tr. W. A. Haussmann, 1909, p.50). *The Birth of Tragedy*, which deplores opera while praising *Tristan und Isolde*, went to the making of TSE's preceding poem in the Notebook, *Opera*.

10, 12 experience . . . So immediate: compare TSE's *Knowledge and Experience in* *the Philosophy of F. H. Bradley* (completed 1916, published 1964), ch. 1: *On Our Knowledge of Immediate Experience.*

11–12 **That were so broad and deep, / So immediate and steep**: compare *Paradise Lost* VII 288–9, after the dividing of the waters (see 3–4 note), with 'broad and deep' at the line-end, and with a repeated 'so':
> So high as heaved the tumid hills, so low
> Down sunk a hollow bottom broad and deep,

Other possible filaments to Milton's Creation: TSE's 'immediate', with 'Immediate are the acts of God' (VII 176); TSE's 'steep', of waters, with 'If steep, with torrent rapture' (VII 299); and the conjunction of TSE's title, *Silence*, his 'waves' (3), 'deep' (12) and 'peace' (15), in Milton's line: 'Silence, ye troubled waves, and thou deep, peace' (VII 216). Swinburne has 'and steep', rhyming with 'and deep', *A Leave-Taking* (1866) 24–6. Perhaps also (given TSE, 14, at the line-end, 'will'), Donne, *Satire* III 79–81:
> On a huge hill,
> Cragged, and steep, Truth stands, and he that will
> Reach her, about must, and about must go;

15 **I am terrified**: given TSE's title (*Silence*), compare Pascal: 'Le silence éternel de ces espaces infinis m'effraye' (*Pensées*, section III, No.206). Pater quoted this in *The Renaissance* (1873, p.30), and TSE marked it in his copy (Hayward Bequest). In *UPUC* (p.133), TSE dissented from I. A. Richards ('The inconceivable immensity of the Universe'): 'It was not, we remember, the "immense spaces" themselves but their *eternal silence* that terrified Pascal. With a definite religious background this is intelligible. But the effect of popular astronomy books (like Sir James Jeans's) upon me is only of the insignificance of vast space.'

16 **There is nothing else beside**: in Laforgue's *Le Concile féerique* (1886), Le Monsieur, déclamant, ends his set speech: 'Vrai, il n'y a pas autre chose'; the setting of the playlet, announced at the beginning, is 'Nuit d'Etoiles' (see the note to TSE's previous line). Laforgue adapted the line to end his poem *Esthétique* (1890): 'Car il n'y a pas autre chose'.

Mandarins 1: Stands there, complete

Dated Aug. 1910 – 'the 4' (poems in the sequence). Title: the third poem of the sequence begins: 'The eldest of the mandarins'. Laforgue mentions mandarins three times, once as 'le Grand Mandarin', in his *Salomé*, which begins: 'Il faisait ce jour-là deux mille canicules qu'une simple révolution rythmique des Mandarins du Palais avait porté le premier Tétrarque' (*Moralités légendaires*, 1992 edn, p.97). Some features of TSE's sequence are to be found in a poem by Gustave Kahn in *Poètes d'aujourd'hui*, the anthology edited by Van Bever and Léautaud which TSE owned in the two-volume edition (1908 and reprinted); compare *Votre domaine est terre de petite fée* 9 (1895): 'vos oiseaux, vos tasses et vos mandarins'.

Compare a run of four stanzas in Byron, *Don Juan* (XIII xxxiii–xxxvi), where the Mandarin is taken as a type of cultivated indifference ([xxxiv] 269–72):

> Just as a Mandarin finds nothing fine, –
>   At least his manner suffers not to guess
> That any thing he views can greatly please.
> Perhaps we have borrowed this from the Chinese –

This stanza has 'That calm Patrician polish in the address' (266; compare TSE, 2, 'addressed'); the previous stanza (259–60) imagines a scene similar to TSE's:

>   Gaze
> Upon the Shades of those distinguished men,
>   Who were or are the puppet-shows of praise.

Byron's following stanzas have 'Indifference' and 'indifferent' ([xxxv] 278, [xxxvi] 281) / TSE, 6, 'Indifferent'.

TSE's poem may recall an essay by W.W. [Watson White] in the *Harvard Advocate*, 25 Nov. 1908 (in which issue TSE published his poem *Circe's Palace*). On *Il Teatro Marionetti* in Boston: 'But "the play's the thing" and we are here to see it. Presently, announced by a burst of chords from the mandolins, the curtain laboriously and unevenly ascends. Behold! There stands a martial figure "armed . . . cap-a-pie," its remarkably small head turned so as to present the audience with a staring, blank expression in shiny paint. Firmly planted on ridiculously fat legs – spread wide apart – it brandishes its tin sword.' Note White's two allusions to *Hamlet* (for *Hamlet*, see the notes to 1, 13–15, 15), and compare TSE, 1–2, 10–11 (and 'Mandarins' / 'mandolins', given OED: '*mandarin*, obs. variant of *mandolin*'). See, too, the notes to *Convictions* 14 and to *Suite Clownesque* 1 13.

1 **Stands there**: a statue, by etymology, immediately 'Stands there'; a statue 'merely stands', 'Stiffly', 'With fixed regardless eyes', 'A hero', the focus of 'the crowds that ran'. For the abrupt opening syntax and stationing, compare *Animula*: ' "Issues from the hand of God, the simple soul" '. But whereas the first line of *Animula* could follow on grammatically from that poem's title, the singular verb of 'Stands there' could not follow from the plural title here, *Mandarins*.

complete: in 1919, TSE contrasted the tragedy and 'the pride of Coriolanus' with *Hamlet*, arguing that Hamlet's tragedy was not 'intelligible, self-complete, in the sunlight' (*SE*, p.144). *OED* 5, 'complete': 'Of persons: Fully equipped or endowed; perfect, accomplished, consummate.' Compare 'complete', also at the line-end, twice, in *Goldfish* IV 23, *Suite Clownesque* III 22. The usage is Shakespearean; at the line-end in *Henry VIII*, I ii 118–21:

> This man so complete,
> Who was enrolled 'mongst wonders, and when we,
> Almost with ravished listening, could not find
> His hour of speech a minute –

Given that TSE's poem is, with whatever irony, about 'A hero! and how much it means' (13), and that it makes play with 'eyes' (10), compare *Troilus and Cressida*, III iii 180–4, Ulysses to Achilles:

> The present eye praises the present object.
> Then marvel not, thou great and complete man,
> That all the Greeks begin to worship Ajax,
> Since things in motion sooner catch the eye
> Than what not stirs.

2 **addressed**: combining *OED* 2: 'Well-ordered, accomplished. *Obs.*' (Spenser, *Faerie Queene*, I ii st.11: 'Full iolly knight he seemde, and well addrest'); with *OED* 4: 'Arrayed, attired, trimmed, dressed. *arch.*' (Shelley, *The Sensitive Plant* I 29: 'And the rose like a nymph to the bath addressed'). **addressed with sword**: compare *Pericles*, II iii 95–6:

> Even in your armours, as you are addressed,
> Will well become a soldier's dance.

Paradise Lost VI 296, 304: 'addressed for fight', 'Now waved their fiery swords'. Compare *Sweeney Erect* 21: 'Sweeney addressed full length to shave'; moreover the abrupt opening syntax above ('Stands there, complete') resembles that which follows a full stop as *Sweeney Erect* 29–30, constituting a complete sentence:

> Tests the razor on his leg
> Waiting until the shriek subsides.

4 **at his feet**: Biblical (the concordance has sixteen instances, nine in the New Testament). Contrast Revelation 19:10: 'And I fell at his feet to worship him'; and *Paradise Lost*, again (by contrast) in submission: 'In adoration at his feet I fell' (VIII 315), 'at his feet / Fell humble' (X 911–12), 'Now at his feet submissive in distress' (X 942).

5 **Keen to appropriate the man**: compare *Merchant of Venice*, III ii 278: 'So keen and greedy to confound a man'.

6 **all these baits**: Miltonic; compare *Areopagitica*: 'vice with all her baits', and *Comus* 537, 700: 'Yet have they many baits', 'lickerish baits'. Given the 'hero',

and TSE's preoccupation with the play and its hero (*A Cooking Egg*: 'Coriolanus / And other heroes'), compare *Coriolanus*, IV i 33: 'cautelous baits'. (Coriolanus is speaking of what alone might ensnare him.)

7 **popular**: four times in *Coriolanus*, likewise pejoratively (*OED* 5a: 'Studious of, or designed to gain, the favour of the common people. *Obs.*'). II i 204: 'Do press among the popular throngs.' II iii 97–8: 'I will counterfeit the bewitchment of some popular man.' III i 106: 'His popular "shall".' v ii 40: 'a violent popular ignorance.'

8 **merely stands and waits**: compare Milton, *Sonnet: When I consider* 14, 'They also serve who only stand and wait'. TSE's syntax (with 'wait' poised at the line-end, something of a pun, not simply 'waits' but 'waits / Upon . . .') may recall too another moment in Milton, *Paradise Lost* v 351–5, where the passage on Adam's dignity shares with TSE not only this effect but 'his own' (9) and 'complete' (at the line-end in TSE too, 1):

> without more train
> Accompanied than with his own complete
> Perfections, in himself was all his state,
> More solemn than the tedious pomp that waits
> On princes,

8–12 **He merely stands and waits / Upon his own intrepid dignity; / With fixed regardless eyes – / Looking neither out nor in – / The centre of formalities**: compare *Coriolan I: Triumphal March* 28–31:

> There he is now, look:
> There is no interrogation in his eyes
> Or in the hands, quiet over the horse's neck,
> And the eyes watchful, waiting, perceiving, indifferent.

Compare 3–5 above ('What of the crowds that ran'), together with *Triumphal March* 4, 6: 'And such a press of people', 'and we so many crowding the way'.

10 **With fixed regardless eyes**: compare Keats, *Eve of St. Agnes* 64: 'She danced along with vague, regardless eyes'; Keats's previous stanza (57–62) has further affinities, not only as to fixed eyes, but in its imagined scene:

> her maiden eyes divine,
> Fixed on the floor, saw many a sweeping train
> Pass by – she heeded not at all: in vain
> Came many a tip-toe, amorous cavalier,
> And back retired – not cooled by high disdain
> But she saw not.

regardless eyes: compare *Burbank with a Baedeker: Bleistein with a Cigar* 17: 'lustreless protrusive eye'.

11 **neither out nor in**: compare the grand old Duke of York, his men 'neither up nor down'.

12 **The centre of formalities**: like the heroic statuesque figure ('some divinely gifted man') in Tennyson, *In Memoriam* LXIV 15–16:
> The pillar of a people's hope,
> The centre of a world's desire;

Dickens (*Barnaby Rudge*, ch. 80) has 'the centre of the system', for a hero just mobbed ('plumpness of his legs', 'tea-table', 'round-faced mandarins', 'reposed upon a shady table', 'red and white' – compare TSE's sequence).

13–14 **how much it means; / How much**: compare *Goldfish* III 14–15:
> How much one knows
> How much one means

Portrait of a Lady I 19–20:
> 'You do not know how much they mean to me, my friends,
> And how, how rare [. . .]

13–15 **A hero! and how much it means; / How much – / The rest is merely shifting scenes**: compare *Humouresque (After J. Laforgue)* 23: 'A hero! – Where would he belong?' Laforgue has the Prince brood upon shifting scenes in his *Hamlet*: 'Un héros! et que tout le reste fût des levers de rideau!', and again 'Un héros!' (*Moralités légendaires*, 1992 edn, p.12; 'des levers de rideau': curtain-raisers); for this in relation to Shakespeare's Hamlet, see the next note. Compare TSE in 1933: 'It has often been said that no man is a hero to his own valet; what is much more important is that no honest man can be a hero to himself; for he must be aware how many causes in world history, outside of abilities and genius, have been responsible for greatness' (*VMP*, p.289).

15 **The rest is**: compare *Hamlet*, V ii 350: 'the rest is silence'. TSE's immediately preceding poem in the Notebook is *Silence*. For Laforgue ('le reste fût . . .'), see the previous note. Compare TSE's ending with that of Verlaine's *Art poétique* (1885): 'Et tout le reste est littérature'; and with the lines quoted by Symons in *Théodore de Banville* (*Studies in Two Literatures*, 1897, p.265):
> Aimer le vin,
> La beauté, le printemps divin,
> Cela suffit. Le reste est vain.

shifting scenes: rhyming likewise with 'means', Tennyson, *The Play* 2, 4: 'the shifting scenes', 'what this wild Drama means'. Compare *The Love Song of J. Alfred Prufrock* 113: 'start a scene or two', in a passage which starts from Prince Hamlet. Compare perhaps TSE's strong linking of shifting scenes and public scrutiny with Hawthorne, *The Scarlet Letter*, ch.11: 'Lastly, in lieu of these shifting scenes, came back the rude market-place of the Puritan settlement, with all the townspeople assembled and levelling their stern regards at Hester Prynne'.

Mandarins 2: Two ladies of uncertain age

Dated Aug. 1910, the sequence. Some details suggest Laforgue's *Locutions des Pierrots* VII (1886): 1, 'douillette' / TSE, 7, 'delicate'; 11, 'peignoir' / TSE, 8, 'gowns'; 7, 'silhouettes' / TSE, 7, 'outlines'; 2–3, 'Comme on trempe, en levant le petit doigt, / Dans son café au lait' / TSE, 2, 'drinking tea', and 14, 'while one lifts her hand to pour'. *Locutions des Pierrots* XVI 6: 'Mes manches de mandarin pâle' (TSE's title for his sequence is *Mandarins*); XII was the source of *Humouresque (After J. Laforgue)*.

1 **ladies of uncertain age**: compare Byron, *Beppo* [xxii] 169–71:
> She was not old, nor young, nor at the years
>   Which certain people call a *"certain age"*,
> Which yet the most uncertain age appears.

An epigraph to *The Sacred Wood* (1920) is from *Beppo* (337: 'I also like to dine on becaficas'). *OED*, 'certain', 11 7e: 'Sometimes euphemistically: Which it is not polite or necessary further to define. *a certain age*: an age when one is no longer young, but which politeness forbids to be specified too minutely: usually, referring to some age between forty and sixty (mostly said of women)'. Compare *The smoke that gathers blue and sinks* 16: 'A lady of almost any age'.

1, 4, 13 **uncertain . . . assured tranquillity . . . sunset**: compare *Preludes* IV 6–7:
> And evening newspapers, and eyes
> Assured of certain certainties,

3 **persiflage**: *OED* cites a severe characterizing by Hannah More, 1799: 'The cold compound of irony, irreligion, selfishness, and sneer, which make up what the French . . so well express by the term *persiflage*'. Its pronunciation (as in 'massage', within both American and British English) declines to rhyme with 'age' (1). Given the likely presence of Byron in the poem (see 1 note, and that to the title of the sequence), compare *Don Juan*, XVI [lii] 462–3:
> Whether the mode be persiflage or piety,
> But wear the newest mantle of hypocrisy.

(TSE, 8, 'gowns' / 'mode', 'wear', and 'mantle'.)

4, 6 **tranquillity . . . sea**: a rhyme dear to Shelley. *Epipsychidion* 457–8:
> It is an isle 'twixt Heaven, Air, Earth, and Sea,
> Cradled, and hung in clear tranquillity;

Rosalind and Helen 971–2:
> Like the tide of the full and weary sea
> To the depths of its tranquillity.

5 **Regard**: equivocal as to its being indicative ('Two ladies . . . Regard . . .'), or imperative as it is in *Rhapsody on a Windy Night* 16, 50: 'Regard that woman',

'Regard the moon'. The fastidious imperative feels and is French; Laforgue has two lines in *Dimanches: C'est l'automne* (1890) 61–2 which strongly influenced TSE's *La Figlia Che Piange* 2–3, 7:

Penche, penche ta chère tête, va,
Regarde les grappes des premiers lilas;

But English too, in its other way: 'Regard thyself' (*Samson Agonistes* 1333), and 'Regard the weakness of thy peers', 'Regard gradation' (Tennyson, *Love thou thy land* 24, 67).

6 **A distant prospect of**: a common phrase; Byron, *Childe Harold's Pilgrimage* IV 285: 'a distant prospect'; Thomas Gray, *Ode on a Distant Prospect of Eton College*.

6, 9–10 **the sea . . . patterns . . . the floor**: compare *Animula* 10–11:

the sea;
Studies the sunlit pattern on the floor

7 **outlines delicate and hard**: compare Symons on Rimbaud: 'in whom dream is swift, hard in outline' (*The Symbolist Movement in Literature*, p.71). **delicate and hard**: compare *Interlude: in a Bar* 8: 'Visionary, and yet hard'.

8 **gowns that fall from neck and knee**: compare *The Love Song of J. Alfred Prufrock* 67, 102: 'Arms that lie along a table', 'skirts that trail along the floor'.

9 **Grey and yellow**: given the 'sunsets' in *Portrait of a Lady* II 12 ('sunset', 13 here), compare *Portrait of a Lady* III 32: 'Afternoon grey and smoky, evening yellow and rose'.

12–13 **they approve / The abstract sunset**: *OED* 6, 'approve': 'To pronounce to be good, commend'. Pope, *Essay on Criticism* 391: 'For fools admire, but men of sense approve'. Shelley, *Rosalind and Helen* 769–70, likewise has 'approve' at the line-end, issuing in a large approval:

I woke, and did approve
All nature to my heart.

Ladies who approve the sunset resemble the couple in Symons, *Scènes de la Vie de Bohème* I (1889), admiring handsomely:

But she yawned prettily. "Come then," said he.
He found a chair, Veuve Cliquot, some cigars.
They emptied glasses and admired the stars,
    The lanterns, night, the sea,

(TSE, 6, 'the sea', likewise ending the line.)

13 **abstract**: *OED* 4d: 'In the fine arts, characterized by lack of or freedom from representational qualities'; the first citation is 1915, *Forum* (N.Y.), but the *New Shorter OED* (1993) amalgamates 4d and 4e, making available this from 1868,

on decorative wood carving: 'treated after a thoroughly abstract fashion'. The *Trésor de la langue française* gives 'abstrait', of fine art, in opposition to 'expressioniste', with a 1904 citation. **The abstract sunset** (**rich**: compare Tennyson, *The Wreck* 136: 'Rich was the rose of sunset there'. **rich, not crude**: compare *Hamlet*, I iii 71 (Polonius on apparel): 'But not expressed in fancy; rich, not gaudy'. Compare *The Love Song of J. Alfred Prufrock* 43: 'rich and modest'. Given 'sea' here (6), compare the phrase from *The Tempest* which haunted TSE, not only in *The Waste Land*: 'rich and strange'.

14 **And while one lifts her hand**: compare the 'one . . . her' sequence in *The Love Song of J. Alfred Prufrock* 96: 'If one, settling a pillow by her head' (modulated in 107). Resembling *Mandarins 2*, *The Love Song of J. Alfred Prufrock* 101–8 has 'sunsets', 'teacups', and 'toward the window'.

15 **You have the other raise**: compare *Portrait of a Lady* I 2: 'You have the scene arrange itself'. For such a 'have', compare *Nocturne* 7: 'Behind the wall I have some servant wait'; *La Figlia Che Piange* 8–9:
So I would have had him leave,
So I would have had her stand and grieve,
These self-addressed creative injunctions resemble those voiced in the 'Instructions' genre (*Instructions to a Painter*), which TSE adopts in *Sweeney Erect* 1–5: 'Paint me [. . .]', 'Paint me [. . .]', 'Display me [. . .]'.

16–17 **porcelain, / Murmurs a word**: compare *The Love Song of J. Alfred Prufrock* 89: 'Among the porcelain, among some talk of you and me'.

Mandarins 3: The eldest of the mandarins

Dated Aug. 1910, the sequence.

1 **the mandarins**: see the sequence's title, and note. But here the setting also suggests *OED* 1b: 'A toy representing a grotesque seated figure in Chinese costume, so contrived as to continue nodding for a long time after it is shaken'. *OED* 1c: '*transf*. A person of much influence, a great man. Often used *colloq*. of Government officials, leading politicians or writers, etc.' This from 1907, with 1908: the 'mandarins of London letters'.

1–2, 4 **eldest . . . in obese repose . . . Regards**: compare Thomas Gray, *The Bard* 74–6:
> Youth on the prow, and Pleasure at the helm;
> Regardless of the sweeping Whirlwind's sway,
> That, hushed in grim repose,
The Bard is in *The Golden Treasury*, which TSE knew well.

2 **repose**: so placed at the line-end in *La Figlia Che Piange* 24. Here coloured by *OED* 5b, from 1695, Dryden: '*Painting*, etc. Harmonious arrangement of figures or colours, having a restful effect upon the eye'. Irving Babbitt, in *The New Laokoon* (1910, pp.229–33) praised 'vital repose' and defended it against 'the romanticists'; TSE dated his copy 1910 (Houghton Library).

2–4 **repose . . . intellectual double chins . . . nose**: compare Byron, *Don Juan* II [lviii] 461: '(dogs have such intellectual noses!)', rhyming with 'reposes'. Compare *Suite Clownesque I* 8, 11, rhyming 'nose' / 'repose', again of someone obese ('His belly sparkling and immense', 14). **intellectual double chins**: compare Wordsworth, *Prelude* (1850) XIII 52: 'Again I took the intellectual eye'.

4 **Regards the corner of his nose**: compare *Rhapsody on a Windy Night* 21: 'see the corner of her eye'.

5 **The cranes that fly**: TSE quoted from Dante the simile before the episode of Paolo and Francesca (*Inferno* V 46–8): 'And as the cranes go chanting their lays, making themselves a long streak in the air, so I saw the wailing shadows come, wailing, carried on the striving wind' (*Dante*, 1929, *SE*, p.245, where the translation begins as that of the Temple Classics and then diverges).   **a screen**: so placed at the line-end in *The Love Song of J. Alfred Prufrock* 105: 'But as if a magic lantern threw the nerves in patterns on a screen' (with 'patterns' in the preceding poem in TSE's sequence here).

6 **Pert, alert**: given that this describes birds, compare perhaps Chaucer's hen Pertelote (*The Nun's Priest's Tale*). Compare the gratifying rhyme with Laforgue,

who rhymes 'Meurtres, alertes' / 'pertes' (losses), in *Complainte de l'automne monotone* (1885) 29, 33.

7 **mien**: often so placed at the line-end by Tennyson (as by Wordsworth), but there invoking the dignified and handsome. (i) *The Beggar Maid* 11–12:
   One praised her ancles, one her eyes,
   One her dark hair and lovesome mien.
   – where 14 has 'all that land' (TSE, 11, 'all that'). (ii) *Freedom* 6: 'But scarce of such majestic mien'.

8 **Attentive intuitionist** (variant): to recognize how important the terms 'attention' and 'intuition' are to Bergson, see the index to *Creative Evolution* (*L'Evolution créatrice*, 1907; tr. A. Mitchell, 1911). Bergson was the intuitionist to end intuitionism. *Introduction à la métaphysique* (1903): 'Il suit de là qu'un absolu ne serait être donné que dans une *intuition*, tandis que tout le reste relève de l'*analyse*. Nous appelons ici intuition la *sympathie* par laquelle on se transporte à l'intérieur d'un objet pour coincider avec ce qu'il a d'unique et par conséquent d'inexprimable'. Again: 'La science et la métaphysique se rejoignent donc dans l'intuition. Une philosophie véritablement intuitive réaliserait l'union tant désirée de la métaphysique et de la science' (*Oeuvres*, pp.1395, 1424). In *Eeldrop and Appleplex*, Appleplex reports: 'Mrs. Howexden recommends me to read Bergson', and Eeldrop retorts that 'A philosophy about intuition is somewhat less likely to be intuitive than any other' (*Little Review*, iv, May 1917, 10). For TSE's later thinking about intuition, see *The Criterion*, vi (Oct. 1927) 340–7, *Mr. Middleton Murry's Synthesis*: 'I mean that intuition must have its place in a world of discourse; there may be room for intuitions both at the top and the bottom, or at the beginning and the end; but that intuition must always be tested, and capable of test, in a whole of experience in which intellect plays a large part'. TSE here called Murry 'a perfect pupil of his master, Bergson'. **intellectualist** (variant): compare *Eeldrop and Appleplex*: 'just as Bergson is an intellectualist' (p.11).

9 **World**: given the context (direct and exclamatory), compare *KEPB* (p.136): 'We can never, I mean, wholly explain the practical world from a theoretical point of view, because this world is what it is by reason of the practical point of view and the world which we try to explain is a world spread out upon a table – simply *there!*' (compare *The Love Song of J. Alfred Prufrock* 2–3: 'spread out [. . .] upon a table'). **World in fist**: *OED*, 'fist', 1400: 'He . . hooldith the world in his feest'. Compare the iconography in, for instance, Emile Verhaeren, *L'Ivresse* 7: 'Des aigles noirs, tenant le globe entre leurs pattes'. (This volume of Verhaeren, *Les Visages de la vie*, 1899, is listed among TSE's books in 1934.) **fist**: Laforgue uses 'poing' laconically like this, as in *Pétition* (1890) 3–6:

Jamais franches,
Ou le poing sur la hanche:
Avec toutes, l'amour s'échange
Simple et sans foi comme un bonjour.
(The last line, Laforgue used in more than one setting; TSE adapted it, *La Figlia Che Piange* 16: 'Simple and faithless as a smile and shake of the hand'.)

10 **Screen and cranes**: compacting 'The cranes that fly across a screen' (5), this may have been furthered by 'écran', the French for screen; Laforgue has 'l'écran des horizons', *Complainte des Mounis du Mont-Martre* (1885) 50 – and Laforgue contributed to the next line here.

11 **And what of all that one has missed!**: for the exclamation and the final word, compare the poem by Laforgue which TSE quotes in *The Metaphysical Poets* (1921, *SE*, p.289), *O géraniums diaphanes* (1890) 51: 'Oh, qu'ils sont pittoresques les trains manqués! . . .' (In *Dimanches: J'aurai passé ma vie*, 1890, 4, there is a variant: 'Oh! qu'ils sont chers les trains manqués'.) In his *Baudelaire* (1930), TSE links Laforgue's line with (as here) flight, direction and beatitude: 'Laforgue exclaims: *Comme ils sont beaux, les trains manqués*. The poetry of flight [. . .] is, in its origin in this paragraph of Baudelaire, a dim recognition of the direction of beatitude' (*SE*, p.428).

12 **And how life goes on different planes!**: compare the last line of the next poem in the sequence, *Mandarins 4*: 'How life goes well in pink and green!' **different planes**: compare Bergson, *Matière et mémoire* (1896), ch. III: 'S'il y a ainsi des *plans différents*, en nombre indéfini'. The running head for these pages was 'Les divers plans de conscience'; and in his *Résumé*, Bergson said: 'Entre le plan de l'action, – le plan où notre corps a contracté son passé en habitudes motrices, – et le plan de la mémoire pure, où notre esprit conserve dans tous ses détails le tableau de notre vie écoulée, nous avons cru apercevoir au contraire mille et mille plans de conscience différents.' TSE returned to the philosophical application in a paper on politics and metaphysics (1913–14?; Houghton Library; bMS Am 1691 (25), p.13): 'the compounding of theories belonging to different planes'. TSE's later dramatic criticism repeatedly pondered different planes. He compared Chapman ('the sense of a "double world" ') and Dostoevsky: 'In *The Revenge of Bussy D'Ambois*, for example, there runs the curious theme of reconciliation, quite inconsistent with the motives and intentions of the personages, but never ludicrous, because it seems to belong to another plane of reality from which these persons are exiles' (*VMP*, pp. 151–2). 'But "the greatest poetry", like the greatest prose, has a doubleness; the poet is talking to you on two planes at once' (Introduction to G. Wilson Knight, *The Wheel of Fire*, 1930, p.xv). 'We sometimes feel, in following the words and behaviour of some of the characters of Dostoevsky, that they are living at once on the plane that we know and on some

other plane of reality from which we are shut out' (*John Marston*, 1934, *SE*, p.229). 'It is in fact the privilege of dramatic poetry to be able to show us several planes of reality at once' (*The Aims of Poetic Drama, Adam*, no. 200, Nov. 1949, p.16). Compare *The Family Reunion* II i, where Harry says:

They don't understand what it is to be awake,
To be living on several planes at once
Though one cannot speak with several voices at once.

planes!: compare the exclamatory Laforguean ending of *Humouresque (After J. Laforgue)*: 'But, even at that, what mask *bizarre!*'

Mandarins 4: Still one more thought for pen and ink!

Dated Aug. 1910, the sequence.

1–2 thought . . . spleen: compare TSE in 1926, on Donne: 'in this loose and desultory form of Satire he found a type of poetry which could convey his random thoughts and reflections, exercise his gift for phrasing, his interest in the streets of London, his irritability and spleen' (*VMP*, p.144). Donne's *Satire III* begins: 'Kind pity chokes my spleen'. Compare TSE's *Spleen*. Baudelaire and Verlaine wrote poems called *Spleen*, and there is much of it in Laforgue, including *Le brave, brave automne!* (1890) 17–20:

> Puis rien ne saurait faire
> Que mon spleen ne chemine
> Sous les spleens insulaires
> De petites pluies fines . . .

Laforgue, like TSE here, parenthesizes spleen just after the start of a poem, *Arabesques de malheur* (1890), which begins:

> Nous nous aimions comme deux fous;
> On s'est quittés sans en parler.
> (Un spleen me tenait exilé
> Et ce spleen me venait de tout.)

But the French did not enjoy a monopoly of spleen, and not only because of Donne and because Ernest Dowson took it up; it had been important to Pope, as well as being Keatsian (six times at the line-end) and Tennysonian too (five times, plus two compounds). At the line-end in *Maud* I [ii] 87: 'From which I escaped heart-free, with the least little touch of spleen', where 90 has 'golden' (TSE, 9, 'goldwire'). Given that this poem is in the sequence *Mandarins*, compare Austin Dobson, *On a Nankin Plate* (1883) 16–19:

> 'That is why, in a mist of spleen,
> I mourn on this Nankin Plate.
> Ah me, but it might have been!' –
> Quoth the little blue mandarin.

1, 3 thought for pen and ink . . . How . . . think: compare Thomas Hood, *Lines in a Young Lady's Album* 9–10:

> Pray only think for pen and ink
>   How hard to get along.

(Hood's poem was reprinted in Carolyn Wells's *A Vers de Société Anthology*, 1907.)

4 Who see their outlines on the screen: compare *Convictions* 3: 'They see the outlines of their stage'; and *The Love Song of J. Alfred Prufrock* 105: 'But as if a magic lantern threw the nerves in patterns on a screen'. (Robert Crawford suggests as a source for the *Prufrock* line an article in the *St. Louis Daily Globe-Democrat*, 'Seeing the Brain', with its illustration of a head lanterned, outlined, on a screen; *The Savage and the City*, pp.8–9.) Compare *The Waste Land MS*, p.29, *The Fire Sermon* (insertion) 14: 'Sees on the screen'. *OED* has as its first cinematic citation, 1d, 1910, *Moving Picture World*: 'People . . like to see on the screen what they read about'. **Arrange and comprehend the scene.** (variant, *2nd reading*): compare *Portrait of a Lady* I 2: 'You have the scene arrange itself'. **conscient** (variant): Laforgue was especially occupied with this and its opposite ('inconscient' is everywhere in his poems); Symons wrote in *The Symbolist Movement in Literature* (p.107): 'He sees what he calls *l'Inconscient* in every gesture'. Symons quoted *Autre complainte de Lord Pierrot* (1885) 11: 'Et moi, d'un oeil qui vers l'Inconscient s'emballe'. TSE said of Laforgue in 1926: 'It is noticeable how often the words "inconscient", "néant", "L'absolu" and such philosophical terms from the vocabulary of Schopenhauer and Hartmann [. . .] recur' (*VMP*, p.215).

5–7 good . . . demoiselles: compare Byron, *Don Juan*, XV [xlii] 330: 'A dashing demoiselle of good estate'.

7, 9 demoiselles . . . dragons: the movement of mind may owe something to demoiselle, both in French and in English, as a dragon-fly. Corbière plays with this double sense in *Idylle coupée* 85 and *Rondel* 11 (both 1873). *OED* 2b, 'demoiselle', 'A dragon-fly'. 1816: 'The name given to them in England, "Dragon flies", seems much more applicable than "Demoiselles" by which the French distinguish them'; and Gosse, 1844: 'an acquaintance with these *demoiselles*'. Compare Remy de Gourmont, *Physique de l'amour: essai sur l'instinct sexuel* (1904), ch.XIII: 'La libellule, joliment appelée la demoiselle'. TSE enquired of Pound for a copy of his translation, 28 July 1922 (*Letters* i 553).

8–9 cherry . . . dragons: both Oriental, but perhaps catching the love-conjunction in Tennyson, *The Princess* V 161–2:
> To such as her! if Cyril spake her true,
> To catch a dragon in a cherry net,

10 Expanded by the breeze: usually nautical, as in Pope, *Odyssey* XII 104–5:
> expand thy sails,
> Ply the strong oar, and catch the nimble gales;

Shelley, *Alastor* 398: 'the expanded sail'. But Shelley also has, *Ginevra* 125: 'The matin winds from the expanded flowers'. **by the breeze:** as at *Maud*, I [iv] 104, where the previous line has 'gay' (as in TSE, 13).

12 Nor intellectual nor mean: compare perhaps Marvell, *An Horatian Ode* 57: 'He nothing common did or mean'.

12–13 Nor intellectual nor mean, / And graceful, not too gay: compare Wordsworth, *Excursion* II 180–2:

An intellectual ruler in the haunts
Of social vanity, he walked the world,
Gay, and affecting graceful gaiety.

(TSE, 8, 'Walk'; TSE's is a scene of 'social vanity'; and 'Mandarins' are rulers.) For the aspiration, compare *Little Gidding* V 6–9: 'neither diffident nor ostentatious', 'exact without vulgarity', 'precise but not pedantic'. TSE praised eighteenth-century prose: 'style neither strained nor relaxed, neither ascetic nor luxurious' (*New English Weekly*, 20 June 1935). **Nor . . . nor:** *OED* 2b, 'Chiefly *poet.*'; no instance after 1852.

15 How life goes well in pink and green!: compare the end of the previous poem in the sequence, *Mandarins* 3: 'And how life goes on different planes!' Also *Ash-Wednesday* III 15: 'in blue and green', and IV 3–4: 'green / Going in white and blue'.

Easter: Sensations of April [1]:
The little negro girl who lives across the alley

Dated April 1910. Title for the paired poems: TSE's mother, Charlotte Eliot, 'throughout her life wrote poems, some of which, like "Easter Songs", were printed in the *Christian Register*' (*Letters* i 5); there is a copy of *Easter Songs* (1899) in the Houghton Library. Subtitle, **Sensations of April**: compare 'our sensations', in the refrain of *First Debate between the Body and Soul*. The phrase *Sensations of April* may owe something to Laforgue: 'O paria! – Et revoici les sympathies de mai', the first line of *Simple agonie* (1886), a poem which has 'Se crucifie', 17 (compare TSE's title **Easter**). Compare also Rimbaud, *Sensation* (1889) 1–6, on 'les soirs bleus d'été', 'la fraîcheur', and 'l'amour infini'. TSE wrote (of Dadaism, loosely): 'It prefers in fact, things which are not art, because the sensation of enjoying something ugly is more amusing than the worn out enjoyment of something beautiful. [. . .] and in the end, if we pursue only sensation, we shall cease to have even sensation' (*Modern Tendencies in Poetry*, a talk circa October 1919; *Shama'a*, April 1920, p.17). And in his *London Letter* (*The Dial*, Aug. 1921, p.216), TSE wrote that Lytton Strachey 'has invented new sensations from history, as Bergson has invented new sensations from metaphysics'. In his Clark Lectures (1926), TSE said, apropos of metaphysical poetry: 'Humanity reaches its higher civilisation levels not chiefly by improvement of thought or by increase and variety of sensation, but by the extent of co-operation between acute sensation and acute thought' (*VMP*, pp.220–1). With the subtitle's *Sensations*, given 'the smell of heat' (7), compare TSE on Kipling: 'for the first condition of right thought is right sensation: the first condition of understanding a foreign country is to smell it, as you smell India in *Kim*' (1941, *OPP*, p.247).

Beginning 'The little negro girl', TSE's poem asks comparison with Blake, *The Little Black Boy*, which four times mentions the 'heat' (TSE, 7), and twice 'God' (TSE, 3); it too has 'flowers' (TSE, 2, 13, 'geranium'). Blake's poem is about being 'taught' a childlike religious lesson (compare TSE, 14, 'Sunday school').

C. F. G. Masterman begins ch.VII of *From the Abyss* (1902, p.72) with a scene with many elements of TSE's poem: 'It is Sunday evening, and the tinkling of numerous church bells is fretfully protesting the desirability of public worship. The temperature has been anything over a hundred and twenty in the sunshine, the asphalt has become soft and bubbly, and in the narrow street [. . .]'; Masterman mentions in the next few lines 'the heat', 'upper windows', and 'children, the girls in white'. (*From the Abyss* has been proposed by James Kissane as a source for *The Waste Land*; *Yeats Eliot Review*, vi, 1, 1979, 24–8.) Compare John Gray's sonnet, *Poem* (1893); beginning 'Geranium', it has 'A wistful child', and 'The asphalt burns'.

  1 **The little negro girl who lives across the alley**: in a letter to Aiken, 25 July 1914 (*Letters* i 44), TSE mentions, as among 'the themes for the "Descent from the

Cross" or whatever I may call it', 'a recurring piece quite in the French style beginning

"The married girl who lives across the street
Wraps her soul in orange-coloured robes of Chopinese." '

3 **formulae**: an equivocal word, given its also being authentically religious. *OED* 1a: 'A set form of words [. . .] to be used on some ceremonial occasion'. TSE wrote: 'The true critic is a scrupulous avoider of formulae'; 'The things of which we are collectively certain, we may say our common formulae, are certainly not true' (*KEPB*, pp.164–5). But he did not disown the word when he italicized it: 'The fundamental beliefs of an intellectual conservatism, that man requires an askesis, a *formula* to be imposed upon him from above' (of Paul Elmer More, *New Statesman*, 24 June 1916).

4 **Geraniums**: compare *Rhapsody on a Windy Night* 12, 63: 'a dead geranium', and 'sunless dry geraniums'. The geraniums here are likewise 'Withered and dry' (10). TSE said of *Rhapsody on a Windy Night*: 'I recognize the geraniums; they were Jules Laforgue's geraniums, not mine, I'm afraid, originally' (*Columbia University Forum*, Fall 1958, p.13). Laforgue, *Pierrots* 1 (1886) 7–8:

La bouche clownesque ensorcèle
Comme un singulier géranium.

(Compare TSE's *Suite Clownesque*.) *Rigueurs à nulle autre pareilles* (1890) 1–4:

Dans un album,
Mourait fossile
Un géranium
Cueilli aux Iles.

Derniers Vers x (1890) begins: 'O géraniums diaphanes'; TSE quoted this (with the first ten lines of the poem) in *The Metaphysical Poets* (1921): 'Jules Laforgue, and Tristan Corbière in many of his poems, are nearer to the "school of Donne" than any modern English poet' (*SE*, pp.289–90). In his Clark Lectures (1926), TSE said of Laforgue: 'he is at once the sentimentalist day-dreaming over the *jeune fille* at the piano with her geraniums, and the behaviourist inspecting her reflexes'; TSE rephrased this for the Turnbull Lectures in 1933: 'he is at once the sentimentalist dreaming about the *jeune fille* at the piano or with her geraniums, and the pathologist commenting on her reflexes' (*VMP*, pp.216, 285).

6 **perfume**: *OED*: 'Orig., like the vb., stressed *per'fume*: so in 18th c. dicts., and in Webster 1828; usu. in 17–18th c., and freq. in 19th c. poets'. US English continued to permit this stress on the second syllable; possibly on the first syllable here.

6–7 **perfume . . . heat**: since these are *Sensations of April*, compare Shakespeare's Sonnet 104:7: 'Three April perfumes in three hot Junes burned'.

7–8 **smell . . . street**: compare *Rhapsody on a Windy Night* 65: 'Smells of chestnuts in the streets' ('street' similarly at the line-end).

9–12 **Geraniums geraniums / Withered and dry / Long laid by / In the sweepings of the memory**: contrast the close of Apollinaire, *J'ai eu le courage* (Nov.–Dec. 1908) 11–12:
Et les roses de l'électricité s'ouvrent encore
Dans le jardin de ma mémoire
Apollinaire's previous line speaks of 'une mulâtresse'; Eliot's next line, of 'The little negro girl'.

10, 12 **Withered . . . memory**: compare Shelley, *Epipsychidion* 4: 'wreaths of withered memory'. **dry . . . sweepings**: compare Tennyson, *Locksley Hall* 131: 'So I triumphed ere my passion sweeping through me left me dry'; with 'dry' at the line-end and with 'passion' possibly touching TSE's title *Easter*.

12 **sweepings**: *OED* 'sweeping', 2a: 'That which is swept up; matter, esp. dust or refuse, that is swept together or away'; but possibly with the memory also engaging in 'sweeping', 1b: 'Dragging for something'. **memory**: at the line-end in *Rhapsody on a Windy Night* 55, 62–3: 'The moon has lost her memory';
The reminiscence comes
Of sunless dry geraniums

13–14 **girl . . . Brings a geranium from Sunday school**: given the Laforguean associations of the geranium (see 4 note), this suggests Laforgue on the girls going to church, *Dimanches: C'est l'automne* (1890) 9–10:
Les Jeunes Filles inviolables et frêles
Descendent vers la petite chapelle
TSE quoted this in his Clark Lectures (*VMP*, pp.214–5).

14] **She is very sure of God.** *deleted, following* 14. Symons, in *The Symbolist Movement in Literature* (pp.57–8), ends his chapter on Villiers de l'Isle-Adam: 'He affirms; he "believes in soul, is very sure of God;" requires no witness to the spiritual world of which he is always the inhabitant; and is content to lose his way in the material world, brushing off its mud from time to time with a disdainful gesture, as he goes on his way (to apply a significant word of Pater) "like one on a secret errand." ' Compare the end of *Bacchus and Ariadne*: 'I am sure'. Given this manifest borrowing from Symons by TSE, compare 'formulae of God' (3) with Symons, earlier in this chapter (p.41): ' "I am far from sure," wrote Verlaine, "that the philosophy of Villiers will not one day become the formula of our century" '.

Easter: Sensations of April II: Daffodils

Dated May 1910. Printed in the limited edition (1989) of *Letters* i, with (tipped in) a facsimile of the page from the Notebook.

1 **Daffodils**: for a literary (as well as the seasonal) association of daffodils with Easter, compare Housman, *A Shropshire Lad* (1896) XXIX 18–20:

> And bear from hill and valley
> The daffodil away
> That dies on Easter day.

If there is some continuity with the child of the previous poem of the pair, TSE may have remembered what Van Wyck Brooks said about 'A child's comments', in *The Wine of the Puritans* (1908), which TSE reviewed in the *Harvard Advocate* (7 May 1909): 'It is the kind of criticism which one receives from a bowl of daffodils on one's desk or the breeze that rustles in the window curtains' (pp.27–8). Brooks later mentions 'the poetry of George Herbert' (p.94); see 4, 5 notes. The 'Daffodils' of TSE's opening may join the 'imagination' at the end, via Wordsworth, whose daffodils were placed by him among 'Poems of the Imagination'. (The poem carried the title *Daffodils* in the *Oxford Book of English Verse*.)

2–3, 7 **sunlight fills . . . cool . . . room . . . perfume**: compare Keats, *Eve of St. Agnes* 275: 'Filling the chilly room with perfume light'.

4 **Swept and set in order**: compare Luke 11:25, the house 'swept and garnished'. (*Choruses from 'The Rock'* III 45: 'I have swept the floors and garnished the altars'.) If George Herbert colours the next line, 'swept' here may owe something to 'Who sweeps a room, as for thy laws' (*The Elixir* 19).   **set in order**: compare Exodus 39:37–8: 'even with the lamps to be set in order', 'the oil for light', and 'the sweet incense' (compare the 'light' in TSE, 2, and 'sweet perfume', 7). Also TSE's title-page epigraph to *For Lancelot Andrewes: Essays on Style and Order* (1928): 'Thou, Lord, Who walkest in the midst of the golden candlesticks, remove not, we pray Thee, our candlestick out of its place; but set in order the things which are wanting among us, and strengthen those which remain, and are ready to die.' (*The Preces Privatae of Lancelot Andrewes*, selections from the translation by F. E. Brightman, 1903, ed. A. E. Burn, 1908, p.43, Sunday Morning: Intercession; TSE's epigraph varies slightly from this translation.) Given 'fills' (2), compare D. G. Rossetti's translation of Saint Francis of Assisi, *Cantica: Our Lord Christ: of Order* 1–3:

> Set Love in order, thou that lovest Me.
>   Never was virtue out of order found;
>   And though I fill thy heart desirously,

The syllabus for TSE's 1918 tutorial class in Elizabethan Literature included:

'Read: A few translations of Italian Sonnets in Rossetti's *Early Italian Poets*' (R. Schuchard, *Review of English Studies* n.s. xxv, 1974, 300). Given the theological associations of 'set in order', compare TSE's paper on ethics (Houghton Library; bMS Am 1691.14 (32), p.2): 'But there are all sorts of ways of setting the world in order; from the relative precision of physics to the relative confusion of theology'.

4–5 in order – / Smelling: compare *Paradise Regained* II 351: 'That fragrant smell diffused, in order stood'.

5 Smelling of earth and rain: compare Herbert, *The Flower* 38: 'I once more smell the dew and rain', likewise rhyming with 'again'. (TSE praised this stanza of Herbert's as 'itself a miracle of phrasing'; *George Herbert*, 1962, p.26.) *The Flower* has in its next line 'light' (TSE, 2), and in 1 'sweet' (TSE, 7); the title *The Flower* may touch TSE's daffodils; further, Herbert anticipated TSE here in entitling a poem *Easter* (it shares with TSE 'sun[s]', 'light', 'sweet', 'perfume' and flowers). Moreover, Herbert has 'Guilty of dust and sin' (*Love* III 2, with 'sweetly' in 5 / TSE, 7, 'sweet'); further, in relation to TSE's 'Smelling of earth and rain', compare perhaps Tennyson, *Maud*, I [vi] 234: 'Smelling of musk and of insolence', where the musk may be compared to TSE's perfume, and 'insolence' to TSE's word 'insistent': 'insistent sweet perfume' (7).

6–7 again / The insistent: compare *Portrait of a Lady* II 16: 'returns like the insistent out-of-tune'. **insistent sweet**: compare *Preludes* IV 3: 'insistent feet'.

7 perfume: see *Easter* I 6 note; the stress here is apparently on the second syllable.

9–10 Irritate . . . the nerves: compare Hawthorne, *The Blithedale Romance*, ch. XVIII, when Zenobia is seen in her room through the window: 'It irritated my nerves; it affected me with a kind of heart-sickness'. TSE wrote to his mother, 31 Oct. 1920: 'I have simply not had the time to do a single piece of work, and when one has in mind a great many things that one wants to do, that irritates the nerves more and more' (*Letters* i 419). **the imagination / Or the nerves**: compare perhaps Henry James, 'the imagination, for the nerves' (*The American Scene*, 1907, p.187); eight pages later, James has 'smelling of dust and' (TSE, 5: 'Smelling of earth and'). TSE wrote to his mother, 2 June 1918: 'James was a fine writer – his book of impressions of America, written about 1907 I think, is wonderfully well written' (*Letters* i 233). Compare Symons, *The Symbolist Movement in Literature* (p.24), of Gérard de Nerval: 'Every artist lives a double life, in which he is for the most part conscious of the illusions of the imagination. He is conscious also of the illusions of the nerves, which he shares with every man of imaginative mind.' Similarly, Symons, *A New Art of the Stage*: 'The imagination has been caught; a suggestion has been given which strikes straight to "the nerves of delight"; and be sure those nerves, that imagination, will do the rest' (*Studies in Seven Arts*, 1906, p.354).

10 **the nerves**: compare *The Love Song of J. Alfred Prufrock* 105: 'threw the nerves in patterns on a screen'. Following 'sunlight' (TSE, 2), possibly recalling the opening line from Jonson's *Poetaster* which moved TSE (*Ben Jonson*, 1919, *SE*, p.151): 'Light, I salute thee, but with wounded nerves.' Symons's *Nerves* (1895) begins: 'The modern malady of love is nerves', and it laments: 'Nerves, nerves!' Symons, in *The Symbolist Movement in Literature* (p.108), wrote: 'It is an art of the nerves, this art of Laforgue, and it is what all art would tend towards if we followed our nerves on all their journeys.' (Laforgue was more rueful, as in the Villonesque joke in *Préludes autobiographiques*: 'où sont mes nerfs d'hier?') By 1921 TSE, having journeyed to Lausanne, where he was under the care of Vittoz, averred: 'I never did believe in "nerves", at least for *myself*!' (*Letters* i 490). Yet it was at this time that he was writing what he himself soon called the 'nerves monologue' in *The Waste Land* (to Pound, 24? Jan. 1922, *Letters* i 504). In his Clark Lectures (1926), TSE deprecated an aspect of Donne's *Satires*: 'my main point is that this deliberate over-stimulation, *exploitation* of the *nerves* – for such it is – has in it, to me, something unscrupulous' (*VMP*, p.158). In 1927, he dissented from Symons on Baudelaire: 'We cannot be *primarily* interested in any writer's nerves (and remember please that "nerves" used in this way is a very vague and unscientific term) or in any one's heredity except for the purpose of knowing to what extent that writer's individuality distorts or detracts from the objective truth which he perceives' (*For Lancelot Andrewes*, 1928, p.91).

Goldfish (Essence of Summer Magazines) 1: Always the August evenings come

At the end of the sequence is the date Sept. 1910. Title of the sequence: **Goldfish** is enigmatic, but there is a suggestion of the wealthy leisure class, floating among 'summer magazines' where their essence is catered to. Compare Henry James on American social life (*The American Scene*, 1907, p.456): 'As for the younger persons, of whom there were many, as for the young girls in especial, they were as perfectly in their element as goldfish in a crystal jar: a form of exhibition suggesting but one question or mystery. Was it they who had invented it, or had it inscrutably invented *them*?'

The conjunction, title with subtitle, of **Goldfish** and **Essence** may owe something to 'His glassy essence', *Measure for Measure*, II ii 120; perhaps via the proximity of 'gold-fish' to 'glassy' in Keats, *Fragment of the Castle Builder* 29–30 (1848 text): 'Clear, but for gold-fish vases in the way, / Their glassy diamonding'. If the line from *Maud*, 'Smelling of musk and of insolence', played some part in *Easter: Sensations of April* II 5, compare perhaps *Essence of Summer Magazines* with the same section of *Maud* (I xiii):

> But his essences turned the live air sick
> And barbarous opulence jewel-thick
> Sunned itself .

(TSE, 13, 'turn, return'.)   **Summer Magazines**: given 'the August evenings', compare Francis Jammes, *J'aime dans les temps* 1–4 (*De l'Angelus de l'aube à l'Angelus du soir*, 1898):

> J'aime dans les temps Clara d'Ellébeuse,
> l'écolière des anciens pensionnats,
> qui allait, les soirs chauds, sous les tilleuls
> lire les *magazines* d'autrefois.

Jammes speaks, eight lines later, of 'des fins d'Eté'; and in *On m'éreinte* 2, in the same collection, describes himself as 'moi qui chante les anciens magazines'. (*De l'Angelus* is listed among TSE's books in 1934.) W. G. Tinckom-Fernandez, *Harvard Advocate* (Dec. 1938, p.8): 'It was Eliot who first told me of the Vers Libre movement, of the work of Paul Fort and Francis Jammes.'

  1 **Always the August evenings come / With**: compare the opening of *Preludes* 1: 'The winter evening settles down / With [. . .]'. Also of *The Little Passion* (i) 1: 'Upon those stifling August nights'. Always the August evenings come in Laforgue: 'Aux soirs d'août', *Clair de lune* (1886) 4; 'ce soir d'août', *Dimanches: Le Dimanche, on se plaît* (1890) 23; 'En ce soir d'août', *Complainte des blackboulés* (1885) 15 (where it follows 'L'orchestre', 5); and 'O crépuscules d'août!' (*Les deux Pigeons*, 1888, added to *Moralités légendaires*; 1992 edn, p.178).

1, 4, 6–8 evenings . . . all . . . call, recall / So many nights and afternoons – / . . . all: compare *The Love Song of J. Alfred Prufrock* 49–50:
> For I have known them all already, known them all –
> Have known the evenings, mornings, afternoons,

2 **With preparation for the waltz**: compare *A Cooking Egg* 8: 'An *Invitation to the Dance*', noting Weber's *L'Invitation à la Valse*. **the waltz**: compare Byron's *Waltz*, which likewise rhymes 'waltz' with 'faults' (53–4), and with 'assaults' (13–14), and which shares with TSE's poem the rhyme-words 'turn', 'return', 'tune' ('tunes', TSE), and 'the rest'. Laforgue brought together comic-opera (compare 'The *Merry Widow*', and 'The *Chocolate Soldier*', TSE, 5, 10), the waltz, and the reminiscential, in the opening lines of *Le Miracle des roses*: 'nullement opéra-comique malgré leur costume. Ah! que tout n'est-il opéra-comique! . . . Que tout n'évolue-t-il en mesure sur cette valse anglaise *Myosotis*, qu'on entendait cette année-là (moi navré dans les coins, comme on pense) au Casino, valse si décemment mélancolique, si irréparablement derniers, derniers beaux jours!' (*Moralités légendaires*, 1992 edn, p.49). Compare TSE's *Exequy* 19–21:
> They terminate the festivals
> With some invariable surprise
> Of fireworks, or an Austrian waltz.

– here Pound wrote in the margin: 'This is Laforgue not XVIII' [eighteenth century] (*The Waste Land MS*, p.101).

5 **The *Merry Widow***: by Franz Lehar, 1905. TSE's brother Henry Ware Eliot 'took him to his first Broadway musical, *The Merry Widow*, which remained a favourite' (*Letters* i 54). The issue of the *Harvard Advocate* which included TSE's poem *Before Morning*, 13 Nov. 1908, had an article by E.N.P. on *Free Music* which brings out what this waltz meant, irony and all, to TSE's generation: 'Now a word about the *Merry Widow Waltz*. We have always liked this waltz, and we like it still. It is melodious, graceful, seductive. But no mere amateur should attempt it. Every note of it is stamped indelibly on the tympanum of every human ear. Only a finished artist, a man who has taken honors in Music 23, should play the *Merry Widow Waltz*. It requires a complete mastery of all the resources of the piano, and an ideal grasp of the aesthetic principle, to interpret it adequately before an intelligent audience. Anything else, young ambition, anything else!' **the rest**: similarly ending the line in Byron, *Waltz* 24 and 229; see 2 note.

6 **call, recall**: compare the placing of 'recall' at the line-end with *Portrait of a Lady* II 12:
> 'Yet with these April sunsets, that somehow recall

('April sunsets' and then, II 17, 'an August afternoon'; compare 'August evenings' above, 1).

8 **August, with all its faults!**: compare Cowper, *The Task* II 206–7: 'England, with all thy faults, I love thee still – / My country!' (England was and was not TSE's country, as he soon knew; see, for instance, his letter to Eleanor Hinkley, 8 Sept. 1914, *Letters* i 57.) Byron the traveller (and expatriate) made play with Cowper's line, in *Beppo* [xlvii] 369–70:

> 'England! with all thy faults I love thee still',
> I said at Calais, and have not forgot it;

all its faults: compare Byron, *Waltz* 53–4, on Germany,

> Who sent us – so be pardoned all her faults,
> A dozen Dukes – some Kings – a Queen – and 'Waltz'.

10 **The *Chocolate Soldier***: an operetta by Oskar Straus, performed in Vienna in 1908. It is an adaptation of Shaw's *Arms and the Man*. TSE wrote to Henry Sherek, 3 May 1957 (Harry Ransom Humanities Research Center, Austin): 'I sometimes think that Shaw is best at musical comedy for *The Chocolate Soldier* and *My Fair Lady* are the only two of his works which I should like to see again and again.' **The *Chocolate Soldier* assaults**: rhyming with 'waltz', and likewise invoking a soldier, compare Byron, *Waltz* 12–14:

> *sans armour* thou shalt take the field,
> And own – impregnable to *most* assaults,
> Thy not too lawfully begotten 'Waltz'.

10–11 **Soldier assaults / The . . . sphinx**: perhaps suggested by Napoleon's Egyptian campaign of 1798, via Byron's *Waltz* which mentions both Buonaparte and Egypt (56, 127). In 1902–3, at Smith Academy, TSE studied *L'Expédition de Bonaparte en Egypt* (John J. Soldo, *The Tempering of T. S. Eliot*, 1983, his Appx.A). The popular belief was that a French soldier shot off the nose of the Sphinx. A soldier stands as if to assault a sphinx in James Thomson, *The City of Dreadful Night* (1874) XX 27–9. **assaults / The tired**: compare *The Waste Land* [III] 236, 239: 'she is bored and tired', 'he assaults at once'; in both poems, music follows: 'the waltzes turn' / 'puts a record on the gramophone'.

11 **The tired Sphinx of the physical**: given the musical setting (and a possible chime of the line-end's music, 'physical' / 'musical'), compare *Love's Labour's Lost*, IV iii 338: 'Subtle as Sphinx; as sweet and musical'. ('The *Chocolate Soldier*' would be sweet and musical.) **tired Sphinx**: often so. Compare Gautier, *Nostalgies d'obélisques* (1852) II 31: 'Des sphinx, lassés de l'attitude'. Emerson's *The Sphinx* (1847) begins: 'The Sphinx is drowsy'. Wilde, *The Sphinx* (1894) 13: 'my lovely languorous Sphinx!' (for more Wilde, see 15–16 note); TSE speaks of the 'typographical caprice' of this poem's rhyming in his Introduction to Marianne Moore's *Selected Poems* (1935), p.10. Kipling's story *The Education of Otis Yeere* I (1888, *Under the Deodars*) follows the remark 'You'd be tired yourself. It's only because I'm tired', eight lines later, with 'Mrs. Mallowe smiled in a superior and Sphinx-like fashion'.

12] **For meanings that we not discern.** (variant); **For meanings we cannot discern.** (variant). Compare Tennyson, *Tiresias* 5: 'The meanings ambushed under all they saw', from a poem which likewise invokes the 'sphinx' (TSE, the previous line); TSE may have been interested in Tiresias well before *The Waste Land.* **that we not discern** (variant): in its archaism or foreignness, this sounds closer than the final reading ('We cannot discern') to possible memories of Dante, with whose words 'non discerno' ('discern no further') TSE ended *What is a Classic?* (1944, *OPP*, p.71); similarly suggestive of the Temple Classics translation, as at *Paradiso* IX 103 (marked by TSE in his copy, Houghton Library): 'Yet here we not repent, but smile'.

13–15 **turn . . . Float and fall, / Like the cigarettes**: compare Tennyson, *The Lotos-Eaters* 75–6: 'turning yellow / Falls, and floats'. Tennyson's strophe (Choric Song III) speaks of 'The folded leaf', which TSE may have rolled with 'yellow' for 'Like the cigarettes'. **Float and fall**: compare John Addington Symonds, *In the Key of Blue* (1893) 38: 'Where dingy lamplight floats and falls'.

15–16 **cigarettes . . . marionettes**: compare Wilde, *The Harlot's House* (1908) 22–3:
Sometimes a horrible marionette
Came out, and smoked its cigarette,
With TSE's (threefold) mention of the waltz, compare *The Harlot's House* 31–2:
Then suddenly the tune went false,
The dancers wearied of the waltz,

Goldfish (Essence of Summer Magazines) II: Embarquement pour Cythère

At the end of the sequence is the date Sept. 1910. Title: Watteau's painting, *L'Embarquement pour l'Ile de Cythère* (Louvre), was submitted in 1717. Baudelaire, *Les Phares* (1857) 21–4:

> Watteau, ce carnaval où bien des coeurs illustres,
> Comme des papillons, errent en flamboyant,
> Décors frais et légers éclairés par des lustres
> Qui versent la folie à ce bal tournoyant;

Watteau's *Embarquement pour l'Ile de Cythère* became Baudelaire's *Un Voyage à Cythère* (1857); TSE quoted 'well-known lines' from it in *Baudelaire in Our Time*. (TSE initially distrusted Symons's translation: 'We wonder even whether Mr Symons has not confused (*whose birth*) Cythera with Cytherea'; this stricture was dropped when TSE reprinted his review, from *The Dial*, May 1927, in *For Lancelot Andrewes*, p.97.) The sardonic ending of Verlaine's *Cythère* (1869) may have contributed to TSE's 'And the sandwiches and ginger beer?' (3):

> Et l'Amour comblant tout, hormis
> La Faim, sorbets et confitures
> Nous préservent des courbatures.

Symons wrote: 'In his acceptance of the fragility of things as actually a principle of art, Laforgue is a sort of transformed Watteau, showing his disdain for the world which fascinates him, in quite a different way' (*The Symbolist Movement in Literature*, p.107). Compare Laforgue, *Cythère* (1890) 11–12:

> Et comment quelques couples vraiment distingués
>   Un soir ici ont débarqué . . .

TSE possibly also recalls Laforgue, *Persée et Andromède*: 'Allez, hop! à Cythère!' (*Moralités légendaires*, 1992 edn, p.139); Laforgue's telling of this tale influenced TSE's *Ode*. Also Laforgue, *Pierrot Fumiste* (1903), where Pierrot suddenly exclaims:

> 'Cochers! Tous à Cythère! Au pays de Watteau!' (Il remonte dans la voiture. La noce qui était redescendue remonte. On va partir).

The scene ends: 'Un beau ciel de mai' (*Mélanges posthumes*, p.97). Laforgue's title, *Pierrot Fumiste*, could punningly have lit TSE's 'cigarette'. Austin Dobson, in his *Essays in Old French Forms*, had lightly adapted these properties; *After Watteau* (1893) begins, 'Embarquons-nous!', and ends:

> 'Allons, embarquons pour Cythère';
> You will not? Press her, then, PIERROT, –
>   'Embarquons-nous!'

---

3 **ginger beer**: a nineteenth-century innovation; Leigh Hunt in 1813: 'trying a composition called ginger-beer' (*OED*). A recipe is given in Charles Elmé Francatelli, *A Plain Cookery Book for the Working Classes* (1861). W. S. Gilbert

banters it in *Thespis, or The Gods Grown Old* (produced 1871), Act II: 'There seems to be something unusual with the grapes of Mytilene; they only grow ginger beer.' 'And a very good thing too.' 'It's very nice in its way, but it is not what one looks for from grapes.'

4–5 let us embark – / The night is anything but dark: compare *The Love Song of J. Alfred Prufrock* 1–2:
>   Let us go then, you and I,
>   When the evening is spread out against the sky

Perhaps 'The night is anything but dark' in contrast with what would be spiritually serious; TSE has on a Harvard note-card (Houghton Library) St John of the Cross, The Dark Night of the Soul.

5–6 The night is anything but dark, / Almost as clear as day: compare André Salmon, *Le Festin sous la lune* (1910) 43–4:
>   ô nuit tendre
>   Où je vois si clair en mon coeur.

Given that TSE's poem is a *festin sous la lune*, compare *Le Festin* 3: 'Des artistes boivent et mangent', and see 11–12 note.

11–12 cigarette . . . light it at the evening star: compare Salmon, *Le Festin sous la lune* 10–12:
>   Parmi le clair de lune bleu,
>   L'autre, moins fou, ne se propose
>   Que d'allumer sa pipe aux cieux.

(A similar fancy, or the same topos, is in Apollinaire, *Hôtel* 4: 'J'allume au feu du jour ma cigarette', not published till April 1914.) Compare *Paradise Lost* VIII 518–20:
>   till the amorous bird of night
>   Sung spousal, and bid haste the evening star
>   On his hill top, to light the bridal lamp.

evening star: Tennyson, *Crossing the Bar* 1: 'Sunset and evening star'; with Tennyson, 8, 'Turns again' / TSE, 9, 'return'; 10, 'dark' / TSE, 5; 12, 'embark' / TSE's title.

12–13 star) / To porcelain land, what avatar: compare the end of Browning, *Waring*, [II] 259–62:
>   Oh, never star
>   Was lost here but it rose afar!
>   Look East, where whole new thousands are!
>   In Vishnu-land what Avatar?

Waring is the story of an embarkation ([I] 101: 'Travels Waring East away?'). As to 'Philosophy' (15), compare TSE in 1926: 'It becomes clear after a little inspection that this type of thought, the *Word made Flesh*, so to speak, is more restricted in the times and places of its avatar than is immediately evident' (*VMP*, p.54). **porcelain land**: compare Whistler's *La Princesse du pays de la porcelaine* (1864; Freer Gallery, Washington), and contrast 'the porcelain department' in *In the Department Store* 1 and note.

13–14 **land . . . blue-**: compare Jean Lorrain, *Embarquement* (1887) 5, 26 (embarking for 'Cythère'), twice the 'bleu pays'; the poem is in *Poètes d'aujourd'hui*, which TSE owned in the two-volume edition, 1908 and reprinted.

14 **blue-delft-romance**: blue delft is invoked in Laforgue's mockery of romance, *Le Miracle des roses*, as the heroine's inkwell: 'Et en effet, grâce aux roses, roses si à propos effeuillées là, de cette fillette anonyme, Ruth était exorcisée de ses hallucinations, et pouvait désormais s'adonner sans partage au seul et pur travail de sa tuberculose, dont elle reprit le journal d'une plume trempée dans un encrier à fleurs bleues genre Delft' (*Moralités légendaires*, 1992 edn, p.65). There is another appearance of blue delft in Laforgue's prose (see the note to *The smoke that gathers blue and sinks* 3; *Mélanges posthumes*, 1903, pp.38–9). *Après-dîner torride et stagnante* has 'un bluet bleu, sur une faience de Delft au-dessus d'un empilement d'étoles'. Compare perhaps Laforgue's 'étoles' (via 'étoile') with TSE's 'star' (12). Laforgue has in this vignette 'la cigarette' as well as, in his next brief section (p.40), 'tout le long, le long de dix cigarettes'; compare TSE, 11: 'As long as a cigarette will burn'. **-delft-romance**: 'Delft' and 'romance' are both to be found in Beatrice Hanscom's poem *The Old Collector* (about works of art, and love), in Carolyn Wells's *A Vers de Société Anthology* (1907). **-romance**: US English continued to permit the stress on the first syllable, as often in Middle English.

15 **Philosophy through**: compare *Dante* (1920, *SW*, p.169): 'the philosophy of Aristotle strained through the schools'. **Philosophy through a paper straw**: for philosophy as something to drink, compare Swinburne, *The Queen's Pleasance*, in *Tristram of Lyonesse* (1882):

> and she
> Drank lightly deep of his philosophy
> In that warm wine of amorous words which is
> Sweet with all truths of all philosophies.

Meredith, *A Ballad of Fair Ladies in Revolt* (1883) 4–5:

> through,
> To teach philosophers the thirst of thieves:

(Meredith's title and his address, 13, 'Most gracious ladies', resemble TSE's opening: 'Ladies, [. . .]'.) TSE, *Modern Education and the Classics*: 'Even *philosophy*, when divorced from *theology* and from the knowledge of life and of ascertainable facts, is but a famishing pabulum, or a draught stimulating for a moment, leaving behind drought and disillusion' (1932, *SE*, pp.511–2). TSE's line may have Harvard undergraduate humour behind it; compare the sing-song of W. G. Tinckom-Fernandez (described by TSE as 'a crony of mine', *Paris Review* 21, Spring/Summer 1959, p.52), and his 'exquisite English diction – "a cup of chocolate – one farthing is the rate – you suck it through a straw, a straw, a straw" ' (Aiken, *Ushant*, 1952, p.135).

Goldfish (Essence of Summer Magazines) III:
On every sultry afternoon

At the end of the sequence is the date Sept. 1910.

2 **have the call**: *OED* 'call', 14b: 'to be in chief or greatest demand; to be the favourite: in *Long Whist*, to be entitled to "call honours" '; from 1840: 'Youth has the call'.

3 **White flannel ceremonial**: compare *The Love Song of J. Alfred Prufrock* 123: 'I shall wear white flannel trousers'. **ceremonial**: including *OED* 4: 'A robe or garment worn on some ceremonial occasion (*obs.*)'.

4 **With cakes and tea**: compare *The Love Song of J. Alfred Prufrock* 79: 'after tea and cakes and ices'.

5 **guesses at eternal truths**: *Guesses at Truth*, by Two Brothers (Augustus William Hare and Julius Charles Hare, 1827, much reprinted). Symons has 'guesses at truth' in his account of Réjane and her acting, *Plays, Acting, and Music* (1903; 1909 edn, p.40): 'It is like an accusing confirmation of some of one's guesses at truth, before the realities of the flesh and of the affections of the flesh. Scepticism is no longer possible'. **eternal**: for TSE's suspicion of the word, in relation to 'meaning' ('How much one means', 15), see *The Criterion*, v (May 1927) 190; TSE deplored the new Prayer Book: 'The two words to which we would call attention again are *infinite* and *eternal*, where they have been substituted for *incomprehensible* and *everlasting* [. . .] The word *eternal* evades all difficulties of time'. **eternal truths**: a draft of *Little Gidding* has: 'And with the eternal truth the local error' (Helen Gardner, *The Composition of Four Quartets*, 1978, p.187).

6 **Sounding the depths with a silver spoon**: compare *The Love Song of J. Alfred Prufrock* 51: 'I have measured out my life with coffee spoons'. Bergson used the metaphor of soundings; *Introduction à la métaphysique* (1903): 'plusieurs des grandes découvertes [. . .] ont été de coups de sonde donnés dans la durée pure. Plus vivante était la réalité touchée, plus profond avait été le coup de sonde'; then (like TSE invoking sun, light and sea) 'au fond de la mer', 'le soleil', 'aux rayons de l'entendement'. **with a silver spoon**: as in the proverbial 'to be born with a silver spoon in one's mouth', *OED* 'spoon', 3c, from 1801 (the first instance being US).

7 **And dusty roses, crickets, sunlight on the sea**: compare *A Song for Simeon* 6: 'Dust in sunlight'; *Animula* 10: 'Pleasure in the wind, the sunlight and the sea'; and *Burnt Norton* v 33–4:
   Sudden in a shaft of sunlight

Even while the dust moves
Also *Burnt Norton* I 16–18:
> But to what purpose
> Disturbing the dust on a bowl of rose-leaves
> I do not know.

(Compare Austin Dobson's *Pot-Pourri*, 1873, 1–6, a poem about disturbing the dust on rose leaves.) *Burnt Norton* I 4 has 'eternally' ('eternal', 5, above). Compare *Rhapsody on a Windy Night* 57–8: 'a paper rose, / That smells of dust'. Compare Tennyson, *Maud* I xxii ('Come into the garden, Maud'), for a conjunction of dust and roses. With TSE's line compare Meredith, *A Ballad of Fair Ladies in Revolt* (1883) 22: 'But now they dream like sunlight on a sea'.

11 **Essence of summer magazines**: see the headnote to this sequence on its subtitle. Laforgue has, as the conclusion to his list of Salome's 'tripotages occultes': 'deux dames-jeannes d'essences-bouquets de printemps et d'automne' (*Salomé, Moralités légendaires*, 1992 edn, pp.103–4).

13 **How much is simple**: compare this turn of phrase with TSE in *Nation and Athenaeum*, 21 May 1927: 'Baudelaire is already influenced by Poe – although it is impossible to decide [. . .] how much is influence and how much simple kinship'. TSE was there discussing 'the romantic phase', 'the romantic cult'. (His preceding poem in this sequence has not only its Baudelairean title but a mention of 'romance'; further, Baudelaire's 'romances', in the note to 3, 6 of the next poem in the sequence.) **How much is simple accident**: with 'scenes' (10), and with the repetition of 'how much', possibly recalling Symons, *Studies in Seven Arts* (1906, pp.349, 361), on *A New Art of the Stage*: 'But in what is incalculable there may be equal parts of inspiration and of accident. How much, in Mr. Craig's staging, is inspiration, how much is accident?'; 'Until I read it, I was not sure how much in Mr. Craig's work was intention and how much happy accident.'

13–15 **How much . . . How much . . . How much one means**: compare *Portrait of a Lady* I 19–21:
> 'You do not know how much they mean to me, my friends,
> And how, how rare and strange it is, to find
> In a life composed so much, so much of odds and ends,

Compare *Mandarins* I 13–14:
> A hero! and how much it means;
> How much –

knows . . . means: compare Tennyson, *The Princess* IV 21: 'Tears, idle tears, I know not what they mean'.

18, 20 **Play . . . conscience . . . crown**: ending the poem, as ends a scene of *Hamlet*, II ii:

The play's the thing
Wherein I'll catch the conscience of the King.

19 **means and ways**: a simple twist, but compare *The Love Song of J. Alfred Prufrock* 29, 60: 'works and days' and 'days and ways'.

20 **wear the crown**: compare Tennyson, *To —, After Reading a Life and Letters* 10: 'Of those that wear the Poet's crown'. Compare *Little Gidding* II 77 (on, among so much else, poetic accomplishment, conscience and irony): 'To set a crown upon your lifetime's effort'.

20–2 **crown of your ideal . . . rose**: compare Tennyson, *The Princess* II 36–8:
as though there were
One rose in all the world, your Highness that,
He worships your ideal.

Goldfish (Essence of Summer Magazines) IV:
Among the débris of the year

Dated Sept. 1910.

3, 6 Old letters, programmes, unpaid bills . . . The limbo of a bureau drawer: compare Baudelaire, *Spleen* (1857) 1–5:

> J'ai plus de souvenirs que si j'avais mille ans. //
> Un gros meuble à tiroirs encombré de bilans,
> De vers, de billets doux, de procès, de romances,
> Avec de lourds cheveux roulés dans des quittances,
> Cache moins de secrets que mon triste cerveau.

Compare Laforgue, *Préludes autobiographiques* (1885) 1: 'En voulant mettre un peu d'ordre dans ce tiroir.' Compare Bergson, *L'Evolution créatrice* (1907), ch.1: 'La mémoire, comme nous avons essayé de le prouver [n. *Matière et Mémoire*, Paris, 1896, chap.II et III] n'est pas une faculté de classer des souvenirs dans un tiroir ou de les inscrire sur un registre. Il n'y a pas de registre, pas de tiroir.'

4 tennis shoes: relatively recent, and socially noticeable; the first OED citation is 1887, Kipling's *Plain Tales from the Hills*.

5 postal cards: originally (1872) 'with postage stamps impressed upon them' (*OED*), as is also true of postcard (1870, 'bearing a representation of a postage stamp'; blank from 1894, and then picture postcards).

6 bureau drawer: compare, at the line-end, *Old Possum's Book of Practical Cats*, *The Rum Tum Tugger* 16: 'He likes to lie in the bureau drawer'.

9 Barcarolle: OED: 'A song sung by Venetian *barcaruoli* as they row their gondolas; a song or piece of music composed in imitation or reminiscence of such songs.' Often invoked by the nineteenth-century French poets; Gautier has *Barcarolle* (1838); the first poem in the first book of poems by Villiers de l'Isle-Adam (1859) is *Barcarolle*; and Verlaine begins *A Clymène* (1869): 'Mystiques barcarolles'. Laurent Tailhade was sardonic in his *Barcarolle* (*Poèmes aristophanesques*, 1904; included in *Poètes d'aujourd'hui*, which TSE owned in the two-volume edition, 1908 and reprinted); compare TSE's next two lines with Tailhade's *Barcarolle* 5–6:

> Combien qu'autour d'eux la Seine
> Regorge de chiens crevés,

Because of the Venetian association of Barcarolle, compare perhaps TSE's rhyme, 'Barcarolle' / 'Pole', with Laforgue, *Soirs de fête* (1890) 10–12, which rhymes 'ma gondole' / 'au Pôle'. 'Given his other allusions in this period to Chopin, TSE may have had in mind Op.60, but the Barcarolle from Act IV of Offenbach's *Les Contes d'Hoffmann* may also be relevant, with the mechanical doll in Act II ("marionettes") and the resurrected mother of Act III ("leave their graves")' (Eric Griffiths).

10–11 the wet paths of the sea . . . barking: compare Swinburne, *A Song in Time of Order* (1866) 53–4:
> In the teeth of the hard glad weather,
> In the blown wet face of the sea;

10, 16 wet paths of the sea . . . Walking the waves: compare Shelley, *Prometheus Unbound* II v 106, 110: 'watery paths', and shapes 'Which walk upon the sea'. wet paths: Homer, ὑγρὰ κέλευθα.

11 barking waves: noting the sound-link to 'Barcarolle' (9) and the move from 'bark' as a boat, compare *Comus* 257–8:
> Scylla wept,
> And chid her barking waves into attention,

Virgil, *Aeneid* VII 588: *latrantibus undis*. Also Kirke White, *Christmas-Day* (c.1800, OED): 'He had words / To soothe the barking waves'; compare TSE, 16, 'Walking the waves'. (TSE's 'the sea . . . barking waves' here might be invoked as a gloss on 'the snarled and yelping seas' of *Sweeney Erect* 4, which has 'gales' two lines later – 'winds', 14, here.) waves pursue: compare Milton's translation of Psalm LXXXVIII 68: 'Like waves they me pursue' (where the next two lines are: 'Lover and friend thou hast removed / And severed me from far').

14 neuropathic: OED: 'Relating to, or caused or distinguished by nervous disease or functional weakness of the nervous system', from 1857; the OED instances are strictly medical. TSE adapts the word from Laforgue, who speaks of 'les névropathes' four times within four paragraphs of *Le Miracle des roses* (*Moralités légendaires*, 1992 edn, p.50). neuropathic winds: compare Apollinaire, *Les Colchiques* (1907) 12: 'au vent dément'. Apollinaire's *La Chanson du Mal-Aimé: Voie lactée* 22 has 'La barque au barcarols chantants' (May 1909, it probably influenced others of these poems by TSE). The move from 'the sea' and 'barking waves' to 'the neuropathic' may owe something to Symons's *The Symbolist Movement in Literature* (pp.12–13), on Gérard de Nerval: 'and when, one day, he was found in the Palais-Royal, leading a lobster at the end of a blue ribbon (because, he said, it does not bark, and knows the secrets of the sea), the visionary had simply lost control of his visions, and had to be sent to Dr. Blanche's asylum at Montmartre.' renew: saliently at the line-end in lines which TSE quoted in his Clark Lectures (1926, VMP, p.174), Shelley's *Chorus* ('The world's great age begins anew'), *Hellas* 1062–3:
> The earth doth like a snake renew
> Her winter weeds outworn:

Again 1082–3:
> Although a subtler Sphinx renew

Riddles of death Thebes never knew.
The first poem in TSE's sequence here has 'Sphinx'.

16 **Walking the waves**: compare *Lycidas* 173: 'Through the dear might of him that walked the waves'.

17 **Bringing the news from**: as evangelists, but also perhaps recalling Browning, *How They Brought the Good News from Ghent to Aix*, which has as its end: 'who brought good news from Ghent'. **from either Pole**: as in Herbert, *Content* 18 (*The Quiddity*, the next poem in *The Temple*, has 'news'). **either Pole**: as in Tennyson, *Locksley Hall Sixty Years After* 169–70:
  to either pole she smiles,
Universal ocean softly washing all her warless Isles.
(TSE, 'the waves', in his previous line.) Two lines earlier in Tennyson, there is 'madness'; compare 'neuropathic' (13). John T. Mayer: 'news from the poles – that is, news of the polar explorations of Peary, Amundsen, and Shackleton (which impressed Eliot enough to recall them in the Notes to *The Waste Land* and to use an expedition incident in Part V of the poem), which made headlines in 1909–1910' (*T. S. Eliot's Silent Voices*, p.61). Given TSE's 'either Pole' and 'Old letters' (3), compare Kipling's 'Answers to Correspondents', appended to *With the Night Mail: A Story of 2000 A.D.* (1909): 'PICCIOLA – Both Poles have been overdone in Art and Literature. Leave them to Science for the next twenty years. You did not send a stamp with your verses.'

18 **fourth dimension**: *OED* from 1875, G. H. Lewes; W. D. Howells, 1895; and in 1904 Bertrand Russell: 'The merit of speculations on the fourth dimension . . is chiefly that they stimulate the imagination, and free the intellect from the shackles of the actual.' Much pondered at the time: C. H. Hinton, *The Fourth Dimension* (1904); early P. D. Ouspensky; and C. B. Patterson's 'thought studies in the fourth dimension', *A New Heaven and a New Earth* (1909).

21, 23 **neat . . . complete**: compare *Suite Clownesque III* 22: 'Neat, complete'. See *Mandarins I* 1 note on 'complete'.

28 **sybil**: compare the sibyl in the epigraph to *The Waste Land*.

29 **four crossroads**: compare the end of Hood's *Faithless Nelly Gray* 67: 'And they buried Ben in four cross-roads'. **crossroads**: given 'oracle' in the next line, compare perhaps the story of Oedipus (though a fork in the road, not a crossroads).

30 **oracle**: compare TSE's paper on ethics (Houghton Library; bMS Am 1691.14 (32), p.1): 'The task of philosophy, it appears to me, is largely one of simplification: to disentangle the riddling oracles [muddled knots *1st reading*] of the world, to paragraph and punctuate them and insert the emphases.'

33 **theoretic**: given 'contemplate' (27), theoretic (from the Greek, contemplative) may be understood as opposed to active or practical. Symons wrote of 'theoretic intelligences' (*The Symbolist Movement in Literature*, p.46, on Villiers de L'Isle-Adam). Compare Nietzsche, *The Birth of Tragedy*, tr. W. A. Haussmann (1909, p.131): 'there is an eternal conflict between *the theoretic* and *the tragic view of things*'. The syllabus for TSE's tutorial class on Modern French Literature in 1916 included (for Lecture 11, *The Reaction against Romanticism*): 'It must be remembered that the French mind is highly theoretic – directed by theories – and that no theory ever remains merely a theory of art, or a theory of religion, or a theory of politics' (R. Schuchard, *Review of English Studies* n.s. xxv, 1974, 165).

34 **assuring certainties**: given 'eyes' (28), compare *Preludes IV* 6–7:
>   and eyes
> Assured of certain certainties,

36 **off for some Hesperides**: like, among other poets, Tennyson, *The Hesperides*. Kipling's concluding stanza to *The Second Voyage* (1903) likewise rhymes 'New prows that seek the old Hesperides!' with 'seas'. Compare *Goldfish II: Embarquement pour Cythère*.

36–7 **– I am off for some Hesperides / Of street pianos and small beers!**: contrast the closing lines of *Portrait of a Lady* I:
> Correct our watches by the public clocks.
> Then sit for half an hour and drink our bocks.

– followed by II 39: 'a street-piano'. **street pianos**: see *First Caprice in North Cambridge* 1 note. **small beers**: the plural feels distinctive. To *OED* 'small beer' 1 ('Beer of a weak, poor, or inferior quality') should be added 2 *transf.*, 'Trivial occupations, affairs, etc.; matters or persons of little or no consequence or importance; trifles'. Compare TSE's ending his poem so with Iago's ending his half-dozen sardonic couplets so, *Othello*, II i 158–61:
> She was a wight, if ever such wights were,

DESDEMONA: To do what?

IAGO: To suckle fools, and chronicle small beer.

DESDEMONA: Oh most lame and impotent conclusion.

Suite Clownesque 1: Across the painted colonnades

At the end of the sequence is the date Oct. 1910. **Clownesque** was added to the title in pencil; TSE's practice of putting a full stop after a title means that one cannot be sure that the title, once *Clownesque* was added, should not be *Suite. Clownesque*, but there is no full stop in pencil after *Suite*, and **Suite Clownesque** moves better. *Suite*: *OED*, 2d: '*Mus*. A set of instrumental compositions (orig. of movements in dance style) to be played in succession'. *Clownesque*: French, clownish; see the third poem in this sequence, *If you're walking down the avenue* 14 ∧ 15 and note; and compare *Humouresque (After J. Laforgue)*. Laforgue has 'clownesque' in his suite *Pierrots* (1886), 1 7–8, where it is followed by the flower which meant much to him and to TSE:

> La bouche clownesque ensorcèle
> Comme un singulier géranium.

Laforgue wrote of 'les virtuosités clownesques', and in a letter to his sister in 1884 he gave the word a central place in describing his enterprise as a poet: 'Je trouve stupide de faire la grosse voix et de jouer de l'éloquence. Aujourd'hui que je suis plus sceptique et que je m'emballe moins aisément et que, d'autre part, je possède ma langue d'une façon plus minutieuse, plus clownesque, j'écris de petits poèmes de fantaisie, n'ayant qu'un but: faire de l'original à tout prix' (*Mélanges posthumes*, 1903, pp.214, 315).

1–4 The English reader may see this as the *In Memoriam* stanza, octosyllabics rhyming *a-b-b-a*, as in TSE's *Song: When we came home across the hill*; but it is more germane that this is the stanza often used by Laforgue in his suites; e.g., for four poems in the suite *Pierrots*, and for six in *Locutions des Pierrots* (1886), one of which (XII) is the source of TSE's *Humouresque (After J. Laforgue)*. Laforgue, like TSE here, does not indent the two central lines of the stanza, unlike Tennyson and TSE in *Song*.

1 **Across the painted colonnades**: compare Pope, *Odyssey* III 511: 'Beneath the pompous Colonnade'.

1, 4 **colonnades . . . serenades**: compare Villiers de l'Isle-Adam, *Guitare* (1859), which begins:

> Voici l'heure des sérénades
> Où brille, loin des colonnades,

Also Stuart Merrill (the American who made himself a French symbolist), rhyming 'colonnades' and 'sérénades' in *Le Palais désert* (1891) 6, 9.

2–4 **the terra cotta fawns . . . lawns . . . serenades**: a fawn is not a faun, but compare Verlaine, *Le Faune* (1869) 1–4:

> Un vieux faune de terre cuite

Rit au centre des boulingrins,
Présageant sans doute une suite
Mauvaise à ces instants sereins

TSE's poem forms part of a *Suite*; compare Verlaine's 'boulingrins' with 'lawns', and his 'Rit' with TSE's 'comedian' (5). Verlaine also has, in his eight-line poem, 'au son des tambourins'; compare TSE's 'orchestra' as well as his 'serenades', also Verlaine's 'sereins' and the first line of his next poem in *Fêtes galantes*, *Mandoline*: 'Les donneurs de sérénades'. Compare also John Gray's version of Verlaine, from the same sequence, *Claire de Lune* (1893) 12–13:

The fountains tall that leap upon the lawns
Amid the garden gods, the marble fauns.

(In TSE, not marble fauns, whether Gray's or Hawthorne's, but terra cotta fawns.) Compare TSE's variant in *Mr. Apollinax* 4, where that lusty figure Priapus was at one stage 'terra cotta in the shrubbery' (see Appendix B). Laforgue (whose word 'clownesque' is) brings together terra cotta, music and clowns: 'Les virtuoses en musique, en terre cuite, en langues, en peinture, etc . . . en plastique personnelle (les clowns)' (*Critique d'art, Mélanges posthumes*, p.178).

3 **Among the potted palms, the lawns**: compare Tennyson, *Enoch Arden* 589: 'Among the palms and ferns and precipices'. Given the placing of 'the lawns' at the line-end, following 'the deer' (TSE, 'fawns'), along with the move into mockery of bodily ungainliness, with laughing and legs (TSE, 13, the 'legs' of the comedian), compare Tennyson, *The Last Tournament* 720–4:

Now talking of their woodland paradise,
The deer, the dews, the fern, the founts, the lawns;
Now mocking at the much ungainliness,
And craven shifts, and long crane legs of Mark –
Then Tristram laughing caught the harp and sang:

4 **The cigarettes and serenades**: given TSE's rogue, compare Tennyson, *The Princess* IV 117: 'A rogue of canzonets and serenades'.

5 **comedian**: OED: 'A professional entertainer who makes his audience laugh by telling jokes, acting foolishly, etc.'; the first instance is 1898, *N.Y. Journal*: 'Wearing spats, front crease in trousers and throwing out one's chest is the receipt followed by Dan Daly, the comedian, to gain height'. Given 'lawns' (3), compare *Afternoon* 8: 'Like amateur comedians across a lawn'.

6 **broad dogmatic vest**: the churchy but absurd associations of the epithets (for a Broad Church is less dogmatic) may suggest the ecclesiastical sense of vest (*OED* 2) added to OED 3b: 'a waistcoat. Now *N.Amer*.'

6–8 **nose / Nose . . . nose**: compare *"Rhetoric" and Poetic Drama* (1919, SE, pp. 40–1): 'the propriety of Cyrano on Noses', 'in the particular case of Cyrano on

Noses, the character, the situation, the occasion were perfectly suited and combined'. TSE's original title of this essay had been *Whether Rostand Had Something about Him*; the finding was discriminatingly positive. As a child of ten, TSE had included in his magazine *Fireside* (No.1, 28 Jan. 1899; Houghton Library) a note on 'The Theatre': 'Cryno de Bergerac has created a great sensation'. TSE supplied 'an picture by our funny artist', of 'Cryno de Bergerac' (with nose in profile, hat, and sword).

6, 8–10 vest . . . scarlet . . . real . . . jellyfish: compare Byron, *Don Juan*, XVI [x] 77–9:
> No real likeness, – like the old Tyrian vest
>   Dyed purple, none at present can tell how,
> If from a shell-fish

7 Nose that interrogates the stars: compare *Humouresque (After J. Laforgue)* 18: '(Feebly contemptuous of nose)'. Nose that interrogates, not mouth – or eye; compare *Coriolan I: Triumphal March* 29: 'There is no interrogation in his eyes' (plus *II: Difficulties of a Statesman* 39: 'Noses strong to break the wind'). Compare the paragraph from Henry James that influenced *Prufrock's Pervigilium* 1–4 (see the note); eleven lines of James's *Siena Early and Late* I (1873) have: 'standing with finger on nose and engaging your interrogative eye', this as though in 'an acted play': 'The speaker seems actually to establish his stage and face his foot-lights' (TSE, 20, 'Inside a ring of lights!'; James, *Italian Hours*, 1909, p.351). Rimbaud's *Accroupissements* (1891) ends with a nose questing the sky: 'Fantasque, un nez poursuit Vénus au ciel profond'. TSE's glimpse of the comically haughty may owe something to a Jacobean intersection; TSE compared Massinger with Webster, to Massinger's disadvantage: ' "Here he comes, / His nose held up; he hath something in the wind", is hardly comparable to "the Cardinal lifts up his nose like a foul porpoise before a storm" ' (*Philip Massinger*, 1920, SE, p.208). The porpoise could have suffered a sea-change into TSE's jellyfish.

8, 11 nose . . . repose: rhyming, 'repose' / 'nose', in *Mandarins* 3 2, 4, again of someone obese.

10, 11 jellyfish: *OED* 2 *fig.*, from 1883: 'A person of "flabby" character, or deficient in energy, steadfastness, or "backbone" '. But given that 'It's all philosophy and art' (15 and note), and 'real' (10), compare TSE's invokings of the jellyfish in philosophical contexts: essay on objects and points of view (1914–15; Houghton Library; bMS Am 1691.14 (21), p.5): 'We are not to say that there is one real world to which the system corresponds, for so far as the system is complete and exact, it *is* the real world. But it is not the same world as that of the plowboy or the jellyfish, except *for* the metaphysician who is inside of his own system' (compare 24, 'A self-embodied rôle'). Similarly *KEPB* (p.166): 'Truth on our level is a different thing from truth for the jellyfish, and there must certainly be analogies for truth and error in jellyfish life.'

11 **without repose**: likewise at the line-end in Shelley, *The Triumph of Life* 140: 'Outspeed the chariot, and without repose'; Shelley has, in the immediate vicinity (136–42), phrases apt to TSE's scene: 'ribald crowd', 'obscene', 'wild dance', 'savage music'. Compare, too, with TSE's clownesque comedian (and 'scarlet', 8), Théodore de Banville, *Harlequin*: 'his red shoes [. . .] trace without repose the figure of a lawless dance'; translated by Stuart Merrill in *Pastels in Prose* (1890), which TSE owned and wrote about (see *First Debate between the Body and Soul* 15 note).

12 **the orchestra**: bearing in mind still that 'It's all philosophy and art' (15), compare TSE's paper on ethics (Houghton Library; bMS Am 1691.14 (32), p.3): 'In a work like the "Principle of Individuality and value" for example, you find the author at the greatest pains to defend the mechanistic conception, until suddenly the theme is taken up by another group of instruments in the orchestra.' (Revised by TSE: 'until suddenly he stands the whole structure on its head – a procedure, to say the least, disconcerting to one's semi-circular canals'. Of the ear, that is.)

13 **legs apart**: TSE's comedian resembles his puppets and marionettes; compare W.W. [Watson White] in the *Harvard Advocate*, 25 Nov. 1908, on *Il Teatro Marionetti* in Boston: 'Firmly planted on ridiculously fat legs – spread wide apart'. (On this essay, see *Convictions* 14 note, and the headnote to *Mandarins* 1.)

14–15 **His belly sparkling and immense:** / **It's all philosophy**: compare Wordsworth, *Ode: Intimations of Immortality* 109–11:
> Thou, whose exterior semblance doth belie
>> Thy Soul's immensity;
> Thou best Philosopher,

(TSE, 24, 'his soul'.)

14, 17–18 **immense . . . the audience . . . suspense**: compare the rhyme in *Convictions* 4, 7 ('immense' / 'suspense'), its 6–7: 'an audience open-mouthed / At climax and suspense'.

15 **philosophy and art**: TSE wrote that 'Solipsism has been one of the dramatic properties of most philosophical entertainers' (*KEPB*, p.141). The dramatic comedian ('A self-embodied rôle', 24) is the supreme solipsist.

19 **entities**: to the comedian, they may be nonentities; *OED* 3: 'A person or thing of no significance, consequence, or importance', from *Tatler*, 1710. Given 'lights' at the end of the next line, compare W. S. Gilbert, *The Pantomime "Super" to His Mask* 13–14:

Before the lights,
Swamped in thine own preposterous nonentity.

(*The Bab Ballads*, 1869.) But, given 'It's all philosophy', note TSE's attention to the philosophical term 'entities'; as in a paper on objects (Houghton Library; bMS Am 1691.14 (24), p.4) where he discusses 'neutral entities', and writes of immediate experience: 'It is certainly neutral, but what ground have [we?] for speaking of it as "entities"?' Likewise his paper on T. H. Green (Houghton Library; (31), p.6): 'It is equally possible to look upon consciousness as the cause or as the effect of a peculiar grouping of entities, though really I suppose that it is neither, but is the group itself.' Compare the conclusion to *Whispers of Immortality*:

And even the Abstract Entities
Circumambulate her charm;
But our lot crawls between dry ribs
To keep our metaphysics warm.

20 **a ring of lights**: compare *Portrait of a Lady* I 5: 'Four rings of light upon the ceiling overhead'. *Murder in the Cathedral*, Part II, the second chorus:

I have seen
Rings of light coiling downwards, descending
To the horror of the ape.

20–1 **lights! . . . the world at rights**: compare *The Waste Land MS*, p.33, *The Fire Sermon* 130, 132: 'lights', rhyming with 'sets the room to rights'. *OED* 14, 'to rights', gives 'at rights' as rare (one instance, 1641: 'to set all things at rights').

22 **Here's one who gets away with it**: given Byron's likely presence in the poem (see the note to 6, 8–10), consider TSE's saying of Byron that he 'not only gets away with it, but gets away with it *as narrative*'. TSE grants Byron 'a kind of knowledge: of the world outside, which he had to learn something about in order to play his role in it, and of that part of himself which was his role'; compare in this poem 'the world', 21; and 'A self-embodied rôle', 24, which (said of a 'comedian') further suggests TSE's Byron, 'an actor who devoted immense trouble to *becoming* a role that he adopted'. Also 'the bust of Byron is that of a man who was every inch the touring tragedian' (*Byron*, 1937, *OPP*, pp.198, 194, 205). In the Clark Lectures (1926), TSE said of the 'rebirth of Good and Evil in the nineteenth century': 'Byron (I believe) had something to do with it. With Byron, if you like, everything was pose, but the existence of a pose implies the possibility of a reality to which the pose pretends' (*VMP*, p.209); compare TSE, 9, 'The most expressive, real of men' (repeated as *Suite Clownesque IV* 15), with TSE, 12, 'repose', perhaps in touch with 'pose'.

23 **spreading of the toes**: compare *Sweeney Among the Nightingales* 1: 'Apeneck Sweeney spreads his knees' ('legs apart', 13 above, is Sweeneyesque).

23, 25 spreading of the toes . . . vest and nose: combining Lewis Carroll and Edward
Lear. Carroll, *'Tis the voice of the Lobster* 3–4:

> so he with his nose
> Trims his belt and his buttons, and turns out his toes.

(*Alice's Adventures in Wonderland*, ch. x.) Lear, *The Pobble Who Has No Toes*
15–16:

> And it's perfectly known that a Pobble's toes
> Are safe, – provided he minds his nose.

Lear rhymes his title-line with his 11–12:

> But before he set out he wrapped his nose,
> In a piece of scarlet flannel.

(And 28, 'scarlet flannel' again.) TSE, 8, 'scarlet nose'. Also Lear, 7, 20, 'The
World', 'the world' / TSE, 21, 'the world'. (As to Lear's 'Porpoise', 27, compare 7
note above; and his 'crawfish', 37 / TSE's 'jellyfish', 10–11.) TSE rhymes 'nose' /
'toes' in *Dirge* 8, 10 (*The Waste Land MS*, p.121).

24–5 self . . . Concentred: compare Scott, *Breathes there the man with soul so dead*
12: 'The wretch, concentred all in self'. Scott's poem is in Quiller-Couch's *Oxford
Book of English Verse* (1900). TSE's context invites the phrase 'centred in
himself', from *The Possibility of a Poetic Drama* (1920, *SW*, p.69): 'The
intervention of performers introduces a complication of economic conditions
which is in itself likely to be injurious. A struggle, more or less unconscious,
between the creator and the interpreter is almost inevitable. The interest of a
performer is almost certain to be centred in himself: a very slight acquaintance
with actors and musicians will testify.' **Concentred:** given 'lights' (20), compare
Paradise Lost IX 105–7:

> Light above light, for thee alone, as seems,
> In thee concentring all their precious beams
> Of sacred influence.

Concentred in his vest and nose: compare Shelley (who often has 'embodied', as
24), *Peter Bell the Third* [VII] 718–20:

> But in his verse, and in his prose,
>   The essence of his dulness was
> Concentred and compressed so close,

– where the rhyming 'prose' / 'close' / 'doze' resembles that of TSE, 'toes' /
'nose'. **his vest and nose:** given 'scarlet nose' (8) and 'legs apart' (13), compare
the killers in John Gray, *Saint Sebastian: On a Picture* (1896) 40, 43–5: 'his vest',
'reddest hose' rhyming with 'nose', 'legs akimbo'. (Gray's poem probably
influenced TSE's *The Love Song of St. Sebastian*.)

Suite Clownesque II: Each with a skirt just down to the ancle

At the end of the sequence is the date Oct. 1910.

1 **with a skirt just down to the ancle**: as with Tennyson, *The Beggar Maid* 11: 'One praised her ancles', a variant spelling of ankle (TSE has it, *Letters* i 70, 73; 27 Nov. 1914); as to the fashion, compare *OED*'s first citation for this compound, *Daily Chronicle*, 25 July 1903: 'Ankle-length ones [skirts] have gained votaries across the Channel'.

3–4 **centre . . . venture . . . dissenter**: compare a scene (quoted by TSE in *Cyril Tourneur*, 1930), of pimping and sexual seduction in *The Revenger's Tragedy*, II i 111–12 ff.; there 'venture' is historically a truer rhyme with 'enter'. There are many possible filaments to TSE's poem. Tourneur has 'Holla!' (TSE, 5–6, 'Hello . . . hello!'); 'people . . . people' in one line (TSE, 5–6); 'finger' at the line-end (TSE, 7); 'ride', 'coach' and 'coaches' (TSE, 13, 'Here's a street car – let's jump in'); 'soldiers' (TSE, 14); and money handed over (TSE, 16); all in a scene which sardonically has a mother abusing her decent girl for her 'childish haviours'. TSE, who speaks of Tourneur's characters as 'almost childish caricatures', describes the playwright's vision as like that of 'a highly sensitive adolescent with a gift for words' (*SE*, pp.185, 189). 'The form in which I began to write, in 1908 or 1909, was directly drawn from the study of Laforgue together with the later Elizabethan drama; and I do not know anyone who started from exactly that point' (Introduction to Pound's *Selected Poems*, 1928, p.viii).

7 **linger . . . finger**: compare *The Love Song of J. Alfred Prufrock* 76–7:
Smoothed by long fingers,
Asleep . . . tired . . . or it malingers,

11 **Seven little girls run away from school**: compare Gilbert, *The Mikado* (produced 1885), Act I:
Three little maids from school are we,
Pert as a school-girl well can be,
Filled to the brim with girlish glee,
    Three little maids from school!
Everything is a source of fun.
[. . .]
From three little maids take one away.
(TSE, 2, 'Everybody is under age'.) But also compare Wordsworth, *We are Seven*: Wordsworth, 1, 'A simple Child' / TSE, 10, 'a simple hat'; Wordsworth, 52, 'she went away' / TSE, 'girls run away'; Wordsworth, 59, 'forced to go' / TSE, 22, 'Where shall we go'.

11, 14 **little . . . descend:** compare *Burbank with a Baedeker: Bleistein with a Cigar* 1–2:

> Burbank crossed a little bridge
> Descending at a small hotel;

TSE's review of *The Education of Henry Adams* describes Henry Adams and Henry James who 'descend at the same hotel' (*Athenaeum*, 23 May 1919). **descend:** *OED* 1c: 'to alight from a horse, carriage, etc. *Obs.* (as a specific sense)', the last citation, 1600. Contrast the Descent in TSE's letter to Aiken about these poems, 25 July 1914, and 'some of the themes for the "Descent from the Cross" or whatever I may call it' (*Letters* i 44).

13 **street car:** *OED* 1, from 1862: '*N.Amer.* A passenger car, running through the streets, usually on rails; a tram-car'.

15–16 The manner and matter, as with 12, suggest *Sweeney Agonistes: Fragment of a Prologue,* for instance 'We hit this town last night for the first time', and the closing lines:

> Sam of course is at *home* in London,
> And he's promised to show us around.

21–2 **text . . . next:** Byron ends, not a poem, but a stanza, *Don Juan,* ix [xli] 326–8:

> Men should know why
> They write, and for what end; but, note or text,
> I never know the word which will come next.

Kipling ends a poem so, and – like TSE – with a question, *The Undertaker's Horse* (1886):

> But to insult, jibe, and quest, I've
> Still the hideously suggestive
> Trot that hammers out the unrelenting text,
> And I hear it hard behind me
> In what place soe'er I find me:–
> "'Sure to catch you soon or later. Who's the next?"

See the next poem in the sequence, *Suite Clownesque III* 8–9 note.

22 **'Where shall we go to next?':** compare *The Death of the Duchess* 12 (*The Waste Land MS,* p.105): 'What is there for us to do?' Also *The Waste Land* [II] 133–4:

> What shall we do tomorrow?

'What shall we ever do?'

Suite Clownesque III: If you're walking down the avenue

At the end of the sequence is the date Oct. 1910.

1 **the avenue:** compare *The Waste Land MS*, p.5, *The Burial of the Dead* 49: 'The next I know the old cab was hauled up on the avenue'. Compare Henry James: 'Hadn't it been above all, in its good faith, the Age of Beauties – the blessed age when it was so easy to *be*, "on the Avenue", a Beauty, and when it was so easy, not less, not to doubt of the unsurpassability of such as appeared there?' (*The American Scene*, 1907, p.220). The avenue and Broadway (TSE, 6, 14) may suggest a flash in *The Education of Henry Adams*, ch.XXXV: 'A traveller in the highways of history looked out of the club window on the turmoil of Fifth Avenue, and felt himself in Rome, under Diocletian, witnessing the anarchy, conscious of the compulsion, eager for the solution, but unable to conceive whence the next impulse was to come or how it was to act. The two-thousand-years failure of Christianity roared upward from Broadway, and no Constantine the Great was in sight.'

3–4 **meet you . . . greet you:** see 10–11 note. Compare *The Cubanola Glide* (1909), quoted by TSE in *The Waste Land MS*, pp.5, 125, *The Burial of the Dead*:
   Tease, Squeeze lovin & wooin
   Say Kid what're y' doin'
Of the two epigraphs to the Clark Lectures (1926, *VMP*, p.40), one is from Dante, and the other:
   I want someone to treat me rough.
   Give me a cabman.
   Popular song
Compare the songs in *Sweeney Agonistes: Fragment of an Agon*, 'Under the bamboo' and 'My little island girl'.

6–7 **Broadway . . . moon:** compare Nathaniel Parker Willis, whose *Unseen Spirits* (1844) begins: 'The shadows lay along Broadway', and whose *City Lyrics* (1844) begins:
   Come out, love – the night is enchanting!
   The moon hangs just over Broadway.
Willis, 10, 'Mint juleps from City Hotel!' / TSE, 13, 'cocktails'.

6, 14 **Broadway . . . Broadway after dark:** compare Phoebe Cary's parody of Poe's *Annabel Lee*, *Samuel Brown* (1854) 36–8:
   And the night's never dark, but I sit in the park
   With my beautiful Samuel Brown.
   And often by day, I walk down in Broadway.
In the previous stanza, Cary twice has 'the girls' (TSE, 16).

7 **Under the light of the silvery moon**: the song, *By the light of the silvery moon*, was introduced in 1909 by the child singer Georgie Prince (words by Edward Madden, music by Gus Edwards). It formed part of Edwards's vaudeville sketch, *School Boys and Girls* (compare TSE, 9, 16, 'the girls'). Compare TSE, *The Song of the Jellicles* 24: 'by the light of the Jellicle Moon'.

8–9 **You may find me / All the girls behind me**: compare Kipling, the end of *The Undertaker's Horse* (1886):
> And I hear it hard behind me
> In what place soe'er I find me:–
> "'Sure to catch you soon or later. Who's the next?"
(See the end of the previous poem in this sequence, *Suite Clownesque II* 21–2 note.) Compare *The smoke that gathers blue* 18: ' "*Throw your arms around me – Aint you glad you found me*" '.

10 **Euphorion**: there are three candidates. (i) 'Of Chalcis in Euboea, a Hellenistic Greek poet of the third century BC'; the *Oxford Companion to Classical Literature* (ed. M. C. Howatson, 1989) adds that 'he seems mostly to have written epic-style poetry on mythological subjects. He exercised a considerable influence on later poets; at Rome his epyllia were greatly admired by Catullus and his contemporaries (hence Cicero's description of these poets as *cantores Euphorionis*, "those who sing the praises of Euphorion")'. (ii) The dramatist son ('First born child'?, TSE, 21) of Aeschylus, whose name twice figures in Browning, *Aristophanes' Apology* 1241, 2254, at the head of the verse-line as in TSE. (iii) the son of Faust (another 'First born child'?) in the Second Part of Goethe's *Faust*, a Byronic figure. In *Three Philosophical Poets* (1910), a book which TSE praised in 1926 as 'one of the most brilliant of Mr. Santayana's works' (*VMP*, p.48), Santayana summarized: 'Faust retires with her [Helen] to Arcadia, – the land of intentional and mid-summer idleness. Here a son, Euphorion, is born to them, a young genius, classic in aspect, but wildly romantic and ungovernable in temper. He scales the highest peaks, pursues by preference the nymphs that flee from him, loves violence and unreason, and finally, thinking to fly, falls headlong, like Icarus, and perishes' (p.177). TSE's poem has its nymphs, and ('on the beach') it is devoted to 'intentional and mid-summer idleness'. Pater, in *The Renaissance* (1873; 1910 edn, pp.226–7), had suggested a role for Euphorion pertinent to TSE's poem: 'Goethe illustrates a union of the Romantic spirit, in its adventure, its variety, its profound subjectivity of soul, with Hellenism, in its transparency, its rationality, its desire of beauty – that marriage of Faust and Helena, of which the art of the nineteenth century is the child, the beautiful lad Euphorion, as Goethe conceives him, on the crags, in the "splendour of battle and in harness as for victory", his brows bound with light'. Compare Pater's reiterated 'modern' (four times in his next two paragraphs) with TSE, 'Euphorion of the modern time'; and contrast 'the crags' with 'the beach',

and the battledress of Euphorion with 'the quintessential flannel suit' (in Pater's next sentence are the words 'its true essence') of TSE's Prufrockian figure. If Goethe's is the Euphorion, then, along with 'Improved' in the next line, compare TSE, *Nation and Athenaeum* (12 Jan. 1929): 'Only earnest devotion to self-improvement could carry one through some of the dreary wastes in the second part of Faust'. The doubt as to which Euphorion may reflect TSE's liking for compounding – St Narcissus / Narcissus (and his St John among the Rocks? See the headnote to *The Love Song of St. Sebastian*). **Euphorion of the modern time**: for such in a different sense, consider the bland appropriator, Euphorion, who is contested by George Eliot in her essay on plagiarism, *The Wasp Credited with the Honeycomb* (*Theophrastus Such*).

10–11 **of the modern time / Improved and up to date – sublime**: compare Tennyson, *In Memoriam* LXI 1, 4: 'If, in thy second state sublime' (noting the line-end and the way in which 'state sublime' would rhyme with TSE's 'date – sublime'); Tennyson's line is followed, as its rhyming line, by 'The perfect flower of human time'. In Tennyson's next stanza (5–8), compare 'And if thou cast thine eyes below' and 'darkness' with TSE's 12 ∧ 13 ('Seen from the depths') and 14 ('dark'). TSE associated Tennyson and his time with the up to date: 'Tennyson lived in a time which was already acutely time-conscious [. . .] That was a time busy in keeping up to date' (*In Memoriam*, 1936, *SE*, p.337). For the rhyme here, compare TSE to Virginia Woolf, dated Twelfth Night 1935 (Berg Collection): 'I have another good song, it goes:

I met you first at Spring St.
  And then upon my word
I thought I'd known you all my life
  When we reached 23d.
I won your heart at Haarlem,
  At the Bronx you murmured Yes:
We lost no time
On that ride sublime
  On the Subway
      Ex*press*.'

time / Improved: compare *Paradise Lost* V 498: 'Improved by tract of time, and winged ascend'. Milton's passage, 496–500, would furnish a contrast to the nutriments, depths, and heights of TSE's New York-scape:

And from these corporal nutriments perhaps
Your bodies may at last turn all to spirit,
Improved by tract of time, and winged ascend
Ethereal, as we, or may at choice
Here or in heavenly Paradises dwell.

up to date: recent in the slangy sense. *OED*, under 'date', from 1890, with 1893:

'who invented the Gaiety burlesque "up to date" – and gave this detestable phrase to the language'. Under 'up to date': 1889, Sims and Pettitt (title) 'Faust Up to Date. Burlesque Opera'; 1889, W. S. Gilbert, *The Gondoliers* I: 'A Grand Inquisitor is always up to date'; and 1894: 'and keep them, as the odious modern phrase is, up to date'. TSE begins *The Local Flavour*, within *Imperfect Critics*: 'In a world which is chiefly occupied with the task of keeping up to date with itself [. . .]' (1919, *SW*, p.32). 'Many people give the appearance of progress by shedding the prejudices and irrational postulates of one generation only to acquire those of the next: by "keeping up to date" ' (contrasting Paul Elmer More, *Princeton Alumni Weekly*, 5 Feb. 1937). TSE sought to rescue the praiseworthy aspect by varying the phrase: *The Criterion* 'was to be up-to-time in its appreciation of modern literature' (V, May 1927, 188).

12 **Quite at home in the universe**: compare Tennyson, *The Princess* VII 37: 'Quite sundered from the moving Universe' (with 'Deeper' in Tennyson's preceding line, and 'depths' in TSE's immediately following line which he added and then cancelled; see variants). With the placing of 'the universe' at the line-end, compare *The Love Song of J. Alfred Prufrock* 45–6:
Do I dare
Disturb the universe?
at home: the transferred sense (*OED* 11c: 'At one's ease') was not recent or trivial; for instance, 1528, Tindale: 'The mayde was at home also in heuenly pleasures'. In his copy of Hegel's *Lectures on the Philosophy of History* (tr. J. Sibree, 1905; Houghton Library), TSE underlined the last twelve words of the following reflection: 'Nature is a system of known and recognized Laws; Man is at home in it, and that only passes for truth in which he finds himself at home' (p.459, on 'The Eclaircissement').

12 ∧ 13 (variant) **Seen from the depths of**: compare Tennyson, *The Princess* IV 22: 'Tears from the depth of some divine despair'.

13 **Shaking cocktails on a hearse**: the conjunction of shaking, alcohol and a hearse (after dark, too) is found in Wilde, *The Ballad of Reading Gaol* (1898) III 105–7:
The troubled plumes of midnight shook
    The plumes upon a hearse:
And bitter wine
Compare the gallows humour of the imperilled ship in *The Waste Land MS*, p.61, *Death by Water* 80: 'Where's a cocktail shaker, Ben, here's plenty of cracked ice'.

14 ∧ 15 Stage direction **sandboard**: not given as a musical instrument in *OED* or Webster's Dictionary, so perhaps here it forms part of the hearse: *OED* 10 (b), 1875, 'a bar over the hind axle'; 1895, 'in car-building, a spring-plank'. For music, compare washboard, *OED* 3c: 'used as a percussion instrument'. **clownesque**: see *Suite Clownesque*. **bones**: *OED*: 'pieces of bone struck or rattled,

to make rude music; *esp.* two pieces of bone or ivory held between the fingers of each hand and rattled together as an accompaniment to the banjo or other instrument; chiefly used by "nigger minstrels" '. *Sweeney Agonistes: Fragment of an Agon*, Song, stage-direction: 'Swarts as Tambo. Snow as Bones'. Compare W. S. Gilbert, *The Three Kings of Chickeraboo* 5: 'The first was a highly-accomplished "bones" ' (*The Bab Ballads*, 1869).

15, 19, 23 walking on the beach . . . the girls . . . flannel suit: suggesting *The Love Song of J. Alfred Prufrock* 123, 130: 'I shall wear white flannel trousers, and walk upon the beach', and 'sea-girls'. Seaside girls were often invoked in music-hall songs, as recalled in Joyce's *Ulysses* (1922, 1937 edn, p.60):

Those girls, those girls,
Those lovely seaside girls.

21, 23 First born child . . . quintessential: compare *Paradise Lost* III 1, 6: 'offspring of Heaven first-born', 'bright essence'; Milton has 'quintessence', both at III 716, 'And this ethereal quintessence of Heaven', and (note 'first') at VII 244–5:

Ethereal, first of things, quintessence pure
Sprung from the deep,

(TSE, 12 ∧ 13 variant, 'depths'.) See Pater's 'essence' in 10 note above. **quintessential**: slangy, *OED*, 1887: 'Eldon's quintessential Toryism'.

22 complete: see the note to *Mandarins 1* 1: 'Stands there, complete'.

24–5 nothing the matter with us! / – But say, just be serious: Laforgue ended *Autre complainte de Lord Pierrot* (1885):

J'aurai un: 'Ah ça, mais, nous avions De Quoi vivre!
        C'était donc sérieux?'

Laforgue's poem influenced TSE's *Portrait of a Lady* (with 'Enfin, si, par un soir, elle meurt'). In *Hamlet* (*Moralités légendaires*, 1992 edn, p.30), Laforgue has Hamlet follow 'devenu si sérieux' with: 'Soyons sérieux ici!' TSE ends *Conversation Galante* with 'serious': 'And – "Are we then so serious?" ' (Relatedly, *Nocturne* begins: 'Romeo, *grand sérieux*'.)

26 Do you think that I'm all right?: compare *Portrait of a Lady* II and III, both of which likewise end with rhetorical questions turning on 'right': 'Are these ideas right or wrong?'; 'And should I have the right to smile?'

Suite Clownesque IV: In the last contortions of the dance

Dated Oct. 1910.

5 **Columbine:** *OED*: 'A character in Italian Comedy, the mistress of Harlequin, transferred to our Pantomime or Harlequinade'. For *the* Columbine, compare *All the Year Round*, 13 Sept. 1862: 'Joey and I both fell in love with the columbine'. Verlaine has a poem *Colombine* (*Fêtes galantes*, 1869); *Le Faune*, from the same sequence, influenced *Suite Clownesque I* (see its 2–4 note).

6 **hat in hand:** compare, describing Romeo, *Nocturne* 2: 'Guitar and hat in hand'; and *Spleen* 13: 'Waits, hat and gloves in hand'. Reminiscent of Symons on Laforgue: 'He composes love-poems hat in hand', *The Symbolist Movement in Literature* (p.109).

6, 8 **hand . . . saraband:** compare Lovelace on this formal dance, concluding *To Lucasta: I laugh and sing* 11–12:
> So you but with a touch from your fair hand,
> Turn all to saraband.

10 **cigarettes and compliments:** given another affinity ('immense', 12, at the line-end, rhyming), compare the line-end of *Convictions* 12: 'promises and compliments'.

12 **dense:** given the philosophical play, particularly ('It's all philosophy and art') in the first poem of this sequence to which this concluding poem returns, note that for TSE 'dense' has philosophical application: 'It is this contrast between the tenuous and the dense which is the contrast between thought and ideality'; 'a loss of density and richness'; 'the greatest philosophies have themselves something of this density and richness, and consequently are themselves subject-matter for study almost as difficult and inexhaustible as the world itself'. This early Harvard essay, *The validity of artificial distinctions* (Houghton Library; bMS Am 1691.14 (27), p.4), is on acting and knowing.

14 **Explodes in laughter:** the first *OED* instance of this particular transferred sense is 1867 ('made the crowd explode with laughter'). For his comedian, TSE summons the original (and etymological) sense, which survived until the nineteenth century: 'To clap and hoot (a player, play, etc.) off the stage'. *Paradise Lost* x 545–6:
> Thus was the applause they meant,
> Turned to exploding hiss, triumph to shame
OED: Swift, 'exploded plays'; Johnson, 'the exploded scene'.

Prufrock's Pervigilium

See the note (p.41), following the opening lines of *The Love Song of J. Alfred Prufrock*.

The indenting of the opening lines of *Prufrock's Pervigilium* is uncertain in the MS. *Prufrock's Pervigilium* ends high on the page, with 'P.T.O' [Please Turn Over]; overleaf, after a scrolled rule, *The Love Song of J. Alfred Prufrock* resumes with its line 75: 'And the afternoon, the evening, sleeps so peacefully!' Within *Prufrock's Pervigilium* there figure (33–4) the two immediately preceding lines of *The Love Song of J. Alfred Prufrock*:

I should have been a pair of ragged claws
Scuttling across the floors of silent seas.

In a letter to John Pope (8 March 1946), about the influence of *Crime and Punishment*, TSE wrote: 'The poem of Prufrock was conceived some time in 1910. I think that when I went to Paris in the autumn of that year I had already written several fragments which were ultimately embodied in the poem, but I cannot at this distance remember which. I think that the passage beginning "I am not Prince Hamlet," a passage showing the influence of Laforgue, was one of these fragments which I took with me, but the poem was not completed until the summer of 1911' (*American Literature*, xviii, 1947, 319–20).

Conrad Aiken wrote, in a letter to the *TLS* (3 June 1960) about TSE's early development: 'Mr. Eliot maintains to this day that on my suggestion a certain passage – now presumably lost – had been dropped from the poem. I can only say that I have no recollection of this, but if so, what a pity!' TSE wrote in reply (*TLS*, 8 July 1960), that *The Love Song of J. Alfred Prufrock* was written 'over a period of time in 1910–11, that is to say all that survives in the printed version. I did, I think, in 1912, make some additions to the poem and I am grateful to Mr. Aiken for having perceived at once that the additions were of inferior quality. The suppressed parts, however, have not disappeared from view like the script of *The Waste Land*; I am pretty sure that I destroyed them at the time, and I have enough recollection of the suppressed verses to remain grateful to Mr. Aiken for advising me to suppress them.' By 1960, TSE had forgotten that the lines of *Prufrock's Pervigilium* were in this Notebook of which he had seen the last in 1922; but there may have been other 'additions' which he successfully destroyed.

TSE wrote to Eudo C. Mason, 21 Feb. 1936: '*J. Alfred Prufrock* was written in 1911, but parts of it date from the preceding year. Most of it was written in the summer of 1911 when I was in Munich. The text of 1917, which remains unchanged, does not differ from the original version in any way. I did at one time write a good bit more of it, but these additions I destroyed without their ever being printed' (Harry Ransom Humanities Research Center, Austin).

Lyndall Gordon noted: ' "Prufrock's Pervigilium" is undated but it was probably copied into Eliot's Notebook in 1912. The rest of "Prufrock" (i.e. the poem as it was eventually published) was copied into the Notebook, in his spiky hand, in July–August 1911. But Eliot deliberately left four pages in the middle of the poem blank which suggests he had a rough draft of the "Pervigilium" which awaited completion' (*Eliot's Early Years*, p.45).

Title: **Pervigilium**: the eve, while suggesting a watching through the night; not in OED. The *Pervigilium Veneris* is described in the *Oxford Companion to Classical Literature*:

("eve of Venus"), a poem preserved in the Latin Anthology written in trochaic tetrameters, ninety-three lines long; the author and date are unknown, but it was written after the second century AD, perhaps as late as the fourth century. The setting is Sicily, on the eve of the spring festival of Venus; the poem celebrates the triumph of spring, the resurgence of life in the world, and the next day's festival, its spirit summed up by the passionate refrain, *cras amet qui nunquam amavit, quique amavit cras amet* ("tomorrow he who has never loved and he who has loved, let them both love").

This exquisitely compacted refrain would have its poignancy for J. Alfred Prufrock. The poem ends: *illa cantat; nos tacemus; quando ver venit meum?* ("[the nightingale] sings; we are silent; when will my own springtime come?").

TSE alludes to the *Pervigilium Veneris* in *The Waste Land*, where his Notes, line 428 ('*Quando fiam uti chelidon* – O swallow swallow'), have: 'V. [Vide] *Pervigilium Veneris*'. He also refers to it, albeit within 'a matter beyond my competence', in relation to 'the native measure of Latin poetry', in *The Music of Poetry* (1942, OPP, p.28).

The *Pervigilium Veneris* enjoyed much attention in the years immediately preceding *Prufrock's Pervigilium*: W. H. Porter translated it, as *The Watch-Night of Venus*, in 1909; Ezra Pound praised it and quoted most of it, in translation, in *The Spirit of Romance* in 1910, in which year J. W. Mackail's edition was printed by T. J. Cobden-Sanderson for the Doves Press; and there was an edition, with translation, by Cecil Clementi in 1911. Pound's chapter, the first, in *The Spirit of Romance* bore the suggestive title *The Phantom Dawn*; his remark that the poem 'celebrates a Greek feast, which had been transplanted into Italy, and recently revived', is apt to the further transplanting and revival, by TSE, into other lands, American and European.

But the crucial evocation of the *Pervigilium Veneris* for TSE's generation was that by Pater, who had elaborately fantasized an author for the anonymous Latin poem, in Part I, ch. VI–VII of *Marius the Epicurean* (1885). (For TSE on *Marius the Epicurean*, see 12 note.) Hugh Ross Williamson, commenting on the allusion to the *Pervigilium Veneris* in *The Waste Land* and in its notes, quoted six lines of Pater on the Latin poem, adding: 'And, though its authorship is unknown, for most of us it can have been written only as Pater has described it in "Marius the Epicurean" – by the dying Flavian', etc. (*The Poetry of T. S. Eliot*, 1932, pp.148–9; Williamson's book carries a note: 'I should like to express my gratitude to Mr. Eliot for his kindness in supplying certain facts of which I have made use in this book, and for the stimulus of his

conversation'). On the one hand, there is an ironical relation of *Prufrock's Pervigilium* to Pater's initiating scene:
It was a snatch from a popular chorus, something he had heard sounding all over the town of Pisa one April night, one of the first bland and summer-like nights of the year, that Flavian had chosen for the refrain of a poem he was then pondering – the *Pervigilium Veneris* – the vigil, or 'nocturn', of Venus.

(1910 edn, i 99)

On the other hand, Flavian at once catches the plague brought back from foreign lands:
There had been something feverish, perhaps, and like the beginning of sickness, about his almost forced gaiety, in this sudden spasm of spring; and by the evening of the next day he was lying with a burning spot on his forehead, stricken, as was thought from the first, by the terrible new disease.

(i 110)

Flavian then writes the *Pervigilium Veneris* ('a kind of nuptial hymn', i 113) while dying; Marius keeps a nightlong vigil as Flavian dies, and then again over his dead body. Pater's diseased description has the effect of invoking the dark sense of *Veneris*, not only Venus but the venereal (Pater i 112: 'depositing various degrees of lifelong infirmity in this member or that'); and this may have been not only a link intimated within *Prufrock's Pervigilium* but also the link between the poem and some other works which influenced it.

For, like *The Love Song of J. Alfred Prufrock* but more so, *Prufrock's Pervigilium* is influenced by Charles-Louis Philippe's novel (1901) about the ravages of venereal disease, *Bubu de Montparnasse* (which TSE read in 1910 when he came first to Paris, as he says in his preface to a translation in 1932, and from which he took the epigraph, ' "Son âme de petite putain": Bubu', which appears in the Notebook for *Preludes III*). The old song of smallpox (and of pox) comes to mind there as if it were itself the old song to Venus.

Tout à coup il se rappela la chanson. Chanson qui console, ô vieille chanson des véroles, qui fais de la musique sur les malades, tu nous rends doux et poétiques comme la souffrance des blessés:
    De l'hôpital, vieille pratique . . .

(ch.iv)

Philippe's character Pierre rises to walk the sordid streets by night:
Et souvent ses désirs l'avaient mené. Certains soirs, ayant travaillé jusqu'à onze heures, il fermait ses livres et se sentait triste à côté de leur science. Tous les diplômes ne valaient pas le bonheur de vivre. Deux ou trois images de femmes rencontrées lui apparaissaient à l'imagination et ils les suivait, d'abord pour se délasser. Puis tout le feu de ses vingt ans s'animait, tous ses sens sentaient ce que contient une femme qui passe. Alors il se dressait, la gorge sèche et le coeur serré, éteignait sa lampe et descendait dans la rue.
Il marchait. Des prostituées pirouettaient à des coins de rue, avec de pauvres

jupes et des yeux questionneurs: il ne les regardait même pas. Il marchait comme
marche l'espérance.

(ch.1)

Another Parisian pervigilium, Laforgue's sonnet *La première Nuit* (1903), has in
common with *Prufrock's Pervigilium* an old man in a sexual setting ('old drunken
man', 30 / 'vieillard lubrique'); children ('enfants', and 'l'enfant', praying in Laforgue,
whimpering in TSE, 5); and, below the gas-light, prostitutes who are soliciting men
(TSE, 6–8):

Ses filles aux seins froids qui, sous le gaz blafard
Voguent, flairant de l'oeil un mâle de hasard.

Laforgue's speaker muses from his window: 'je rêve à ma fenêtre' (TSE, 28, 'I
fumbled to the window to experience the world'). Like the movements of the fog in
The Love Song of J. Alfred Prufrock, the movements of darkness in *Prufrock's
Pervigilium* (though clearly with other elements too, since what darkness stretches
out is tentacles, not claws) resemble those of a cat – crawling, leaping, darting,
flattening itself, stretching out, and even hissing (20–4); so there should be noted
Laforgue's twice referring in his sonnet to 'mon chat Mürr', a name the suggestions of
which may have contributed to TSE's line 22: 'And darted stealthily across the wall'.
See, below, the notes to 21 (on the lines from *The Love Song of J. Alfred Prufrock*),
and to 23 ('the cat which flattens itself', *Rhapsody on a Windy Night*).

In his *Notes sur Baudelaire* (*Mélanges posthumes*, 1903, p.111), Laforgue praised
Baudelaire's originality: 'Le premier, parla de Paris en damné quotidien de la capitale
(les becs de gaz que tourmente le vent de la Prostitution qui s'allument dans les rues
[. . .] et les chats)'. Compare TSE, 6–8. (This, the text of 1903 available to TSE, has
since been corrected by P. Bonnefis in his edition of *Mélanges posthumes*, 1979,
p.111.)

TSE was to write to Aiken, 31 Dec. 1914:
How much more self-conscious one is in a big city! Have you noticed it? Just at
present this is an inconvenience, for I have been going through one of those
nervous sexual attacks which I suffer from when alone in a city. Why I had almost
none last fall I don't know – this is the worst since Paris. I never have them in the
country. [. . .] I am very dependent upon women (I mean female society); and feel
the deprivation at Oxford – one reason why I should not care to remain longer –
but there, with the exercise and routine, the deprivation takes the form of
numbness only; while in the city it is more lively and acute. One walks about the
street with one's desires, and one's refinement rises up like a wall whenever
opportunity approaches. I should be better off, I sometimes think, if I had
disposed of my virginity and shyness several years ago: and indeed I still think
sometimes that it would be well to do so before marriage.

(*Letters* i 74–5)

In *The Waste Land*, TSE was to twist this feeling of the city streets by night, with
the woman in *A Game of Chess* [II] 132–3 exclaiming at night:

'I shall rush out as I am, and walk the street
'With my hair down, so.

To Laforgue's poem and Philippe's novel should be added Wilde, *The Picture of Dorian Gray* (1891), ch.VII:

He remembered wandering through dimly-lit streets, past gaunt black-shadowed archways and evil-looking houses. Women with hoarse voices and harsh laughter had called after him. Drunkards had reeled by cursing, and chattering to themselves like monstrous apes. He had seen grotesque children huddled upon doorsteps, and heard shrieks and oaths from gloomy courts.

(Richard Shusterman related this passage to *The Love Song of J. Alfred Prufrock* and to *Rhapsody on a Windy Night*, in *Wilde and Eliot, T. S. Eliot Annual No.1*, ed. S. Bagchee, 1990, p.123.)

Further, there is James Thomson, *The City of Dreadful Night* (1874), about which Paul Elmer More used the phrase 'fierce nocturnal vigils': 'For this poem of unrelieved pessimism is simply the impressions of an insomniac changed from self-complaining to a phantom evocation of the London as he came to know it from his fierce nocturnal vigils – "the City is of Night, but not of Sleep" ' (*Shelburne Essays*, fifth series, 1908, p.184).

Pervigilium: in the manuscripts of *Little Gidding* II, TSE was to invoke 'The agony and the solitary vigil'; this revised 'The dark night in the solitary bedroom', and at once continued: 'Remember also fear, loathing and hate' (Helen Gardner, *The Composition of Four Quartets*, p.183). Other filaments are *Little Gidding* II, 'I fought the darkness', and 'evil' (manuscript readings, Gardner, p.186); compare *Prufrock's Pervigilium* 10, 15–19: 'fought', 'evil', and (three times) 'the darkness'. The epigraph to *Prufrock's Pervigilium* was to be crucial to this Dantesque section of *Little Gidding*. TSE wrote to Hayward, 27 Aug. 1942 (Gardner, p.65):

That brings us to the reference to swimming in fire which you will remember at the end of Purgatorio 26 where the poets are found. The active co-operation is, I think, sound theology and is certainly sound Dante, because the people who talk to him at that point are represented as not wanting to waste time in conversation but wishing to dive back into the fire to accomplish their expiation.

The passage from Dante on which the epigraph draws, *Purgatorio* XXVI 142–8, recurs in TSE. Compare *Dante* (1929, *SE*, p.256):

The canto ends with the superb verses of Arnaut Daniel in his Provençal tongue:

'*Ieu sui Arnaut, que plor e vau cantan;*
consiros vei la passada folor,
e vei jausen lo jorn, qu'esper, denan.
Ara vos prec, per aquella valor   [145]
que vos guida al som de l'escalina,
sovegna vos a temps de ma dolor.'
POI S'ASCOSE NEL FOCO CHE GLI AFFINA.
'*I am Arnold, who weeps and goes singing. I see in thought all the past folly. And I*

see with joy the day for which I hope, before me. And so I pray you, by that Virtue
which leads you to the topmost of the stair – be mindful in due time of my pain'.
Then dived he back into that fire which refines them.
Ara Vos Prec, misgiven as *Ara Vus Prec,* is the title of a volume of TSE's poems
(1920). Line 148 is quoted in *Dante* (1920, *SW*, p.167). Dante's last line stands as
The Waste Land [V] 427, where it is followed by the line from *Pervigilium Veneris*; in
his Notes, TSE quotes Dante's last four lines (with *condus* for *guida*). Dante's
penultimate line, which is the first line of the epigraph to *Prufrock's Pervigilium,*
constitutes the last line of *Exequy*; TSE replaced it with that which comes four lines
earlier (*consiros* . . .), but then deleted both (*The Waste Land MS*, p.101). Line 146
provided the original title *Som de l'escalina* (1929) for section III of *Ash-Wednesday.*

On *Prufrock's Pervigilium* and its eroticism in relation to Arnaut Daniel's lust, see
Grover Smith (*Eliot and the Ghost of Poe*, in *T. S. Eliot: A Voice Descanting*, ed.
S. Bagchee, 1990, pp.159–61).

1 **Shall I say**: compare Isaiah 38:15: 'What shall I say?'; John 12:27: 'Now is my
soul troubled; and what shall I say?'

1, 3–4 **at dusk through narrow streets . . . lonely men in shirtsleeves . . . windows**
. . . woke: one paragraph in Henry James's *Siena Early and Late* I (1873) has
'narrow streets – that vague historic dusk', and 'I not only don't curse my
wakefulness, but go to my window to listen. Three men come carolling by,
trolling and quavering with voices of delightful sweetness, or a lonely troubadour
in his shirt-sleeves draws such artful love-notes' (*Italian Hours*, 1909, pp.350–1);
TSE's lines fall within a 'Love Song'.

5 **the children whimpering in corners**: compare *The Burnt Dancer* 20–1:
  Children's voices in little corners
  Whimper whimper through the night
in corners: compare, at the line-end, *A Song for Simeon* 6: 'Dust in sunlight and
memory in corners'. Compare Philippe, *Bubu de Montparnasse*, ch.VIII: 'parce
que dans nos âmes il y a le bon coin qui, du temps où nous ne faisions pas le mal,
était plein de sentiments simples et qui reste toujours à sa place et où des voix
parfois descendent et viennent crier commes des enfants abandonnés'.

5–7 **in corners / Where women took the air, standing in entries – / Women, spilling**
out of corsets, stood in entries: compare *Rhapsody on a Windy Night* 16–21:
  'Regard that woman
  Who hesitates toward you in the light of the door
  Which opens on her like a grin.
  You see the border of her dress
  Is torn and stained with sand,
  And you see the corner of her eye

entries: not only doorways, but passages between houses. Compare Laurent Tailhade, *Vieilles Actrices* (1904) 34: 'Vous dont la gorge flotte en amont du corset'. The actresses there are whorish. (For TSE and Tailhade, see *Afternoon* note.)

8 **gas-jet flickered**: compare *Rhapsody on a Windy Night* 14: 'street-lamp sputtered'.

8–9 **flickered / And the oil cloth curled up stairs**: compare Keats, *The Eve of St. Agnes* 355–60: 'the wide stairs', 'lamp was flickering', 'And the long carpets rose along the gusty floor'. **oil cloth**: defined in Webster (1828): 'cloth oiled or painted for covering floors'.

10, 13 **when the evening . . . spread out**: compare *The Love Song of J. Alfred Prufrock* 2: 'When the evening is spread out against the sky'. **the evening fought itself awake**: compare *Preludes II* 1: 'The morning comes to consciousness'.

11–12 **peeling oranges and reading evening papers . . . smoking cigarettes**: compare *Preludes IV* 5–6: 'stuffing pipes, / And evening newspapers'.

12 **drifted**: of *Marius the Epicurean* (see headnote), TSE wrote: 'Marius merely *drifts* towards the Christian Church'. Compare TSE's criticisms of Pater and his novel (*Arnold and Pater*, 1930, *SE*, pp.439–42) with *Prufrock's Pervigilium*: 'Pater is inclined to emphasize whatever is morbid or associated with physical malady'; '*Marius* itself is incoherent; its method is a number of fresh starts'; 'To the end, Marius remains only a half-awakened soul'; 'The true importance of the book, I think, is as a document of one moment in the history of thought and sensibility in the nineteenth century'. Also 'dissolved' and 'dissolution' – *Prufrock's Pervigilium* ends 'Then suddenly dissolve and fall away'.

13 **drugstore**: pharmacy, *OED*: 'orig. *U.S.* and chiefly *N.Amer.*', from 1810; by the end of the century, established as 'often also dealing extensively or mainly in other articles'.

15 **evil houses**: including the sense, houses of evil fame or repute, brothels. **evil houses leaning all together**: compare *The Waste Land* [II] 105–6:
> staring forms
> Leaned out, leaning, hushing the room enclosed.

The Hollow Men I 2–3:
> We are the stuffed men
> Leaning together

Leanings are often sinister in TSE. *Whispers of Immortality* 3–4:
> And breastless creatures under ground
> Leaned backward with a lipless grin.

Sweeney Among the Nightingales 29–30:

Leaves the room and reappears
Outside the window, leaning in,
The Death of the Duchess 18, 30–1 (*The Waste Land MS*, p.105):
In the square they lean against each other
and
The people leaning against another in the square
Discuss the evening's news,
(above, 10, 'the evening', and 17, 'Whispering').

16 **Pointed a ribald finger**: the paragraph of Henry James quoted in the note to 1, 3–4 has in the one sentence 'their points' (and 'their point') and 'standing with finger on nose'.   **ribald**: for the associations with brothels and with loose women, see *OED* 1b and 3b.

16–24 Compare the devilish visions with Tennyson, *St Simeon Stylites*, 168–73:
    Devils plucked my sleeve,
Abaddon and Asmodeus caught at me.
I smote them with the cross; they swarmed again.
In bed like monstrous apes they crushed my chest:
They flapped my light out as I read: I saw
Their faces grow between me and my book;
In addition to Tennyson, TSE had read *The Picture of Dorian Gray*, which remembered Tennyson – Wilde adopts 'like monstrous apes' – in evoking another evil pervigilium; see the quotation in the headnote.

16–17 **in the darkness / Whispering all together**: contrast *Hidden under the heron's wing* 3: 'Evening whisper of stars together'; and compare *Murder in the Cathedral* Part I: 'whispers in darkness'.   **Whispering all together, chuckled at me**: compare Psalm 41:5–8: 'speak evil of me', 'When he goeth abroad', 'All that hate me whisper together against me: Against me do they devise my hurt. An evil disease [. . .]' (TSE, 15, 'evil').   **at me in the darkness**: compare Job 17:13–14: 'I have made my bed in the darkness. I have said to corruption, Thou art my father.'

19 **I tossed the blankets back, to watch the darkness**: compare *Preludes III* 1–6:
You tossed a blanket from the bed,
You lay upon your back, and waited;
You dozed, and watched the night revealing
The thousand sordid images
Of which your soul was constituted;
They flickered against the ceiling.
watch the darkness: Symons wrote of the supreme artist: 'when he looks into the darkness, he sees' (*The Symbolist Movement in Literature*, p.25).

19–21 the darkness / Crawling . . . to the floor: compare *Oh little voices of the throats of men* 39: 'Across the floor the shadows crawled and crept'.

21 It leapt to the floor and made a sudden hiss: given 'leap' (24), compare *The Love Song of J. Alfred Prufrock* 20: 'Slipped by the terrace, made a sudden leap'. The sequence 'leapt . . . made . . . darted . . . Flattened . . . Stretched' recapitulates *The Love Song of J. Alfred Prufrock* 17–22: 'Licked . . . Lingered . . . Let fall . . . Slipped . . . made . . . Curled'.

21–2 sudden hiss . . . across: compare Swinburne, *Laus Veneris* (1866) 116: 'sudden serpents hiss across her hair'. TSE quoted *Laus Veneris* in a letter to Aiken, 19 July 1914 (*Letters* i 40–1).

23 Flattened itself: compare *The Picture of Dorian Gray*, ch.xvi: 'the squat misshapen figure that flattened itself into the shadow as he passed.' This opium-den night-scene has its resemblances to TSE's poem of night-life, 'pipes' (TSE's 'drugstore'), with 'gas-jets' (TSE, 8, 'gas-jet'), 'an old man' (compare TSE, 30), and 'chattered' (TSE, 36, 'chatter'). **Flattened itself upon the ceiling**: compare *Rhapsody on a Windy Night* 35: 'the cat which flattens itself in the gutter'; and *Preludes* iii 6: 'They flickered against the ceiling' (see 19 note above). **Flattened itself upon the ceiling overhead**: compare *Portrait of a Lady* i 5: 'Four rings of light upon the ceiling overhead'. Shelley often has 'overhead' at the line-end, preceded by light in some form, as in *The Revolt of Islam* [ii] 670: 'And the green light, which, shifting overhead'; [vi] 2746: 'Flooded with lightning was ribbed overhead'.

24 Stretched out its tentacles: given its grimness, compare perhaps Shelley, *The Sensitive Plant* iii 54–7:
And thistles, and nettles, and darnels rank,
And the dock, and henbane, and hemlock dank,
Stretched out its long and hollow shank,
And stifled the air till the dead wind stank.
Compare Shelley's 'thistles, and nettles, and darnels' with TSE's 'tentacles'. **prepared to leap**: the syntax ('Flattened . . . Stretched out . . . prepared'), given that 'prepared' could be preterite or adjectival participle, anticipates *The Waste Land*, where the sequence in *A Game of Chess* – 'lurked . . . troubled, confused / And drowned . . . stirred' – similarly suspends decision, as William Empson drew out ('Mr. T. S. Eliot provides a grand example of this trick', *Seven Types of Ambiguity*, 1930, 1947 edn, pp.77–9).

24–5 Stretched out . . . And when the dawn at length: given the devilish atmosphere, compare *Paradise Lost* i 208–9:
and wished morn delays:
So stretched out huge in length the arch-fiend lay

And when the dawn: compare *Preludes III* 7 (continuing the lines quoted in 19 note): 'And when all the world came back' ('the world', 37 below). For the evil presences, compare perhaps Shelley, *Prometheus Unbound*, III iv 73–7:
and when the dawn
Came, wouldst thou think that toads, and snakes, and efts,
Could e'er be beautiful? yet so they were,
And that with little change of shape or hue:
All things had put their evil nature off:

25 **And when the dawn at length had realized itself:** compare again (see the note to 10, 13) *Preludes II* 1: 'The morning comes to consciousness'.

25–7 **the dawn . . . to see what it had stirred; / The eyes and feet of men:** compare *Sweeney Erect* 9: 'Morning stirs the feet and hands'. *Suppressed Complex* 7 (variant): 'When morning stirred the long nasturtium creeper'. *Oh little voices of the throats of men* 38: 'Stirred by the morning air'.

25, 28 **And when the dawn at length had realized itself . . . the world:** in F. H. Bradley, 'realize itself' is a recurrent philosophical concept; for instance, 'an idea's general tendency to realize itself'; 'Truth is the whole Universe realizing itself in one aspect [. . .] For it is the whole Universe which, immanent throughout, realizes and seeks itself in truth'; 'The Universe is nowhere apart from the lives of the individuals, and, whether as truth or otherwise, the Universe realizes itself not at all except through their differences'; 'That which we call our real world [. . .] It is the Universe realizing itself as truth within finite centres' (respectively, July 1904; April 1907, the two; and July 1911; *Essays on Truth and Reality*, 1914, pp.80, 116, 121, 332). Again for 'realized itself' and 'the world', compare TSE's paper on 'the self-realisation ethics of Green': 'and we may think, in rather mythological language, of a consciousness gradually realising itself by the effort of making itself its own objects; so that the term of the process would be an infinite consciousness contemplating the whole world' (Houghton Library; bMS Am 1691.14 (31), pp.1, 8–9). Compare TSE's 'dawn . . . world' with *The Picture of Dorian Gray* (see the headnote and 23 note), ch.XI: 'we watch the dawn remaking the world'. (For this passage of Wilde and *Oh little voices of the throats of men*, see 38–40 note there.)

25, 28–9 **realized itself . . . experience . . . singing:** *The Music of Poetry*, which mentions *Pervigilium Veneris*, includes one of TSE's central statements on poetry and music: 'a poem, or a passage of a poem, may tend to realize itself first as a particular rhythm before it reaches expression in words [. . .] and I do not believe that this is an experience peculiar to myself' (1942, *OPP*, p.38).

25, 30 **realized itself . . . blind:** compare *The Education of Henry Adams*, ch.XVI: 'Society in America was always trying, almost as blindly as an earthworm, to realize and understand itself; to catch up with its own head, and to twist about in search of its own tail'. Cat-like, like TSE's preceding lines.

28–9 the world . . . my Madness: compare TSE, paper on T. H. Green: 'the real world is quite mad, and it is the self-appointed task of ethics and metaphysics to organise it' (Houghton Library; bMS Am 1691.14 (31), p.16).

28, 30–3 fumbled . . . blind . . . man . . . gutters . . . fall: compare *The Education of Henry Adams*, ch.xxv: 'one fumbled over it as feebly as ever. In such labyrinths, the staff is a force almost more necessary than the legs; the pen becomes a sort of blind-man's dog, to keep him from falling into the gutters'.

29 hear my Madness singing: compare *The Love Song of J. Alfred Prufrock* 124: 'heard the mermaids singing'. (And behind both, Donne, *Song: Go, and catch a falling star* 5: 'Teach me to hear mermaids singing'.) Compare *King Lear*, IV iv 2: 'As mad as the vexed sea, singing aloud' (Lear in his madness, an 'old . . . man', in a play with a 'blind old . . . man' too, TSE's next line). Given 'hiss' (21) and 'my Madness chatter' (36), compare the forms which harass Caliban, *The Tempest*, II ii 9, 14: 'Sometime like apes that mow and chatter at me', 'Do hiss me into madness'. (Compare Tennyson, and Wilde, 'like monstrous apes', quoted in the headnote and 16–24 note.) Hearing his madness singing suggests Arnaut Daniel in Dante's *Purgatorio* XXVI 142–3:
> 'Ieu sui Arnaut, que plor e vau cantan;
>   consiros vei la passada folor
TSE rendered this: 'I am Arnold, who weeps and goes singing. I see in thought all the past folly'; but the Temple Classics translation, which he used when young, has '. . . in thought I see my past madness'. This Arnaut Daniel passage furnished, among much else in TSE, the epigraph for *Prufrock's Pervigilium*; see the headnote.

29–31 hear . . . mutters . . . in many gutters: compare *Preludes* III 8–9 (following the line quoted in 24–5 note):
> And the light crept up between the shutters
> And you heard the sparrows in the gutters,

30–1 [A blind old drunken man who sings and mutters, / With broken boot heels stained in many gutters]: compare *First Debate between the Body and Soul* 2–3:
> A blind old man who coughs and spits sputters
> Stumbling among the alleys and the gutters.
Since the singing of the old man is also that of the poet ('my Madness singing'), compare Baudelaire, *Spleen: Pluviôse* (1857) 7–8:
> L'âme d'un vieux poète erre dans la gouttière
> Avec la triste voix d'un fantôme frileux.
Also (for 'blind') Corbière, *Décourageux* (1873) 31: 'quel aveugle a chanté!', and

La Fin (1873) 37: 'O poète, gardez pour vous vos chants d'aveugle'. In *Madame Bovary*, Emma Bovary is haunted by the recurrent figure of the blind old man, half-mad, who sings. Part III v; Part III vii; and then Part III viii, her dying moment:

– L'Aveugle! s'écria-t-elle.

Et Emma se mit à rire, d'un rire atroce, frénétique, désespéré, croyant voir la face hideuse du misérable, qui se dressait dans les ténèbres éternelles comme un épouvantement.

(TSE, 35, 'the darkness'.) **old drunken man**: compare *The Death of Saint Narcissus* 29: 'a drunken old man'. Compare Kipling, *Gentleman-Rankers* (1892) 29: 'When the drunken comrade mutters and the great guard-lantern gutters'; TSE included *Gentleman-Rankers* in his *Choice of Kipling's Verse*. **With broken boot heels stained in many gutters**]: in syntax, rhythm, and something of subject, suggesting the second line of Wyatt's *They flee from me*: 'With naked foot stalking in my chamber', recalled in *Paysage Triste* 12: 'With naked feet passing across the skies', and in *Hidden under the heron's wing* 5: 'With evening feet walking across the grass'. In *The Oxford Book of English Verse* (1900), Wyatt's line was given Tottelly smoothed: 'With naked foot stalking within my chamber'.

33 **I should have been a pair of ragged claws**: compare Darwin's *Descent of Man*, a passage (marked by TSE in his copy) on the 'sexual characters' of crabs: 'The development of these hook-like processes has probably followed from those females who were the most securely held during the act of reproduction, having left the largest number of offspring.' TSE's copy is of the 1913 edn (Houghton Library; Part II, ch.IX, p.412), but he might have read the book before that. The poetic scuttle, submarine and profound, to the claws, presumably of a crab, may have been prompted not only by the restaurants earlier in *The Love Song of J. Alfred Prufrock*, but by some association with the crab as crab-louse ('The Pubic Louse . . which is known by the common name of "Crab Louse" ', 1861, *OED*); see the headnote to *Prufrock's Pervigilium*, on the *Pervigilium Veneris* and the venereal, and note 'les morpions' of *Petit Epître* 17. One further cluster, which may be no more than a coincidence but does have several affinities, is a scene in Turgenev's *Smoke* (ch.XV). (TSE admired Turgenev: 'he is one of the very greatest', *Letters* i 217, 31 Dec. 1917, and see *The Egoist*, Dec. 1917.) In *Smoke*, at a lavish social occasion, there is, first, this moment:

Countess Liza, a lady of superstitious bent, [. . .] wound up by asking him whether there were animals which could be influenced by mesmerism.

'There is one such animal any way,' Prince Kokó declared from some way off. 'You know Melvanovsky, don't you? They put him to sleep before me, and didn't he snore, he, he!'

'You are very naughty, *mon prince*; I am speaking of real animals, *je parle des bêtes.*'

'*Mais moi aussi, madame, je parle d'une bête. . . .*'

'There are such,' put in the spiritualist, 'for instance – crabs'.

A servant is sent out for a crab, which is brought in on a dish:

The spiritualist ruffled up his hair, frowned, and approaching the table, began waving his hands in the air; the crab stretched itself, backed, and raised its claws. The spiritualist repeated and quickened his movements; the crab stretched itself as before.

'*Mais que doit-elle donc faire?*' inquired the countess.

'*Elle doâ rester immobile et se dresser sur sa quiou,*' replied Mr. Fox, with a strong American accent, and he brandished his fingers with convulsive energy over the dish; but the mesmerism had no effect, the crab continued to move. [. . .] Then the waiter was called, and told to take away the crab, which he accordingly did, grinning from ear to ear, as before; he could be heard exploding outside the door. [The Constance Garnett translation, 1896, as of the right period]

Perhaps this memorable scene struck TSE, for, in addition to the sudden arrival of a crab's claws in his social poem (itself having a strong American accent, and being both French and Russian – see the headnote, p.176, on *The Love Song of J. Alfred Prufrock*), there is here in *Smoke* a cluster resembling the consecutive sequence of lines, *The Love Song of J. Alfred Prufrock* 71–6:

And watched the smoke that rises from the pipes
Of lonely men in shirt-sleeves, leaning out of windows? . . .

I should have been a pair of ragged claws
Scuttling across the floors of silent seas.

.   .   .   .   .

And the afternoon, the evening, sleeps so peacefully!
Smoothed by long fingers,

– followed, six lines later, by 'brought in upon a platter' (82), and then by 'And I have seen the eternal Footman hold my coat, and snicker' (85). Note Turgenev's title *Smoke*; his evening scene with a crab to be put to sleep by movements of the fingers; his servant bringing the crab in upon a dish, and later grinning and exploding into laughter.

34 **across the floors of silent seas**: compare *Interlude: in a Bar* 4: 'Across the floors that soak'. Compare *The Ancient Mariner* [II] 106: 'that silent sea'.

35 **seen . . . creep along the**: given 'Whispering' (17), and the women, compare Keats, *Isabella* 345–6:

See, as they creep along the river side,
How she doth whisper to that aged Dame,

35–6 **I have seen the . . . my Madness chatter**: compare *The Love Song of J. Alfred Prufrock* 84: 'I have seen the moment of my greatness flicker'.   **I have seen . . . I have heard**: compare *The Love Song of J. Alfred Prufrock* 124, 126: 'I have heard the mermaids singing, each to each', and 'I have seen them'. Given 'darkness', compare *The Waste Land MS*, p.43, *The Fire Sermon* 93–4:
> Unreal City, I have seen and see
> Under the brown fog of your winter noon

'I have seen' is repeatedly Biblical – the concordance has thirty-six occurrences, among them Job 5:3: 'I have seen the foolish taking root: But suddenly I cursed his habitation'; and Psalm 37:35–6: 'I have seen the wicked in great power, And spreading himself like a green bay tree. Yet he passed away, and lo, he was not' ('suddenly dissolve and fall away'?, 38). The repetition of 'I have seen' (35, 37) resembles Symons, *Time and Memory* (1906) 5–7:
> I have seen love, that was so quick a flame,
> Go out in ashes; I have seen desire
> Go out in smoke, that was so bright a fire;

Symons's preceding line ends 'away', as does TSE, 38. Behind Symons (and TSE) there may be the reiterated 'J'ai vu' of Rimbaud, *Le Bateau ivre* (1883).   **seen . . . darkness . . . creep**: compare *Samson Agonistes* 75: 'They creep, yet see, I dark in light exposed' (with the 'blind . . . man' of TSE, 30).   **I have seen . . . along the wall . . . I have heard . . . chatter**: compare Tennyson, *Maud*, I [xviii] 599, 606–7: 'I have led her home';
> Just now the dry-tongued laurels' pattering talk
> Seemed her light foot along the garden walk,

my Madness chatter: compare *Maud*, II [v] 257–8:
> And then to hear a dead man chatter
> Is enough to drive one mad.

Isaiah 38:14 (see 1 note) has 'so did I chatter'.

37 **I have seen the world roll up into a ball**: compare *The Love Song of J. Alfred Prufrock* 92–3:
> To have squeezed the universe into a ball
> To roll it towards some overwhelming question,

– TSE's two renderings (with 'the world' in one, 'squeezed' in the other) divide the debt to Symons, *The Symbolist Movement in Literature* (p.109): 'In Laforgue, sentiment is squeezed out of the world before one begins to play at ball with it'. Compare Marvell, *To His Coy Mistress* 41–2:
> Let us roll all our strength, and all
> Our sweetness, up into one ball:

Close to *Prufrock's Pervigilium*, because of 'world', is Bergson's *L'Evolution créatrice* (1907), ch.IV: 'Aristote les pressa [les Idées] les unes dans les autres, les ramassa en boule, et plaça au-dessus du monde physique une Forme.'

37–8 I ... the world ... dissolve ... fall away: compare Keats, *Ode to a Nightingale* 19–21:

> That I might drink, and leave the world unseen,
>   And with thee fade away into the forest dim: //
> Fade far away, dissolve, and quite forget

the world roll . . . a ball . . . away: compare Blake, *The Mental Traveller* 63–5:

> The Senses roll themselves in fear
> And the flat Earth becomes a Ball //
> The Stars Sun Moon all shrink away

the world . . . fall away: compare the blind man, in this poem (30) and in *First Debate between the Body and Soul*, with TSE on blindness: 'I am interested in braille, however, for a personal reason. I do not know whether the thought of possible blindness haunts other writers, but I know that it has always haunted me. And this, without any physical premonition: my sight, I am thankful to say, is as reliable as most people's. For a writer, blindness need not be, of course, the end of his activity, as it must be for a painter: but it involves re-adjustments so great as to frighten *me*.' TSE then discussed the difference it makes that the eye *reads* poems: 'That is why, if I were suddenly blinded, or if I found the world slowly dimming before my eyes, I should be thankful for the invention of braille' (*The New Beacon*, 15 Aug. 1952).

Entretien dans un parc

Dated Feb. 1911. Title: **Entretien dans un parc**: unidentified, but perhaps deriving from J.-B. Pater's painting, *Conversation galante dans un parc* (note TSE's *Conversation Galante* in the Notebook). Compare Watteau's *Assemblée dans un parc* (Louvre), with, to the left, a couple moving away; on the right, a seated couple talking; and a woman in tension with a suitor. Compare TSE's *Embarquement pour Cythère* (*Goldfish 11*), from Watteau's *L'Embarquement pour l'Ile de Cythère*, which *Assemblée dans un parc* foreshadows. Compare TSE's cancelled title for *First Debate between the Body and Soul: Reflections in a Square*. Verlaine's *Colloque sentimental* (1869) begins:

> Dans le vieux parc solitaire et glacé
> Deux formes ont tout à l'heure passé.

Situation (cancelled title): compare *The Waste Land* [I] 49–50:

> Here is Belladonna, the Lady of the Rocks,
> The lady of situations.

TSE's cancelled title is likely to add to *OED* 1 ('place, position, or location') and to 9 ('Position of affairs'), 9b: 'A particular conjunction of circumstances (*esp.* one of a striking or exciting nature) under which the characters are presented in the course of a novel or play'; from 1779, including 1864: 'wildly melodramatic, and full of "situations" from end to end'. 9c, without article, has 1779, Sheridan, *The Critic*: 'This scene goes entirely for what we call situation and stage effect [. . .] There's situation for you! there's an heroic group!' TSE has 'All the scene's absurd!' (19). TSE, to Eleanor Hinkley, 1 April 1918, on Henry James: 'I think he has about the keenest sense of Situation of any novelist, and his always alert intelligence is a perpetual delight' (*Letters* i 227).

Situation prompts the possibility that *Entretien dans un parc* may be diffusedly indebted to a Browning poem to which Pater, in *The Renaissance* (1873; 1910 edn, pp.214–5), repeatedly devoted the word 'situation': 'His poetry is pre-eminently the poetry of situations. The characters themselves are always of secondary importance; often they are characters in themselves of little interest; they seem to come to him by strange accidents from the ends of the world. His gift is shown by the way in which he accepts such a character, throws it into some situation, or apprehends it in some delicate pause of life, in which for a moment it becomes ideal. In the poem entitled *Le Byron de nos Jours*, in his *Dramatis Personae*, we have a single moment of passion thrown into relief after this exquisite fashion. Those two jaded Parisians are not intrinsically interesting: they begin to interest us only when thrown into a choice situation. But to discriminate that moment, to make it appreciable by us, that we may "find" it, what a cobweb of allusions, what double and treble reflexions of the mind upon itself, what an artificial light is constructed and broken over the chosen situation.' In Browning's *Dîs Aliter Visum: or, Le Byron de Nos Jours*, a woman speaks, deploring a long-lost opportunity in love. The poem begins:

> Stop, let me have the truth of that!
>   Is that all true? I say, the day
> Ten years ago when both of us
>   Met on a morning, friends – as thus
> We meet this evening, friends or what? – //
> Did you – because I took your arm
>   And sillily smiled,

Compare TSE, 1, 'Was it a morning or an afternoon'; 9, 'seize her hand'; 13, 'She smiles'. Also TSE, 10, 'we walk on' / Browning, 12, 'walked'. TSE, 33, 'Some day, if God – ' / Browning, 129–30:

> For us and love
>   Failure; but, when God fails, despair.

(Compare likewise TSE's closing lines with Browning's title, from *Aeneid* II 428: 'The gods' thought was [or seemed] otherwise'.) TSE, 34, 'souls' / Browning, 139, 145, 'soul', 'souls'. Browning's failed lovers invoke Paris, as Pater remarked, so theirs would be an *Entretien*; note that Browning's subtitle is in French, like TSE's title. The cancelled title, *Situation*, might or might not have been French; compare Laforgue's closing word in the shorter version of *Dimanches: C'est l'automne* (1890): 'Ah! faudrait modifier cette situation . . .'

3 **We walked along**: compare *So through the evening* 12, variants (*The Waste Land MS*, p.113): 'through which we walked along'.

3–4 **April . . . uncertainties**: with the love-setting and its clouding over, compare *Two Gentlemen of Verona*, I iii 84–7:

> O, how this spring of love resembleth
> The uncertain glory of an April day,
> Which now shows all the beauty of the sun,
> And by and by a cloud takes all away!

Since this is an *Entretien dans un parc*, in April, compare perhaps TSE's *How to Pick a Possum* 21–2 (1937; *Noctes Binanianae*, 1939):

> From April to middle-December
>   He is apt to occur in the parks,

4 **certain uncertainties** (variant): compare *Preludes* IV 7: 'Assured of certain certainties'.

5 **becomes intense**: compare, at the line-end, Browning, *Fifine at the Fair* 881: 'While, oh, how all the more will love become intense'.

6 **I wonder if it is too late or soon**: compare *Portrait of a Lady* III 36–7:

> Not knowing what to feel or if I understand
> Or whether wise or foolish, tardy or too soon . . .

Gerontion 39–42:

Gives too late
What's not believed in, or if still believed,
In memory only, reconsidered passion. Gives too soon
Into weak hands,
late or soon: given 'the world has not been changed' (11), and 'God' (33),
compare Wordsworth's sonnet, *The world is too much with us; late and soon*,
which has 'Proteus', the changer, and 'God'.

12, 15 revision . . . decision: compare the rhyme 'indecisions' / 'revisions', *The Love
Song of J. Alfred Prufrock* 32–3.

13 She smiles: compare *Portrait of a Lady* II 10: 'I smile, of course' (the previous line
has 'smiles at situations'; note the cancelled title *Situation* here).

14 So little: Miltonic, particularly at the head of the line, in *Paradise Regained* IV 6:
'So little here, nay lost; but Eve was Eve', and in *On Time* 7–8:
So little is our loss,
So little is thy gain.
composure: compare Eve, *Paradise Lost* IX 272: 'With sweet austere composure
thus replied'.

17 And yet this while we have not spoken a word: combining two lines of Browning.
The Last Ride Together 100: 'And yet – she has not spoke so long!', and the last
line of *Porphyria's Lover*: 'And yet God has not said a word!' (TSE, 33, 'God').
Compare Symons, *The Dogs* (1899) 26: 'But he has not spoken a word'. (He is
God.)

18 It becomes at last a bit ridiculous: compare *The Love Song of J. Alfred Prufrock*
118: 'At times, indeed, almost ridiculous'.

19–20 All the scene's absurd! / She and myself: compare *As You Like It*, II vii 139–
40:
All the world's a stage,
And all the men and women merely players;

21 And what we feel, or not: see the note to *Do I know how I feel?* 1.

22, 25 pot . . . ridicule: compare Ecclesiastes 7:6: 'For as the crackling of thorns
under a pot, so is the laughter of the fool: this also is vanity'. TSE's hot pot,
within a vernal park, may owe something to Henry James, *The American Scene*
(1907), pp.116–18, the sequence from 'The fusion, as of elements in solution in a
vast hot pot', to: 'and do we not feel ourselves feeding, half the time, from the
ladle, as greasy as he chooses to leave it for us, that he holds out? Such questions
were in my ears, at all events, with the cheerful hum of that babel of tongues
established in the vernal Park.'

22–5 Round and round, as in a bubbling pot . . . cool . . . fire . . . fire: compare the scene ('All the scene's absurd!', TSE, 19) of the witches, *Macbeth*, IV i 4, 9, 11, 37: 'Round about the cauldron go', 'pot', 'Fire burn and cauldron bubble', 'Cool'. Given love (and God) in the poem, compare TSE's Note to *The Waste Land* 307: 'V. St. Augustine's *Confessions*: "to Carthage then I came, where a cauldron of unholy loves sang all about mine ears".' For this metaphor within philosophical discussion, compare TSE's paper on politics and metaphysics (1913–14?; Houghton Library; bMS Am 1691 (25), p.17): 'When this author [Walter Lippmann] is describing fact or criticising human affairs, he is apt to be right; when he philosophises, he is not wholly wrong. When he stirs the two ingredients together in his witches cauldron, a foul vapour rises.'

26 a blind alley . . . walls: compare Gérard de Nerval, *Vers dorés* (1845) 9: 'Crains, dans le mur aveugle, un regard qui t'épie'. TSE said in 1926: 'In so baffling a poet as Gérard de Nerval, about whom I have never yet been able to make up my mind, there are passages obviously of the daydream type [. . .] as well as the line so admired by Arthur Symons – "Crains, dans le mur aveugle, un regard qui t'épie!" – which seems to me consciously of the double-world type' (*VMP*, pp.153–4). Symons had said, in *The Symbolist Movement in Literature* (p.18): 'The sun, as he mentions, never appears in dreams; but, with the approach of night, is not every one a little readier to believe in the mystery lurking behind the world? "Crains, dans le mur aveugle, un regard qui t'épie!" he writes in one of his great sonnets; and that fear of the invisible watchfulness of nature was never absent from him.' Compare TSE, two lines later: 'But if we could have given ourselves the slip'. **blind alley**: given the philosophical elements in the poem, note how TSE used the phrase, first, in an essay on ethics (Houghton Library; bMS Am 1691.14 (31), p.11): 'the blind alleys of taboo and superstition'. Second, of logical positivism, on a page where he recalls the time of these poems, 'the time when I myself was a student of philosophy – I speak of a period some thirty-five to forty years ago': 'even if some of its avenues turn out to be blind alleys, it is, after all, worth while exploring a blind alley, if only to discover that it *is* blind' (Introduction to Josef Pieper, *Leisure the Basis of Culture*, 1952, p.12). Given that in this poem TSE has 'ants' six lines later (32), compare Bergson, *L'Evolution créatrice* (1907) ch.II, in two consecutive sentences: 'beaucoup d'impasses', 'les sociétés [. . .] de Fourmis'. **stopped with**: given 'April' (3) and 'dusty' (34), compare *King John*, IV ii 120: 'stopped with dust: the first of April'. **broken walls**: compare Isaiah 22:5: 'in the valley of vision, breaking down the walls' (TSE, 8, 'vision').

26–7 Up a blind alley . . . childish scrawls!: TSE may have unconsciously summoned these early lines of his when he later wrote to Robert Waller, 21 Sept. 1942: 'I do fear that Dylan Thomas has been up a blind alley, an alley choked with rather rank vegetation of verbiage' (British Library). **walls . . . chalked**

with childish scrawls: compare Shelley, *Letter to Maria Gisborne* 265–71, a cityscape which touches TSE's poems:

> But what see you beside? – a shabby stand
> Of Hackney coaches – a brick house or wall
> Fencing some lonely court, white with the scrawl
> Of our unhappy politics; – or worse –
> A wretched woman reeling by, whose curse
> Mixed with the watchman's, partner of her trade,
> You must accept in place of serenade –

TSE quoted, as having 'a distinct originality', a scene of degradation from Marston's *The Wonder of Women*, or *Sophonisba* (*John Marston*, 1934, *SE*, pp.231–2), beginning (IV i 154–6):

> Where statues and Jove's acts were vively limned
> Boys with black coals draw the veil'd parts of nature,
> And lecherous actions of imagin'd lust.

28 **given ourselves the slip**: *OED* 'slip', III 8a, 'to give (one) the slip: To evade or escape from (a person)'; from 1567. Not ordinarily reflexive, but suicide would be one way of managing it; along with the *Hamlet* associations (30), compare Thackeray, *Henry Esmond* III iv: '[I] thought to put an end to myself, and so give my woes the slip'.

30 **No stumbling**: compare 1 John 2:10: 'He that loveth his brother abideth in the light, and there is none occasion of stumbling in him'. **ends unshaped**: compare *Hamlet*, V ii 10: 'There's a divinity that shapes our ends' (and 'unshapèd', *Hamlet*, IV v 8; see also 32 note). Compare Shelley, *The Boat on the Serchio* 31: 'Who shaped us to His ends and not our own'. Compare *The Engine 1*: 'ends unknown'.

30, 32 **ends . . . moles**: compare TSE, Introduction to Pound's *Selected Poems* (1928), p.xii: 'The mole digs and the eagle flies, but their end is the same, to exist'. Recalling Blake, *The Book of Thel*, *Thel's Motto* 1–2:

> Does the Eagle know what is in the pit?
> Or wilt thou go ask the Mole?

32 **keep ahead, like ants or moles**: compare Proverbs 6:6–8: 'Go to the ant, thou sluggard; Consider her ways, and be wise: Which having no guide, Overseer or ruler, Provideth her meat in the summer, And gathereth her food in the harvest.' That moles keep ahead is puzzling, but, given 30 note, compare *Hamlet*, I v 162–3:

> Well said, old mole, can'st work i' th' earth so fast?
> A worthy pioner.

(Granted, 'pioner', pioneer, has there a military meaning.) In an early Harvard essay, TSE uses the word 'pioneers' in a philosophical context of what is ahead:

'truth is forward and not behind. But in the work of any one, or any group of pioneers, the advance [. . .]' (*The validity of artificial distinctions*; Houghton Library; bMS Am 1691.14 (27), p.4). **keep . . . ants or moles**: compare John Webster's Dirge, from *The White Devil* v iv:

The ant, the field-mouse, and the mole
To rear him hillocks that shall keep him warm
And (when gay tombs are robbed) sustain no harm;
But keep the wolf far thence, that's foe to men,
For with his nails he'll dig them up again.

The Dirge was in Palgrave's *Golden Treasury*, and it supplied TSE with *The Waste Land* [I] 74–5:

'O keep the Dog far hence, that's friend to men
'Or with his nails he'll dig it up again!

For ants and moles in an erotic context, see Remy de Gourmont, *Physique de l'amour: essai sur l'instinct sexuel* (1904). The ant, ch.x: 'Il meurt sur place, la femelle se relève, gagne son nid, pond, avant d'accueillir la mort. Les noces des fourmis, c'est toute une fourmilière à la fois; la chute des amants simule une cascade dorée et la résurrection des femelles jaillit au soleil comme une écume rousse.' The mole, ch.IX: 'il n'est peut-être aucune femelle qui ait, autant que la taupe, de justes motifs pour craindre le mâle.' The male mole 'finit par l'acculer dans une impasse, et, tandis qu'elle enfonce dans la terre son museau aveugle, il l'agrippe, l'opère et la féconde.' 'Et quelle vierge humaine montra jamais une telle constance à garder sa vertu? Et laquelle, seule dans la nuit d'un palais souterrain, userait ses mains à ouvrir les murs, toute sa force à fuir son amant?' Compare TSE, 26, 'blind alley . . . walls'. TSE enquired of Pound for a copy of his translation, *The Natural Philosophy of Love* (*Letters* i 553, 28 July 1922).

34 **But then what opening out of dusty souls!**: compare Meredith, *Modern Love* (1862) L 11–12:

Ah, what a dusty answer gets the soul
When hot for certainties in this our life!

TSE, 4, 'uncertainties', and 15, 'life'. TSE's 'moles' / 'souls': Meredith ended *Hard Weather* (1888) with the rhyme 'soul' answering 'mole'. (TSE incorporated in *Cousin Nancy* a line of Meredith: 'The army of unalterable law'; and compare 'The one who read George Meredith' in *The Waste Land MS*, p.5, *The Burial of the Dead* 51.) **souls**: given the cancelled title *Situation*, compare TSE's comment on Edgar Lee Masters: 'Mr. Masters sometimes fails in a situation ("Arabel") because he does not fix before you the contact and cross-contact of souls' (*Manchester Guardian*, 9 Oct. 1916).

Interlude: in a Bar

Dated Feb. 1911.

2 forms that pass: compare Tennyson, *A Dream of Fair Women* 23: 'forms that passed', with 27, 'the wall', 1, 'the . . . walls', and 31, '-scattered' / TSE, 6, 'The walls . . . scattered'.

4 Across the floors that soak: compare *The Love Song of J. Alfred Prufrock* 74: 'across the floors of silent seas'.

4–5 floors that . . . glass: compare Tennyson, *In Memoriam* LXXXVII 20: 'That crashed the glass and beat the floor'. Tennyson's section has several affinities with TSE's poem: 1, 'I past [passed]' / TSE, 2, 'pass'; 1, 'walls' / TSE, 6; 16, 'the rooms' / TSE, 1, 'the room'; 19, 'hands' / compare TSE, 12, 'finger nails'; 37, 'form' / TSE, 2, 'forms'; and perhaps – bizarrely – Tennyson's concluding line, 'The bar of Michael Angelo', in relation to TSE's setting (*in a Bar*) and his concluding words: 'Tapping the bar', a phrase which might sardonically invite another poem by Tennyson, *Crossing the Bar*.

5 from broken glass: compare *The Hollow Men* I 9: 'Or rats' feet over broken glass'. (I 11 has 'form' / here, 2, 'forms'.)

6–8 fling back the scattered streams . . . Visionary, and yet hard: compare Shelley, *The Question* 6–7:

> flung
> Its green arms round the bosom of the stream,

Shelley has 'visionary' (33). (Also a mention of his 'hand' in 38; compare TSE, 12.) **the . . . streams / Of life . . . Visionary**: compare Wordsworth, *Prelude* (1850) VI 439: 'the sister streams of Life and Death' (recreating his *Descriptive Sketches* 72: 'the mystic streams of Life and Death'); 'visionary' is very frequent in Wordsworth, including 'life's visionary stir', *On the Power of Sound* 212 (where the next line has 'intoxicate'; compare TSE's setting and details). **scattered streams / Of life**: compare Byron, *Corsair* I 127–8:

> Whose scattered streams from granite basins burst,
> Leap into life, and sparkling woo your thirst;

TSE's setting, *in a Bar*, is one to woo your thirst. Byron has four lines later 'that red hand'; compare the subsequent lines in TSE. **Visionary, and yet hard**: compare *Mandarins* 2 7: 'delicate and hard'. **yet hard**: when Milton ended a line with those last two words, 'Enjoyment of our right as Gods; yet hard', it was immediately following a description of 'his riven arms to havoc hewn' (compare TSE, 11, 'scarred'), *Paradise Lost* VI 449, 452.

10 But hard . . .: compare *Paradise Lost* III 200: 'But hard be hardened, blind be blinded more'. (Milton's next line has 'stumble'; TSE in *Entretien dans un parc* has 'stumbling', 30, and blind 'moles', 32.)

11 **Broken and scarred**: compare (given TSE's preoccupation with the play) *Coriolanus*, IV v 108–9: 'broke / And scarred'. Shakespeare's lines might then have precipitated two strange turns, the one upon 'ash' – akin to the 'smoke' (1) of TSE's setting, but meaning the weapon-wood in *Coriolanus*, and the other upon 'moon' in relation to TSE's 'finger nails':

> that body, where-against
> My grained ash an hundred times hath broke
> And scarred the moon with splinters.

12 **Like dirty broken finger nails**: compare *The Waste Land* [III] 303: 'The broken fingernails of dirty hands'.

12–13 **nails / Tapping**: compare Tennyson, *Maud*, II [ii] 69–70:

> Slight, to be crushed with a tap
> Of my finger-nail on the sand,

See 4–5 note.

Paysage Triste

Donald Gallup suggests that this is probably to be dated 1914 (*T. S. Eliot and Ezra Pound*, 1970, p.5). Title: Verlaine has a sequence of seven poems, *Paysages tristes* (1866). The fourth, *Nuit du Walpurgis classique*, mentions the opera *Tannhäuser* (compare TSE, 19), and three times 'les cors', the horns (TSE, 15). The first and last stanzas of Verlaine's poem end with something of the spirit of TSE's: 'Correct, ridicule et charmant'. J.-K. Huysmans' use of 'paysage triste' in *A rebours* (1884), ch.xv, has not only a musical allusion (to Schubert) but also an overt love-sadness: 'Jamais, sans que de nerveuses larmes lui montassent aux yeux, il n'avait pu se répéter "les Plaintes de la jeune fille", car il y avait dans ce lamento, quelque chose de plus que de navré, quelque chose d'arraché qui lui fouillait les entrailles, quelque chose comme une fin d'amour dans un paysage triste.'

   1 **mounted in the omnibus**: perhaps to be distinguished from 'mounted the omnibus', as going upstairs within it. Reassurance for ladies was offered by Baedeker's *London and Its Environs* (1908), which TSE owned (his copy, in the Hayward Bequest, is dated October the 14th, 1910), p.20: 'The "garden seats" on the top (same fares as inside) are pleasant enough in fine weather and are freely patronized by ladies.' But this is a 'rainy day'. **in the omnibus**: long a conventionally unconventional poetic setting. Nathaniel Parker Willis published in 1844 *The Lady in the White Dress, Whom I Helped Into the Omnibus*, beginning 'I know her not!' Willis, 9, 'And in the blue depths of her stainless eyes' / TSE, 6, 'faint blue eyes' (likewise at the line-end); Willis, 19, 'on my knee' / TSE, 16, 'on my knees' (both at the line-end); Willis, 26, 'Wear, if they will [. . .]' / TSE, 9 and 14, 'what to wear'. More recently for TSE, there was Symons, *In an Omnibus* (1892), rhyming (10–12) 'when to wear' with 'hair' – compare the internal rhyming in TSE 5–6, 9–11. (Pound was to publish in 1916 a poem in French: *Dans un Omnibus de Londres*.) The full form 'omnibus' was not then affected, though formal; Baedeker's *London and Its Environs* (1908), although it concedes 'familiarly known as a '*bus*' (p.20), regularly uses the word 'omnibus'. As a child of ten, TSE had included in his magazine *Fireside* (No.1, 28 Jan. 1899; Houghton Library), within *Poet's Corner*, an adaptation of Lewis Carroll's comic turns in *Sylvie and Bruno*. TSE:

> I thought I saw a elephant
> A-riding on a 'bus
> I looked again, and found
> Alas! 'Twas only us.

He included another of these with a 'bus, from Carroll (as 'Anon.'), in next day's *Fireside* (No.2, 29 Jan. 1899). In *Paysage Triste*, TSE may have preferred the full form 'omnibus' not only for its air of formality but also for its preserving the etymology ('for all'), one which might further the poem's hint that the girl may be of easy virtue ('An almost denizen of Leicester Square'). The poem's movement of mind, and of sensibility, 'the omnibus . . . the box . . . opera-glasses' (1, 8, 19), may owe something to the term 'omnibus box' (of theatres and opera-houses), OED 'omnibus', 2a, from 1853. 'The famous *omnibus* boxes were filled, towards the conclusion of the opera, with the fashionable allies' (1864); 'He was in the omnibus box at the opera' (1882).

2 **a penny fare**: Baedeker's *London and Its Environs* (1908), p.20: 'The fares vary from 1*d.* to 6*d.* or 7*d.*'

4 **averted**: not in itself a remarkable word, but TSE may owe something to Keats, *Sleep and Poetry* 105–6:
> Catch the white-handed nymphs in shady places,
> To woo sweet kisses from averted faces, –

For 'Leicester Square' (7) is one of the 'shady places' in both senses (compare 'Here I am in Shady Bloomsbury', TSE, 8 Sept. 1914, *Letters* i 56); and 'An almost denizen of Leicester Square' suggests *Sleep and Poetry* 48–9:
> That am not yet a glorious denizen
> Of thy wide heaven – Should I rather kneel

(of which the first line and a half are promptly repeated by Keats as 54–5); with, perhaps, 'kneel' /TSE, 16, 'knees'.

7 **An almost**: OED 2b: 'qualifying a sb. with implied attribute', including Southey, 1808: 'an almost Quaker'. **denizen of Leicester Square**: see 4 note, but also Pope, *The Rape of the Lock* II 55–6:
> He summons strait his denizens of air;
> The lucid squadrons round the sails repair:

Following 'denizens', 'squadrons' could have participated in TSE's 'Square', both in sound and in etymology. (Pope presumably took pleasure in 'squadrons round', squaring the circle.) The whole passage in *The Rape of the Lock* (II 47–56) is pertinent to TSE's poem, in likeness and unlikeness; whereas Pope's attractive woman is sunnily (and operatically) transported on the Thames –
> But now secure the painted vessel glides,
> The sun-beams trembling on the floating tides;

TSE's girl has 'mounted in the omnibus / The rainy day' (1–2). In Pope, 'melting music steals upon the sky' (II 49; also 'of the skies', II 65); compare the music heard in TSE, 15–19, and his 'across the skies' (12). TSE has 'fan' (17), and *The Rape of the Lock* makes great play with fans (II 112, III 17, V 7). In Pope, too, 'the box' in the theatre (TSE, 8, at the opera) is of consequence (I 44, V 14, V 17). Moreover, mention is twice made in TSE of the attractive woman's hair. (For the lock of hair flying 'through the skies', see Pope V 127–32, and compare TSE, 11–12.) Compare, further, *Paysage Triste* with the pastiche-Pope passage in *The Waste Land MS* draft (p.23) of *The Fire Sermon*; this was adapted by 'F.M.'

(Vivien Eliot), in collaboration with TSE, for an article in *The Criterion*, ii (April 1924) 360–1, *Letters of the Moment – II*, which includes the following lines:
"My dear, I missed you last night at the Play;
Were you not there? Or did you slip away?
Or were you in the seats of cheaper price?
Dorilant sat with me, and I looked nice.
Once settled in my box, he never stirred –
I told him you were there, but I don't think he heard. . . ."
Leicester Square: with 'ease' at the end of 13, compare TSE's *Cat Morgan Introduces Himself* (1952, added to *Old Possum's Book of Practical Cats* in 1953), where 3 ends with 'ease' and 4 with 'Bloomsbury Square'.

8–9, 19 in the box . . . what to wear . . . opera-glasses: TSE, to Virginia Woolf, 27 April 1937: 'To go to the Opera in a box is the only endurable way of going to the Opera: I have not been under such conditions for many a long year. Perhaps I shall go to Vienna and see if they have any cheap Opera there' (Berg Collection). Baedeker's *London and Its Environs* (1908), p.44: 'Evening-dress is [. . .] *de rigueur* in most parts of the opera-house during the opera season.'

10–11 eyes . . . loosened hair: compare Browning, *Pauline* 2–3: 'thy sweet eyes, / And loosened hair'. **with loosened hair**: compare Landor, *Gebir* II 136: 'His chaplets mingled with her loosened hair'. (TSE: 'I wonder whether many people ever read *Gebir*; and yet Landor, the author of that dignified long poem, was a very able poet indeed'; *What is Minor Poetry?*, 1944, *OPP*, p.43.) D. G. Rossetti mentions the 'loosened hair' of the prostitute, *Jenny* (1870) 47 (TSE alluded to this poem in *The Waste Land MS*, p.27, *The Fire Sermon* 45: 'The lazy laughing Jenny of the bard'); and Meredith, *Modern Love* (1862) XIII has 'loosened hair', in a Meredithian sonnet which remarks: 'She drops a look of fondness, and goes by' (compare the 'look' in TSE, 4).

12 With naked feet: TSE's opera-house, a pleasure-house, may have been coloured by a poem which he admired (*What is Minor Poetry?*, 1944, *OPP*, p.42), Sir Edwin Arnold's *The Light of Asia* (1879), Book the Seventh, pp.183–4:
So went those merchants to the Pleasure-House,
Full softly pacing through its golden ways
With naked feet, amid the peering maids,
Much wondering at the glories of the Court.
With naked feet passing across the skies: following 'her chamber' at the previous line-end, this suggests (in syntax, rhythm, and something of subject) the line by Wyatt, 'With naked foot stalking in my chamber' (*They flee from me*), that is recalled in *Prufrock's Pervigilium* 31: 'With broken boot heels stained in many gutters'; and in *Hidden under the heron's wing* 5: 'With evening feet walking across the grass'. (Wyatt's next line, 'I have seen them' / TSE's preceding line, 'I

see her'.) In *The Oxford Book of English Verse* (1900), Wyatt's line was given smoothed: 'With naked foot stalking within my chamber'. Compare also *Preludes* IV 1: 'His soul stretched tight across the skies'.

13–14 crudely ill at ease . . . sit: compare Symons, *Fête Champêtre* (1895) 2–3:
> We sat together, you and I;
> Our hearts were sweetly ill at ease

The association of 'ill at ease' (at the line-end) with the theatrical, with behaviour, and with roles, recurs in *The Family Reunion*, I i, the first chorus:
> Why do we feel embarrassed, impatient, fretful, ill at ease,
> Assembled like amateur actors who have not been assigned their parts?

13, 16 ill at ease . . . knees: compare *Portrait of a Lady* III 2–4:
> Except for a slight sensation of being ill at ease
> I mount the stairs and turn the handle of the door
> And feel as if I had mounted on my hands and knees.

With 'mounted' and 'mount' ('mounted', 1, above), and the homophonic 'stairs' / 'stare' (3, above).

16 leaned: pronounced by TSE, when he read *The Waste Land* [II] 106, as rhyming with 'screened', not as 'lent' (leant).

18 The smiling stripling with the pink soaped face: compare *Paradise Lost* III 636–8:
> And now a stripling cherub he appears,
> Not of the prime, yet such as in his face
> Youth smiled celestial,

The cherub, two lines later, has 'flowing hair' / TSE, 11, 'loosened hair'. Compare Byron, *Don Juan*, XI [xxxv] 277: 'Who, seeing a handsome stripling with smooth face'. **pink soaped face**: compare *Sweeney Erect* 22–4:
> pink from nape to base,
> Knows the female temperament
> And wipes the suds around his face.

(*Sweeney Erect* 17, 'knees', at the line-end, as here, 16.)

19 in his care: compare, at the line-end, *Paradise Lost* IX 318: 'So spake domestic Adam in his care'.

Afternoon

Donald Gallup suggests that this is to be dated 1914 (*T. S. Eliot and Ezra Pound*, 1970, p.37). Compare *Morning at the Window*. Printed in *Letters* i; sent by TSE, 25 Feb. 1915, from Oxford (with *Suppressed Complex*), to Aiken (*Letters* i 88–9). (Aiken, after making typescripts, later sold the manuscripts of the poems; their whereabouts are apparently now unknown, but to Aiken's typescripts may be added those made by Jane Quinby, now in the possession of Donald Gallup.) TSE to Aiken:
> I will put one or two small verses into this letter. Pound is still trying to get two of my things into print. [viz. *The Love Song of J. Alfred Prufrock* and *Portrait of a Lady*]
>
> Affectionately
>
> TSE

The idea of a submarine world of clear green light – one would be attached to a rock and swayed in two directions – would one be happiest or most wretched at the turn of the tide?

In his copy of Baedeker's *London and Its Environs* (1908, dated by TSE October the 14th, 1910; Hayward Bequest), TSE might have noticed the sequence on p.290, about the British Museum: '[. . .] Assyrian, and American Collections and the Waddesdon Room. The Museum is open on Sun. afternoon from 2 o'clock, but is shut on Good Friday and Christmas Day. – Sticks and umbrellas are left in the hall'. TSE's 'drying rubber overshoes' recall the advice of Baedeker (p.81, 'Disposition of Time'): 'Rainy days had better be devoted to the galleries and museums'. Further to 'the sombre Sunday afternoon' (6), Baedeker, p.84: 'The movement for the Sunday opening of museums, galleries, and other large public collections has recently made great strides in London; and that day need no longer count as practically a *dies non* in the traveller's itinerary'.

Richard Aldington published in *The Egoist*, 1 June 1915, a poem, *At the British Museum*, which brings out that it may be impossible to distinguish influence (whichever way it might run) from the poeticalities of the day. TSE had sent *Afternoon* to Aiken four months earlier. TSE shares with Aldington a crucially postponed 'Vanish' at the head of the line, and both have at the line-end 'lawn[s]'. The poems would constitute a critique of one another, given Aldington's romantic colouring (his 'cobalt-blue', 'umber', 'rosy', and his swallows, as against TSE's 'green and purple feathers on their hats'). *At the British Museum*:
> I turn the page and read:
> "I dream of silent verses where the rhyme
> Glides noiseless as an oar."
>
> The heavy musty air, the black desks,
> The bent heads and the rustling noises
> In the great dome

Vanish. . . .

And

The sun hangs in the cobalt-blue sky,
The boat drifts over the lake shallows,
The fishes skim like umber shades through the undulating weeds,
The oleanders drop their rosy petals on the lawns,
And the swallows dive and swirl and whistle
About the cleft battlements of Can Grande's castle.

Aldington, 'The heavy musty air' / TSE, 'The faint perfume'. Aldington, 'over [. . .]
shallows' / TSE, 'overshoes'. Aldington, 'Fishes skim like umber' / TSE, 'Vanish in
the sombre'. Aldington's sequence of line-openings: Vanish > And; TSE's, And >
And > Vanish. Did the one poet influence the other, or was all this in the air? (Or are
the coincidings too slight?)

Of the ladies who gather, poetically, in the British Museum, TSE may have
remembered Louise Imogen Guiney and her poem *In the Reading Room of the British
Museum* (1893). But TSE's debt is to Laurent Tailhade, who in his *Poèmes
aristophanesques* (1904) had two consecutive poems, which later occupied one page
in an anthology which TSE owned in the two-volume edition (1908 and reprinted),
Poètes d'aujourd'hui (ed. Van Bever and Léautaud). *Musée du Louvre* mentions
'manteaux verts', and with 'Ses anglaises' it contrasts 'les rouges Yankees'. 'Ces
voyageurs ont des waterproofs d'un gris jaune / Avec des brodequins' (boots). 'Ils
s'arrêtent, pour consulter le *Guide Joanne*' (compare TSE and Baedeker). Tailhade,
'l'antique pucelle au turban de vizir'; TSE, 'And the green and purple feathers on their
hats'. Tailhade's other poem, *Place des Victoires*, begins, like TSE here, by stationing
'The ladies who . . .' – ladies in relation to an art (though music in Tailhade's lines,
where the 'Pianiste hongrois' prompted TSE to the foreign pianist in *Portrait of a
Lady*):

Les femmes laides qui déchiffrent des sonates
Sortent de chez Erard,

– and like TSE it ends with the women under the gaze of statuary:

Leur silhouette court, falote, au ras d'un mur,
Cependant que Louis, le Vainqueur de Namur,
S'assomme à regarder les portes de la Banque.

(In *Poètes d'aujourd'hui*, 'd'un mur'; in *Poèmes aristophanesques* 'du mur'.) TSE
included Tailhade among 'a number of admirable poets much of whose work has
permanent value', in his Foreword to Joseph Chiari's *Contemporary French Poetry*
(1952).

Pound had an article on Tailhade, among others, in *New Age*, 2 Oct. 1913; he
quoted the first six lines of *Place des Victoires*, commenting in terms apt to TSE: 'This
is what is called "rendering one's own time in the terms of one's own time". Heine
wrote in this manner, and so did Catullus, and so for that matter did Aristophanes for
whom M. Tailhade names the present volume. M. Tailhade has translated Petronius;

it is what one would expect him to do.' Pound also quoted the four lines about 'des waterproofs' and the 'Guide Joanne' from the other poem adapted by TSE, Musée du Louvre: 'The Louvre itself is versified with no less aptness.' Pound's praise of Tailhade might have struck TSE: 'It is a pleasing and erudite irony such as should fill the creative artist with glee and might well fill the imitator with a species of apostolic terror.'

1 **The ladies who are interested in Assyrian art:** compare *The Love Song of J. Alfred Prufrock* 13–14:

> In the room the women come and go
> Talking of Michelangelo.

Like TSE's poem, Ezekiel 23 associates women with Assyrians, art, the commanding figures of men, and costume, hats even: 'she doted on her lovers, on the Assyrians her neighbours, which were clothed with blue, captains and rulers'; 'the chosen men of Assyria, and with all on whom she doted'; 'the Assyrians, upon whom she doted'; 'she saw men pourtrayed upon the wall, the images of the Chaldeans pourtrayed with vermilion'; 'exceeding in dyed attire upon their heads, all of them princes to look to'; 'captains and rulers, great lords and renowned'.

1, 3, 5 **Assyrian . . . perfume . . . hats:** compare Tennyson, *Maud*, I [vi] 231–4:

> What if that dandy-despot, he,
> That jewelled mass of millinery,
> That oiled and curled Assyrian Bull
> Smelling of musk and of insolence,

Tennyson too was responding specifically to the Assyrian art of the British Museum. **Assyrian . . . purple:** compare Byron, *The Destruction of Sennacherib* 1–2:

> The Assyrian came down like the wolf on the fold,
> And his cohorts were gleaming in purple and gold;

1, 4–5 **The ladies . . . steam from drying rubber overshoes . . . hats:** compare two consecutive sentences in Henry James, *The Bostonians*, ch.IV: 'The ladies, who were much the more numerous, wore their bonnets [. . .] Two or three had retained their overshoes, and as you approached them the odour of the india-rubber was perceptible.'

3 **perfume:** stressed here on the second syllable; see *Easter I* 6 note and *Easter II* 7. **last year's tailor suits:** the fashion (and the new term) of the previous decade; OED has as its first instance of the noun, *Westminster Gazette*, 1907: 'We do not soar beyond the new tailor-suit for a week or two longer'; also *Westminster Gazette*, 1906: '*Elégantes* of Paris who were tailor-suited'. TSE was interested in fashions: 'I have not seen this costume on the street and I don't think it will be a

success' (*Letters* i 17, 24 March 1911, with a note by Valerie Eliot: '*La jupe-culotte*, or divided skirt'); Jean Verdenal described to him 'la "jupe fendue à la mode" ' (*Letters* i 22, mid-July 1911). Given the poem's philosophical destination, and last year's fashions and hats, compare TSE on philosophy in 1912: 'it must be admitted that the New Realism, like most pre-War philosophies, seems now as demoded as ladies' hats of the same period' (*New English Weekly*, 6 June 1935).

4 **overshoes:** OED has as its first instance Melville, *Moby-Dick*, 1851: 'Hat, coat, and overshoes were one by one removed'. See the note to 1, 4–5.

6–7 **Vanish in . . . fade . . . statuary:** Keatsian. *Endymion* II 375: 'Vanished in elemental passion' (head of the line); *Fairy's Song* 18: 'I vanish in the heaven's blue'. *Ode to a Nightingale* 20–21: 'fade away', 'Fade far away'; *Ode on a Grecian Urn* 19: 'She cannot fade'. *Fall of Hyperion* I 336: 'I marked the goddess in fair statuary' (likewise stationed at the line-end).

8 **Like amateur comedians across a lawn:** compare *Suite Clownesque I* 5: 'Here's the comedian again', with 'lawns' two lines earlier.

9 **the absolute:** similarly concluding *Spleen*: 'On the doorstep of the Absolute' (rhyming there with 'suit', as here rhyming at a distance with 'suits'). TSE may have recalled one of the hugely popular Hans Breitmann ballads, in pidgin Germanic English, by Charles Godfrey Leland, whose *Wein Geist* (1871) ends:
> In Madchenlieb or Schnapsenrausch
> Das Absolut ist dein.

('Translated' by John Hollander as: 'In the love of a girl or drunken fit, the Absolute is yours'; *American Poetry: The Nineteenth Century*, 1993, ii 149, 969.) But more important than American pastiche-German was the French of Laforgue. In TSE's *Spleen*, the ending on 'the Absolute' follows 'hat and gloves in hand', reminiscent of Symons on Laforgue: 'He composes love-poems hat in hand', *The Symbolist Movement in Literature* (p.109): note 'hats' here (5). Compare *Conversation Galante* 14, again at the line-end, bantering a woman: 'The eternal enemy of the absolute' (as also at the line-end in *Suite Clownesque III* 21: 'First born child of the absolute'). Laforgue placed the word there: 'Me laisser éponger mon Moi par l'Absolu?', *Préludes autobiographiques* (1885) 106; and he proclaimed in *Lohengrin* (*Moralités légendaires*, 1992 edn, p.86):
> Nul Absolu;
> Des compromis;
> Tout est pas plus;
> Tout est permis.

TSE in 1926, of Laforgue: 'It is noticeable how often the words "inconscient", "néant", 'L'absolu" and such philosophical terms from the vocabulary of Schopenhauer and Hartmann [. . .] recur' (*VMP*, p.215); compare 'the unconscious' and 'the absolute' in this poem, as also with TSE's saying of Corbière: 'he has less direct feeling of "the absolute", "the unconscious", and the other abstractions which aroused Laforgue's passion' (*VMP*, p.217). Publishing, at last, his Harvard doctoral dissertation (completed 1916) in 1964, as *Knowledge and Experience in the Philosophy of F. H. Bradley*, TSE wrote in his Preface (p.11): 'The last page of the typescript ends with an unfinished sentence: *For if all objectivity and all knowledge is relative* . . . I have omitted this exasperating clause: it is suitable that a dissertation on the work of Francis Herbert Bradley should end with the words "the Absolute".' More; for TSE's final sentence then becomes: 'And this emphasis upon practice – upon the relativity and the instrumentality of knowledge – is what impels us toward the Absolute.' The poem ends: 'Towards the unconscious, the ineffable, the absolute'. With no final full stop to the poem, apparently. TSE wrote to Norbert Wiener, 6 Jan. 1915 (*Letters* i 80–1): 'one can have a relative absolute if one likes, for it is all one if one call the Absolute, Reality or Value. It does not exist for me, but I cannot say that it does not exist for Mr. Bradley. And Mr. Bradley may say that the Absolute is implied *for* me *in* my thought – and who is to be the referee?' This same letter makes something of 'toward': 'I am content to say figuratively that the goal to which "reality" strives is the world of the materialist. One is equally free to say that it "strives" toward the other end too. Of course it does not get there, in either case.' On this sense of 'Towards . . . the absolute', compare Symons on Rimbaud: 'It is for the absolute that he seeks, always; the absolute which the great artist, with his careful wisdom, has renounced seeking' (*The Symbolist Movement in Literature*, p.70). Richard Wollheim, without lessening the Absolute of F. H. Bradley, remarks of TSE's education in philosophy that 'the term is also central to Royce's version of Idealism' (*Eliot in Perspective*, ed. Graham Martin, 1970, p.192). For another's Absolute, see TSE on politics and metaphysics (1913–14?, Houghton Library; bMS Am 1691 (25), p.2): 'Professor Bosanquet is the prophet who has put off his shoes and talked with the Absolute in a burning bush.' TSE returns often to the Absolute in his Clark Lectures, 1926: 'You know how the Absolute of Bergson is arrived at: by a turning back on the path of thought, by divesting one's mind of the apparatus of distinction and analysis, by plunging into the flow of immediate experience'; 'whether you seek the Absolute in marriage, adultery or debauchery, it is all one – you are seeking in the wrong place'; 'In these lines of Donne there is a great deal of the modern *recherche de l'absolu*, the disappointed romanticism, the vexation of resignation at finding the world other than one wanted it to be' (*VMP*, pp.99, 115, 128).

Suppressed Complex

Printed in *Letters* i 87–9. Sent in letters by TSE from Oxford: first, to Pound, 2 Feb. 1915:

> I enclose one small verse. I know it is not good, but everything else I have done is worse. Besides, I am constipated and have a cold on the chest. Burn it.

Second, to Aiken, 25 Feb. 1915; see the headnote to *Afternoon*. 'Aiken sold these two poems, copied on the first and third pages of a single folded sheet, but made typescripts, which are in the Huntington Library' (*Letters* i 89). Donald Gallup tentatively proposed that *Suppressed Complex* might have been the poem sent by Pound to Wyndham Lewis in 1915 for *Blast* (*T. S. Eliot and Ezra Pound*, 1970, p.5); but W. K. Rose's *The Letters of Wyndham Lewis* (1963), on which this supposition was based, has since been superseded here by Timothy Materer's *Pound/Lewis* (1985, pp.12–13), which makes clear that the poem was *Portrait of a Lady*.

Title: **Suppressed Complex**: TSE wrote to his brother Henry, 2 July 1915, about Vivien and himself: 'I am much less suppressed, and more confident, than I ever have been' (*Letters* i 104). 'Suppressed' in a psychological and psychoanalytic application is not specifically given in *OED* (even the Second Edition), but there is 'suppression', 7a, '*Psychol.*' 1880, William James: 'What do we mean by "suppression"? Either complete oblivescence, or such presence as to evoke the steady sentiment of aversion or negation'. Also 7b, '*Psychoanal.* The action or result of (consciously) inhibiting an unacceptable feeling, desire, or memory'; from 1913, A. A. Brill, tr. Freud *Interpretation of Dreams*: 'Language has hit upon the truth when it speaks of the "suppression" of such impulses'.

complex: *OED* 3, from 1907: '*Psychol.* A group of emotionally charged ideas or mental factors, unconsciously associated by the individual with a particular subject, arising from repressed instincts, fears, or desires'. The conjunction, *Suppressed Complex*, remains teasing, not least because 'suppressed' may posit consciously, and 'complex' unconsciously. TSE's use of the noun 'complex', given the procedures of the poem, may owe something to Pound: 'An "Image" is that which presents an intellectual and emotional complex in an instant of time. I use the term "complex" rather in the technical sense employed by the newer psychologists, such as Hart, though we might not agree absolutely in our application' (*A Retrospect*, 1913, *Literary Essays of Ezra Pound*, 1954, p.4).

The poem has affinities with Baudelaire's prose poem, *Les Bienfaits de la Lune* (*Le Spleen de Paris*, 1869), especially as translated by Stuart Merrill in *Pastels in Prose* (1890, p.176), which TSE owned (Houghton Library) and wrote about (see *First Debate between the Body and Soul* 15 note): Merrill, 'as thou wert sleeping' / TSE, 'She stirred in her sleep'; 'extraordinarily pale' / TSE, 'very pale'; 'through the windows', 'passed noiselessly through the panes', and 'joy' / TSE 'passed joyously out through the window'. Plus 'eyes' in both, 'thought' / TSE, 'think', 'light' / TSE, 'firelight', and with 'clasped' / TSE, 'clutched'.

In *The Savage and the City* (p.103), Robert Crawford comments: 'On 29 October 1914, he heard Collingwood, lecturing on Aristotle's *de Anima*, talk of how the soul might be supposed to leave the body and return to it later. Eliot scribbled a reference to Frazer's treatment of such experiences in *The Golden Bough*. By February 1915, he was sending Aiken "Suppressed Complex", a poem about a soul-like shadow dancing in the firelight of a woman's room, before passing out of the window. In 1916 Eliot recalled "Tylor's dreaming aborigine who finds that his soul in sleep can part company with his body and roam the forests".' (Sir Edward Tylor, 1832–1917, anthropologist, author of *Primitive Culture*, 1871.) To this anthropological possibility might be added a philosophical one; in *Appearance and Reality*, F. H. Bradley had offered 'a fiction': 'Suppose a collection of beings whose souls in the night walk about without their bodies, and so make new relations. On their return in the morning we may imagine that the possessors feel the benefit of this divorce; and we may therefore call it truth. But, if the wrong soul with its experience came back to the wrong body, that might typify error. On the other hand, perhaps the ruler of this collection of beings may perceive very well the nature of the collision. And it may even be that he provokes it. For how instructive and how amusing to observe in each case the conflict of sensation with imported and foreign experience. Perhaps no truth after all could be half so rich and half so true as the result of this wild discord – to one who sees from the centre. And, if so, error will come merely from isolation and defect, from the limitation of each being to the "this" and the "mine" ' (1893; 1897 edn, pp.171–2).

1 **stubborn eyes**: as against the usual knees; *Hamlet*, III iii 70: 'stubborn knees'; Samuel Butler, *Hudibras*, I i 17–18:
> That never bent his stubborn knee
> To any thing but chivalry,

6–7 **She was very pale and breathed hard. / When morning**: compare, as diffusedly apt to TSE, Keats, *Isabella* 41, 49–53: 'So said he one fair morning';
> So once more he had waked and anguishèd
>   A dreary night of love and misery,
> If Isabel's quick eye had not been wed
>   To every symbol on his forehead high;
> She saw it waxing very pale and dead,

TSE, 1, 3: 'bed . . . I was a shadow' / *Isabella* 302, 305: 'bed', 'I am a shadow'.

7 **morning shook the long nasturtium**: compare *Rhapsody on a Windy Night* 12: 'madman shakes a dead geranium'. **morning stirred** (variant): compare *Sweeney Erect* 9: 'Morning stirs the feet and hands'. *Oh little voices of the throats of men* 38: 'Stirred by the morning air'. *Prufrock's Pervigilium* 25–6: 'the dawn . . . to see what it had stirred'. **the tawny bowl**: contrast TSE's love-scene with Robert Stephen Hawker, *King Arthur's Waes-hael* 1–6:
> Waes-hael for knight and dame!

O merry be their dole!
Drink-hael! in Jesu's name
  We fill the tawny bowl;
But cover down the curving crest,
Mould of the Orient Lady's breast.

Hawker's poem, which has 'breathe' and 'shadowy' (18–19 / TSE, 2–3, 6, 'breath', 'shadow', 'breathed'), is in the *Oxford Book of English Verse* (1900).

8 **I passed joyously . . . through**: compare Shelley, *Rosalind and Helen* 525–7:

Nor noticed I where joyously
Sate my two younger babes at play,
In the court-yard through which I passed;

In the Department Store

Donald Gallup suggests that this is to be dated 1915 (*T. S. Eliot and Ezra Pound*, 1970, p.37). Title: *OED* has 'department store', 'orig. *U.S.*', from 1887. H. G. Wells in *Mr. Polly* (1910) still finds it necessary to explain the term: 'One of those large, rather low-class establishments which sell everything from pianos and furniture to books and millinery – a department store.'

In the Department Store: compare Henry James's love-story with a similar setting (a shop), *In the Cage* (1898). TSE's line, 'The summer evenings in the park' (5), recalls James's central elaborated scene (occupying three chapters), which takes place on a summer evening in the park; in James, the phrase 'in the Park' comes half a dozen times, and 'the Park' often too. (James's story contributed to the cancelled title, *In the Cage*, which TSE had at first for *A Game of Chess* in *The Waste Land*.) TSE wrote, *New English Weekly*, 12 Sept. 1935: 'What the help and encouragement of men of an older generation may be like, what it feels like, what useful stimulus or perhaps misdirection it may give, I do not know. At a time which may be symbolised by the figures 1910, there was literally no one to whom one would have dreamt of applying. One learnt something, no doubt, from Henry James, and might have learnt more. But Henry James was a novelist, and one who gave the most formidable appearance of exclusive concentration on his own kind of work.' Virginia Woolf reported TSE in her Diary, 20 Sept. 1920: 'A personal upheaval of some kind came after Prufrock, & turned him aside from his inclination – to develop in the manner of Henry James.' TSE's poem belongs, in kind, with one by his Harvard friend, W. G. Tinckom-Fernandez, *The Waitress* (*Harvard Advocate*, 31 Jan. 1908); the poems share mention of the lady, her eyes, her hair, her smile, and her being business-like / busy. For the smile of a stranger, compare *Morning at the Window* 7–8.

1 **The lady of the porcelain department**: compare Whistler's *La Princesse du pays de la porcelaine* (1864; Freer Gallery, Washington), noting TSE's 'To porcelain land' (*Goldfish ii: Embarquement pour Cythère* 13). Compare too 'the porcelain department' with the tower or pavilion of porcelain, much invoked in poetry and prose. Given the Jamesian elements in TSE's poem (see headnote), and Whistler's *La Princesse du pays de la porcelaine*, compare *The Golden Bowl* (1904), where, in the first chapter of Book Fourth (*The Princess*), the Princess contemplates her insufficiently-happy marriage under the image of 'some wonderful beautiful but outlandish pagoda, a structure plated with hard bright porcelain', with its 'rare porcelain plates'. Compare Longfellow, *Kéramos* (1878), strophe 27:
And yonder, by Nakin, behold!
The Tower of Porcelain, strange and old.
But particularly a property of the French. Compare Gautier, *Chinoiserie* (1838), which begins somewhat as TSE's poem ends: 'Ce n'est pas vous, non, madame, que j'aime'. *Chinoiserie* 5–7:

Celle que j'aime, à présent, est en Chine;
Elle demeure avec ses vieux parents,
Dans une tour de porcelaine fine,

Again Gautier, *Le Sommet de la tour* (1838) 113: 'Dans la Chine bizarre, aux tours de porcelaine'. Compare also Judith Gautier, *The Emperor (After Thoo-Foo)*. In translation, the second part of this prose poem begins: 'In her pavilion of porcelain, like a resplendent flower, surrounded by leaves, the Empress is sitting among her women'; and the whole concludes: 'And the Emperor, radiant with precious stones, walks towards the pavilion of porcelain, leaving the astonished Mandarins to stare at one another in silence.' This translation by Stuart Merrill is in his *Pastels in Prose* (1890), which TSE owned (Houghton Library) and wrote about (see *First Debate between the Body and Soul* 15 note); and compare TSE's sequence *Mandarins* (Mandarins are thrice mentioned in *The Emperor*). Also Merrill's *Ballade of the Chinese Lover* (1889) 9: 'Past the porcelain towers of Keou-Kang'. A sardonic rhyme obtains in André Salmon, *Odelette Chinoise* (1910) 33–6:

Dans une tour de porcelaine
O n'être de rien occupé
Que des vers de Li-Taï-Pé
Et d'un petit magot obscène.

Note the association of 'ladies' with 'porcelain' in *Mandarins* 2 1, 16; and the exotic–erotic in *Goldfish II: Embarquement pour Cythère* 13–14:

To porcelain land, what avatar
Where blue-delft-romance is the law.

Pound sardonically treated of porcelain, a lady, and love, in *The Bath Tub* (1913, collected 1916):

As a bathtub lined with white porcelain,
When the hot water gives out or goes tepid,
So is the slow cooling of our chivalrous passion,
O my much praised but-not-altogether-satisfactory lady.

2 **Smiles at the world**: compare *Paradise Lost* v 124, 'smiles on the world', where Milton's lines share some words with TSE's poem ('kept' / 'keeps', 'her hair', 'eye[s]', 'night[s]') and include other words ironically apt to *In the Department Store*: 'in store' itself, and 'fresh employments'. Milton in paradise pictures a happier scene than that of TSE's poem: 'So cheered he his fair spouse, and she was cheered'. But *but*, both Milton and TSE are moved to say. *Paradise Lost* v 124–31:

Than when fair morning first smiles on the world,
And let us to our fresh employments rise
Among the groves, the fountains, and the flowers
That open now their choicest bosomed smells

Reserved from night, and kept for thee in store'.
So cheered he his fair spouse, and she was cheered,
But silently a gentle tear let fall
From either eye, and wiped them with her hair.

3 **pencil in her hair:** 'business-like', but – given the oriental touch in 'porcelain' – perhaps calling to mind a formal oriental hair-style with a large pin.

4 **sharpened eyes:** as in Pope, *Odyssey* V 505. Compare Browning, *Sordello* IV 690: 'All eyes were sharpened'. *OED* 2a: 'To render more acute (a person's wits, sight [. . .] etc.)'. TSE, *Dante* (1929, *SE*, pp.243–4): 'There is a well-known comparison or simile in the great XVth canto of the *Inferno* [XV 20–1], which Matthew Arnold singled out, rightly, for high praise; which is characteristic of the way in which Dante employs these figures. He is speaking of the crowd in Hell who peered at him and his guide under a dim light:

> *e sì ver noi aguzzevan le ciglia,*
> *come vecchio sartor fa nella cruna.*

and sharpened their vision (knitted their brows) at us, like an old tailor peering at the eye of his needle.' There, 'sharpened their vision' is the Temple Classics translation, which TSE owned when young; TSE's gloss is in parentheses. Adduced, too, by TSE in the Clark Lectures (1926, *VMP*, p.122).

5, 7 **The summer evenings in the park . . . dark:** compare Clough, *Dipsychus*, scene IV 128–9:

> (Written in London, standing in the Park,
> An evening in July, just before dark.)

Compare *Portrait of a Lady* II 31: 'any morning in the park'.

6 **And heated nights in second story dance halls:** compare *The Love Song of J. Alfred Prufrock* 6: 'Of restless nights in one-night cheap hotels'. **second story:** *OED* 'story' 1: 'while in England [as against the U.S.A.] the term FIRST-FLOOR is applied to the floor above the ground floor, the numbering of "stories" (so named) usually begins with the ground-floor, so that the "first-floor" is identical with the "second story" '.

7 **Man's life is powerless and brief and dark:** from Bertrand Russell, *The* [later *A*] *Free Man's Worship* (1903): 'Brief and powerless is Man's life; on him and all his race the slow, sure doom falls pitiless and dark.' (Russell owed something to Shelley, *Queen Mab* III 220–1: 'Man's brief and frail authority / Is powerless'.) TSE, *Nation*, 23 March 1918: 'We know the passage as well as the conclusion to the "Studies in the Renaissance":– "Brief and powerless is man's life . . ." [TSE's ellipsis]. It is quite as good prose as Pater's, but it is not Mr. Russell's best prose. It presents a mood which could be made poignant in one of only two ways. We might be allowed to guess the sadness between the lines of a plain statement of

philosophic creed; or we might realize it through the plain statement of the tragedy of a particular individual man or woman.' TSE's poem seeks such a realization in the plain statement of his next and final line: 'It is not possible for me to make her happy' – the tragedy of a particular individual man and woman. Russell went on, in the next sentence of this his closing paragraph, to invoke love: 'for Man, condemned to-day to lose his dearest, and to-morrow himself to pass through the gate of darkness.' (TSE probably compounds Russell with Hobbes, *Leviathan*: 'and the life of man, solitary, poor, nasty, brutish, and short'; TSE's copy of *Leviathan*, 1907 edn, was dated by him February 1914.) In *Revelation* (ed. John Baillie and Hugh Martin, 1937, p.7), TSE remarked: 'Readers will be reminded, by the turgid style rather than by the ill-constructed sentences, of that remarkable effusion of twenty years ago, Mr. Bertrand Russell's *Free Man's Worship*.' Again, in 1948: 'One may become a Christian partly by pursuing scepticism to the utmost limit. I owe much, in this way, to Montaigne; something, in this way, to Bertrand Russell's essay *A Free Man's Worship*: the effect this essay had upon me was certainly the reverse of anything the author intended' (*A Sermon preached in Magdalene College Chapel*, 1948, p.5). TSE's cancelling of the inversion in Russell (who wrote 'Brief and powerless is Man's life') brings two further suggestions. (i) *Man's life is*: as in *King Lear*, II iv 266: 'Man's life is cheap as beast's'; TSE's 'powerless . . . dark' may – after 'sharpened eyes' (4) – suggest the blinding of Gloucester, III vii 85: 'All dark and comfortless'. (ii) (given TSE's context) Byron, *Don Juan*, I [cxciv] 1545–6:

'Man's love is of man's life a thing apart,
'Tis woman's whole existence;'

The Little Passion: From "An Agony in the Garret"

Donald Gallup suggests that this is to be dated 1915 (*T. S. Eliot and Ezra Pound*, 1970, p.37). On 25 July 1914, TSE wrote to Aiken with a tentative title for a sequence: 'I enclose some *stuff* – the *thing* I showed you some time ago, and some of the themes for the "Descent from the Cross" or whatever I may call it' (*Letters* i 44). Note the 'cross' in 15. Title: **The Little Passion**: compare *Easter*. *Little* used in this way suggests Corbière, whose *Petit Mort pour rire* (1873) was one of the Corbière poems which TSE transcribed on leaves laid into the Notebook. **Agony in**: compare *The Waste Land* [V] 323–4:
> After the frosty silence in the gardens
> After the agony in stony places

Agony, not like Christ's in the garden, but in the garret. Compare *The Family Reunion*, Part I Scene iii: 'The agony in the dark'; and Part II Scene i: 'The agony in the curtained bedroom'. *Little Gidding* II had in manuscript 'The agony and the solitary vigil' (Helen Gardner, *The Composition of Four Quartets*, p.183). **Passion . . . Agony**: TSE corrected the Theological Editor of the *New English Weekly*, 29 March 1934: 'And when he speaks of "agony and passion" he is transferring to the Incarnation two terms which are properly applicable to the Atonement.' **in the Garret**: compare *He said: this universe is very clever* 11: 'They did not crucify him in an attic'. *The Waste Land* [III] 194: 'in a little low dry garret'.

(i)
1 **Upon those stifling August nights**: *Goldfish (Essence of Summer Magazines)* 1 begins: 'Always the August evenings come'.

2–4 **streets . . . retreats**: compare *The Love Song of J. Alfred Prufrock* 4–5:
> Let us go, through certain half-deserted streets,
> The muttering retreats

The rhyme is in James Thomson, *The City of Dreadful Night* (1874) III 1, 3.

7 **cross**: for the 'Descent from the Cross', see headnote. Compare *He said: this universe is very clever* 9: 'He said: "this crucifixion was dramatic" '.

(ii) [Another draft including these lines]
1 **those ideas** (**these ideas** Gallup): compare the closing line of *Portrait of a Lady* II: 'Are these ideas right or wrong?'

1, 3 **ideas . . . seldom well digested**: compare *Inside the gloom* 25–6:
> Said Are not all these questions
> Brought up by indigestions?

6 **That spun around him like a wheel**: with the martyrdom in 15–16, suggesting St Catherine.

7–8 "I feel / As if I'd been a long time dead": compare *So through the evening* 24–5 (*The Waste Land MS*, p.113):

A man lay flat upon his back, and said [*revised to* cried]
"It seems that I have been a long time dead:

TSE to Aiken, 31 Dec. 1914: 'In Oxford I have the feeling that I am not quite alive – that my body is walking about with a bit of my brain inside it, and nothing else' (*Letters* i 74). Noting 'streets' repeatedly in the poem, compare *Eeldrop and Appleplex*: 'In Gopsum Street a man murders his mistress. The important fact is that for the man the act is eternal, and that for the brief space he has to live, he is already dead' (*Little Review*, iv, May 1917, 9). Also *Sweeney Agonistes: Fragment of an Agon*:

He didn't know if he was alive
> and the girl was dead
He didn't know if the girl was alive
> and he was dead
He didn't know if they both were alive
> or both were dead
If he was alive then the milkman wasn't
> and the rent collector wasn't
And if they were alive then he was dead.

In *The Family Reunion* II iii, Mary says: 'It takes so many years / To learn that one is dead!'

16 our souls are spread: compare *Preludes* IV 1: 'His soul stretched tight'.

17 across the bar: given the proximity of death, and with 'cross' (15), compare Tennyson, *Crossing the Bar*.

18–19 hopeless . . . withered face: compare Wordsworth, *The Old Cumberland Beggar* 176–7: 'his withered face. / Reverence the hope'.

19, 21 face . . . A washed-out: compare *Rhapsody on a Windy Night* 56: 'A washed-out smallpox cracks her face'.

21 unconscious half-disgrace (variant): compare James Thomson, *In the Room* (1880) 190: 'Unconscious of the deep disgrace'. Thomson, 198, 'hopeless' / TSE, 18. (Valerie Eliot, in a letter to the present editor, 20 April 1995, reports that *In the Room* was 'another favourite' of TSE's, among Thomson's poems.)

Introspection

Title: **Introspection:** *OED* 2: '*spec.* (with no object expressed): The action of looking within, or into one's own mind'; anticipated by Dryden, 1695, 'introspection into mine own mind', and then from 1807. TSE: 'There is certainly an important field for psycho-physics and the study of behaviour, and there are even certain processes where introspection is not without value' (*KEPB*, p.82). In the preface to *Appearance and Reality* (1893; 1897 edn, p.xii), Bradley set down 'of Introspection that "The one self-knowledge worth having is to know one's mind" '; and in *On Our Knowledge of Immediate Experience* (Jan. 1909), in his account of 'a kindred difficulty attaching to what is called Introspection', he asked 'Can I observe my own present state, and, if not that, what in the end can I observe?' Here Bradley resisted a certain kind of struggling (compare TSE's 'struggling'): 'To myself, when I try to observe exhaustively, say, some internal sensations, the idea that I am struggling to remember them seems even ridiculous' (*Essays on Truth and Reality*, 1914, p.166). TSE wrote to his mother, 11 April 1917: 'I have some ideas for an Article on Introspective Consciousness' (*Letters* i 175).

For other prose poems of TSE, see *Hysteria* and *The Engine I–II*. For TSE on the prose poem, see *The Borderline of Prose* (*New Statesman*, 19 May 1917). There he wrote of the Nineties and of Stuart Merrill's volume of translations from the French, *Pastels in Prose* (1890; TSE's copy is in the Houghton Library): 'I have remarked recently a recrudescence of the poem in prose – not only in France, but in England; not only in England, but in America; perhaps not only in America, England, and France [. . .]'. 'Now, reverting for a moment to the 'Nineties, it must be observed that the prose poetry of this epoch was probably based upon the work of a man much greater than any poet then living – and that is Arthur Rimbaud.' On inevitability of form: 'There could be no prose equivalent for *The Rape of the Lock*. There could be no verse equivalent for *Madame Bovary* or *Bubu de Montparnasse*'. In *The Athenaeum*, 11 April 1919, TSE wrote of Aldous Huxley: 'In his prose poems, he has made the mistake of going for a model to Laforgue instead of to Rimbaud. The prose poem is an aberration which is only justified by absolute success.' Again, on *Prose and Verse*, *The Chapbook* (April 1921, p.3): 'I have not yet been given any definition of the prose poem, which appears to be more than a tautology or a contradiction. Mr. Aldington, for example, has provided me with the following: "The prose poem is poetic content expressed in prose form." Poetic content must be either the sort of thing that *is usually*, or the sort of thing that *ought to be*, expressed in verse. But if you say the latter, the prose poem is ruled out; if you say the former, you have said only that certain things can be said in either prose or verse, or that anything can be said either in prose or verse. I am not disposed to contest either of these conclusions, as they stand, but they do not appear to bring us any nearer to a definition of the prose poem.' Later, TSE has a page on poetry, verse and prose, and what it is 'to write poetry in what is called prose', in his Preface to his translation of St.-J. Perse, *Anabasis* (1930), p.9.

1 **six feet deep**: the traditional depth of a grave.

3–4 **head having swallowed his tail**: given the title *Introspection*, compare *The Death of the Duchess* 43–4 (*The Waste Land MS*, p.107):
My thoughts in a tangled bunch of heads and tails
One suddenly released, fell to the floor
Compare TSE on 'introspectiveness', *The Egoist*, July 1919, about Aiken's *The Charnel Rose*: 'Mr Aiken has gone in for psycho-analysis with a Swinburnian equipment; and he does not escape the fatal American introspectiveness; he is oversensitive and worried. He is tangled in himself.' It was to Aiken that TSE sent his self-swallowing Laforguean burlesque, which concludes: 'they turned a flip flop somersault and disappeared down their own throats, leaving the assembly in darkness' (21 Aug. 1916, *Letters* i 146). Compare TSE on the impossible feat of 'translating' Indian thought into the European tradition: 'However, some such study (as far as one can) is I believe profitable, as getting outside of one's own skin, or jumping down one's own throat' (to I. A. Richards, 9 Aug. 1930; Magdalene College, Cambridge). Two moments in Henry Adams may come together in TSE's poem. From ch.xvi of *The Education of Henry Adams*: 'Society in America was always trying, almost as blindly as an earthworm, to realize and understand itself; to catch up with its own head, and to twist about in search of its tail.' And from ch.xxix: 'He knew no tragedy so heartrending as introspection [. . .] One's own time had not been exempt. Ever since 1870 friends by scores had fallen victim to it. Within five-and-twenty years, a new library had grown out of it. Harvard College was a focus of the study; France supported hospitals for it; England published magazines of it.'

While you were absent in the lavatory

2–4 a negro . . . Bringing a dish with oranges and bananas / And another brought coffee and cigars: compare *Sweeney Among the Nightingales* 17–20:

> The silent man in mocha brown
> Sprawls at the window-sill and gapes;
> The waiter brings in oranges
> Bananas figs and hothouse grapes;

There the 'man in mocha brown' may emanate from 'coffee' and 'a negro', and 'gapes' recalls 'wide mouth' (6). Compare TSE's letter to Eleanor Hinkley from Paris, 26 April 1911 (see *Interlude in London* 1 note): 'And one looked through the windows, and the waiter brought in eggs and coffee, and the *Graphic* (which I conscientiously tried to read, to please them)' (*Letters* i 18). The poem's incident (a man, a waiter, a woman, a mouth) asks comparison with *Hysteria*.

6–7 wide mouth . . . suspended on the: compare Shelley, *Alastor* 362: 'Suspended on the sweep of the smooth wave', where two lines later is 'Yawned'.

6, 8 wide mouth . . . rabbit: compare Tennyson, *Maud*, I [x] 360: 'A rabbit mouth that is ever agape'. **white rabbit:** suggesting *Alice's Adventures in Wonderland*; see the introductory note on TSE's title *Inventions of the March Hare*. TSE, again to Eleanor Hinkley, 3 Jan. 1915, about his boarding-house: 'Mrs. Nichols an elderly white rabbit with a very small timid daughter who plays solitaire when it rains' (*Letters* i 78).

The Burnt Dancer

Dated June 1914. Title: compare *The Death of Saint Narcissus* 17: 'but became a dancer before God'. Symons has *The Armenian Dancer* (1906); see the notes to 3, 5 and 37–8. This Dantesque poem of TSE's, **The Burnt Dancer**, points towards the Dantesque section of *Little Gidding*, including II 92–3:

> unless restored by that refining fire
> Where you must move in measure, like a dancer.'

– lines indebted to Dante (Arnaut Daniel, *Purgatorio* XXVI 133–48). The epigraph is *Inferno* XVI 6: 'beneath the rain of the sharp torment' (Temple Classics, reading *sotto*, where the Argument of the Canto makes clear that this is 'burning rain'). TSE marked this line in his copy (Houghton Library).

1–2 **flame / A black moth**: compare *The Bhagavad-Gita*, Lesson the Eleventh, verse 29: 'As moths with exceeding speed pass into a lighted fire to perish, so pass the worlds with exceeding speed into Thy mouths to perish.' The previous verse has 'Thy blazing mouths', and the next verse 'flaming mouths'; compare TSE, 17, 'the ragged teeth of flame'. Translated by Lionel Barnett (1905); TSE's copy, dated 1912 and with his markings, is in the Houghton Library. *The Bhagavad-Gita* is a source of TSE's *I am the Resurrection and the Life* (*The Waste Land MS*, p.111). For a link with Dante (who provides more than the epigraph to *The Burnt Dancer*), consider TSE: 'the *Bhagavad-Gita*, which is the next greatest philosophical poem to the *Divine Comedy* within my experience' (*Dante*, 1929, SE, p.258).

2–3, 12 **moth . . . night . . . desire . . . star**: the cluster is in Shelley. (i) *One word is too often profaned* 13–14:

> The desire of the moth for the star,
>   Of the night for the morrow,

(ii) *Epipsychidion* 218–24:

> I sprang, as one sandalled with plumes of fire,
> And towards the lodestar of my one desire,
> I flitted, like a dizzy moth, whose flight
> Is as a dead leaf's in the owlet light,
> When it would seek in Hesper's setting sphere
> A radiant death, a fiery sepulchre,
> As if it were a lamp of earthly flame.

TSE has 'flight' (4) and 'flame' (7). (iii) *Epipsychidion* 53: 'Sweet Lamp! my moth-like Muse has burned its wings'.

3 **Caught in the circle of desire**: as Arnaut Daniel is caught in the circle of lust, *Purgatorio* XXVI 133–48, and Paolo and Francesca in the circle of the carnal

sinners, *Inferno* V 73–142. Compare Blake, *And did those feet* 10: 'Bring me my arrows of desire'.

3–4 desire / Expiates his heedless: compare the exchange between the Third Tempter and Thomas in *Murder in the Cathedral* I:

'[. . .] in timeless torment,
Parched passion, beyond expiation'.
       'No!
Who are you, tempting with my own desires?'

3, 5 desire . . . that do not tire: compare *In Memoriam* CX 18–19:

But mine the love that will not tire,
And, born of love, the vague desire

CX 6 has 'pride' (TSE, 9). D. G. Rossetti's translation of Cavalcanti, *Canzone, He laments the Presumption and Incontinence of his Youth* 4–9 (a poem that begins 'The devastating flame'), rhymes 'desire' with 'that shall not tire' – and with 'fire'. The syllabus for TSE's 1918 tutorial class in Elizabethan Literature included: 'Read: A few translations of Italian Sonnets in Rossetti's *Early Italian Poets*' (R. Schuchard, *Review of English Studies* n.s. XXV, 1974, 300). Symons, for the closing speech in *The Lover of the Queen of Sheba* (1899), borrowed from Tennyson 'desire' rhyming with 'Man loves that love which shall not tire'; as also in *The Armenian Dancer* (1906) 21, 'I dance, and shall not tire', rhyming with 'desire' (and with 'fire'; compare TSE, 34, 36). Similarly deriving from Tennyson, there is Christina G. Rossetti, *Later Life* 5 (1881) 10–13:

O Love exhaust, fulfilling my desire:
Uphold me with the strength that cannot tire,
Nerve me to labour till Thou bid me rest,
Kindle my fire from Thine unkindled fire,

4 Expiates: TSE drew the attention of John Hayward to 'the reference to swimming in fire which you will remember at the end of *Purgatorio* 26 where the poets are found. The active co-operation is, I think, sound theology and is certainly sound Dante, because the people who talk to him at that point are represented as not wanting to waste time in conversation but wishing to dive back into the fire to accomplish their expiation' (letter, 27 Aug. 1942; Helen Gardner, *The Composition of Four Quartets*, p.65). See the headnote.

6–7 more vital values / To golden values: given 'desire' (3) in a poem about self-sacrifice and taboo, compare TSE, essay on ethics: 'It is the business of descriptive ethics to follow the slow expansion of primitive desires into the various systems of values, indicating the bypaths of prejudice and the blind alleys of taboo and superstition, noting the categories or the general form into which value articulates itself; the various genres of art, the various satisfactions of religion, the subordinate moral values, as benevolence, sympathy, or self-sacrifice' (Houghton Library; bMS Am 1691.14 (31), pp.11–12).

6, 28 Distracted from . . . but not with human meaning: compare *Burnt Norton* III 12–13:
> Distracted from distraction by distraction
> Filled with fancies and empty of meaning

7, 9 flame . . . shame: compare Shelley, *The Revolt of Islam* [x] 3977, 3979: 'the agony of the flame', rhyming with 'shame'. (TSE, 23, 'agony'.) Symons, *Modern Beauty* (1899) 1–6, has affinities with Shelley (see the note to 2–3, 12) and with TSE's poem:
> I am the torch, she saith, and what to me
> If the moth die of me? I am the flame
> Of Beauty, and I burn that all may see
> Beauty, and I have neither joy nor shame,
> But live with that clear life of perfect fire
> Which is to men the death of their desire.

For his moth, TSE rhymes 'the flame' and 'or shame', and compare 'the end of his desire' (TSE, 36).

9 (repeated in 10) a world too strange for: *Little Gidding* II 51, 69, has 'Too strange to each other for misunderstanding', and 'Between two worlds become much like each other'; this, in a section which (among much else) contemplates pride or shame, and praise and blame. Compare Pater, *The Poetry of Michelangelo*, *The Renaissance* (1873; 1910 edn, p.90): 'in a world too coarse', with 'strange' in the previous sentence.

12–13 star / For mirthless dance: compare Tennyson, *Maud*, I [xviii] 675, of the stars: 'Beat to the noiseless music of the night' (TSE, 5, 'beat', and 2, 'the night'). **mirthless dance**: compare Chaucer, *Parlement of Foules* 592: 'Daunseth he murye that is myrtheles'. **mirthless dance and . . . revel**: compare *Paradise Lost* IV 763–70: 'loveless, joyless', 'dance', and 'revels'; the passage also has 'wings' / TSE, 5; 'golden' / TSE, 7; and 'proud' / TSE, 9, 'pride'.

14 The French line: unidentified. **papillon noir**: in the plural, papillons noirs are dark thoughts. Littré: 'visions noires, idées lugubres; locution tirée de ces paroles de Patelin feignant le délire: "Ma femme, chasse, chasse ces papillons noirs, qui volent autour de moi", BRUEYS, *Avocat Patelin*, II, 3.' For a link of this French idiom with fierce burning, compare *Madame Bovary*, the penultimate paragraph of Part I, when she throws her wedding bouquet into the fire: 'Elle le regarda brûler [. . .] et les corolles de papier, racornies, se balançant le long de la plaque comme des papillons noirs, enfin s'envolèrent par la cheminée'. 'racornies': hardened as horn (in the flames); compare TSE, 35, the 'horns' of fire.

15 **The tropic odours**: since the 'odours' here derive from *Paradise Lost* (see the next note), compare *Paradise Lost* X 675: 'the Tropic Crab'. **odours of your name**: compare *Romeo and Juliet*, II ii 44–5 (this First Quarto reading has proved popular):

> That which we call a rose
> By any other name would smell as sweet.

15–16 **odours . . . Mozambique**: compare *Paradise Lost* IV 160–2:

> past
> Mozambic, off at sea north-east winds blow
> Sabaean odours from the spicy shore

Mozambique: French, as when the last word of TSE's *Mélange Adultère de Tout*, rhyming with 'Afrique'. **Nicobar**: the Nicobar Islands, in the Bay of Bengal, are often mentioned in Frazer, *The Golden Bough*; compare *The Scapegoat* (1913), ix 201–2, with TSE, whose evil, waters, flame, and flight have counterparts in the Nicobar Islanders' ritual: 'The demon-laden barks being now launched, the women threw ashes from the shore, and the whole crowd shouted, saying, "Fly away, devil, fly away, never come again!" ' On TSE and Frazer, whom he studied at Harvard, see Robert Crawford, *The Savage and the City*; and TSE, *A Prediction in Regard to Three English Authors* (*Vanity Fair*, Feb. 1924). Compare the sequence 'tropic', 'From Mozambique to Nicobar', with Corbière, the last stanza of *Le Novice en partance et sentimental* (1873) 110: 'Du Tropique ou Noukahiva'. Compare, taken from Corbière, TSE's *Mélange Adultère de Tout*, which has as a rhyme-word, not 'Nicobar', but 'Omaha': 'De Damas jusqu'à Omaha'. Note also Kipling's 'from Novastoshnah to Lukannon', in a passage which brings together (like TSE) in a fire-dance at night, flame and oil and water: 'That night Kotick danced the Fire-dance with the yearling seals. The sea is full of fire on summer nights all the way down from Novastoshnah to Lukannon, and each seal leaves a wake like burning oil behind him' (*The White Seal*, *The Jungle Book*, 1894). Compare Coleridge, *The Ancient Mariner* 128–30:

> The death-fires danced at night;
> The water, like a witch's oils,
> Burnt green, and blue, and white.

15, 17 **name . . . teeth of flame**: Wilde rhymes 'teeth of flame' with 'name', *The Ballad of Reading Gaol* (1898) VI 4–6.

15, 20–1 **name . . . in little corners / Whimper**: compare *Maud*, I [vi] 261: 'And my own sad name in corners cried'.

17–18 **the ragged teeth of . . . upon the waters**: compare Symons, *Giovanni Malatesta at Rimini* (1906) 14–16:

> he saw
> The ragged teeth of the sharp Apennines

Shut on the sea;

Symons's poem is about Paolo and Francesca (see 3 note, above), and therefore desire and flames. **flame / Like perfumed**: compare *Maud*, I [xviii] 622: 'perfumed altar-flame', with 'delight' two lines later. TSE has 'delight' (23), and his 'acolyte' (32) would attend upon an altar. **flame . . . perfumed . . . upon the waters**: compare *Antony and Cleopatra*, II ii 195–200:

> The barge she sat in, like a burnished throne,
> Burned on the water. The poop was beaten gold;
> Purple the sails, and so perfumèd that
> The winds were love-sick with them; the oars were silver,
> Which to the tune of flutes kept stroke, and made
> The water which they beat to follow faster,

TSE has 'golden' (7), 'beat' (5), and 'faster' (24). He later refashioned Enobarbus's speech, both in *Burbank with a Baedeker: Bleistein with a Cigar* 11–12:

> Her shuttered barge
> Burned on the water all the day.

and in *The Waste Land* [II] 77–8:

> The Chair she sat in, like a burnished throne,
> Glowed on the marble,

perfumed oil: 'perfumed oils', in a poem which TSE admired, Sir Edwin Arnold's *The Light of Asia* (1879), Book the Fourth, p.83. **upon the waters**: as twice in Tennyson, *Enoch Arden* 590, 592, describing the tropical island (TSE, 15, 'tropic'). Shelley has in the one stanza of *The Revolt of Islam* [XII] 4611, 4607–8: 'A shadow, which was light, upon the waters shed', with 'golden' / TSE, 7; 'strange and star-bright' / TSE, 9, 10 and 11, 'strange'; 12 and 27, 'star'; and 'odour' / TSE, 15, 'odours'.

18–19 oil upon the waters . . . secret: combining pouring oil upon (troubled) waters, with Ecclesiastes 11:1: 'Cast thy bread upon the waters', and with Proverbs 9:17: 'Stolen waters are sweet, And bread eaten in secret is pleasant'.

20–1 Children's voices in little corners / Whimper whimper: compare *Prufrock's Pervigilium* 5: 'I heard the children whimpering in corners'. For children's voices elsewhere in TSE, see *First Caprice in North Cambridge* 4 note. Given the fire, compare Moloch's cruelty, *Paradise Lost* I 395: 'Their children's cries unheard, that passed through fire'.

22, 24 what disaster do you warn us . . . Dance fast dance faster: compare Symons's poem from Verlaine, *Colombine* (1913) 28–9:

> O tell me toward what
> Disaster unthought

– with 'speed' as the immediately preceding word, and 'Leads this dance' in 35.

23 Agony nearest to delight: the one word nearest to the other in John Davidson's *Insomnia* (1905) 10–11:

> The Seraph at his head was Agony;
> Delight, more terrible, stood at his feet.

Compare *The Love Song of St. Sebastian* 6: 'And torture and delight', likewise rhyming with 'night'.

24–5 Dance fast dance faster . . . mortal disaster: compare Poe, *The Raven* 63–4:

> whom unmerciful Disaster
> Followed fast and followed faster

Poe, 79, 'perfume' / TSE, 18, 'perfumed'. (TSE: 'And yet one cannot be sure that one's own writing has *not* been influenced by Poe. I can name positively certain poets whose work has influenced me, I can name others whose work, I am sure, has not; there may be still others of whose influence I am unaware, but whose influence I might be brought to acknowledge; but about Poe I shall never be sure.' *From Poe to Valéry*, 1948, *TCTC*, p.27.) Compare also Christina G. Rossetti, *Brother Bruin* (1888) 22–5:

> He danced indeed, but danced in dudgeon,
> Capered in fury fast and faster:–
> Ah, could he once but hug his master
> And perish in one joint disaster!

Compare (given 'mortal') *Five-Finger Exercises* IV: *Lines to Ralph Hodgson Esqre.* 5–7:

> Which, just at a word from his master
> Will follow you faster and faster
> And tear you limb from limb.

25 no mortal: compare Shelley, *Alastor* 640: 'no mortal pain'; *The Revolt of Islam* [VII] 2998: 'no mortal fears'. **disaster:** alert to the etymology, from *astrum*, a star ('your hidden star', 27).

28 but not with human: compare *Paradise Lost* IX 561: 'I knew, but not with human voice endued'. TSE, 20, 'voices'.

30 Within the circle of my brain: compare *Hamlet*, I v 103: 'Within the book and volume of my brain', with 'globe' six lines earlier.

32 acolyte: *OED* 1: '*Eccl.* An inferior officer in the church who [. . .] performed subordinate duties, as lighting and bearing candles, etc'. The candle-duties are stressed throughout the *OED* instances, and are crucial to TSE's poem. Given 'star' both earlier and later in the poem, perhaps 'acolyte' reflects *OED* 2c: 'An attendant star', 1876. Compare TSE's poem and the juxtaposition within the one line, 'The martyr, the wan acolyte', in Browning, *Johannes Agricola in Meditation* 53; Browning's poem has 'waves of flame' (compare TSE, 17–18) and 'broken-' (52; compare TSE, 40), and it twice mentions 'stars' and twice a 'star' (TSE, 12, 39). **of pain:** Swinburne, *Dolores* (1866), concluding every other stanza of the fifty-five: 'Our Lady of Pain'.

34 **The singèd reveller:** compare Arnold, *The Strayèd Reveller* (1849). **reveller:** compare Young, *Night Thoughts* IX 679–80:
> For other ends they shine,
> Than to light revellers from shame to shame,

Compare the 'star' in TSE (39), and 'end' (36), 'shame' (9).

34, 37 **fire . . . loss:** compare 1 Corinthians 3:15: 'If any man's work shall be burned, he shall suffer loss: but he himself shall be saved; yet so as by fire.'

35 **Caught on those horns:** many kinds of horn: (i) because of 'toss', those of a bull. (ii), with 'caught', 1 Kings 2:28: 'and caught hold on the horns of the altar'. (iii) the horns of the monster, Daniel 7:7, and Revelation 17:16: 'And the ten horns which thou sawest upon the beast, these shall hate the whore, and shall make her desolate and naked, and shall eat her flesh, and burn her with fire.' (TSE, 34–5, 'fire . . . horns', and 38, 'burn'.) The passage in Revelation has 'golden' (TSE, 7), and 'strength' (TSE, 33, 'strong'). (iv) Dante, *Inferno* XXVI 85, quoted by TSE (*Dante*, 1929, *SE*, pp.247–8): 'So Ulysses, unseen in the hornèd wave of flame,
> *Lo maggior corno della fiamma antica* [. . .]
> *The greater horn of the ancient flame*'
(TSE gives the Temple Classics translation.) Given 'whiter flames' (38), compare Keats, *The Fall of Hyperion* I 237–8:
> I looked upon the altar, and its horns
> Whitened with ashes, and its languorous flame,

36–7 **the end of his desire:** compare Dante, *Paradiso* XXXIII 46: 'al fine di tutti i disii'. Also *Paradise Lost* VIII 417: 'the cause of his desire' (414 has 'human' / TSE, 28). **the end of his desire / Desires completion:** compare Tennyson, *The Gardener's Daughter* 232–4:
> That my desire, like all strongest hopes,
> By its own energy fulfilled itself,
> Merged in completion?

TSE has 'strong' (33). **completion:** *OED* 1b: 'Accomplishment, fulfilment (of a prophecy, wish, etc.)'. **desire / Desires:** Luke 22:15: 'With desire I have desired'. With the succession 'desire / Desires' (rhyming with 'fire', in martyrdom), compare Christina G. Rossetti, *A Martyr* (1881) 34: 'Thy Will I will, I Thy desire desire'. Elements of TSE's lines recur in the drafts of *Little Gidding* III and IV: 'the death of desire', with (two lines later) 'completion'; and 'The culmination of desire', rhyming – as here – with 'fire'. (Helen Gardner, *The Composition of Four Quartets*, pp.198, 213.)

37–8 Desires . . . whiter flames that burn: compare Symons, *The Armenian Dancer* 16–18:

> I dance, and as I dance
> Desires as fires burn white
> To fan the flame delight;

(TSE, *The Burnt Dancer*.) Symons, 2, 'ends' / TSE, 36, 'end'; Symons, 35, 'grave' / TSE, 28; Symons, 7, 'flight' as rhyme / TSE, 4; and see the note to 3, 5.

38–9 strayed . . . vagrant: describing birds (another, albeit different, 'beat of wings'), compare Pope, *Odyssey* II 212: 'Vagrants of air, and unforeboding stray'. **vagrant . . . star:** compare Kipling, *Dedication* to *Barrack-Room Ballads* (1892) 2: 'vagrant star-dust'. Kipling's next two lines have: 'our world. // They are purged of pride'; compare TSE, 9, 'world too strange for pride'. TSE included the Dedication in his *Choice of Kipling's Verse*.

38, 40 burn not . . . return not: characteristic of Swinburne, who has, for instance, as rhymes 'know not' / 'flow not' / 'grow not' (*Anima Anceps*, 1866, 9–11); 'falls not' / 'calls not' (*A Forsaken Garden*, 1878, 25–7); 'close not' / 'knows not' (*In Memory of Barry Cornwall*, 1878, 19–21); 'bent not' / 'lent not', 'give not' / 'forgive not', 'care not' / 'were not', 'give not' / 'live not' (*A Song in Season*, 1878, stanzas x, xiv–xv, xx).

40 broken guest: compare the opening of Donne's *The Relic*:

> When my grave is broke up again
> Some second guest to entertain,

TSE returned to this opening stanza: *Reflections on Contemporary Poetry: I, The Egoist* (Sept. 1917); *The Metaphysical Poets* (1921, *SE*, p.283); the Clark Lectures (1926, *VMP*, p.125).

41 O danse danse mon papillon noir!: compare 'chasse, chasse ces papillons noirs' (14 note, above).

First Debate between the Body and Soul

Dated Jan. 1910. Title: *Reflections in a Square* was added above the title and cancelled. *Debate* was written over an indecipherable word (possibly *Reflection* or *Reflections*); *First Debate* then added. With the cancelled title, compare *Entretien dans un parc*. Ronald Bush maintained that TSE 'was still thinking of going on with the "Debate" as late as March 1918' (*T. S. Eliot: A Study in Character and Style*, 1983, p.19), but this misinterprets TSE's 'my dialogue' in the letter Bush cites; TSE was referring to *Eeldrop and Appleplex*, published the previous year in the *Little Review*, in 'two parts', and this letter to Quinn (4 March 1918) distinguishes this (prose) from verse, 'if I do any verse': 'I have been very keenly interested in the success of *The Little Review*, and Pound's enthusiasm on the subject is infectious. I hope to continue my dialogue (not that I was at all satisfied with the first two parts), and if I do any verse Pound shall have it' (*Letters* i 223).

Compare Marvell, *A Dialogue between the Soul and Body*. On this literary kind, see Rosalie Osmond, *Mutual Accusation: Seventeenth-Century Body and Soul Dialogues in Their Literary and Theological Context* (1990). TSE's poem and Marvell's share some words (listed here in their order within TSE): 'blind[ed]', 'square', 'Forced' / 'forces', 'to endure' (TSE, 'Forced to endure' / Marvell, 'Constrained not only to endure'), 'trees', 'dies' / 'die', 'eye', 'will not react' / 'will not forgo', 'physical' / 'physic', 'Here's' (variant) / 'Here', 'soul', 'fear', and 'Standing' / 'stands'.

TSE called his poem not a dialogue but a debate. Compare *Bacchus and Ariadne: 2nd Debate between the Body and Soul*; *Silence* 6, on incidents 'debated'; and *Inside the gloom* 21: 'while the debate was rife'. In *First Debate*, the debating is muted, but the intercalated quatrains all ending with 'our sensations' create an antiphonal effect such as is characteristic of many a debate-poem by Laforgue (for whom the relations of body to soul are a recurrent concern), for instance his *Complainte des printemps* (1885) where there is a play of longer lines against five compact quatrains all rhyming on the same termination (the first runs: 'sirène' / 'haleine' / 'verveine' / 's'amène'). The other (varied) refrain in TSE, 'The street pianos through the trees', suggests the similar return of the rhyming couplets on 'ritournelles' in Laforgue's *Complainte des pianos qu'on entend dans les quartiers aisés* (1885); the opening of Laforgue's poem asks the pianos to lead the soul:

Menez l'âme que les Lettres ont bien nourrie,
Les pianos, les pianos, dans les quartiers aisés!

– to lead the soul into what becomes a debate between the body and soul; compare the juxtaposition of 'the soul' and 'pianos' in TSE, 29–31. Laforgue has (in the order within TSE) 'nos étranges rues' ('the street', TSE, 1); 'pure' and 'pur' (TSE, 15, 40); 'l'Idéal' ('The pure Idea' and 'idealist', TSE, 15, 36); and 'pauvres' ('Poor', TSE, 33). Another poem by Laforgue is behind TSE's 44–5 (see the note). Laforgue has *Complainte des débats mélancoliques et littéraires* (1885), but this is not antiphonal.

See Anne Holmes, *Jules Laforgue and Poetic Innovation* (1993), p.74, on Laforgue's *Avant-dernier mot* (1890): 'The form of the poem clearly builds on the counterpoint technique developed in the *Complaintes*: a third voice offers comments on the central debate, which is expressed in the poem's disyllabic quatrains.' Also compare with TSE's quatrains the observation by Holmes, p.162: 'The "quatrain populaire" was the only regular element that Laforgue intended to retain in his free verse, and in many of the *Derniers Vers* he quite simply transposes quatrains from the *Fleurs*.'

In 1933, TSE said of Laforgue: 'What he wants, of course, is some way of salvation in which both the mind and the feelings, the soul and the body, shall cooperate towards fulness of life' (*VMP*, p.285).

TSE persistently put his mind to the soul and the body. Compare *La Figlia Che Piange* 11–12:

As the soul leaves the body torn and bruised,
As the mind deserts the body it has used.

In *La Figlia* 18, 23, there is the internal rhyming 'imagination' / 'cogitations'; compare TSE's refrain.

In his copy of Charles Bakewell, *Source Book in Ancient Philosophy* (1907, pp.241–2, Houghton Library), TSE underlined in the account of Aristotle the remark that the 'soul may be regarded as a sort of form and idea'; the previous sentence had spoken of 'our sensation', and on the next page TSE jotted down six terms, including sensation and Imagination. Compare the poem's refrain 'Imaginations' (and 'Imagination's') / 'our sensations', and its 'Idea' (15, 40).

TSE's Clark Lectures in 1926 were devoted to body and soul. In his edition (*VMP*, p.114), Ronald Schuchard quotes TSE's annotation in his Plotinus (*Enneades*, ed. R. Volkmann, 1883; Hayward Bequest), on the fourth Ennead: 'He looks at soul 1st as possessed of faculties wh. refer to sensible world (Aristotle) 2 as rising above the world to union with God [. . .] Plotinus is a two substance man as against Aristotle's reduction of the soul to functions of the body.' TSE on the last twelve lines of Donne's *The Ecstasy*: 'Here is posited, as clearly as may be, a distinction, a disjunction, between soul and body of which I think you will find no expression whatever in the *trecento*, and for which I do not think you will find much authority in Aquinas' (*VMP*, p.112). Again on *The Ecstasy*: Aquinas 'would in no case accept anything like the virtual *duplication* of the human animal effected in the poem of Donne, into two beings, one called the soul and the other called the body, whose only essential difference is that one is admirable and the other slightly shameful' (*VMP*, p.113). 'The separation of soul and body in this way is a modern conception; the only ancient parallel that occurs to me is the attitude of Plotinus toward the body as quoted by Porphyry; and in the form employed by Donne represents a far cruder state of philosophical speculation than that of Aquinas' (*VMP*, p.114).

In creating his *First Debate between the Body and Soul*, TSE may have been thinking not only of Donne and Marvell but of another seventeenth-century poet of whom he wrote in the year of the Clark Lectures, 1926: Sir John Davies. 'The poem of *Nosce Teipsum* is a long discussion in verse of the nature of the soul and its relation to the body.' As to Davies's theories, 'it is evident that we cannot take them very seriously' (*OPP*, p.133).

The Dantesque section of *Little Gidding* (II) is in some ways a re-imagination of *First Debate*, and constitutes TSE's *last* 'debate between the body and soul' ('As body and soul begin to fall asunder', *LG* II 81), encountering an old man in the street ('A blind old man', even, given the presence of Milton and of Joyce within the 'familiar compound ghost'); and in its MS drafts, *Little Gidding* shares much with the early poem. (For MS details, see Helen Gardner, *The Composition of Four Quartets*, pp.172–95.) *First Debate* 1: 'The August wind is shambling down the street' / *Little Gidding* II 35: 'the urban dawn wind'. *First Debate* 5: 'patience' / *LG* II prose draft: 'impatience'. *First Debate* 6: 'The withered leaves' / *LG* II 30: 'the dead leaves'. *First Debate* 12 and *LG* II prose draft: 'turpitude'. *First Debate* 15: 'pure' / *LG* II 74: 'purify'. *First Debate* 15: 'dies' / *LG* II variant: 'dying'. *First Debate* 22: 'The eye' / *LG* II 42: 'The eyes'. *First Debate* 25 and *LG* II prose draft: 'fact'. *First Debate* 26 and *LG* II 78: 'sense'. *First Debate* 39: 'a shabby square' / *LG* II variant: 'the shabby road'. *First Debate* 41 and *LG* II prose draft: 'nature'. A variant of *LG* II 76 has 'Reflect'; the cancelled title for *First Debate* was *Reflections in a Square*. A memory of the quatrains rhyming on -ations may have contributed to *Little Gidding* II, where the MS drafts have – as line-endings – 'revelation', 'observation', 'desolation', 'expectation', and 'salutation'. (Plus, within lines, the plural 'desolations', and 'precipitation', 'preparation'.) The only such ending in the final version of *Little Gidding* II, 'laceration', was suggested by John Hayward (Gardner, p.193), but TSE had had the sound running in his head.

Coming between *First Debate* and *Little Gidding* is another poem about an old man, *A Song for Simeon*; compare the -ations rhymes in *First Debate* with the crucial line-endings in *A Song for Simeon*: 'lamentation' / 'desolation' / 'consolation' / 'generation' / 'salvation'.

2–3 A blind old man who coughs and spits sputters / Stumbling among the alleys and the gutters: compare *Prufrock's Pervigilium* 30–1:
> [A blind old drunken man who sings and mutters,
> With broken boot heels stained in many gutters]

blind . . . man . . . Stumbling . . . the gutters: compare *The Education of Henry Adams*, ch.xxv: 'one fumbled over it as feebly as ever. In such labyrinths, the staff is a force almost more necessary than the legs; the pen becomes a sort of blind-man's dog, to keep him from falling into the gutters'. *First Debate* anticipates somewhat a paragraph by TSE on a blind man who sang, Milton: 'Had Milton been a man of very keen senses – I mean of *all* the five senses – his blindness would not have mattered so much. But for a man whose sensuousness, such as it was, had been withered early by book-learning, and whose gifts were naturally aural, it mattered a great deal' – this followed at once by two mentions of 'visual imagination' (*Milton I*, 1936, *OPP*, p.139). Compare *First Debate*: 'withered', 'sensations', 'Imaginations', 'sense'.

2–4 old man . . . Stumbling . . . the gutters. // He pokes: compare *Gerontion* 14–15:

> poking the peevish gutter.
>
> I an old man,

5 With senile patience: compare *Paradise Lost* II 569: 'With stubborn patience' (in Hell).

5, 7 With senile patience . . . sensations: given 'gutters' in 3, compare *First Caprice in North Cambridge* 9–10: 'gutter with sordid patience', rhyming with 'considerations'. Similarly, *O lord, have patience* 1, 3 rhyming 'patience' / 'irritations'. *The Waste Land* [v] 330, 'With a little patience', takes up 'reverberation' (326). *How to Pick a Possum* 17, 19: 'stations' / 'patience' (*Noctes Binanianae*).

6–7 The withered leaves / Of our sensations: compare Hawthorne, in *Buds and Bird Voices* (*Mosses from an Old Manse*): 'On the soil of thought and in the garden of the heart, as well as in the sensual world, lie withered leaves – the ideas and feelings that we have done with.' (*TSE*, 15, 'Idea'.) Given TSE's 'August wind' (1), compare Shelley, *Ode to the West Wind* 64–5:

> Like withered leaves to quicken a new birth!
> And, by the incantation of this verse,

The sound of Shelley's 'incantation' may have assisted TSE's 'sensations' (and 'Imaginations', etc., in the quatrains). Compare also, for the syntax of TSE's six words, Byron, *Don Juan*, IX [lxxv] 598–9:

> the languid rout
>
> Of our Sensations.

sensations: compare *Easter: Sensations of April*. The word has a wide range; compare perhaps, in this poem's pondering of imagination, Bergson, *Essai sur les données immédiates de la conscience* (1888): 'Si l'art qui ne donne que des sensations est un art inférieur, c'est que l'analyse ne démêle pas souvent dans une sensation autre chose que cette sensation même'; this has its affinity with 'Imaginations / Masturbations' (18–19). Bergson's *Matière et mémoire* (1896) had as subtitle *Essai sur la relation du corps à l'esprit*.

6, 9 withered leaves . . . vacant square: compare *Preludes I* 7–8:

> Of withered leaves about your feet
> And newspapers from vacant lots;

Usual enough, 'withered leaves', yet perhaps recalling not only Shelley (see 6–7 note) but Keats, *Endymion* II 564–5, 'throw / Himself on withered leaves', because Keats has in the previous line 'blind' (TSE, 2, 10), and has two lines later 'muttered' (TSE, 2, variant, 'mutters').

8 **devoted to the pure idea**: compare *Inside the gloom* 12: 'Explained the Pure Idea'. Remy de Gourmont was devoted to, and explained, the pure idea. In *La Dissociation des idées*, he wrote: 'il y a des gens qui se dévouent à l'Idée'. He analysed 'l'idée pure, une, et par conséquent inattaquable', 'l'idée pure de liberté comme l'idée pure de justice'. 'L'idée pure est plus ou moins contaminée par le souci des intérêts personnels'. 'L'idée de beauté n'est pas une idée pure; elle est intimement unie à l'idée de plaisir charnel.' In *Du Style ou de l'écriture*: 'Une bonne analyse des procédés naturels du style commencerait à la sensation pour aboutir à l'idée pure – si pure qu'elle ne correspond à rien, non seulement de réel, mais de figuratif' (*La Culture des idées*, 1901). This, like de Gourmont's belief that the idea is an image that has gone dead, contributed to TSE, 15, 'The pure Idea dies of inanition'. The pure form of what is quizzed within these two early poems may be glimpsed in TSE's translation of St.-J. Perse, *Anabasis* 1: 'and the idea pure as salt' ('et l'idée pure comme un sel').

9–10 **in the vacant square . . . blind**: compare D. G. Rossetti's translation of Cavalcanti, *To Guido Orlandi: Sonnet, Of a Consecrated Image* 8–9:
> Over the curse of blindness she prevails,
> And heals sick languors in the public squares.

TSE assigned some translations of Italian sonnets from Rossetti's *The Early Italian Poets* for his 1918 tutorial class. **vacant square . . . stare**: TSE's contribution to *Gala Day London* (1953) was an eight-line poem, facing a photograph of a cat on a park bench, ending:
> The Sage, disposed to sit and stare
> With a vacant mind in a vacant square.

10 **inconscient**: adapting Laforgue; see *Afternoon* 9 note.

11–12 **exude / The odour**: *ex-sudare*, 'To ooze out like sweat' (*OED*). Compare *Lune de Miel* 4: 'La sueur aestivale, et une forte odeur'.

12 **turpitude**: given the '-ations' rhyming refrain, compare *Choruses from 'The Rock'* v: 'these abominations, the turpitudes'. The word 'turpitude' has a markedly sexual emphasis in French; compare Remy de Gourmont: marriage as 'la bonté de Dieu à la turpitude humaine', and 'La vieille opposition entre la virginité et la turpitude' (*La Morale de l'amour, La Culture des idées*). Also Flaubert, *Bouvard et Pécuchet*, ch.VII, where 'sa turpitude' reveals itself in syphilis, 'une maladie secrète'.

13 **And a street piano through the dusty trees**: compare *First Caprice in North Cambridge* 1: 'A street-piano, garrulous and frail'. (See the note there.) *Portrait of a Lady* II 39–40:

> when a street-piano, mechanical and tired
> Reiterates some worn-out common song

The street piano is reiterated in *First Debate between the Body and Soul* (13, 16, 31, 46). **dusty trees**: compare, at the line-end, *The Waste Land* [III] 292: 'Trams and dusty trees'.

15 **The pure Idea dies of inanition**: see 8 note. Compare the close of the translation from a prose poem by Louis Bertrand in Stuart Merrill's *Pastels in Prose* (1890), p.18: 'the salamander died of inanition'. TSE owned a copy of *Pastels in Prose* (Houghton Library), and referred to it in *The Borderline of Prose* (*New Statesman*, 19 May 1917); he was interested in Merrill as an American who had become a French symbolist poet (*Paris Review* 21, Spring/Summer 1959, p.56). In an essay on ethics (Houghton Library; bMS Am 1691.14 (32), p.1), TSE wrote: 'Idealism, having sold his mess of pottage for a birth-right, is perhaps beginning to show signs of inanition; and it is possible too that materialism, toughened by an age of lusty beggary, will fall upon his brother and leave him naked.' (*First Debate* has its relations to age, lusty beggary, idealism – 'complete idealist', 36 – and materialism, 'The emphatic mud of physical sense', 26; see also 49 note.) Given TSE's reference to the 'brain' (23), compare Bergson, *L'Evolution créatrice* (1907), ch.II: 'C'est un fait remarquable que, chez des animaux morts de faim, on trouve le cerveau à peu près intact'; with note: 'Récemment, des observations analogues ont été faites sur un homme mort d'inanition'. Emerson's *Blight* (1847) begins:

> Give me truths;
> For I am weary of the surfaces,
> And die of inanition.

Blight is apt to TSE's poem. *Blight* 23, 'The old men' / TSE, 2, 'A blind old man'. *Blight* 36, 'And haughtily return us stare for stare' / TSE, 10, 'Forced to endure the blind inconscient stare'. *Blight* 50, 'The stunted trees' / TSE, 13, 'the dusty trees'. Emerson might be judged 'A supersubtle peasant / (Conception most unpleasant)' (37–8), 'Regarding nature' (41).

18 **Imaginations**: in the plural like this (but see the textual note above), faintly French, but also Biblical and Shakespearean, where it is often dark. *Merry Wives of Windsor*, IV ii 138–9: 'you must pray, and not follow the imaginations of your own heart'. *Hamlet*, III ii 81–2: 'And my imaginations are as foul / As Vulcan's stithy'. *King Lear*, IV vi 283: 'wrong imaginations'.

18–19 **Imaginations / Masturbations**: Byron's letter (to John Murray, 9 Nov. 1820) about such a rhyming relation in Keats's poetry used to be printed in an expurgated text: 'such writing is a sort of mental **** [masturbation] – [he is always] ******** [f—gg—g] his *Imagination*.—I don't mean [that] he is *indecent*, but viciously soliciting his own ideas into a state' (*Letters and Journals*, ed. R. E. Prothero, V, 1901, 117; what was then omitted is here supplied from Leslie Marchand's *Byron's Letters and Journals*, vii, 1977, 225). Contrast 'the pure Idea' in 15. In a letter to Aiken, 19 July 1914, TSE makes play with 'Dr. Hans Frigger (the celebrated poet)' (*Letters* i 42). **Masturbations**: for the rhyme, compare one of the Columbo verses (Appendix A):

> On Sunday morning after prayers
> They took their recreation
> The crew assembled on the deck
> And practiced masturbation.

Compare *The Death of Saint Narcissus* 24–7:

> Then he knew that he had been a fish
> With slippery white belly held tight in his own fingers,
> Writhing in his own clutch, his ancient beauty
> Caught fast in the pink tips of his new beauty.

23, 25 The . . . brain . . . dull: compare Keats, *Ode to a Nightingale* 34: 'the dull brain'. *Five-Finger Exercises I: Lines to a Persian Cat* 4: 'the dull brain'. (See the cat in 9–10 note.)

27 The cosmic smudge of an enormous thumb: twice to be compared with Henry James. (i) *The American Scene* (1907), pp.31–2, on *New England: An Autumn Impression*: 'Charming places, charming objects, languish, all round him, under designations that seem to leave on them the smudge of a great vulgar thumb – which is precisely a part of what the pleading land appears to hint to you when it murmurs, in autumn, its intelligent refrain.' TSE's 'withered leaves' suggest autumn (despite his 'August'), and his poem both has and hears a refrain. (ii) *Siena Early and Late* (which coloured the opening of *Prufrock's Pervigilium*, lines also in *The Love Song of J. Alfred Prufrock*): 'the month of August; a spectacle that I am far from speaking of as the finest flower of my old and perhaps even a little faded cluster of impressions, but which smudges that special sojourn as with the big thumb-mark [. . .].' (TSE, 1, 'August'; 2, 'old'.) Further, James on this same page (*Italian Hours*, 1909, p.364) mentions a 'square', 'patience' and 'position'; as TSE, 9, 5, 14. Compare TSE's cadence, 'The cosmic smudge of an enormous thumb', with Shelley, *The Cyclops* 376: 'The knotty limbs of an enormous oak' ('through the trees', TSE, 16, 31, 46), especially as 'limbs' sometimes has masturbatory connections (*The Death of Saint Narcissus* 9: 'made him aware of his limbs smoothly passing each other'; see 18 note).

29 the sanctuary of the soul (variant): compare *At Graduation 1905* 49: 'For in the sanctuaries of the soul'. Compare Samuel Rogers, *The Sleeping Beauty* 15–16:

> And may the secret of thy soul
> Remain within its sanctuary!

Rogers's poem is in *The Golden Treasury*.

32–3 Imagination's / Poor Relations: *Rhapsody on a Windy Night* 4, 6, rhymes 'incantations' and 'clear relations'. See Bradley on 'The relation of body to soul' in 36–7 note. Henry James, devotee of city squares, has both 'poor relation' and 'imagination' in the second paragraph of *The Beast in the Jungle* (1903). **poor relation:** *OED*, under 'poor' 8: 'relative or kinsman in humble circumstances (also *transf.*)'; from 1720.

33, 35 Relations . . . our sensations: in his copy of T. H. Green's *Prolegomena to Ethics* (1906, p.30, Houghton Library), TSE marked the first two sentences of this from Green: 'A sensation is the unalterable effect of its conditions, whatever those conditions may be. It is unalterably related to other sensations. Our opinion about its conditions or relations may vary, but not the conditions or relations themselves, or the sensation determined by them.'

36–7 Absolute! . . . supersubtle: together with the refrain's 'Imaginations' (and 'Imagination's'), compare TSE: 'The Absolute, we find, does not fall within any of the classes of objects: it is neither real nor unreal nor imaginary. But I do not think that supersubtle defence is necessary' (*KEPB*, p.169). Ch.XXIII of Bradley's *Appearance and Reality* is *Body and Soul* (compare TSE's title): 'The relation of body to soul presents a problem which experience seems to show is really not soluble. And I may say at once that I accept and endorse this result [. . .] For body and soul are mere appearances' (1893; 1897 edn, p.261). **Absolute! complete idealist . . . peasant:** compare Symons, in *The Symbolist Movement in Literature* (p.53), on Villiers de l'Isle-Adam: 'Villiers was too sincere an idealist, too absolute in his idealism, to hesitate'; a dozen lines earlier, Symons adduces 'a peasant'.

37, 39 A supersubtle peasant: compare *Othello*, I iii 352: 'a super-subtle Venetian'. Henry James is very fond of 'supersubtle'. In 1926 TSE twice invoked the word: 'Donne, or a supersubtle heroine of one of Racine's tragedies'; 'I am not presenting Marino as a supersubtle Italian who led the simple Englishman Crashaw astray' (*VMP*, pp.88, 177–8). **supersensitive** (variant): compare two cognate forms: Tennyson, *Merlin and Vivien* 107: 'a supersensual sensual bond'; and TSE in 1926, 'a supersensuous experience', 'many super-sensuous feelings' (*VMP*, pp.120, 133).

38 No conception (variant): as in *Othello*, III iv 157.

40 Assist me: given 'love' (41), and 'fact' (25) rhyming with 'react', compare Shakespeare, *The Rape of Lucrece* 349–51:
> The powers to whom I pray abhor this fact;
> How can they then assist me in the act? //
> Then Love and Fortune be my gods,

Given TSE's preoccupations here and in others of these poems, and his next line

('Regarding nature without love or fear'), compare Wordsworth, *Maternal Grief*
11–12:
> Death, life, and sleep, reality and thought,
> Assist me, God, their boundaries to know,

42–3 **a little while / Standing**: compare Wordsworth, *Nutting* 21: 'A little while I
stood' (Wordsworth, 18, 'withered leaves', as four times in TSE; Wordsworth,
25, 'the trees' / TSE, 46).

42, 44 **a little while . . . life . . . a smile**: compare Shelley, *Rosalind and Helen* 315–7:
> My father lived a little while,
> But all might see that he was dying,
> He smiled with such a woeful smile!

(Compare, Shelley, three lines earlier, 'I walked about like a corpse alive', with,
for instance, *The Little Passion* (ii) 7–8: ' "I feel / As if I'd been a long time
dead" '.)   **a little while, a little while**: the second and third quatrains of Philip
Bourke Marston's *After* (1875) both begin: 'A little while'.

44 **Till life evaporates into a smile**: compare *Opera* 12: 'Life departs with a feeble
smile'. When life evaporates into a smile it suggests Lewis Carroll's Cheshire Cat,
especially given the title *Inventions of the March Hare*; compare *Morning at the
Window* 8–9:
> An aimless smile that hovers in the air
> And vanishes along the level of the roofs.

44–5 **a smile / Simple and profound**: compare *La Figlia Che Piange* 16: 'Simple and
faithless as a smile', and *Mr. Apollinax* 8: 'His laughter was submarine and
profound'. Laforgue, *La vie qu'elles me font mener* (1890) 11–12, has, in
addition and adjacent, the suggestion of 'a little while' (TSE, 42):
> tant que l'Amour
> S'échange par le temps qui court,
> Simple et sans foi comme un bonjour,

Emile Verhaeren ended *L'Attente*, on the spirit and the world:
> Et réunir notre esprit et le monde,
> Dans les deux mains d'une très simple loi profonde.

This volume of Verhaeren's, *Les Visages de la vie* (1899), was listed among TSE's
books in 1934.

49 **Defecations**: in an essay on ethics (Houghton Library; bMS Am 1691.14 (31),
p.19), TSE wrote: 'Mind in this pure and defecated state is a figment; and true as
these laws may be of mind, they are not true of the world as *I* experience it, at
least, for this world contains many things besides mind, and it does not even
contain mind unadulterated.' Compare this poem's concern with 'the Pure Idea'
and with imagination. Similarly TSE's essay on metaphysics (Houghton Library;

(30), p.3): 'the world would be pure form defecated of particularity'. TSE has 'defecate' in an account of the imagination, to Robert Nichols, 8 Aug. 1917: 'I am not anxious to write more – or rather I feel that the best promise of continuing is for one to be able to forget, in a way, what one has written already; to be able to detach it completely from one's present self and begin quite afresh, with only the technical experience preserved. This struggle to preserve the advantages of practice and at the same time to defecate the emotions one has expressed already is one of the hardest I know' (*Letters* i 191). Similarly in an interview for the *Yorkshire Post* in Aug. 1961: 'I think that what stimulates me to write a poem is that I have something inside me that I want to get rid of. I have to get it out. It is almost a kind of defecation, if you like' (*The Bed Post*, ed. Kenneth Young, 1962, p.44). The word 'defecations' possibly sets against the excremental the redemptive, in the theological sense, *OED* 2: 'Purification of the mind or soul from what is gross or low'; 1649, Jeremy Taylor: 'A defecation of his faculties and an opportunity of Prayer'. Compare Coleridge, *Reason*, two lines of which gained particular currency because Matthew Arnold quoted them, and applied them to one form of poetic achievement, in *On Translating Homer* I:

> Coleridge says, in his strange language, speaking of the union of the human soul with the divine essence, that this takes place
>> Whene'er the mist, which stands 'twixt God and thee,
>> Defecates to a pure transparency;
> and so, too, it may be said of the translator with his original, which alone can produce a good translation, that it takes place when the mist which stands between them – the mist of alien modes of thinking, speaking, and feeling on the translator's part – 'defecates to a pure transparency,' and disappears.

Coleridge follows his quatrain with Dante's *Paradiso* I 88–90, invoking imagination:

> tu stesso, ti fai grosso
> Col falso immaginar, sì che non vedi
> Ciò che vedresti, se l'avessi scosso.

'Thou thyself makest thyself dense with false imagining, and so thou seest not what thou wouldst see, if thou hadst cast it off' (Temple Classics translation). **desquamations** (variant): this too with the possibility of something better, as not only *OED* 2: 'A coming off in scales or scaly patches', but also the more positive aspect of this 'removal of scales'; compare 'The scales are fallen from their eyes', in *Airs of Palestine, No.2* 39.

Bacchus and Ariadne: 2nd Debate between the Body and Soul

Dated Feb. 1911. TSE has written *Fragment* before the title. Title: Lemprière: 'According to some writers, Bacchus loved her [Ariadne] after Theseus had forsaken her, and he gave her a crown of seven stars, which, after her death, was made a constellation.' A. D. Moody suggested that the final stanza of *Sweeney Erect* 'may allude to a variant of Ariadne's tale, which has it that she did not die of a broken heart, but was loved by Bacchus' (*Thomas Stearns Eliot, Poet*, 1979, p.61). Robert Crawford linked this with the present poem, 'probably inspired by Titian's painting in the National Gallery. He [TSE] ticked this picture in his London *Baedeker* whose commentary singles it out for its great "exuberance" ' (*The Savage and the City*, p.108). In his Baedeker, *London and Its Environs* (1908, which he dated October the 14th, 1910), TSE read on p.175:

> *Titian*, Bacchus and Ariadne, painted in 1514 for Alphonso, Duke of Ferrara.
>
> 'This is one of the pictures which once seen can never be forgotten . . . Rich harmony of drapery tints and soft modelling, depth of shade and warm flesh all combine to produce a highly coloured glow; yet in the midst of this glow the form of Ariadne seems incomparably fair. Nature was never reproduced more kindly or with greater exuberance than it is in every part of this picture. What splendour in the contrasts of colour, what wealth and diversity of scale in air and vegetation; how infinite is the space – how varied yet mellow the gradations of light and shade!' (C. & C.) [Joseph Crowe and Giovanni Battista Cavalcaselle, *The Life and Times of Titian*, 1877, 2nd edn 1881.]

TSE's notes on Italy (Houghton Library, bMS Am 1691 (131); summer 1911, slightly later than this poem), on Venice, interior of the Palace of Doges: 'Only painting that I note is the Bacchus & Ariadne of Tintoretto. As near to feeling as T. ever came'. Subtitle: see *First Debate between the Body and Soul* and headnote.

1 **lives . . . like a wave**: compare Shelley, *Ode to the West Wind* 53–4:
> Oh, lift me as a wave, a leaf, a cloud!
> I fall upon the thorns of life!

like a wave: compare, at the line-end, Tennyson, *The Vision of Sin* 125: 'Rising, falling, like a wave'. Compare TSE in 1933, on Donne, *The Ecstasy* 2 ('A pregnant bank swelled up'): 'he means rather, "was swollen" or perhaps swells like a wave' (*VMP*, p.269).

1, 3 **their lives curl . . . wave . . . grave**: compare Ernest Dowson, *In a Breton Cemetery* (1899) 5–8:
> Beneath the long curled wave,
> So quiet a grave. //
> And they sleep well
> These peasant-folk, who told their lives away.

('told'; contrast 'never spoken', TSE, 4.) **curl . . . wave . . . break**: given 'resistant' (13), perhaps remodelled by TSE in *Eeldrop and Appleplex*: 'a wave of excitement curled into the street and broke', where the previous sentence has 'irresistible' (*Little Review* iv, May 1917, 7).

4 **tendencies unknown**: compare *The Engine 1*: 'ends unknown'.

5 **The drums of life were beating on their skulls**: TSE ended *The Beating of a Drum* (*Nation and Athenaeum*, 6 Oct. 1923): 'It is equally possible to assert that primitive man acted in a certain way and then found a reason for it. An unoccupied person, finding a drum, may be seized with a desire to beat it; but unless he is an imbecile he will be unable to continue beating it, and thereby satisfying a need (rather than a "desire"), without finding a reason for so doing. The reason may be the long continued drought. The next generation or the next civilization will find a more plausible reason for beating a drum. Shakespeare and Racine – or rather the developments which led up to them – each found his own reason. The reasons may be divided into tragedy and comedy. We still have similar reasons, but we have lost the drum.' Robert Crawford: 'The primitive ceremony which came soonest to Eliot's mind, whether in his "Beating of a Drum" or in 1926 when he spoke of savages who "believe [*may believe* Introduction to *Savonarola*] that the ritual is performed in order to induce a fall of rain", was rain-making, probably because he had read about it for his 1913 seminar paper. Frazer's *Dying God* describes rituals where drums are beaten to beg rain from heaven' (*The Savage and the City*, p.117). Note 'The floods' (6) and 'desert plains' (9). Given TSE's subtitle, compare perhaps Marvell, *A Dialogue between the Soul and Body* 6: 'Deaf with the drumming of an ear'.

5–6 **drums . . . in their brains**: compare *Portrait of a Lady* 1 32: 'Inside my brain a dull tom-tom begins'.

7, 9 **ring . . . annuls . . . railway-**: joining *ad nullum* ('to nothing') with *annulus*, a ring (*OED* 'annular': ringlike). The movement across to 'Like railway-engines' may have been suggested by the annular railway; R. L. Stevenson, *The Ebb-Tide* (1894), Part II ch.VII: 'like the embankment of an annular railway'. (The unexpected sight of an island-settlement soon gives the men the sense 'of a blow impending'; compare the next line in TSE: 'The world of contact sprang up like a blow'.) TSE praised *The Ebb-Tide* in his Harvard essay, March 1909, on Kipling (J. Donald Adams, *Copey of Harvard*, 1960, p.160), and had it among his books (*Letters* i 399).

8 **insights**: *OED* 2c, the plural, from Coleridge, 1817; 2d, *Psychol.*, 'the sudden perception of the solution to a problem or difficulty', from William James, 1909: 'insight-giving passion'.

9 **Like railway-engines over desert plains**: as very often in Kipling, for instance

'William the Conqueror' (1898): 'skirting the edge of the desert on a narrow-gauge railway'. Compare TSE on Stravinsky's music for *Sacre du Printemps*: 'it did seem to transfer the rhythms of the steppes into the scream of the motor horn, the rattle of machinery, the grind of wheels, the beating of iron and steel, the roar of the underground railway, and the other barbaric cries of modern life; and to transform these despairing noises into music' (*Dial*, Oct. 1921, p.48). The rites of spring had been suggested earlier in the poem, and the beating of iron recalls the beating of a drum; see 5–6 note. **over desert plains**: compare *The Waste Land* [v] 369: 'Over endless plains, stumbling in cracked earth'.

10 **The world of contact sprang up**: compare Tennyson, *In Memoriam* CXII 10, 15–16: 'Sprang up for ever at a touch':
   And world-wide fluctuation swayed
   In vassal tides that followed thought.
(With the fluctuation and tides, compare 'like a wave', 1; and 'swaying', 6.) **contact sprang up like a blow**: for a way in which contact may be like a blow, compare TSE's line of thought in 1926: 'Donne throughout his life was in contact with Jesuitism; directly in his early family life, later by his studies, and not least by his battle with the Jesuits. For you can hardly fight anyone for very long without employing his weapons and using his methods; and to fight a man with ideas means adapting your ideas to his mind. Conflict is contact' (*VMP*, p.89).

11 **The winds beyond the world**: William Morris's *The Wood Beyond the World* (1894) was listed among TSE's books in 1934. TSE perhaps combined this with Kipling's phrase, 'The Wind that blows between the Worlds', three times in *Tomlinson* (1892), which TSE included in his *Choice of Kipling's Verse*. (*Tomlinson* later mentions 'a caddis-case' / TSE, 17, 'a chrysalis'.) For such combining (Morris and Kipling again), compare TSE's letter, *TLS* (10 Jan. 1935): 'I do not think that I got the title "The Hollow Men" from Dowson. There is a romance of William Morris called "The Hollow Land." There is also a poem of Mr. Kipling called "The Broken Men." I combined the two.'

11–12 **world . . . passed . . . trace . . . Time began**: all heard in *In Memoriam* XLIII (though 'past', 'traces'), together with 'pure' (TSE, 16, 'purity') and with 'Soul' (as in TSE's subtitle). **the world had passed without a trace**: compare Laforgue, *Soir de carnaval* (1903) 8: 'La terre crève aux cieux, sans laisser nulle trace'.

14 **to burst out**: given 'sudden' (8), compare Milton, *Lycidas* 74: 'And think to burst out into sudden blaze'. **burst out . . . ingenuous**: availing itself of the etymology of 'ingenuous', free-born / TSE, 16, 'set free'.

14, 16 **ingenuous . . . set free**: compare Symons, *The Symbolist Movement in Literature* (p.89), on Verlaine: 'The verse murmurs, with such an ingenuous confidence, such intimate secrets. That "setting free" of verse [. . .].'

14, 16–17 pure ... purity ... chrysalis: compare Laforgue, *Complainte des crépuscules célibataires* (1890) 28: 'chrysalide', with 'Purs' two lines later.

16 to set free the purity that clings: compare *So through the evening* 7–8 (*The Waste Land MS*, p.113):
> The word that frees
> The inspiration that delivers
– with 'wings' eight lines later (here, two lines later).   purity that clings: given the mimetic enjambment ('that clings / To') and 'pure', compare Tennyson, *Maud*, II [iv] 171–5:
> 'Tis a morning pure and sweet,
> And a dewy splendour falls
> On the little flower that clings
> To the turrets and the walls;
> 'Tis a morning pure and sweet,

17 cautious midnight: compare *Paradise Lost* IX 58–9:
> and at midnight returned
> From compassing the earth, cautious of day,
Three lines before, Milton has 'meditated' ('meditates', two lines later in TSE). *The Waste Land MS*, p.27, *The Fire Sermon* 64, 66, has 'nights' with 'cautious' two lines later.

17–18 midnight of its chrysalis ... meditates its wings: compare *Choruses from 'The Rock'* x: 'Small lights of those who meditate at midnight'. Here 'midnight' because in the dark and asleep; compare Bergson, *L'Evolution créatrice*, ch.II: 'D'une part, en effet, la conscience a dû s'assoupir, comme la chrysalide dans l'enveloppe où elle se prépare des ailes.'   chrysalis ... wings: Tennysonian in spiritual contexts (as invoked in *The Two Voices* 8–15); *St Simeon Stylites* 153–4:
> Courage, St Simeon! This dull chrysalis
> Cracks into shining wings,
In Memoriam LXXXII 8: 'Or ruined chrysalis of one'.

18 cell: religiously lit by 'meditates' (and 'wings').   meditates: *OED* 1b: 'To fix one's attention upon', as in Dryden: 'With inward rage he meditates his prey'; but in TSE proleptic, contemplative. If an earlier reminiscence of *Lycidas* be credited (see 14 note), compare *Lycidas* 66: 'And strictly meditate the thankless Muse'.   meditates its wings: compare *Burbank with a Baedeker: Bleistein with a Cigar* 29–32:
> Who clipped the lion's wings
> And flea'd his rump and pared his claws?
> Thought Burbank, meditating on
> Time's ruins, and the seven laws.

TSE's first draft had 'the lion's mane'; ' "wings" is supplied in Pound's hand' (*The Waste Land MS*, p.131). Some association of meditation with the winged, and with night, is in Marvell's stanza on the nightingale, *The Mower to the Glowworms* 3–4:

And studying all the summer night,
Her matchless songs does meditate;

Again with night, in Meredith, *The Night-Walk* (1901) 31–2:

She flew on it, then folded wings,
In meditation

Coleridge has 'Meditation's heaven-ward wing', *Religious Musings* 413. Given 'The world . . . the world' (10–11), and 'chrysalis' (18), compare TSE's early Harvard essay, *The validity of artificial distinctions* (Houghton Library; bMS Am 1691.14 (27), p.3): 'The world is not simply there, for metaphysics to play upon; it is itself metaphysical, and meditating upon its own nature, spins itself out of its own belly'. (Nine lines later TSE has 'take the wing', and he goes on to speak of 'philosophic flights'; compare 'meditates its wings'.)

19 **Nourished . . . by manure**: compare Browning, *The Inn Album* 711: 'nourished with manure'. **stimulated by manure**: *OED* has under 'stimulating', 1842, *Suburban Horticulture*: 'hence this manure is stimulating as well as enriching'.

20–2 **I am sure it is like this / I am sure it is this / I am sure**: such lineation (with what *Ash-Wednesday* III 19 calls 'stops and steps of the mind') anticipates, for example, the opening of *Ash-Wednesday*:

Because I do not hope to turn again
Because I do not hope
Because I do not hope to turn

With this ending 'I am sure', compare the cancelled ending (it would seem) of *Easter I*: 'She is very sure of God'.

The smoke that gathers blue and sinks

Dated Feb. 1911.

1–2 The smoke that gathers blue . . . cigars: compare TSE's opening with that of Kipling's story *A Conference of the Powers* (*Soldiers Three*, 1888): 'The room was blue with the smoke of three pipes and a cigar'. Compare Kipling's title, its 'Conference' and 'Powers', with TSE, 4–5, rhyming 'immense' / 'insolence' (and 'Existence'), and with 'overpowering' (4). **gathers blue:** *OED* 'gather' 6: 'Of material objects: To be the means of bringing together or accumulating; to receive addition of'. Instanced from 1611 Bible, Joel 2:6: 'all faces shall gather blacknesse', and also from the first Tennyson quotation which follows in this note. But smoke is not exactly a material object, and TSE may be modifying this transitive into an intransitive usage. For 'gather' with a colour, Tennyson: (i) *In Memoriam* CI 3–4:

> that beech will gather brown,
> This maple burn itself away;

– 'burn itself away' connecting with TSE's 'smoke of rich cigars'. (ii) *Sir Launcelot and Queen Guinevere* 8–9:

> The topmost elm-tree gathered green
>   From draughts of balmy air.

– where 6 has 'Blue' and where the immediately following line (10) is 'Sometimes the linnet *piped* his song' (italics added; one of the best burlesquings of Tennyson, riling him, was his being found smoking, first thing in the morning, and being hailed with the observation, 'The earliest pipe of half-awakened bards' – as against the 'birds' of *Tears, idle tears*). In both of the Tennyson instances there are leaves, with something grotesquely apt to smoking and its tobacco leaves. Compare, for gathering and burning, the closing line of *Preludes*: 'Gathering fuel in vacant lots'.

3 torpid after-dinner: compare the epigraph to *Gerontion*, *Measure for Measure*, III i 32–4 (modified here by TSE):

> Thou hast nor youth nor age
> But as it were an after dinner sleep
> Dreaming of both.

(TSE, 16, 'of almost any age'.) The conjunction 'after dinner . . . just about to die' (7) may owe something to this epigraph, since Claudio fears that he is just about to die: 'prepared to die', 'I seek to die', III i 4, 42. Within the prose *Paysages et impressions* (in *Mélanges posthumes*, 1903, pp.38–9), Laforgue has a vignette, *Après-dîner torride et stagnante*; 'la cigarette', 'des seins', 'ces musiciens' and 'une vieille fille' resemble TSE (2, 'cigars'; 17, 'chiefly breast'; 14, his musicians; and

16, 'A lady of almost any age'), and Laforgue's *Après-dîner torride* may have prompted 'torpid after-dinner'.

3, 5 **after-dinner drinks . . . insolence**: compare *Paradise Lost* I 502: 'flown with insolence and wine'. Also perhaps FitzGerald, *Rubáiyát of Omar Khayyám* xxx (1872 text):
> Oh, many a Cup of this forbidden Wine
> Must drown the memory of that insolence!

6 **matter "going by itself"**: a belief anathema to Bergson. *L'Evolution créatrice* (1907), ch.i: 'nous réprendrions que la vie est, avant tout, une tendance à agir sur la matière brute'. Compare *Inside the gloom* 20: 'Explained the relation of life to matter'. Contrasted with Bergson, and aligned with what these poems scorn, is Bertrand Russell, as in the closing paragraph of *The Free Man's Worship* (1903): 'Blind to good and evil, reckless of destruction, omnipotent matter rolls on its relentless way'. For TSE and this peroration of Russell's, see *In the Department Store* 7 note. In his copy of T. H. Green's *Prolegomena to Ethics* (1906, p.13, Houghton Library), TSE marked this: 'If it could be admitted that matter and motion had an existence *in themselves*, or otherwise than as related to a consciousness, it would still not be by *such* matter and motion, but by the matter and motion which we know, that the functions of the soul, or anything else, can for us be explained' (Green's italics). **"going by itself"**: presumably TSE had a source for the particular phrase, somewhere in animist or vitalist philosophy as to 'matter'. Thoughts of the self-mobile might, in these years, have been tempered by the 'automobile'; *OED* has *Encycl. Brit.*, 1902: 'On the Continent of Europe and in the United States the usual expression for these vehicles is "automobile" '. TSE's quotation marks suggest perhaps an advertisement for such overpowering (horsepowering) overoiled machinery and its insolence.

8 **Stifled with glutinous liqueurs**: compare Milton, *Comus* 917: 'Smeared with gums of glutinous heat'; after this, the Lady is freed from her immobility, able to go by herself. **glutinous**: given the drinks, compare Keats, *Lamia* I 209–10:
> Or where God Bacchus drains his cups divine,
> Stretched out, at ease, beneath a glutinous pine;

liqueurs: the first instance in *OED* (1a) is Pope, *Dunciad* IV 317–8:
> Tried all hors d'oeuvres, all liqueurs defined,
> Judicious drank, and greatly-daring dined.

9 **sensation**: see *First Debate between the Body and Soul* 6–7 note.

10 **overoiled**: including 'oiled', *OED* 3: '*slang*. Drunk'; from 1737, *Pennsylvania Gazette*. Compare TSE's letter to Virginia Woolf, Twelfth Night 1935 (Berg Collection), from 'one of my songs' about drinking Wurzburger: 'It's allright to oil up a sewing-machine'. **machinery**: including *OED* 1, *Theatr. and literary*,

from 1687, including Pope, Dedication to *The Rape of the Lock*, 1714: 'a term invented by the Critics, to signify that Part which the Deities, Angels, or Daemons, are made to act in a Poem'. (TSE has 'action' in his next line.) In *The Wine of the Puritans* (1908; TSE reviewed it in the *Harvard Advocate*, 7 May 1909), Van Wyck Brooks deplored the American obsession with 'the machinery of life': 'Efficiency is the well-oiled machinery' (pp.55, 50).

11 **action**: OED does not have any citations with exactly the force of the US slang 'you want action?' here. 1e: 'Activity considered noteworthy or important; freq. with *the*. *spec.* in gambling or betting'; but this from 1933. Tinged with OED 4: 'The thing represented as done in a drama'.

12 **attraction**: OED 9: 'A thing or feature which draws people by appealing to their desires, tastes, etc.; *esp.* any interesting or amusing exhibition which "draws" crowds'; from 1829.

16 **A lady of almost any age**: compare *Mandarins* 2 1: 'Two ladies of uncertain age'.

18 **"*Throw your arms around me – Aint you glad you found me*"**: the song (copyright 1907, words by Harry Williams, music by Egbert Van Alstyne) has as the superscribed title *Ain't You Glad You've Found Me*, but the title on the front of the sheet music follows the lyrics of the Chorus, having 'You Found'. TSE adapts the Chorus:

Ain't you glad you found me?
I'm so glad that I found you.
When you're near me, dear, you cheer me,
And I hope I cheer you too,
Pur your arms around me,
Just a squeeze or two will do.
Now if you're not glad you found me,
I'm glad I found you.

Compare *Suite Clownesque III* 3–5, 8–9:

I may meet you
Very likely greet you
Show you that I know you [. . .]
You may find me
All the girls behind me.

Compare TSE's most noted and most notable such adaptation, *The Waste Land* [II] 128–30:

O O O O that Shakespeherian Rag –
It's so elegant
So intelligent

(*That Shakespearian Rag*, words by Gene Buck and Herman Ruby, music by

David Stamper, copyright 1912). Compare the popular song in *The Waste Land MS*, pp.5, 125, *The Burial of the Dead*:

> Tease, Squeeze lovin & wooin
> Say Kid what're y' doin'

from *The Cubanola Glide* (1909). Of the two epigraphs to the Clark Lectures (1926, *VMP*, p.40), one is from Dante, the other:

> I want someone to treat me rough.
> Give me a cabman.
>

Popular song

Compare the songs in *Sweeney Agonistes: Fragment of an Agon*, 'Under the bamboo' and 'My little island girl'.

20-1 a negro (teeth and smile) / Has a dance: Van Wyck Brooks puts '*danced*' and 'a negro', two lines apart in *The Wine of the Puritans* (see 10 note), and on the same page (p.109): 'Negroes grin'.

22 That's the stuff!: *OED* 7f, which continues '(*to give them* or *to give the troops*)': 'that is what is particularly appropriate to the situation, that is what is required'; its first instance, though, is 1923, as 'That's the stuff to give the troops', with 1943 for the abbreviated 'that's the stuff'.

23 your gin: possibly with some sense of a trap or stratagem, as in *Faerie Queene* III vii stanza 7:

> The Damzell there arriuing entred in;
> Where sitting on the flore the Hag she found,
> Busie (as seem'd) about some wicked gin:

THE SMOKE THAT GATHERS BLUE AND SINKS 70

He said: this universe is very clever

Dated March 1911. 'Fragment' is jotted in the right hand corner, slanted; a face is sketched, upside down, below the word.

1 **this universe**: frequent in Milton; *Paradise Lost* VII 227, the Creation; VIII 360; IX 684; and *Paradise Regained* I 49.

1, 3 **clever . . . never**: compare Byron, *Don Juan*, XVI [xcviii] 825–8:

This makes your actors, artists, and romancers,
　　Heroes sometimes, though seldom – sages never;
But speakers, bards, diplomatists, and dancers,
　　Little that's great, but much of what is clever;

Byron does not list 'scientists' (TSE, 2), but his next stanza begins: 'The poets of arithmetic' (TSE, 9, 'geometric'); and in a pertinent stanza elsewhere, he speaks of Newton (see the next note).

2, 4 **paper . . . cut an unintentioned caper**: compare Byron, *Don Juan* x [iii] 17–20:

And wherefore this exordium? – Why, just now,
　　In taking up this paltry sheet of paper,
My bosom underwent a glorious glow,
　　And my internal Spirit cut a caper:

Subsequently W. S. Gilbert, *Ruddigore* (produced 1887), Act II:

My ways were strange
Beyond all range –
Paragraphs got into all the papers.
We only cut respectable capers.

Gilbert again, and with 'spiders' / 'insiders' in the same song (compare TSE, 7, 9): 'wall-papers' / 'capers' (*The Grand Duke*, produced 1896), Act I. As to 'the scientists' busy in contemplation of 'this universe', Byron's preceding stanza (x [ii] 11–12) had invoked one of them:

In which Sir Isaac Newton could disclose
　　Through the then unpaved stars the turnpike road,

unintentioned: compare Elizabeth Barrett Browning, *Casa Guidi Windows* II 10–11:

As little children take up a high strain
　　With unintentioned voices,

(Compare *First Caprice in North Cambridge* 3–4: 'strains / Of children's voices'.)

3 **Place in Life** (variant): as in *Inside the gloom* 22.

4 **cut . . . caper**: *OED* sb.2 b: 'to dance in a frolicsome way, to act fantastically', with the first instance *Twelfth Night*, I iii 129: 'Faith, I can cut a caper'. William James had brought together faith, 'caper-cutting', the 'sombre religious person',

the predatory and the divine (compare TSE 6–9), in *The Varieties of Religious Experience* (1902), lecture III: 'The constitutionally sombre religious person makes even of his religious peace a very sober thing. Danger still hovers in the air about it. Flexion and contraction are not wholly checked. It were sparrowlike and childish after our deliverance to explode into twittering laughter and caper-cutting, and utterly to forget the imminent hawk on bough. Lie low, rather, lie low; for you are in the hands of a living God.'

6 **syphilitic**: Byron mentions 'pseudo-syphilis', *Don Juan*, I [cxxxi] 1048, where he has in the next stanza 'intentions' (TSE, 4, 'unintentioned'). **syphilitic spider**: perhaps with a memory of Donne, 'The spider love', *Twicknam Garden* 6; TSE quoted the lines in *The Listener*, 19 March 1930. (TSE's scabrous French poem ribbing John Hayward – *Vers pour la Foulque*, in *Noctes Binanianae*, 1939 – mentions both 'la Tarentule [. . .] au vénin sûr' and 'des chats avariés'; translated by TSE as the 'spider with [. . .] deadly poison', and – in the manuscript, Hayward Bequest – bizarrely, 'syphilitic cats'; in the printed text, more faithfully, 'damaged cats'.) Compare the oath in one of the Columbo verses (Appendix A): ' "Fuck Spiders" was his chief remark'. The thought in this poem may be that syphilis deals death in love and sex, and so – in some species – does the female spider (destroying the male once he has served her turn). Compare Remy de Gourmont, *Physique de l'amour: essai sur l'instinct sexuel* (1904), ch.XIII, an elaborated account of spider-love, including: 'A peine la fécondation est-elle opérée que l'ogresse se retourne, bondissante, et dévore l'amant sur le lieu même de ses amours.' TSE enquired of Pound about a copy of his translation, *The Natural Philosophy of Love*, 28 July 1922 (*Letters* i 553). The association of the spider with philosophy (though not with its Absolute), and with love, is in Emerson, *Philosopher* (1884); 'his philosophy' impels him to watch coldly and damagingly his love and his grief (8, 10–12):

> Is't not like
> That devil-spider that devours her mate
> Scarce freed from her embraces?

6–7 **in the middle, like a syphilitic spider . . . sits**: in *Sir John Davies* (1926, OPP, p.134), comparing Pope, and finding Davies's 'spider the more alive', TSE quoted Davies, *Nosce Teipsum* 1061–2:

> Much like a subtill spider, which doth sit
> In middle of her web, which spreadeth wide.

spider / The Absolute: Bergson's Absolute more than Bradley's. TSE evoked Paris 'during the first decade and more of this century': 'and over all swung the spider-like figure of Bergson' (*The Criterion* xiii, April 1934, 451–2). Aiken thought likewise, in a letter of March 1913, congratulating TSE 'that you have shunted Bergson down the hill [. . .] It seemed to me that he was not in contact with life: or if he was, in his first premises, he soon lost it in images of light and sound. And I always wax impatient with these withered little spiders who spin endless subtleties out of their own inner consciousness, merely using the external world as attacking-points, or points of suspension' (*Selected Letters*, ed. Joseph Killorin, 1978, pp.29–30). A relation of philosophy to the spider was suggested in a metaphor of TSE's in an early Harvard essay, *The validity of artificial distinctions* (Houghton Library; bMS Am 1691.14 (27), p.3): 'The world is not simply there, for metaphysics to play upon; it is itself metaphysical, and meditating upon its own nature, spins itself out of its own belly.' For a relation of the spider to the divine absolute, compare Diderot, *Le Rêve de d'Alembert*:

Mlle de Lespinasse: Et qui est-ce qui vous a dit que ce monde n'avait pas aussi ses méninges, ou qu'il ne réside pas dans quelque recoin de l'espace une grosse ou petite araignée dont les fils s'étendent à tout.

Bordeu: Personne. Moins encore si elle n'a pas été, ou si elle ne sera pas.

Mlle de Lespinasse: Comment cette espèce de Dieu-là . . .

Bordeu: La seule qui se conçoive . . .

Mlle de Lespinasse: Pourrait avoir été ou venir et passer?

Bordeu: Sans doute; mais puisqu'il serait matière, dans l'univers, portion de l'univers, sujet à vicissitudes, il vieillirait; il mourrait.

TSE reviewed a translation of Diderot's *Early Philosophical Works* in the *New Statesman*, 17 March 1917.

9 **crucifixion**: given the chairs, compare Aiken's reminiscence of TSE at the end of 1911: 'He had taken a room in Ash Street, installing in it a small stove – "something to point the chairs at" – and a Gauguin *Crucifixion*, brought from Paris' (*King Bolo and Others*, in *T. S. Eliot*, ed. Richard March and Tambimuttu, 1948, p.21). (TSE's 'Yellow Christ', 'your hoisted Jesus', Aiken to TSE, 23 Feb. 1913, *Selected Letters*, pp.25–6.) TSE to Aiken, 25 July 1914: 'I enclose some *stuff* – the *thing* I showed you some time ago, and some of the themes for the "Descent from the Cross" or whatever I may call it' (*Letters* i 44). Compare *The Little Passion* (ii) 15: 'some inevitable cross'.

10 **passed his life on officechairs**: compare *The Love Song of J. Alfred Prufrock* 51: 'measured out my life with coffee spoons'.

12 **abysmal**: *OED* 2: 'In weakened sense: of an exceptionally poor standard or quality; extremely bad'. The first instance is 1904, Henry James, *The Golden Bowl*. TSE plays the slangy sense against the sublime and its paradoxical perspectives ('Up . . . abysmal'). **broken stairs**: at once contrasted, in their sordid dailiness, with the spiritual heights of crucifixion, and suggestive of them: 'As in the figure of the ten stairs', *Burnt Norton* v 24, where the figure derives from St John of the Cross, *The Dark Night of the Soul* and *The Ascent of Mount Carmel*. Compare Tennyson, *In Memoriam* LV 15–16:

Upon the great world's altar-stairs

That slope through darkness up to God,

13 **pot:** *OED* 1a: 'Often with defining word, as *glue-pot*'.

14 **clippings:** *OED* 2b: 'A press cutting, orig. *U.S.*'; from 1857.

15 **an article:** compare perhaps Byron, *Don Juan*, xi [lx] 479–80 (a stanza about 'the Gods' and a 'Poor fellow'):

> 'Tis strange the mind, that very fiery particle,
> Should let itself be snuffed out by an Article.

TSE alluded to this in a review of J. T. Merz in Oct. 1916: 'Is personality equivalent to this totality of experience, or is it only a (very fiery) particle?' (*International Journal of Ethics* xxvii 126).

Inside the gloom

Compare Laforgue, *Litanies des premiers quartiers de la lune* (1886), which similarly contemplates the heavens in fourteen sardonic couplets, not unlike the rhythm of TSE's opening couplets:

> Lune bénie
> Des insomnies,
>
> Blanc médaillon
> Des Endymions,
>
> Astre fossile
> Que tout exile,

TSE was twice to return to a serious burlesque of the constellations. First, *Sweeney Among the Nightingales* 7–10: 'Death and the Raven drift above', 'Gloomy Orion and the Dog / Are veiled'. Second, including (compare 7) the Scorpion, in *East Coker* II 8–13 (lines ruefully dubbed 'A periphrastic study in a worn-out poetical fashion'), where the rhymes – like many in *Inside the gloom* – are on edge:

> Thunder rolled by the rolling stars
> Simulates triumphal cars
> Deployed in constellated wars
> Scorpion fights against the Sun
> Until the Sun and Moon go down
> Comets weep and Leonids fly

John T. Mayer, considering *The Little Passion*, remarks of the fourteen couplets: 'The idea of zodiacal stations recalls another ancient pattern, that of the Stations of the Cross, a series of meditations upon the fourteen stages of Christ's Passion that coincide with fourteen stations, or stopping places, along the Via Dolorosa, the Way of the Cross' (*T. S. Eliot: The Modernist in History*, ed. Ronald Bush, p.74). He extends his claim with an insistence upon 'the city series, which, if Eliot had used all the city poems in the Notebook, would have consisted of fourteen poems, fourteen stations of a modern, diminished Way of the Cross' (p.76); this number, though, is arrived at without specifying the principle of inclusion, and by excluding, for instance, *Silence*, which is in the Notebook and would have to be counted a city poem, beginning as it does 'Along the city streets'.

1–2 **gloom . . . room**: compare Milton, *On the Morning of Christ's Nativity* 77–9:

> And though the shady gloom
> Had given day her room,
> The sun himself withheld his wonted speed,

– an astronomical glimpse. *Whispers of Immortality* 26, 28, rhymes 'gloom' and 'drawing-room'; and *Animula* 29–30 'in its own gloom' and 'in a dusty room'.

1, 3–4 **gloom . . . constellations . . . stations**: compare *Paradise Lost* VII 562–3 (1667 text; 1674 has 'station'):

> The heavens and all the constellations rung,
> The planets in their stations listening stood,

On the Morning of Christ's Nativity 121–2:

> His constellations set,
>   And the well-balanced world on hinges hung,

(TSE, 14, 'Balanced'.) Given 'gloom', compare W. S. Gilbert, *Thespis, or The Gods Grown Old* (produced 1871), which begins with a Chorus of Stars:

> Throughout the night
>   The constellations
> Have given light
>   From various stations.
> When midnight gloom

9 **tail on fire**: perhaps playing with the legend that the scorpion, when ringed with fire, stings itself to death with its tail.

11 **Cassiopea**: TSE may have taken a hint for his poem from the close of Laforgue's *Persée et Andromède* (*Moralités légendaires*), where the map of the heavens is scanned, and mention made of Cassiopeia, the Great Bear and other constellations. (TSE adapted *Persée et Andromède* in his *Ode*.)

11–12 **Cassiopea / Explained the Pure Idea**: compare *Paradise Lost* VII 557, the Creation: 'Answering his great idea'. Compare Tennyson, *The Princess* IV, where 'Cassiopeia' (418) is preceded by 'Ida, Ida, Ida' (413), 'Ida' (416). **the Pure Idea**: compare *First Debate between the Body and Soul* 8, 15: 'And yet devoted to the pure idea', 'The pure Idea dies of inanition' (see the notes).

13 **Major Bear**: Ursa Major. **The dancing bear** (variant): compare *Portrait of a Lady* III 28: 'Like a dancing bear', followed two lines later by 'chatter' (27 below, 'chattered'). TSE's childhood journal *Fireside* (No. 13–14, Feb. 1899; Houghton Library), when he was ten, includes chapters of *A Voyage to the Great Bear*.

14 **Balanced a chair**: as at a circus, balancing a chair on its nose. Compare *Paradise Lost* IV 1000: 'balanced air' (with the astronomical 'Scorpion' two lines earlier, as in 7 above). **chair**: Cassiopeia, invoked in the previous couplet, is the Lady's Chair (rhymed by Hardy with 'Greater Bear' in *Shut out that moon*, 1909). TSE repeatedly delighted in George Chapman, *Bussy d'Ambois*: 'Beneath the chariot of the snowy Bear', from Seneca, *Hercules Furens*: 'sub cardine / glacialis ursae'; see *The Egoist* (July 1919); *Shakespeare and the Stoicism of Seneca* (1927, *SE*, p.74); the Clark Lectures in 1926 (*VMP*, p.152); *The Listener* (12 March 1930); and *UPUC*, p.147. Compare *Gerontion* 68: 'Beyond the circuit of the shuddering Bear'.

16 intellection: *OED* 1: 'the exercise or activity of the intellect'. *OED* 1b (*Obs.*) has a different direction to intellection: 'Applied *spec.* to the kind of immediate knowledge or intelligence ascribed to divine or angelic beings'. Berkeley, 1732: 'As reason is of kind peculiar to man, so by intellection he [Picus] understands a kind or manner of knowledge peculiar to angels'. TSE wrote of Marianne Moore's poems: 'To the moderately intellectual the poems may appear to be intellectual exercises; only to those whose intellection moves more easily will they immediately appear to have emotional value' (Introduction to her *Selected Poems*, 1935, p.8). There the angelic suggestion possible to 'intellection' may be supported by 'immediately' ('immediate knowledge', above).

17 **Pegasus the winged horse**: given the other filaments to *Paradise Lost* VII (noted above and below), compare VII 4: 'Pegasean wing'.

18 **Vital Force**: translating Bergson's *élan vital* in *L'Evolution créatrice* (1907); often rendered 'life-force'. The term 'vital force' does not figure in the 1911 translation (A. Mitchell, *Creative Evolution*), though 'vital principle' does (p.42); Mitchell's index has under its very long entry for 'vital': *activity, current, impetus* and *order* (but not *force*); and under 'force' it has 'limitedness of vital force', but none of the pages listed has specifically 'vital force'. Compare *Reflections on 'Vers Libre'* (1917, *TCTC*, p.183): '*Vers libre* does not exist, and it is time that this preposterous fiction followed the *élan vital* and the eighty thousand Russians into oblivion'. TSE wrote in *Revelation* (ed. John Baillie and Hugh Martin, 1937, p.4): 'in spite of the appearance of Bergson – whose mind does not seem to me characteristically French – I am inclined to believe that philosophies which admit the inclusion of the irrational, or of anything which eludes rational grasp – such as *vitalism* – are more natural to non-"Latin" countries where the decay of Christianity has followed a different route.' Contrast the address given by Charles Eliot, President of Harvard and distant cousin of TSE, to the Harvard Summer School of Theology in July 1909, on the forthcoming God: 'the Jewish Jehovah, the Christian Universal Father, the modern physicist's omnipresent and exhaustless Energy, and the biological conception of a Vital Force', a religion that would 'not be gloomy' (compare TSE, 1). *The Religion of the Future* (1909), *Charles W. Eliot: The Man and His Beliefs*, ed. W. A. Neilson (1926), ii 576–601.

19 **Cetus**: constellation, the Whale.

20 **the relation of life to matter**: Bergson's *L'Evolution créatrice*, passim; in the translation, the index-entry under 'matter' summarizes Bergson's position well: 'see "inert matter" '. *L'Evolution créatrice*, ch. 1: 'nous réprendrions que la vie est, avant tout, une tendance à agir sur la matière brute'. See *The smoke that gathers blue and sinks* 6–7:
>Of matter "going by itself"
>Existence just about to die

21 while the debate was rife: compare *Silence* 6, on incidents 'debated'; *First Debate between the Body and Soul*; *Bacchus and Ariadne: 2nd Debate between the Body and Soul*.

21–2 a fork and knife [variant] . . . **Place**: because of some suggestion of laying a place? *Mr. Mistoffelees* 33–4:

> If you look for a knife or a fork
> And you think it is merely misplaced –

Compare Theodore Hook's *Clubs* 11–12:

> The very waiters answer you with eloquence Socratical,
> And always place the knives and forks in order mathematical.

(*A Vers de Société Anthology*, ed. Carolyn Wells, 1907, p.48.)

22 Place in Life: as in *He said: this universe is very clever* 3 (variant).

23 Bootes: OED, 'A northern constellation, the Wagoner, situated at the tail of the Great Bear and containing the bright star Arcturus'. Pope, *Thebais* 521: 'When clouds conceal Bootes' golden wain'.

23, 25–6 unsettled . . . questions . . . indigestions: compare TSE, *The Idealism of Julien Benda*: 'I think that one can admit that ours is an unsettled age'; and later in the same paragraph: 'We are conscious of these questions as a man with indigestion is conscious of his stomach' (*Cambridge Review*, 6 June 1928).

25–6 questions . . . indigestions: compare *The Little Passion* (ii) 1–3:

> Of those ideas in his head
> Which found me always interested
> Though they were seldom well digested –

Byron twice rhymes 'question' and 'indigestion' in *Don Juan*; XI [iii] 17–24 is apt to TSE (as bringing metaphysical questions into relation with 'stars'):

> For ever and anon comes Indigestion,
>   (Not the most 'dainty Ariel') and perplexes
> Our soarings with another sort of question:
>   And that which after all my spirit vexes,
> Is, that I find no spot where man can rest eye on,
>   Without confusion of the sorts and sexes,
> Of being, stars, and this unriddled wonder,
> The World, which at the worst's a glorious blunder –

(In a letter to Aiken, 16 Nov. 1914, *Letters* i 69, TSE quoted *Don Juan*, IV [v] 36–9, the passage about which he later jested in *UPUC*, pp.30–1.) W. S. Gilbert took up Byron's rhyme in *The Mountebanks* (produced 1890), Act I:

> Commencing with a gentle pain
>   Scarce worth a question,
> It grows apace, till you complain

Of indigestion.
Austin Dobson rhymes 'Your cynic question' with 'due / To indigestion' (*A Gage d'Amour*, 1873, 16, 11–12). For the thought in 25–6, compare *Paradise Lost* VII 126–30, in reply to Adam's questions: 'But knowledge is as food', 'Wisdom to folly, as nourishment to wind'.

27–8 chattered . . . mattered: compare *The Waste Land MS*, p.23, *The Fire Sermon* 27–8:
> Oh, Lady Kleinwurm's monde – no one that mattered –
> Somebody sang, and Lady Kleinwurm chattered.

Oh little voices of the throats of men

Printed in *Letters* i 45–6. TSE had told Aiken, 19 July 1914 (*Letters* i 42):
> I have written some *stuff* – about 50 lines, but I find it shamefully laboured, and am belabouring it more. If I can improve it at all I will send it you.

Sent by TSE in a letter to Aiken, from Marburg, 25 July 1914, with *The Love Song of St. Sebastian*. (The typescript of the poems sent to Aiken is now in the McKeldin Library, University of Maryland; 'This letter [now in the Huntington Library] and the poems became separated when Aiken sold the latter to a private collector', *Letters* i 44.)

> I enclose some *stuff* – the *thing* I showed you some time ago, and some of the themes for the "Descent from the Cross" or whatever I may call it. I send them, even in their present form, because I am disappointed in them, and wonder whether I had better knock it off for a while – you will tell me what you think.

For Aiken, TSE marked the margin at three places. 1–14 (lacking 6), with a brace: 'Introduction. To be amplified at the end also'. 15–34 (it seems; alongside 20–30): 'This theme to recur twice, in variations' ('theme' added with a caret). 37–end, with a brace: 'finale to the foregoing'.

TSE wrote to Aiken, 30 Sept. 1914, about this poem and *The Love Song of St. Sebastian*: 'The stuff I sent you is not good, is very forced in execution, though the idea was right, I think' (*Letters* i 58).

Diffused through lines 5–36 of the poem is some likeness to *The Waste Land* [I] 60–8. In the order of *Oh little voices*: 5 and *WL* 65, 'feet'; 9, 'roads' / *WL* 66, 'Street'; 10 (twice) and 28, 'keep' / *WL* 67, 'kept'; 26 and *WL* 60, 'unreal' / 'Unreal'; 33 and *WL* 68, 'dead'; 8 and 34, 'time' / *WL* 67, 'the hours'; and 36, 'morning broke' / *WL* 61, 'dawn'.

1 **little voices**: as in two successive poems by Symons in *Images of Good and Evil* (1899, and *Poems*, 1902): *The Coming of Spring* 1 and *September Idyl* 2. The former, like TSE, has the phrase in its first line, and has 'song' in 3 (TSE, 2), as well as 'men', 6 (TSE, 1); 'world', 9 (TSE, 16); 'well-', 9 ('well', TSE, 9 and 10); and 'is it death or sleep?', 11 (TSE, 14, 'death and sleep?'). Compare 'little voices' with Verlaine, *Romances sans paroles* (1874) I 6: 'Le choeur des petites voix'; translated by Symons (1913), 'Little voices that sing' (TSE, 2, 'song'). In *The Symbolist Movement in Literature* (p.155), Symons quoted, in translation, from Maeterlinck 'the little voice of light' (from *Le tragique quotidien*). TSE deprecated the Georgian poets' recourse to the adjective: 'it is not unworthy of notice how often the word "little" occurs: and how this word is used, not merely as a necessary piece of information, but with a caress, a conscious delight' (*The Egoist* iv, Sept. 1917, 118).

1–2 throats of men . . . the singer and the song: compare Byron, *Farewell Petition to J.C.H.* 41–2:

> why should I prolong
> My notes, and vex a *Singer* with a *Song*?

Byron has 'men' in the previous line, and his 'notes' may have prompted 'throats'.

3, 5–6, 8 men . . . undirected feet . . . ways . . . paths: compare Proverbs 3:6: 'In all thy ways acknowledge him, And he shall direct thy paths'. Proverbs 16:9: 'A man's heart deviseth his way: But the LORD directeth his steps.'

3–4 hands . . . rend the beautiful and curse: compare *Richard III*, I ii 126: 'These nails should rend that beauty', with 'Curse' in 132 (and with 144 in this exchange, 'Why dost thou spit at me?' / TSE, 12, 'spit').

5 Impatient tireless . . . feet: given 'paths' (8), compare Sir Edwin Arnold, *The Light of Asia* (1879), Book the Fourth, p.94: 'To tread its paths with patient, stainless feet'. TSE admired *The Light of Asia*.

6 wrinkled: *OED* 1: 'Formed or disposed in convolutions, sinuosities, or windings. *Obs.*'; from 1403, with 1407: 'The house of Dedalus . . is so wrynkled to and froo'; and 1513, Douglas, *Aeneid*: 'wrinkillit walls' (of a labyrinth). Compare 'wrinkled ways' with *So through the evening* 9 (*The Waste Land MS*, p.113): 'This wrinkled road which twists'.

5, 7–9 feet . . . heaven and hell . . . paths . . . do well: compare D. G. Rossetti, the closing lines of *Dante at Verona* (1870):

> those stairs
> Which, of all paths his feet knew well,
> Were steeper found than Heaven or Hell.

(TSE, 48, 'stair'.)

7 frontier of heaven and hell: compare Symons on Gérard de Nerval: 'For Gérard, so sharp an awakening was but like the passage from one state to another, across that little bridge of one step which lies between heaven and hell, to which he was so used in his dreams' (*The Symbolist Movement in Literature*, pp.20–1). Compare Pascal: 'Entre nous, et l'enfer ou le ciel, il n'y a que la vie entre deux, qui est la chose du monde le plus fragile' (*Pensées*, section III, no.213).

8 divers: *OED* 3: 'Now somewhat *archaic*, but well known in legal and scriptural phraseology'.

9 you do well: since 'do well', like 'ways' and 'paths', is repeatedly Biblical, compare – given TSE's 'voices' (1), 'heaven' (7), and 'you do well' – 2 Peter 1:18–19: 'And this voice which came from heaven we heard, when we were with him in the holy mount. We have also a more sure word of prophecy; whereunto ye do well that ye take heed.'

10 **to keep the ways you keep**: compare *The Love Song of J. Alfred Prufrock* 27: 'to meet the faces that you meet'.

11–12 **pleasure and pain . . . wind . . . rain**: compare *Paradise Lost* II 586–9:
> Forgets both joy and grief, pleasure and pain.
> Beyond this flood a frozen continent
> Lies dark and wild, beat with perpetual storms
> Of whirlwind and dire hail,

The landscape of Hell ('hell', TSE, 7).

11–13 **balance pleasure and pain . . . rain . . . sun**: compare Tennyson, *Sir Launcelot and Queen Guinevere* 1–4:
> Like souls that balance joy and pain,
> With tears and smiles from heaven again
> The maiden Spring upon the plain
> Came in a sun-lit fall of rain.

TSE, 7, 'heaven'. Tennyson, 13, 'fear of wrong' / TSE, 6, 'ways of wrong'. In *Appearance and Reality* (compare TSE, 15, 'Appearances appearances'), F. H. Bradley elaborated an argument about 'a balance of pain' and 'a balance of pleasure' (1893; 1897 edn, p.138), and he italicized '*balance*'. 'In the world, which we observe, an impartial scrutiny will discover more pleasure than pain, though it is difficult to estimate, and easy to exaggerate, the amount of the balance' (p.175).

12 **blow against the wind**: compare *Paradise Lost* XI 311–3:
> But prayer against his absolute decree
> No more avails than breath against the wind
> Blown stifling back on him that breathes it forth.

blow against the wind and spit against the rain: given TSE's rhyme with 'pain', compare Blake, *Mock on* 1–4:
> Mock on Mock on Voltaire Rousseau
> Mock on Mock on tis all in vain
> You throw the sand against the wind
> And the wind blows it back again

Blake has 'paths' (8 / TSE, 8, 30), and 'Particles of light' (10 / TSE, 40, 'the thin light').

13 **more real than**: compare Shelley, *Prometheus Unbound* I 748: 'Forms more real than living man'.

15 **Appearances appearances**: religious, philosophical and artistic. (i) 1 Samuel 16:7: 'for man looketh on the outward appearance, but the LORD looketh on the heart'. John 7:24: 'Judge not according to the appearance'. (ii) TSE on F. H. Bradley, notably on *Appearance and Reality*: 'The attitude of science, then, involves the

constitution of a larger and larger limbo of appearance [. . .] Economics is appearance for the biologist, biology for the chemist. Similarly, social psychology is appearance to the individual psychologist'; 'This seems to me essentially the position of the critical philosophy: the thing is known through its appearances, but as soon as the distinction is made appearance and thing fall apart, and appearance replaces thing as a point of attention' (*KEPB*, pp.73, 96). 'Whenever we desire to *explain* we will think of a reality which causes the appearances, but as soon as we have clearly formulated it, it turns out to be itself appearance' (TSE on causality, probably 1914, Houghton Library; bMS Am 1691.14 (18) p.4). On Bradley's understanding of appearance, see further Richard Wollheim, *F. H. Bradley* (1959), pp.211–32. In his copy (dated 3 March 1913) of *The Philosophy of Kant* (selected and translated by John Watson, 1908; Houghton Library), TSE underlined on p.37: 'For the truth is, that, however far we may carry our investigations into the world of sense, we never can come into contact with aught but appearances'. On the Eastern contribution to TSE's thinking while at Harvard and later, see Jeffrey M. Perl and Andrew P. Tuck, *The Significance of T. S. Eliot's Philosophical Notebooks*: 'The distinction between appearance and reality Eliot took to be the founding presupposition of Western philosophy – most European philosophers were seeking to ferret out truths, not obviously and immediately true – and much of Eliot's own philosophical labour aimed at undermining that key distinction'; 'Eliot found in certain Buddhist schools, as he was finding in F. H. Bradley, an option that he believed to be unavailable in the range of previous European philosophy'; 'Eliot held the view that the world of ultimate reality and the world of appearance are not as distinct as had been traditionally held in the West' (*Southern Review*, Winter 1985 and Autumn 1985; subsequently *T. S. Eliot: Essays from the Southern Review*, ed. James Olney, 1988, p.158). (iii) Symons, *Conclusion* to *The Symbolist Movement in Literature* (p.170): 'Knowing so much less than nothing, for we are entrapped in smiling and many-coloured appearances'. TSE, Introduction to G. Wilson Knight, *The Wheel of Fire* (1930), p.xx: 'In a work of art, as truly as anywhere, reality only exists in and through appearances [. . .] The work of Shakespeare is like life itself something to be lived through. If we lived it completely we should need no interpretation; but on our plane of appearances our interpretations themselves are a part of our living.' TSE in the Turnbull Lectures (1933): 'The artist is the only genuine and profound revolutionist, in the following sense. The world always has, and always will, tend to substitute appearance for reality. The artist, being always alone, being heterodox when everyone else is orthodox, and orthodox when everyone else is heterodox, is the perpetual upsetter of conventional values, the restorer of the real' (*VMP*, pp.288–9).

15, 21–2 **Appearances appearances . . . Contradiction . . . contradiction**: compare Nietzsche, *The Birth of Tragedy*, on Raphael: 'the "appearance" here is the counter-appearance of eternal Contradiction, the father of things' (tr. W. A. Haussmann, 1909, p.39).

16 **world through dialectic**: compare TSE's paper on T. H. Green: 'it is only by an abuse of transcendental dialectic that he can reduce the world to the one or the other' (Houghton Library; bMS Am 1691.14 (31), p.4). *Dante* (1929, *SE*, p.261): 'It is the philosophy of that world of poetry which we have entered. But with the xxviith canto we have left behind the stage of punishment and the stage of dialectic.' **dialectic**: TSE writes of 'the nature of the "dialectic process" ' in *KEPB* (p.165). Compare *Choruses from 'The Rock'* vii:

and this has never happened before
That men both deny gods and worship gods, professing first Reason,
And then Money, and Power, and what they call Life, or Race, or Dialectic.

dialectic ways: compare F. H. Bradley, 'I wish simply to consider what sort of operation is performed by Dialectic, assuming that it has a real way of its own' (*The Principles of Logic*, 1883; 1922 edn, ii 408). Compare 6, 'wrinkled ways'; the ways of dialectic were for TSE insufficiently wrinkled: 'Much of idealism, which is the philosophy of the historically minded, consists in an attempt to take the delicate and evasive truths of historical and literary criticism, truths which are the intuitive apprehension of a trained mind and a trained taste, and dragoon them into the goose-step of dialectic' (paper on ethics; Houghton Library; bMS Am 1691.14 (32), p.2). Given 'more real' (13), compare p.3 of this paper: 'And in spite of the irresistable current of dialectic I find myself always returning to the feeling (for I do not dignify it by any more honourable name) that what we call the physical universe represents something much more real and permanent than all our structures of thought.'

16–17 **world through dialectic ways . . . nights**: compare *Paradise Lost* iii 543–5:
Of all this world at once. As when a scout
Through dark and desert ways with peril gone
All night,

16–18 **searched the world through . . . questioned . . . nights . . . every**: compare Tennyson, *Demeter and Persephone* 53–67 (Demeter's search and enquiries): 'search', 'Through', 'night', 'And asked the waves that moan about the world', 'every'. **questioned . . . every**: compare *Lycidas* 93: 'questioned every gust'. **the world . . . I . . . questioned restless . . . every . . . where**: compare Shelley, *Epipsychidion* 234–6:
'Where?' – the world's echo answered 'where?'
And in that silence, and in my despair,
I questioned every tongueless wind that flew

17–18 **questioned restless nights . . . followed . . . lead**: compare *The Love Song of J. Alfred Prufrock* 6–10:

Of restless nights in one-night cheap hotels
And sawdust restaurants with oyster-shells:
Streets that follow like a tedious argument
Of insidious intent
To lead you to an overwhelming question . . .

Compare *The Waste Land MS*, p.27, *The Fire Sermon* 62: 'When restless nights distract her brain from sleep'.   **lead**: the past tense (led); for TSE on this, see *The Love Song of St. Sebastian* 11 note.

20 **Intolerable interminable**: compare Shelley, *The Daemon of the World* [I] 176, 198: 'interminable', 'intolerable' (the order in the McKeldin text in *Letters* i).

21 **Contradiction is the debt**: compare TSE's lines with *Samson Agonistes* 300–13:

> Yet more there be who doubt his ways not just,
> As to his own edicts, found contradicting,
> Then give the reins to wandering thought,
> Regardless of his glory's diminution;
> Till by their own perplexities involved
> They ravel more, still less resolved,
> But never find self-satisfying solution.
>   As if they would confine th'interminable,
> And tie him to his own prescript,
> Who made our laws to bind us, not himself,
> And hath full right to exempt
> Whomso it pleases him by choice
> From national obstriction, without taint
> Of sin, or legal debt;

'ways' / TSE, 16; 'found contradicting' / TSE, 19, 'find', and 21, 22, 'Contradiction'; 'still' / TSE, 22; 'never find' / TSE, 19, 'find'; 'interminable' / TSE, 20; 'debt' / TSE, 21. Bradley in *Appearance and Reality* repeatedly ponders contradiction (p.192: 'There is only one way to get rid of contradiction, and that way is by dissolution'), and so does TSE in *KEPB*: 'the real world of practice is essentially vague, unprecise, swarming with what are, from a metaphysical point of view, insoluble contradictions' (p.136). TSE ended a paper on definition (Houghton Library; bMS Am 1691.14 (26), p.4): 'Nothing is contradictory until it has been made a thing, and everything can be made a thing, and everything is contradictory'.

22 **And still**: at the head of the line, compare Milton, *Sonnet: I did but prompt* 10: 'And still revolt when truth would set them free' ('truth', TSE, 31, 32, 33).

23 **know what else you seek**: compare *Paradise Lost* VII 639: 'know; if else thou seek'st'.

26 **nowise**: a favourite word for Browning (more than 130 instances). Swinburne has a similar tone; *Atalanta in Calydon* (1865): 'And these things nowise move me', and 'But nowise through her living' (the speech by Althea beginning 'Look you, I speak not', and that by Plexippus beginning 'Let her come crowned'). TSE's philosophical prose 1911–16 often has recourse to 'no wise' in pondering the 'real' and the 'true' (both invoked in this line of the poem): 'it is no wise true that . . .'; 'Nor do we advance a step farther by affirming that everything is real, for this alteration merely crams all the unreality into thought which was formerly in perception, and in nowise resolves the question'; 'the reality of a "thing" (we are here painfully hampered by language) is in no wise limited to its thinghood'; 'the assertion that "the monads have no windows" in no wise entangles him [Leibniz] in solipsism, for [. . .] our knowledge [. . .] is only through physical appearance within our own world' (with 'Appearances appearances', followed by 'the world' in 15–16 and characterized in 25–26 of the poem, along with 'window' in 37 and 46); 'To say that I can know only my own states, accordingly, is in no wise the foundation of solipsism, unless it were possible that I should know my states as my states, and as nothing else, which would be a palpable contradiction' – compare the nexus in these lines of the poem: 'Contradiction', 21 and 22; 'know' and 'else', 23; 'nothing', 24 (*KEPB*, pp.75, 135–6, 141, 146, 147). TSE's early Harvard essay, *The validity of artificial distinctions*, has: 'They can in no wise pretend to be ultimate'; and a paper on matter and form: 'described only and in no wise explained' (Houghton Library; bMS Am 1691.14 (26), p.5, (27), p.3). **real; unreal**: compare *The Waste Land MS*, p.27, *The Fire Sermon* 53: 'Unreal emotions, and real appetite'.

28 **Hopeful of what?**: compare, at the head of the line, *Samson Agonistes* 1575: 'Hopeful of his delivery' (but Samson is dead; compare TSE's next line). **whether you**: compare TSE in 1926 (*VMP*, p.115): 'for whether you seek the Absolute in marriage, adultery or debauchery, it is all one – you are seeking in the wrong place'; together with 'you seek' (TSE, 23), with the invocation of Bradley pertinent to 'the Absolute', and with 'no other place' (34). **thanksgiving**: OED 2, 'a prayer or religious service used to render thanks for Divine benefits'.

29 **Or pray for earth on tired body and head**: John T. Mayer takes this, with the previous line, to mean: 'whether he follows Western ways (observes thanksgiving) or Eastern ones (prays on his head)' (*T. S. Eliot's Silent Voices*, p.142). But the sense is: pray that earth be on one's head, that one be buried. Compare Pascal: 'On jette enfin de la terre sur la tête, et en voilà pour jamais' (*Pensées*, section III, no.210). Compare Swinburne, *Laus Veneris* (1866) 57–8:
   Ah yet would God that stems and roots were bred
   Out of my weary body and my head,
TSE quoted *Laus Veneris* in a letter to Aiken, 19 July 1914 (*Letters* i 40–1). **tired body and head**: compare *Humouresque (After J. Laforgue)* 2–3:

not yet tired of the game –
But weak in body as in head.

30 **This word . . . the paths:** 'this word' is repeatedly Biblical. Compare Isaiah
30:11–12: 'turn aside out of the path', 'Because ye despise this word'. Hebrews
12:26–7: 'shake not the earth only, but also heaven. And this word, Yet once
more' (TSE, 7, 'heaven'). Isaiah 8:20: 'if they speak not according to this word, it
is because there is no light in them' (TSE, 40, 'light'), with the previous verse:
'should not a people seek unto their God? for the living to the dead' (TSE, 23,
'seek', and 32–3, 'the living . . . the dead').

30–1 **all the paths you tread . . . said:** compare Deuteronomy 11:25: 'all the land
that ye shall tread upon, as he hath said unto you'.

30–3 **true . . . As true as truth . . . truth . . . truth:** *Troilus and Cressida*, III ii 161–
80, has 'true' four times and 'truth' eight times in twenty lines, including 165–6:
I am as true as truth's simplicity,
And simpler than the infancy of truth.

32 **no truth:** as in Hosea 4:1: 'no truth, nor mercy, nor knowledge of God in the
land'. John 8:44: 'because there is no truth in him'.

32–3 **among the living . . . the dead:** placed at the line-ends, compare Shelley, *To
Stella (from the Greek of Plato)* 1, 4: 'Thou wert the morning star among the
living', 'New splendour to the dead'. **the living . . . the dead:** given TSE's setting
(and 'crept', 39), compare Tennyson, *Locksley Hall Sixty Years After* 222–4:
There a single sordid attic holds the living and the dead. //
There the smouldering fire of fever creeps across the rotted floor,
And the crowded couch of incest in the warrens of the poor.
among the dead: compare Milton, Psalm LXXXVIII 18: 'Among the dead to
sleep'.

34 **No other . . . no other:** compare Keats, *Sonnet* XVII 1–3:
Happy is England! I could be content
To see no other verdure than its own;
To feel no other breezes than are blown
Compare 'breeze' (TSE, 45) and 'blow' (12), while registering the sentiment for
the expatriate TSE. The repetition ('no other . . . no other') is found later in TSE
(*Time and Tide*, 19 Jan. 1935), with some affinity with *Oh little voices*, in
invoking salvation and damnation ('heaven and hell', 7): 'The ultimate meaning
of liberty is that each individual should be free to determine his own eternal
salvation or damnation. There is no other final meaning, there is no other final
value, to liberty than this. *La sua voleuntade e nostra pace* is the last word about
free will'.

36 till the morning broke: given 'Until' and the last three words at the line-end, compare Shelley, *The Revolt of Islam* [VII] 2904–5:

Until upon their path the morning broke;
They anchored then, where, be there calm or breeze,

TSE, 8, 'paths'; 45, at the line-end, 'then . . . breeze'. Shelley's next stanza speaks of 'shadows which pursued' / TSE, 39–43, 'the shadows' and their activity.

36, 38–9, 41–2, 44 -chair . . . Stirred . . . crawled . . . leapt . . . crawled . . . lair: compare Wilkie Collins, *The Woman in White* (1860), The Third Epoch viii: 'I had stirred in its lair the serpent-hatred of years – but only for a moment. Like a lurking reptile, it leaped up at me – as she eagerly bent forward toward the place in which I was sitting. Like a lurking reptile, it dropped out of sight again – as she instantly resumed her former position in the chair'. TSE called *The Woman in White* 'the greatest of Collins's novels' (*Wilkie Collins and Dickens*, 1927, SE, pp.463–4).

37 Across the window panes: as in *Interlude in London* 2.

37–8 Across the window panes . . . Stirred by the morning air: compare *The Waste Land* [II] 89–90: 'stirred by the air / That freshened from the window'. *Sweeney Erect* 9: 'Morning stirs the feet'. *Suppressed Complex* 7 (variant): 'morning stirred the long nasturtium'. In *Oh little voices*, shadowy figures immediately threaten, as in *The Family Reunion*, where Harry (scenting the Eumenides – 'the pursuers') asks: 'Do you feel a kind of stirring underneath the air?' (II ii).

37–45 Grover Smith (*Eliot and the Ghost of Poe*, in *T. S. Eliot: A Voice Descanting*, ed. S. Bagchee, 1990, pp.156–8) compared, by contrast, Poe, *The Sleeper* 20–9:

The wanton airs, from the tree-top,
Laughingly through the lattice drop –
The bodiless airs, a wizard rout,
Flit through thy chamber in and out,
And wave the curtain canopy
So fitfully – so fearfully –
Above the closed and fringéd lid
'Neath which thy slumb'ring soul lies hid,
That, o'er the floor and down the wall,
Like ghosts and shadows rise and fall!

38–40 Stirred . . . the shadows crawled and crept . . . through the trees: compare a paragraph of *The Picture of Dorian Gray*, ch.XI: 'Gradually white fingers creep through the curtains, and they appear to tremble. In black fantastic shapes, dumb shadows crawl into the corners of the room, and crouch there. Outside, there is the stirring of birds among the leaves.' 'Out of the unreal shadows of the night comes back the real life that we had known' (TSE, 26, 'real; unreal').

39 **Across the floor the shadows crawled and crept**: compare *Prufrock's Pervigilium*
19–21:
> the darkness
> Crawling among the papers on the table
> It leapt to the floor

and 35: 'the darkness creep along the wall'.

39, 41 **the shadows . . . form**: compare a passage from Shelley of which TSE quoted
nine lines in *The Cocktail Party*, Act III. *Prometheus Unbound* I 195–8:
> For know there are two worlds of life and death:
> One that which thou beholdest; but the other
> Is underneath the grave, where do inhabit
> The shadows of all forms that think and live

The apparitions in 39–44 resemble the devilish forms that harass the saint in
Tennyson, *St Simeon Stylites* 168–76; Tennyson 171, 'In bed like monstrous apes
they crushed my chest', helped to create the passage from *The Picture of Dorian
Gray* (ch.VII) which coloured *Prufrock's Pervigilium*, a poem with many
affinities to *Oh little voices* (itself an imperfect vigil – 'And dozed'): 'He
remembered wandering through dimly-lit streets, past gaunt black-shadowed
archways and evil-looking houses. Women with hoarse voices and harsh laughter
had called after him. Drunkards had reeled by cursing, and chattering to
themselves like monstrous apes.'

39–42 **shadows . . . trees / Around . . . muffled . . . knees**: compare Tennyson, *The
Talking Oak* 149–50 (taking in Tennyson's title and subject):
> O muffle round thy knees with fern,
> And shadow Sumner-chace!

40 **thin light**: compare *Humouresque (After J. Laforgue)* 19: 'thin moonlight'. *OED*
'thin', 3c: 'Wanting depth or intensity; faint, weak, dim, pale. Formerly of light
(*arch.*)'; from 1649. **shivered**: both *OED* 'shiver' verb 1 2: 'To fly in pieces; to
split'; and verb 2 1b: 'To tremble', including 1878, 'The air shivered with noise'.

40–1 **shivered through the trees . . . danced**: compare *Maud*, I [vi] 259–62, which
recurred to TSE:
> Where I hear the dead at midday moan,
> And the shrieking rush of the wainscot mouse,
> And my own sad name in corners cried,
> When the shiver of dancing leaves is thrown

(TSE, 33, 'the dead'.)

44, 48 **lair . . . stair**: compare *Circe's Palace* 8, 10: 'lairs' / 'stairs'.

45 **And then sprang up a little damp dead breeze**: compare *The wind sprang up at
four o'clock*; also *Song for the Opherion* 8 (*The Waste Land MS*, p.99): 'The

wind sprang up and broke the bells'. **dead:** *OED* IV: 'Without motion'; 22a: 'Of water, air, etc.: Without motion or current'. 1861, 'The wind had fallen dead'; but having fallen is the opposite of springing up, and TSE combines a movement through time with a paradox or a resurrection ('sprang up a . . . dead breeze'). Compare Bulwer Lytton, *A Night in Italy* 81: 'The night said not a word. The breeze was dead'; the poem is in Quiller-Couch's *Oxford Book of English Verse* (1900).

46 rattled at the window: compare the title and opening line of *Morning at the Window*: 'They are rattling breakfast plates in basement kitchens'.

47 human voices: compare *The Love Song of J. Alfred Prufrock* 131: 'Till human voices wake us, and we drown'. Compare Tennyson, *The Voyage of Maeldune* 27–8:
And we came to the Isle of Shouting, we landed, a score of wild birds
Cried from the topmost summit with human voices and words;

47, 49 human voices . . . known: compare *Paradise Lost* IX 560–1:
Thee, serpent, subtlest beast of all the field
I knew, but not with human voice endued;
chimneys . . . laughed: compare Whittier, *Snow-Bound* (1866) 164: 'The great throat of the chimney laughed' / TSE, 1, 'throats'. Also (noting too TSE, 41, 'leapt', and 39, 'floor'), W. D. Howells, *Forlorn* (1873) 48–50:
Leaped loud in welcome from the hollow floors; //
But gusts that blew all day with solemn laughter
From wide-mouthed chimney-places

48 along the stair: *OED* B 1: 'Through the whole or entire length of; from end to end of'; as Thomson, *Winter* 186: 'The whirling Tempest raves along the plain'. TSE's usage resists the feeling that 'along' moves horizontally.

49 had not known: 'have not known', 'hast not known', Biblically very frequent. **laughed or wept:** TSE's ending is very close to John Gray's for *The Barber* (1893); compare TSE's rhyme upon 'crept', his 'shoulders' and 'hair', and the suggestions of madness (plus TSE, 1, 'the throats of men'), with Gray's concluding stanza:
So, at the sound, the blood of me stood cold.
Thy chaste hair ripened into sullen gold.
The throat, the shoulders, swelled and were uncouth.
The breasts rose up and offered each a mouth.
And on the belly pallid blushes crept,
That maddened me, until I laughed and wept.
Also Ecclesiastes 3:4: 'a time to weep, and a time to laugh' (the passage reconceived in *The Love Song of J. Alfred Prufrock* 26–34 and at the beginning of *East Coker*).

The Love Song of St. Sebastian

Printed in *Letters* i 46–7. Sent by TSE in a letter to Aiken, from Marburg, 25 July 1914, with *Oh little voices of the throats of men*. (The typescript of the poems sent to Aiken is now in the McKeldin Library; 'This letter [now in the Huntington Library] and the poems became separated when Aiken sold the latter to a private collector', *Letters* i 44.)

> I enclose some *stuff* – the *thing* I showed you some time ago, and some of the themes for the "Descent from the Cross" or whatever I may call it. I send them, even in their present form, because I am disappointed in them, and wonder whether I had better knock it off for a while – you will tell me what you think. Do you think that the *Love Song of St. Sebastian* part is morbid, or forced? Then there will be an Insane Section, and another love song (of a happier sort) and a recurring piece quite in the French style beginning
> "The married girl who lives across the street
> Wraps her soul in orange-coloured robes of Chopinese." –
> Then a mystical section, – and a Fool-House section beginning
> "Let us go to the masquerade and dance!
> I am going as St. John among the Rocks
> Attired in my underwear and socks . . .
> Does it all seem very laboured and conscious? The S. Sebastian title I feel almost sure of; I have studied S. Sebastians – why should anyone paint a beautiful youth and stick him full of pins (or arrows) unless he felt a little as the hero of my verse? Only there's nothing homosexual about this – rather an important difference perhaps – but no one ever painted a female Sebastian, did they? So I give this title *faute de mieux*.

(Also TSE to Aiken, 30 Sept. 1914, about this poem and *Oh little voices of the throats of men*: 'The stuff I sent you is not good, is very forced in execution, though the idea was right, I think'; *Letters* i 58.)

'Only there's nothing homosexual about this': the word *homosexual* was still fairly new; *OED* cites it from 1892, and Shaw used it in the *New Statesman* in 1914. Ian Fletcher notes (*The Poems of John Gray*, 1988, p.325), of John Gray's poem, *Saint Sebastian: On a Picture* (1896): 'Homosexuals had a particular cult of Saint Sebastian. The combination of nudity and the phallic arrows was irresistible. Baron Corvo, for example, has two sonnets [1891] for a pointing [sic; Freudian slip?] of the Saint by Guido Reni in the Capitoline Gallery at Rome.' Of *Saint Sebastian: On a Picture*, Fletcher suggests that the picture is probably that by Albrecht Altdorfer. Gray, 9, 'The stair they stand on' (Altdorfer shows stairs), which may colour TSE, 3, 'at the foot of your stair'; Gray, 35, 'Their ears' / TSE, 28, 'your ears'; and 51, 'Pale Sebastian's feet' / TSE, 12, 'your feet are white'.

The conjunction of *Love Song* and *St. Sebastian* owes something to Gray, whose *Saint Sebastian: On a Picture* is followed, seven poems later in *Spiritual Songs*

(1896), by *Lovesong to the Bridegroom*. This latter, a forty-line translation from Friedrich Spe, might itself have prompted recollection of St Sebastian since it includes 'arrows', 'shoots a thousand darts', 'pain', and 'sharp to kill'. TSE's repetition of 'white', 12–14, might suggest Gray's *Lovesong*, 'White arm of Jesus and white hands'; and Gray's 'my sore breast', 'against his breast' / TSE, 21, 'Between your breasts'.

Wilde's *The Picture of Dorian Gray* (1891), ch.XI, has among its vestments 'medallions of many saints and martyrs, among whom was St. Sebastian'. On the widespread *fin de siècle* fascination with St Sebastian, see Richard Kaye, *Voluptuous Immobility: St. Sebastian and the Decadent Imagination* (1997).

The movement in TSE's letter from the tentative title for his poems, the *Descent from the Cross*, to the 'homosexual' may owe something to the conviction of (among others) Henry James, that the Descent from the Cross is the masterpiece of the painter Sodoma (*Siena Early and Late* I, 1873, an essay which coloured *Prufrock's Pervigilium*; *Italian Hours*, 1909, p.358).

'St. John among the Rocks' in TSE's letter: suggesting St John the Divine, not only the landscape of Patmos but Revelation 6:15: 'And the kings of the earth, and the great men, and the rich men, and the chief captains, and the mighty men, and every bondman, and every free man, hid themselves in the dens and in the rocks of the mountains.' But St John the Baptist should not be excluded (especially given TSE's liking for doublings, as with his Saint Narcissus). For in his Baedeker's *London and Its Environs* (1908, dated by TSE 14 October 1910), he marked on p.170: '*Leonardo da Vinci* (1452–1519), Madonna and Child, with John the Baptist and an angel, a studio-copy, with alterations, of "La Vierge aux Rochers" in the Louvre.' In his Baedeker, TSE also marked, on p.168, '*Antonio Pollaiuolo* (d. 1498), Martyrdom of St. Sebastian' (both in the National Gallery).

TSE had written to Aiken, 19 July 1914 (*Letters* i 41–2):
There are *three* great *St. Sebastians* (so far as I know):
    1) Mantegna (ca d'Oro) [Venice]
    2) Antonello of Messina (Bergamo)
    3) Memling (Brussels)
    I have written some *stuff* – about 50 lines, but I find it shamefully laboured, and am belabouring it more. If I can improve it at all I will send it you.
(On his Italian visit, summer 1911, TSE had visited Venice, Ca d'Oro – 'Mantegna. First quality' – and Bergamo, noting: '*Ant. da Messina: St. Sebastian*'; Houghton Library; bMS Am 1691 (131).) Also to Sydney Schiff, 24 March 1920: 'Mantegna is a painter for whom I have a particular admiration – there is none who appeals to me more strongly. Do you know the St. Sebastian in the Franchetti's house on the Grand Canal?' (*Letters* i 376). The epigraph to *Burbank with a Baedeker: Bleistein with a Cigar* included 'nil nisi divinum stabile est; caetera fumus', the 'Lines on Mantegna's great *St. Sebastian* in the Ca d'Oro Venice', in TSE's words in a copy of *Ara Vos Prec*, 1920 (Houghton Library).

Lyndall Gordon, *Eliot's Early Years*, reproduces the Mantegna painting (plate 9); she remarks that the poem's St Sebastian has 'only tenuous links with the real saint, a Roman martyr in the time of Diocletian who, the fable goes, was sentenced to be shot by archers. Although the arrows pierced his flesh, he did not die but was rescued by a woman and nursed in her lodgings' (p.61). (Gordon believes: 'In the case of Eliot's saint, the martyrdom is not only self-inflicted, but is an exhibitionistic attempt to gain a woman's attention.') St Sebastian suffered a later martyrdom, without rescue; his death by the mace is alluded to in John Gray's other such poem, *Saint Sebastian* (*The Blue Calendar: January*, 1897).

Arrows are strikingly absent from the poem, even covertly; the name of St Sebastian is scarcely more to be deduced from *The Love Song of St. Sebastian* than the name of Prufrock from *The Love Song of J. Alfred Prufrock*. For arrows and another saint, compare a poem of this period, *The Death of Saint Narcissus* 33–7:

So he became a dancer to God.
Because his flesh was in love with the burning arrows
He danced on the hot sand
Until the arrows came.
As he embraced them his white skin surrendered itself to the redness of blood, and satisfied him.

Harvey Gross, *The Figure of St. Sebastian*, noted that of the three paintings (by Mantegna, Antonello and Memling), 'It is clearly Mantegna's painting that makes the strongest impression on Eliot's imagination.' Gross suggests, further, a debt to Gabriele d'Annunzio's sensational dance-drama or mystery play, *Le Martyre de Saint Sébastien*, written in French by d'Annunzio, with music by Debussy and sets by Léon Bakst; it was staged in Paris and danced by Ida Rubinstein, 29 May to 19 June 1911, when Eliot could have seen it. (*Southern Review*, Autumn 1985; *T. S. Eliot: Essays from the Southern Review*, ed. James Olney, 1988, pp.105–9.)

Compare Apollinaire's *La Chanson du Mal-Aimé* (May 1909; *Alcools*, 1913) 48–50:

Pour chauffer un coeur plus glacé
Que les quarante de Sébaste
Moins que ma vie martyrisés

(Apollinaire's poem influenced *Interlude in London* and probably *Fourth Caprice in Montparnasse*.)

John Gray's *Saint Sebastian* (*The Blue Calendar: January*, 1897) praises the saint: 'At thy bright touch their sicknesses were healed' (4). Remy de Gourmont listed 'St. Sébastien' among the 'Saints guérisseurs', as curing 'Peste' (Plague), in *Le Paganisme éternel* (*La Culture des idées*, 1901). This would fit with TSE's having been influenced in his poem's erotic morbidity by a poem which mentions and turns upon 'plague', Swinburne's *The Leper* (1866). TSE picked out *The Leper* as indispensable to any selection of Swinburne (*Swinburne as Poet*, 1920, *SE*, p.323). Compare *The Leper* 18–20:

Yet am I glad to have her dead
Here in this wretched wattled house
Where I can kiss her eyes and head.

Swinburne's sado-masochism is one crucial precedent for the 'torture and delight' (6) in TSE's poem. Another has been suggested by Grover Smith (*Eliot and the Ghost of Poe*, in *T. S. Eliot: A Voice Descanting*, ed. S. Bagchee, 1990, p.163): *The Love Song of St. Sebastian* 'must have been indebted rhetorically to W. B. Yeats's *He Wishes His Beloved Were Dead*' (1899). Compare in particular with TSE (19–23, 34–7), Yeats's opening lines:

Were you but lying cold and dead,
And lights were paling out of the West,
You would come hither, and bend your head,
And I would lay my head on your breast;
And you would murmur tender words,
Forgiving me, because you were dead:

Grover Smith here (p.153) says that *The Love Song of St. Sebastian* 'concerns no authentic saint'; yet there is poetic precedent for self-flagellating saints, for instance Tennyson's *St Simeon Stylites* (on which, see *Oh little voices of the throats of men* 39, 41 note). Smith (pp.153–5) compares Poe's *To Annie*, of which TSE said: 'Only after you find that it goes on throbbing in your head, do you begin to suspect that perhaps you will never forget it' (*The Listener*, 25 Feb. 1943).

TSE wrote to Aiken, 16 Nov. 1914 (*Letters* i 69):

I think that you criticise my verse too leniently. It still seems to me strained and intellectual. I know the kind of verse I want, and I know that this isn't it, and I know why. I shan't do anything that will satisfy me (as some of my old stuff *does* satisfy me – whether it be good or not) for years, I feel it more and more.

Title: compare *The Love Song of J. Alfred Prufrock*, which TSE said (*Kipling Journal*, March 1959) would not have been so named had it not been for Kipling's *Love Song of Har Dyal* (1888).

1 **shirt of hair:** *OED* 1c, = hair-shirt; the last instance being Cowper, *Truth* (1782) 81: 'In shirt of hair and weeds of canvas dress'd'. Cowper distinguishes such 'blood' and 'stripes', 'sore tormented', from true 'saints' and 'prayer'. *Truth* 89–90:

Wearing out life in his religious whim,
'Till his religious whimsy wears out him.

3 **at the foot of your stair:** compare *Do I know how I feel?* 4: 'at the foot of the stair'. Compare *The Death of the Duchess* 29 (*The Waste Land MS*, p.105): 'There will be no footsteps up and down the stair'.

6 **And torture and delight:** likewise rhyming with 'night', compare *The Burnt Dancer* 23: 'Agony nearest to delight'. **and delight:** at the line-end, in Shelley,

Hellas 1036–41, sharing with TSE the rhyme 'delight' / 'light' / 'night', as well as 'lamp' (7), in a setting of 'wild desire' and 'beauty':

> And, like loveliness panting with wild desire
> While it trembles with fear and delight,
> Hesperus flies from awakening night,
> And pants in its beauty and speed with light
> Fast-flashing, soft, and bright.
> Thou beacon of love! thou lamp of the free!

7 **Until my blood should ring the lamp**: to Aiken, TSE wrote of this line, in the margin: 'Does this mean anything to you? I mean stand all about in a pool on the floor'. **ring the lamp**: given 'stair' (3), compare *Rhapsody on a Windy Night* 74: 'The little lamp spreads a ring on the stair'. (The McKeldin text of *The Love Song of St. Sebastian* 2: 'I would come with a little lamp in the night'.)

9 **I should**: previously, thrice, 'I would'; thereafter, both forms. With these and related reiterations throughout the poem, compare *La Figlia Che Piange*, which has 'I would have had' (twice), 'he would have', 'I should', 'we both should', 'they should have been'. **neophyte**: *OED*, 'Not in general use before the 19th c.'; 1a: 'A new convert; one newly admitted to a church or religious body. Used chiefly with ref. to the primitive Christian, or the Roman Catholic, Church; in the latter, also applied to a newly ordained priest, or to a novice of a religious order'.

10 **And then put out the light**: compare *Othello*, v ii 7: 'Put out the light, and then put out the light'; and compare 34 below: 'You would love me because I should have strangled you'. Compare Symons, *In Bohemia* (1892) 13–15:

> put out the light:
> 'Tis morning, let the daylight come.
> God! how the women's cheeks are white,

Compare TSE, 'the morning came' (20), and 'your feet are white' (12). Compare *Choruses from 'The Rock'* x: 'And we must extinguish the candle, put out the light and relight it'.

11 **lead**: to Aiken, TSE wrote in the margin: 'preterite! not present'. The spelling 'led' would have made this clear. *Oh little voices* 18 likewise has 'lead' for the past tense. In his papers on philosophy, TSE has, for 'led' and 'misled', 'lead' and 'mislead' (Houghton Library; bMS Am 1691.14 (29), p.1, and (32), p.6).

11–12 **To follow where . . . To follow where**: compare TSE's poem of a 'cruel I' with Shelley, *Kissing Helena (from the Greek of Plato)* 5–6:

> To follow where the kiss should guide it,
>   Oh, cruel I,

12 **your feet**: Swinburne three times mentions the loved one's feet in *The Leper* 33–4, 43. (See headnote.)

16 you would take me in (repeated in 18): Symons, *Alla Passeretta Bruna* (1891), ends:

> And the light is night above,
> You will let me in,
> You will take me.

17 hideous in your sight: compare Job 18:3: 'Wherefore are we counted as beasts, And reputed vile in your sight?'

18 without shame: given 'torture' (6), compare Shelley, *The Revolt of Islam* [x] 3979: 'Naked they were from torture, without shame', likewise rhyming with 'came'.

20–1 And when the morning came / Between your breasts should lie my head: compare the Song of Solomon 1:13: 'He shall lie all night betwixt my breasts'. Compare Symons, *To Muriel: at the Opera* (1895) 2: 'Nestle between your breasts to-night'.

24, 28 Your ears curl back . . . your ears were curled: contrast Swinburne, *The Leper* 12: 'Her curled-up lips and amorous hair' (see 12 note and headnote).

25 no one's else: compare TSE to Aiken, 30 Sept. 1914: 'The thing is to be able to look at one's life as if it were somebody's else – (I much prefer to say somebody else's)' (*Letters* i 58–9).

26 all the world shall melt: compare Amos 9:13: 'all the hills shall melt'.

29–30 linger . . . finger: compare the rhyme in *The Love Song of J. Alfred Prufrock* 76–7:

> Smoothed by long fingers,
> Asleep . . . tired . . . or it malingers,

32 I think that at last you would understand: compare *La Figlia Che Piange* 15: 'Some way we both should understand'.

34 because I should have strangled you: as in a poem which impelled TSE's as a whole, Browning, *Porphyria's Lover* 41: 'And strangled her'. Compare Wilde, *Ballad of Reading Gaol* (1898) I 37: 'Yet each man kills the thing he loves', a line which figured (as Harvey Gross noted; see headnote), in translation, in d'Annunzio's *Le Martyre de Saint Sébastien*: 'Il faut que chacun / tue son amour'.

34–7 because: crucial in four consecutive lines, the word suggests *KEPB*, p.144: 'for any explanation in terms of "because" (a term made necessary by the weakness of human conceiving) can be only misleading unless we turn it about the other way as well.' Compare *Ash-Wednesday* I, which has 'Because' at the head of eleven of its forty-one lines.

35 **infamy**: as in the epigraph to *The Love Song of J. Alfred Prufrock*, ending 'senza tema d'infamia ti rispondo' (*Inferno* XXVII 66). In his essay on Ben Jonson (1919, *SE*, p.156), TSE quoted from Beaumont and Fletcher a passage which likewise rhymes 'me' with 'infamy':

> Wilt thou, hereafter, when they talk of me,
> As thou shalt hear nothing but infamy,
> Remember some of these things? . . .
> I pray thee, do; for thou shalt never see me so again.

(*A King and No King*, III i.) The same rhyme, manifest though within prose, is strong in a verse of *The Bhagavad-Gita* which TSE marked in pencil (translated by Lionel Barnett, 1905; TSE's copy, dated 1912, is in the Houghton Library). Lesson the Tenth, verses 5–6, is pertinent to *The Love Song of St. Sebastian*, with 'mortification', 'delight' (TSE, 6), 'infamy' / 'Me', followed by 'Saints':

> harmlessness, indifference, delight, mortification, almsgiving, fame, and infamy – these are the forms of born beings' existence severally dispensed by Me.
>
> The seven Great Saints [. . .]

Barnett has a note to Lesson the Second, verse 59: 'Mortification of the flesh in itself (practised without regard to a Deity) may *practically* raise a man above the weaknesses of the flesh; but there still remains in him a potentiality of carnal sin, a relish for the things of the flesh.'

Do I know how I feel? Do I know what I think?

1 **Do I know how I feel? Do I know what I think?**: compare *Portrait of a Lady* III 36: 'Not knowing what to feel'. *The Waste Land MS*, p.31, *The Fire Sermon* 110: 'Knowing neither how to think, nor how to feel'; and p.37, *The Fire Sermon* (insertion) 5: 'Knowing little what they think, and muchless what they feel'. *The Death of the Duchess* 5, 8 (*The Waste Land MS*, p.105): 'They know what they are to feel and what to think', 'They know what to think and what to feel'. Relatedly, *Entretien dans un parc* 21: 'And what we feel, or not'. TSE marked his copy of Bernard Bosanquet, *The Essentials of Logic*, p.11, underlining 'whatever we are obliged to think' and writing in the margin: 'How can I know what I am obliged to think?' (The 1910 edition was bought by TSE, 16 Jan. 1914; Houghton Library.) TSE's address at Milton Academy, 17 June 1933, moved from a warning ('If you want to write poetry, keep away from pencils and paper and typewriters until you have overcome the temptation') to insist in the next paragraph: 'Whatever you think, be sure that it is what you think; whatever you want, be sure that it is what you want; whatever you feel, be sure that it is what you feel' (*Milton Graduates Bulletin*, Nov. 1933, pp.7–8); compare 1–2 here.   I feel . . . think: TSE marked *Dejection* 87–90 in his copy of Coleridge's *Poetical Works* (1907, Houghton Library):

> For not to think of what I needs must feel,
> But to be still and patient, all I can;
> And haply by abstruse research to steal
> From my own nature all the natural man –

1–2 **feel . . . think . . . pen and ink**: twelve days after his father's death, TSE wrote to his mother, reaching back perhaps to this poem about letters (5) and about death (and which repeats 'little', 'little', 20, 24): 'You will know that my thoughts have been with you every day, though it always seems that little, very little, can ever filter through to pen and ink of what one feels. I am waiting as patiently as I can for letters. [*New paragraph*] One keeps thinking of little things – I have been longing to have some little drawings of father's' (19 Jan. 1919, *Letters* i 268). Next month (27 Feb. 1919, *Letters* i 273), writing to his brother Henry about these drawings, TSE said of his father: 'he hardly knew himself what he was like'.

1–3 **Do I know . . . let me take pen and ink . . . with my hat . . . take the air**: compare (in addition to 1 note) *Portrait of a Lady*: 'you do not know, you do not know'; 'me sitting pen in hand'; 'I take my hat'; 'Let us take the air' (twice) (II 4, III 33, II 29, I 36 and III 30).

4 **at the foot of the stair**: compare *The Love Song of St. Sebastian* 3: 'at the foot of your stair'.

5—9 Compare this imagined fearful exchange with *The Death of the Duchess* 51—3 (*The Waste Land MS*, p.107):

> Tomorrow when we open to the chambermaid
> When we open the door
> Could we address her or should we be afraid?

7 second floor: US English would mean by this the British first floor; see *In the Department Store* 6 note.

10 so much beauty: as in Tennyson, *The Lover's Tale* I 206.

10—11 spilled on the open street / Or: compare Symons, *Summer in Spring* (1913) 8: 'Or spilt upon the streets'. **street / Or wasted**: compare Kipling, *The Broken Men* (1903) 69—70:

> Our towns of wasted honour –
> Our streets of lost delight!

TSE acknowledged *The Broken Men* as, with Morris's *The Hollow Land*, the source of his title *The Hollow Men*; see Appendix D, p.395.

10—12 beauty spilled . . . wasted . . . untasted: compare Symons, *Wasted Beauty* (1906) 1—2:

> This beauty is vain, this, born to be wasted,
> Poured on the ground like water, spilled, and by no man tasted.

In TSE, 16, is the variant 'water'. **wasted . . . untasted**: compare Shelley, *Prometheus Unbound* I 528—9:

> From wide cities, famine-wasted;
> Groans half heard, and blood untasted;

Compare the sentiment, as to waste, with Thomas Gray, *Elegy Written in a Country Churchyard* 53—6:

> Full many a gem of purest ray serene,
> The dark unfathomed caves of ocean bear:
> Full many a flower is born to blush unseen,
> And waste its sweetness on the desert air.

TSE, 'wasted' and 'darkened chambers'; also TSE, 'villages' / Gray, 'village-' in his next line.

12 neurasthetic (variant): not in *OED*, but 'neurasthenic'. Neurasthenia: '*Path*. An atonic condition of the nervous system; functional nervous weakness; nervous debility'; from 1856. *The Nature and Diagnosis of Neurasthenia* (1879) by Beard. (There is a pointed beard in TSE, 17.) **darkened chambers**: compare Wilde, *The Picture of Dorian Gray* (1891), ch.XVI, the opium-den: 'a little staircase, leading to a darkened chamber'. Wilde's paragraph influenced *Prufrock's Pervigilium*; see its 23 note, and 16 note below. Given 'on the open street'

(10), compare *Rhapsody on a Windy Night* 63–4 (Notebook text, first reading, Appendix B):

> on the streets
> And female smells in darkened rooms,

13 **restless on winter nights**: compare *The Love Song of J. Alfred Prufrock* 6: 'restless nights', as in *Oh little voices of the throats of men* 17. **who can blame us?**: compare Kipling, *Gentleman-Rankers* (1892) 28: 'Can you blame us if we soak ourselves in beer?' TSE quoted four lines of *Gentleman-Rankers* in a review of Kipling, *The Athenaeum*, 9 May 1919, and included the poem in his *Choice of Kipling's Verse*. See also 21–2 note.

15–16 **slips . . . at my finger tips . . . that drips**: compare *Portrait of a Lady* I 9, 14, rhyming 'finger-tips' / 'slips' – the conversation being about the pianist of Chopin. Symons ends *The Chopin Player*: 'Dying delicately at my finger tips?', rhyming with 'and drips'. (TSE, 19, 'death'.) Symons's sonnet begins: 'The sounds torture me: I see them in my brain'; TSE ends 21: 'in the brain'. Also Symons, 6, 'They die of a touch' / TSE, 'death', and 'touch', 22. Symons gave his poem in full at the end of his essay *Pachmann and the Piano*, in *Plays, Acting, and Music*, 1903, and collected the poem in 1906. Symons would have known Swinburne, *Laus Veneris* (1866), which likewise rhymes 'finger-tips' with 'drips', in lines (149–52) which twice speak of 'death'. TSE quoted *Laus Veneris* in a letter to Aiken, 19 July 1914 (*Letters* i 40–1).

16 **creolin**: a disinfectant; in *OED* within citations for Jeyes' fluid and lysol; 1891, as 'creoline'. **something that drips**: among several suggestions of *The Picture of Dorian Gray* (1891), there is the murder with its consequent suicide:

> Something began to trickle on the floor. He waited for a moment, still pressing the head down. Then he threw the knife on the table, and listened.
> He could hear nothing, but the drip, drip on the threadbare carpet.

There (ch.XIII) is a 'knife' (TSE, 18), and in the next chapter 'a large mahogany chest of chemicals' (TSE, 18, 'chemicals') with which the accomplice disposes of the body. ('There was a horrible smell of nitric acid in the room. But the thing that had been sitting at the table was gone'.) The man whom Dorian Gray blackmails into doing this commits suicide. Dorian has his secret (TSE, 22), one which causes these deaths and which involves a cause of death that was also the cause of the life (TSE, 19).

17 **black bag with a pointed beard and tobacco**: compare TSE's *Tristan Corbière* 4: 'barbe pointue'. Compare perhaps the doctor in Charles-Louis Philippe, *Marie Donadieu* (1904), part II ch.II: 'une barbe noire', 'le jeune homme était médecin', 'on peut fumer son cigare'. For TSE on this book, see Appendix D (p.407).

19 **Will investigate the cause of death**: compare *Eeldrop and Appleplex*: 'In Gopsum

Street a man murders his mistress [. . .] For the man's neighbors the important fact is what the man killed her with? And at precisely what time? And who found the body? For the "enlightened public" the case is merely evidence for the Drink question, or Unemployment, or some other category of things to be reformed. But the mediaeval world, insisting on the eternity of punishment, expressed something nearer the truth' (*Little Review*, iv, May 1917, p.9). Compare Corbière, *Pauvre Garçon* (1873) 11: 'Car il est mort, de quoi?'

19–20 **life . . . in the brain**: given the line-end, compare Tennyson, *In Memoriam* CXXI 8: 'And life is darkened in the brain' (TSE, 12, 'darkened').

20, 24 **a little whisper in the brain . . . a little laughter**: compare Symons, *The Dance of the Seven Sins* (1899), Avarice on imminent death:
Leaving me only, for my part,
A little love within my heart,
A little wisdom in my brain:
The worms of these shall have their gain;

21–2 **the ancient pain . . . touch**: compare W. G. Tinckom-Fernandez, *The Street Organ* 4–6 (published in the *Harvard Advocate*, 25 June 1908):
Still in my heart the ancient pain,
Where, in my heart, old memories lie,
Touched by the songs the organ plays.
(Also Tinckom-Fernandez, 7, 'live', and 10, 'slain' / TSE, 19, 'death' and 'life'.) For *The Street Organ* again, see *Interlude in London* headnote. **ancient pain**: compare Shelley, *Lines Written Among the Euganean Hills* 333: 'And its ancient pilot, Pain'. But note the first instance in *OED*, 'ancient' 5a, 1586: 'the ancient pain of the Head'. **pain . . . secret**: compare Kipling, *Gentleman-Rankers* 31–2:
Every secret, self-revealing on the aching whitewashed ceiling,
    Do you wonder that we drug ourselves from pain?
See 13 note.

23 **My brain is twisted in a tangled skein**: compare *The Death of the Duchess* 43 (*The Waste Land MS*, p.107): 'My thoughts in a tangled bunch of heads and tails'.

23–4 **tangled . . . blinding light**: compare Milton, *Comus* 181: 'In the blind mazes of this tangled wood'; and *On the Morning of Christ's Nativity* 188: 'twilight shade of tangled thickets'.

24, 26 **a little laughter . . . after**: compare Swinburne, *Anima Anceps* (1866) 33–5:
Though time rend after
Roof-tree from rafter,
A little laughter

25 **blackness of ether:** perhaps recalling John Davidson (whom TSE admired), *Insomnia* (1905) 4: 'Only the empty ether hovered black'. **ether:** compare *The Love Song of J. Alfred Prufrock* 3: 'Like a patient etherised upon a table'. *East Coker* III 22: 'Or when, under ether, the mind is conscious but conscious of nothing'. TSE noted, from William James's *Varieties of Religious Experience*, that B. P. Blood had shown how ether might stimulate mystical consciousness (transcriptions on index cards, Houghton Library; Crawford, *The Savage and the City*, p.80).

26 **either:** the relation of the word to 'ether' at the end of the previous line may be clarified by TSE's pronunciation of 'either' (when reading aloud *The Waste Land*) with a long *i*, not a long *e*.

Hidden under the heron's wing

Compare Tennyson, *Tithonus* 56–63:

> Glow with the glow that slowly crimsoned all
> Thy presence and thy portals, while I lay,
> Mouth, forehead, eyelids, growing dewy-warm
> With kisses balmier than half-opening buds
> Of April, and could hear the lips that kissed
> Whispering I knew not what of wild and sweet,
> Like that strange song I heard Apollo sing,
> While Ilion like a mist rose into towers.

TSE (in Tennyson's order): 'crimson'; 'I lie'; 'whisper of'; 'song . . . sing'; 'mist'.

1 **Hidden under the heron's wing**: compare *Coriolan: i. Triumphal March* 32: 'hidden under the dove's wing'; and *ii. Difficulties of a Statesman* 32: 'hidden under the . . . Hidden under the . . .' *Burnt Norton* IV 8: 'After the kingfisher's wing'.

2 **song before daybreak**: compare Swinburne, *Songs before Sunrise* (1871). Compare TSE, *Before Morning*. Jean Verdenal wrote to TSE, 22 April 1912: 'Je suis comme si j'avais toujours vécu à l'aube et comme si bientôt le soleil allait paraître' (*Letters* i 33). **lotos-birds**: *OED*, under 'lotos' 6, 1890: 'The *Parra gallinacea*, which in Australia is called the lotus-bird. It sits on the leaves that float on the water, particularly those of the water-lily'. **the lotos-birds sing**: compare the Song of Solomon 2:12: 'The time of the singing of birds is come'; see 4 note, as also for 'daybreak'.

2–3 **daybreak . . . sing . . . stars together**: compare Job 38:7: 'When the morning stars sang together'.

3 **Evening whisper of stars together**: contrast *Prufrock's Pervigilium* 16–17: 'in the darkness / Whispering all together'; and *Murder in the Cathedral*, Part I, opening chorus: 'whispers in darkness'.

4 **my beloved**: throughout the Song of Solomon (nearly twenty times), which then colours the whole of TSE's poem, as 2:16–17: 'My beloved is mine, and I am his: He feedeth among the lilies. Until the day break, and the shadows flee away, Turn, my beloved'. Compare 'before daybreak' (TSE, 2), and the 'lotos-birds' (2) with the 'lilies'. **what do you bring**: compare the Song of Solomon 8:2: 'bring thee into my mother's house', with 'wine' (compare TSE, 7, though there it might be poison or a drug).

5 **With evening feet walking across the grass**: in syntax, rhythm, and something of subject, suggesting the line by Wyatt, 'With naked foot stalking in my chamber'

(*They flee from me*), which is recalled in *Paysage Triste* 12: 'With naked feet passing across the skies', and in *Prufrock's Pervigilium* 31: 'With broken boot heels stained in many gutters'. In *The Oxford Book of English Verse* (1900), Wyatt's line was given smoothed: 'With naked foot stalking within my chamber'.

6 **fragile arms**: compare *Paradise Regained* III 386–9:

> To whom our Saviour answered thus unmoved.
> Much ostentation vain of fleshly arm,
> And fragile arms, much instrument of war
> Long in preparing, soon to nothing brought,

dividing the evening mist: compare *Paradise Lost* XII 629: 'Gliding meteorous, as evening mist'. Dividing and mist both figure in Genesis 1–2, the Creation (which is invoked too in the quotation from Job, 2–3 note above).

6, 8 **arms . . . crimson fist**: compare *Paradise Lost* II 173–4: 'arm again / His red right hand'. **the housemaid's crimson fist**: compare the maid Amanda in *The Waste Land MS*, p.23, *The Fire Sermon* 7: 'With coarsened hand, and hard plebeian tread'.

7–8 **I . . . the housemaid's crimson fist**: compare this poem (and its 'daybreak') with *Morning at the Window* 3: 'I am aware of the damp souls of housemaids'.

8 **crimson fist**: perhaps with some suggestion of 'red-handed', whether as being caught so, or bloody (from broken glass here?); compare Rider Haggard's *She*, ch.XVIII: 'How will this man take thee red-handed from the slaughter of her who loved and tended him?' (The woman, Ustane, had twice sung to him as 'my Beloved', ch.VII / TSE, 4.) **scarlet** (variant): compare the Song of Solomon 4:3: 'Thy lips are like a thread of scarlet', with 4:6: 'Until the day break' (compare TSE, 2), and 4:16: 'my beloved' (TSE, 4).

O lord, have patience

Epigraph (or superscription): compare TSE, *Dante* (1929, *SE*, pp.244–5):
    We cannot understand the inscription at Hell Gate:
      Giustizia mosse il mio alto Fattore;
      fecemi la divina Potestate,
      la somma Sapienza e il primo Amore.
    Justice moved my high Maker; what made me were the divine Power, the supreme
    Wisdom, and the primal Love.
    until we have ascended to the highest Heaven and returned.
(TSE amends the Temple Classics translation, and leaves 'the primal Love' in roman for emphasis.) The opening of *Inferno* III is quoted again by TSE at the end of the first section of his *Dante* (*SE*, p.251). In his review *Two Studies in Dante*, TSE wrote in *TLS* (11 Oct. 1928) about 'what is certainly the central idea of the Divine Comedy – the idea of Justice'; 'the importance of the conception of Justice in the Divine Comedy can hardly be over-estimated'; 'The Aristotelian "justice" as taken over by Dante is a term with progressive enlargement of meaning, from social or legal justice to Divine justice, which are related but not identical. It is largely due, we believe, to the romantic conception of justice that the Inferno has been, especially among Anglo-Saxon and Northern readers, the most popular and most apparently intelligible part of the Comedy.' Paul Elmer More thought well of TSE's *Dante*, and TSE wrote to him, 2 June 1930, with gratitude and dissent: 'But, equally seriously, I am perturbed by your comments on Hell. To me it *is giustizia, sapienza, amore*. And I cannot help saying, with all due respect of a (somewhat) younger and (much) more ignorant man, that I am really shocked by your assertion that God did not make Hell. It seems to me that you have lapsed into Humanitarianism. The Buddhist eliminates Hell – for I remember the yarn of the Hellpot Prayer, and I know that even Channa shall be saved – only by eliminating everything positive about Heaven (uttama paranibbana being obviously not heaven). Is your God Santa Claus?' (Princeton).
    Robert Crawford noted that TSE probably read James Thomson before reading Dante (and in some ways read Dante in the light of Thomson), and that in *The City of Dreadful Night* Thomson twice adopts the line ('They leave all hope behind who enter there', and 'Leave hope behind, all ye who enter here'), from this inscription at Hell Gate (I 78, VI 21; *The Savage and the City*, pp.42–3).

1 **O lord**: Biblical, especially when followed by an imperative plea or prayer. **O lord, have patience**: compare Matthew 18:26: 'The servant therefore fell down, and worshipped him, saying, Lord, have patience with me, and I will pay thee all.' (And again, 18:29: 'Have patience'.)

1, 3 **patience . . . irritations**: compare *First Caprice in North Cambridge* 9–10, rhyming 'patience' / 'considerations'; and *First Debate between the Body and*

Soul 5–7: 'patience' / 'sensations'. *The Waste Land* [v] 326, 330: 'reverberation' / 'patience'.

2 **derelictions:** *OED* 1: 'The action of leaving or forsaking (with intention not to resume); abandonment. (Now *rare* exc. in legal use.)' The religious application is clear from *OED*, in Donne: 'Desertion, or Dereliction'; and in Jeremy Taylor, though there the word is turned to take in the thought of abandoning sin: 'Repentance and dereliction of sins'. The modern use (*OED* 2), 'implying a morally wrong or reprehensible abandonment or neglect; chiefly in the phr. *dereliction of duty*', dates from 1778, Burke.

2, 4 **derelictions . . . my . . . convictions:** compare Browning, *Christmas-Eve* 1144–7:
> Let me enjoy my own conviction,
>   Not watch my neighbour's faith with fretfulness,
> Still spying there some dereliction
>   Of truth, perversity, forgetfulness!

3 **convince:** *OED* 1: 'To overcome' (*Obs.*), and 2 ('in argument', also *Obs.*); and, given the cast of the poem, with something of 3d: 'To produce a moral conviction *of* sinfulness'. Germane convictions may include *OED* 1, 6, 7, 8: the proving or finding a person guilty; the mental state or condition of being convinced; an opinion or belief held as well proved or established; and the fact or condition of being convicted or convinced of sin.

O LORD, HAVE PATIENCE 83

Airs of Palestine, No. 2

Title: John Pierpont (1785–1866) established his reputation as a poet with *Airs of Palestine* (1816, new edition 1840); 'proceeds from book helped defray cost of attending Harvard Divinity School' (John Hollander, *American Poetry: The Nineteenth Century*, i 1019). 'Greece and her charms I leave, for Palestine'. It includes high-minded riverscapes: 'See at his foot, the cool Cephissus flow'; 'On Arno's bosom, as he calmly flows'; etc.

TSE mentioned in a letter to Aiken, 21 Aug. 1916, his 'reviews for the *New Statesman*, the *Manchester Guardian* and the *Westminster Gazette*' (*Letters* i 143). His review of Durkheim appeared there on 19 Aug. 1916. On 6 Sept. 1916, he wrote to his mother: 'The *Westminster* have given [me] some novels to do', and the next day to J. H. Woods: 'I am doing considerable reviewing for the *Westminster Gazette* – all sorts of things from Durkheim and Boutroux down to *Village Government in India* and even H. de Vere Stacpoole's novels. I got hold of their Indian books by telling them that I was a student of Sanskrit and Pali – whereupon they gave me several books on contemporary Indian politics' (*Letters* i 149, 152). But on 30 Jan. 1917, Pound wrote to Harriet Shaw Weaver: 'I am afraid Eliot has split with *The Westminster*' (*Letters of Ezra Pound, 1907–1941*, ed. D. D. Paige, 1950, p.106). TSE had written to Aiken, 21 Aug. 1916: 'Of poetry I have not written a line; I have been far too worried and nervous. I hope that the end of another year will see me in a position to think about verse a bit' (*Letters* i 144). The combination of these remarks and TSE's splitting with the *Westminster* suggests 1917 for *Airs of Palestine, No.2*, but on the other hand TSE might not have considered these lines 'poetry' and he might have written them while still writing for the *Westminster*. For TSE and newspapers, compare *The 'Boston Evening Transcript'*.

With this satire on the *Westminster Gazette*, compare TSE in 1926 on Donne's satires: 'It does not matter that Donne loved the Court as much as anybody; it does not matter [that] his hatred of courtiers, so far as it is sincere, is that of a man who spent a large part of his life, and wrote a great many of his letters, in courting courtiers. What matters is that in this loose and desultory form of Satire he found a type of poetry which could convey his random thoughts and reflections, exercise his gift for phrasing, his interest in the streets of London, his irritability and spleen. "Here are Gods conduits, grave Divines" ' (*VMP*, pp.143–4).

The quatrain poems of 1920 owe much to Gautier. 'At a certain moment, my debt to [Pound] was for his advice to read Gautier's *Emaux et Camées*, to which I had not before paid any close attention' (*Poetry*, lxviii, 1946, 335). TSE said in the *Paris Review* (21, Spring/Summer 1959, p.54): 'the suggestion of writing quatrains was his [Pound's]. He put me onto *Emaux et Camées*'. Pound wrote to William Carlos Williams, 12 Sept. 1920: 'Eliot is perfectly conscious of having imitated Laforgue, has worked to get away from it, and there is very little Laforgue in his Sweeney, or his Bleistein Burbank, or his "Gerontion," or his Bay State hymn book' (*Letters of Ezra*

Pound, p.161). For the sardonic and even blasphemous hymn, compare *The Hippopotamus* (which, like the present poem, is unusual among TSE's quatrain poems in rhyming the first and third lines as well as the second and fourth).

Compare *Airs of Palestine, No.2* with *The Death of Saint Narcissus* (which was set in type, but not published, in 1915): 'struck' / 'Struck down'; 'the . . . Rock' / 'The . . . rock'; 'writhe' / 'Writhing'; 'green'; 'the Thames' / 'the river'; these with the general sense of 'like a man possess'd'.

In a letter to John Middleton Murry, Nov.? 1919 (*Letters* i 345), TSE adapted the first and third stanzas of *Airs of Palestine, No.2*, bending the poem upon J. C. Squire, who had his editorial or contributory finger in all the printers' pies named here by TSE:

> God from a Cloud to Squire spoke
> And breath'd command: take thou this Rod
> And smite therewith the living Rock;
> And Squire hearken'd unto God.
>
> And Squire smote the living Rock,
> And Lo! the living Rock was wet –
> Whence issue, punctual as the clock
> > *Land and Water,*
> > *The New Statesman,*
> > *The Owl,*
> > *The London Mercury,*
> > And the *Westminster Gazette*

1 **God from a Cloud to Spender spoke**: compare Exodus 24:16: 'and the seventh day he called unto Moses out of the midst of the cloud'. J. A. Spender (1862–1942) was the editor of the *Westminster Gazette* (founded 1893) from 1896 to 1922: 'one of the most remarkable editorships in British journalism' (*DNB*). Spender in 1940 was to express himself at some length on the poems of TSE: 'Eliot, on his own showing, requires the reading of a whole reference library for the understanding of his "Waste Land". I say to him, this may be a curious and interesting new literary product, but there is no definition of poetry to which it corresponds' (Wilson Harris, *J. A. Spender*, 1946, p.60).

2–3 **And breathed command: "Take thou this Rod, / And smite therewith the living Rock"**: compare Numbers 20:8–11: 'And the LORD spake unto Moses, saying, Take the rod'; 'And Moses took the rod from before the LORD, as he commanded him'; 'And Moses lifted up his hand, and with his rod he smote the rock twice: and the water came out abundantly.' Exodus 17:5–6: 'thy rod', 'take in thine hand', 'and thou shalt smite the rock, and there shall come water out of it'.

3 **the living Rock**: *OED* 'living', 2d: 'In various phrases of biblical origin: . . . (c)

Of rock, stone: Native, in its native condition and site, as part of the earth's crust'. Widespread, including Wordsworth, Joanna Baillie and Tennyson. From the living Rock there might have issued living waters (Biblical; OED 2d (a): constantly flowing, refreshing).

4 hearkened unto: very frequent in the Old Testament.

5–6 Cloud . . . the swart tempestuous blast: compare Shakespeare, Sonnet 28:10–11: 'clouds . . . the swart-complexioned night'. Milton, *Lycidas* includes both 'swart' and 'blast', admittedly far apart (ll.138, 97).

5–6, 8 shook . . . Cloud . . . blast . . . quaking . . . aghast: compare Milton, *On the Morning of Christ's Nativity* 158–62 (on Exodus, see 1 note):
> As on mount Sinai rang
> While the red fire and smouldering clouds out-brake:
> The aged earth aghast
> With terror of that blast,
> Shall from the surface to the centre shake,

6 Riding the . . . blast: compare *Macbeth*, I vii 22: 'Striding the blast'. TSE alludes to this speech in *Ode*.

9 struck the living Rock: Matthew Arnold likewise uses the octosyllabic quatrain, rhyming *abab*, for *The Progress of Poesy* (1867), which begins:
> Youth rambles on life's arid mount,
> And strikes the rock, and finds the vein,

TSE, when writing this poem about London journalism (and alluding to Mount Sinai), might perhaps have been affected by the fact that *New Rome* (1881), the next poem in Arnold's collected editions from 1885 (including the standard edition *Poetical Works*, 1890, often reprinted), quotes *The Times*, which had admonished Rome 'O learn of London'.

11–12 henceforth at twelve o'clock / Issues: compare *Paradise Lost* VI 9–10:
> Light issues forth, and at the other door
> Obsequious darkness enters, till her hour

The hour of twelve o'clock (noon) is signal in *Paradise Lost*, thrice in Book IX. The *Westminster Gazette* was issued mid-day; Baedeker's *London and Its Environs* listed it first of the six 'leading evening papers' (1908, p.66; TSE's copy is dated October the 14th, 1910; Hayward Bequest). Issues: frequent with this application in Ezekiel 47:1,8,12: 'and, behold, waters issued out from under the threshold'; 'These waters issue out toward the east country'; 'because their waters they issued out of the sanctuary'. At the head of the line in TSE, compare *Animula* 1: ' "Issues from the hand of God, the simple soul" '.

13 Swift: frequently thus, at the head of the line, in Pope, including *Rape of the Lock*

III 135, IV 17; *Dunciad* II 57, III 234, plus II 177: 'Swift as it mounts . . .' / TSE, 24, 'Mounting'.

14 **The viscid torrents**: recalling the rivers of Hell, *Paradise Lost* II 577–81, particularly 'Abhorred Styx the flood of deadly hate' and 'fierce Phlegeton / Whose waves of torrent fire inflame with rage'. Compare TSE on baptism in such floods: 'And hate the Germans more and more' (36).

15 **long lanes**: commonplace, but compare perhaps Tennyson, *The Princess* IV 457: 'Long lanes of splendour slanted o'er a press' – where the press is other than a printing press, and where 'splendour' might prompt Spender; for Tennyson's preceding lines (450–3) compare invective to a torrent:

a tide of fierce
Invective seemed to wait behind her lips,
As waits a river level with the dam
Ready to burst and flood the world with foam:

(TSE, 20, 'floods'.) **of dogs**: given the Thames (likewise as a rhyme-word), compare Pope, *Dunciad* II 271–4:

To where Fleet-ditch with disemboguing streams
Rolls the large tribute of dead dogs to Thames,
The King of dykes! than whom no sluice of mud
With deeper sable blots the silver flood.

Fleet-ditch would have, via Fleet Street, its journalistic link to TSE's poem. The next line in Pope is: 'Here strip, my children! here at once leap in' / TSE, 'And there they innocently strip' (30). The mock-baptism in both Pope and TSE is in the floods of journalistic dirt; compare Pope, in this scene, II 279–80:

Who flings most filth, and wide pollutes around
The stream, be his the Weekly Journals bound,

(On the affinities of *The Dunciad* with *The Waste Land*, see J. S. Cunningham, in *The Waste Land in Different Voices*, 1974, ed. A. D. Moody.) TSE associates the Thames with journalistic corruption (*The Spectator*) in *Le Directeur*, which begins:

Malheur à la malheureuse Tamise
Qui coule si près du Spectateur.

The words 'of dogs' may evoke the Isle of Dogs in the Thames, which figures in *The Waste Land* [III] 275–6:

Down Greenwich reach
Past the Isle of Dogs.

Praising John Davidson, TSE wrote of having 'a fellow feeling with the poet who could look with a poet's eye on the Isle of Dogs and Millwall Dock' (Preface to *John Davidson: A Selection of His Poems*, 1961; Davidson's *In the Isle of Dogs*, 1899, resembles early TSE in invoking a barrel-organ). **of dogs and men**: frequently together in Homer's war-poem, the *Iliad*; in Pope's translation, XII

164 ('dogs, and voice of men'), XIII 600 ('dogs and men'), XV 308 ('men and dogs'), XVIII 673 ('the dogs, the men').

16–19 **Canning Town and Rotherhithe [Cannon St. and London Wall** variant] . . . **Bermondsey** . . . **Wapping Stair** . . . **Clapham Junction** . . . **Sheen** . . . **Leicester** . . . **Grosvenor Square**: compare the other Londonscapes in TSE. *A Cooking Egg* 28: 'From Kentish Town and Golder's Green'. *The Waste Land* [I] 62–6: 'London Bridge . . . King William Street'; [III] 213: 'the Cannon Street Hotel'; [III] 258: 'And along the Strand, up Queen Victoria Street' (*The Waste Land MS*, p.35: 'up the ghastly hill of Cannon Street'); and [III] 293: 'Richmond and Kew'. *Burnt Norton* III 21–3:

> Driven on the wind that sweeps the gloomy hills of London,
> Hampstead and Clerkenwell, Campden and Putney,
> Highgate, Primrose and Ludgate.

Growltiger's Last Stand brings word of 'The Terror of the Thames' to Rotherhithe, Hammersmith, Putney, Wapping and Brentford. Pope, who mentions Wapping in *The Dunciad* II 384 (1728 edition), anticipates TSE in such Londonscapes. So does W. S. Gilbert:

> The swelling murmurs grew –
> From Camberwell to Kentish Town –
> From Rotherhithe to Kew.

(*Peter the Wag* 34–6, *The Bab Ballads*, 1869.)

18, 20 **Sheen** . . . **green**: a traditional pastoral rhyme (Byron has pleasure in it, *Don Juan*, III [xxvii] 210, 214), but here a capital onomastic pun. Compare Shelley, *The Question* 31–2:

> And bulrushes, and reeds of such deep green
> As soothed the dazzled eye with sober sheen.

Milton's use of the rhyme offers the coincidence, apt to TSE's poem about printjournalism, of the words 'printless' and 'fleet' (Fleet?; see 15 note), along with 'waters'. *Comus* 893–7:

> Thick set with agate, and the azurn sheen
> Of turkis blue, and emerald green
>   That in the channel strays,
> Whilst from off the waters fleet
> Thus I set my printless feet

TSE's next line, 21, describes 'the street of gems'; the lines from *Comus* specify 'set with agate', 'turkis', and 'emerald'. TSE's rhyme and gems may also owe something to John Gray, *The Twelve Precious Stones* (1896):

> EMERALD, exceeding green,
> Doth present an olive sheen.

Gray adds 'BERYL is a liquid gem' (TSE, 21–3, 'gems', 'Thames'), and his final stanza begins: 'O JERUSALEM of peace'; compare this poem about war, *Airs of Palestine, No.2* (and its 'Zion').

20 **bilious green**: the *Westminster Gazette* had a pea-green front page. With a memory of another river of Hell: Baudelaire, *Spleen: Je suis comme le roi* (1857), ends: 'l'eau verte du Léthé'. Also in *Les Fleurs du Mal*, Baudelaire has 'Je te frapperai . . . Comme Moïse le rocher!' (*L'Héautontimorouménos*, 1857, 1, 3); compare TSE, 9. For 'emerald green', rhythmically similar to 'bilious green' in its slight elision, see Milton in the previous note, and compare Pope, *Dunciad* II 156: 'And the fresh vomit run for ever green'.

21, 23 **gems . . . Thames**: rhymed in Spenser's *Prothalamion* 14, 11. Spenser's refrain, 'Sweet Thames run softly, till I end my Song', figures in *The Waste Land*, [III] 176, 183–4, a poem with affinities to *Airs of Palestine, No.2*. TSE's incorporation of the Spenser line in his something-of-a-cento poem *The Waste Land* may owe something to the drunken cento in Kipling's story *Brugglesmith* (*Many Inventions*, 1893):

> Here he stood up in the bows and declaimed:
> 'Ye towers o' Julia, London's lasting wrong,
>   By mony a foul an' midnight murder fed –
> Sweet Thames run softly till I end my song –
>   And yon's the grave as little as my bed.
> I'm a poet mysel' an' I can feel for others'.

25 **And higher still**: compare *Paradise Regained* IV 545–7:

> The holy city lifted high her towers,
> And higher yet the glorious Temple reared
> Her pile,

25–7 **the torrent . . . pearly wall . . . Mary's garden**: with 'gems' (21), these are the commonplaces of such a hymn as *The New Jerusalem* (deriving from Revelation 21–2), in the *Oxford Book of English Verse*, ed. Quiller-Couch: 'Thy walls are made of precious stones'; 'Thy gates are of right orient pearl'; 'Thy gardens'; 'Our Lady sings *Magnificat*'; and, intensifying the contrast with TSE, the river of life:

> Quite through the streets, with silver sound,
>   The flood of Life doth flow;

One of the most famous of nineteenth-century American poems (much sung as a hymn), Robert Lowry's *Beautiful River* ('Shall we gather at the river', 1869) had as its epigraph Revelation 22:1: 'And he showed me a pure River of Water of Life, clear as crystal, proceeding out of the Throne of God and of the Lamb'. TSE may have intended a contrast of his squalid river with Lowry's, and its Chorus:

> Yes, we'll gather at the river,
>   The beautiful, the beautiful river –
> Gather with the saints at the river

That flows by the throne of God.
Compare TSE's wartime poem about bellicosity with Lowry's closing stanza:
Soon we'll reach the shining river,
Soon our pilgrimage will cease,
Soon our happy hearts will quiver
With the melody of peace.

27 **Wherein, by Mary's garden close**: close by / garden close. TSE quoted five lines
from William Morris in *Andrew Marvell* (1921, *SE*, p.299), *The Nymph's Song
to Hylas* (1867), Book IV, beginning:
I know a little garden close
Set thick with lily and red rose.
Similarly Wilde, *Panthea* (1881) 55: 'garden close', rhyming with 'rose', like
TSE's 'flows'; this, despite the pronunciation given in *OED* for the noun 'close':
'as in the adj.'. John Gray too rhymes 'garden close' and 'rose', in *Fleurs: Imitated
from the French of Stéphane Mallarmé*, 6–7 (1893). *OED* 'close', 2d: 'The
precinct of any sacred place'. (*OED* has, under 'garden', 'garden-close'.)
Compare Elizabeth Barrett Browning's *The Lost Bower*, the opening lines of
which appear as the epigraph to Kipling's story *The Education of Otis Yeere*
(1888) and also in his story *They* (1904). TSE wrote to John Hayward, 5 Aug.
1941, about ' "They" which I don't think I had read for 30 years, but the
quotation from E. B. Browning has always stuck in my head, and that may be due
to "They" rather than to the Bardess herself':
In the pleasant orchard closes,
'God bless all our gains', say we;
But 'May God bless all our losses',
Better suits with our degree.
(Helen Gardner, *The Composition of Four Quartets*, pp.29, 40; she points out
TSE's incorporation of 'our losses' in *The Dry Salvages* I 22, and she notes (from
R. Schuchard) that in TSE's tutorial class in 1916 *The Lost Bower* was one of the
poems recommended for study in conjunction with TSE's lecture on E.B.B.)

31 **all their sin**: as in Milton, Psalm lxxxv 7.

32 **navel**: compare Proverbs 3:7: 'fear the LORD [. . .] it shall be health to thy navel'.

34 **Attain . . . the . . . shore**: *OED* 'attain', 6: 'to arrive at'. 1585: 'We quickly shall
attain the English shore'; 1854: 'attained the opposite shore'. **the farther shore**:
at the line-end, as in *The Dry Salvages* III 29: 'Here between the hither and the
farther shore', where the phrase (as often in late TSE) is redeemed from the
sardonic. Compare Pope, *Iliad* XXIII 93: 'Now give thy hand, for to the farther
shore'. From *Aeneid* VI 314: 'ripae ulterioris' (of the dead in the underworld).

35 **Cleansed and rejoiced**: compare *The Hippopotamus* 19, 29: 'But every week we

hear rejoice', 'Blood of the Lamb shall wash him clean'. **rejoiced:** gladdened; given 'the Germans' in the next line, compare *The Education of Henry Adams*, ch.xx: 'Germany was never so powerful, and the Assistant Professor of History had nothing else as his stock in trade. He imposed Germany on his scholars with a heavy hand. He was rejoiced.'

36 **hate the Germans:** this, despite Spender's having been considered a German sympathizer before the war. *DNB*: 'The range of his interests was limited only by the range of contemporary politics, but the cause of Anglo-German friendship stood especially high among them.' TSE's poem about hating the Germans, and about the insufficiently muzzled press, may owe something to John Jay Chapman, *Bismarck* (1898) 46–8, which speaks repeatedly of 'hatred':

we see

The fruits of hatred ripen hourly
And Germany's in bondage – muzzled press –

37–8 **redeemed from . . . frowardness:** compare Tennyson, *Morte d'Arthur* [*The Epic*] 279: 'Redeemed it from the charge of nothingness'. **frowardness:** compare Proverbs 2:14: 'the frowardness of the wicked'; 6:14: 'Frowardness is in his heart'; 10:32: 'the mouth of the wicked speaketh frowardness'.

39 **The scales:** compare Acts of the Apostles 9:18: 'And immediately there fell from his eyes as it had been scales: and he received sight forthwith, and arose, and was baptized.' (TSE, 35, 'Cleansed'.) Compare 'desquamations' in *First Debate between the Body and Soul* 49 (variant).

Petit Epître

TSE wrote to his mother, 11 April 1917 (*Letters* i 175): 'Besides my lectures [. . .] and considerable reviewing [. . .] I have been doing some writing – mostly in French, curiously enough it has taken me that way – and some poems in French which will come out in the *Little Review* in Chicago'. Of the four French poems published by TSE, three (*Le Directeur*, *Mélange Adultère de Tout*, and *Lune de Miel*) were published there in July 1917, along with *The Hippopotamus* (which adapted a poem by Gautier). The fourth, *Dans le Restaurant*, was published in Sept. 1918 in the *Little Review*.

Pound wrote to James Joyce, 19 April 1917: 'I hope to send you Eliot's poems in a few weeks. He has burst out into scurrilous french during the past few weeks, too late for his book, which is in the press, but the gallicism should enrich the review [*Little Review*]. He is "just as bad" as if he had been to Clongowes. But it is perilous trying to manipulate a foreign language' (*Pound/Joyce*, ed. Forrest Read, 1967, p.112).

TSE commented on his French poems in the *Paris Review* interview (21, Spring/ Summer 1959, pp.56–7):

Interviewer: I think it was after *Prufrock* and before *Gerontion* that you wrote the poems in French which appear in your *Collected Poems*. I wonder how you happened to write them. Have you written any since?

TSE: No, and I never shall. That was a very curious thing which I can't altogether explain. At that period I thought I'd dried up completely. I hadn't written anything for some time and was rather desperate. I started writing a few things in French and found I *could*, at that period. I think it was that when I was writing in French, I didn't take the poems so seriously, and that, not taking them seriously, I wasn't so worried about not being able to write. I did these things as a sort of *tour de force* to see what I could do. That went on for some months. The best of them have been printed. I must say that Ezra Pound went through them, and Edmund Dulac, a Frenchman we knew in London, helped with them a bit. We left out some, and I suppose they disappeared completely. Then I suddenly began writing in English again and lost all desire to go on with French. I think it was just something that helped me get started again.

Interviewer: Did you think at all about becoming a French symbolist poet like the two Americans of the last century?

TSE: Stuart Merrill and Vielé-Griffin. I only did that during the romantic year I spent in Paris after Harvard. I had at that time the idea of giving up English and trying to settle down and scrape along in Paris and gradually write French. But it would have been a foolish idea even if I'd been much more bilingual than I ever was, because, for one thing, I don't think that one can be a bilingual poet. I don't know of any case in which a man wrote great or even fine poems equally well in two languages. I think one language must be the one you express yourself in in poetry, and you've got to give up the other for that purpose. And I think that the

English language really has more resources than the French. I think, in other words, I've probably done better in English than I ever would have in French even if I'd become as proficient in French as the poets you mentioned.

Edmund Dulac (1882–1953), French illustrator of English books: there is a letter from TSE to him, 23 Aug. 1918 (*Letters* i 240).

In 1938, TSE wrote – for private circulation only – a scabrous quatrain poem in French, purporting to find John Hayward repulsive and sinister. Addressed to their common friend, Geoffrey Faber, *Vers pour la Foulque* was translated by TSE into preposterous prose, as *Verses for the Coot* (*Noctes Binanianae*, 1939).

Compare Tristan Corbière's sardonic self-portrait, *Le Poète contumace* (1873) 24–30, with its aggressive officials and gossips:

Le curé se doutait que c'était un lépreux;
Et le maire disait: – Moi, qu'est-ce que j'y peux,
  C'est plutôt un Anglais . . . un *Etre*. //
Les femmes avaient su – sans doute par les buses –
Qu'il *vivait en concubinage avec des Muses!* . . .
Un hérétique enfin . . . Quelque *Parisien*
De Paris ou d'ailleurs.

Similarly the interrogation in *Le Renégat* (1873) 15, 22: 'Son nom?', 'Coup de barre du vice?' For TSE and Corbière, see the next poem *Tristan Corbière*, and Appendix D (pp.402–7, 409–10).

1–2 **dégoute / Ou gout d'égout**: Corbière enjoyed his turns hereabouts. *Epitaphe* (1873) 47: ' – Son goût était dans le dégoût'. This poem gave TSE a title and impulse: *Mélange Adultère de Tout*. *Le Poète contumace* 82–3:
      Moi j'en suis dégoûté. –
Dans mes dégoûts surtout, j'ai des goûts élégants;
Le Renégat ends: 'Pur, à force d'avoir purgé tous les dégoûts'. TSE marked in his copy of Pater, *The Renaissance* (1873, p.95), on da Vinci: 'For the way to perfection is through a series of disgusts'.

8 **une odeur fémelle**: compare Corbière's prose story, *L'Américaine* (1874): 'Ce poison, l'odeur de femme, m'emplissait les narines'; and his *Bonne Fortune et fortune* (1873) has as its epigraph *Odor della feminita*. Compare *Rhapsody on a Windy Night* 66: 'And female smells in shuttered rooms'. *Lune de Miel* 4: 'une forte odeur de chienne'. *Dans le Restaurant* 13 ∧ 14 (line in manuscript): 'Elle avait une odeur fraîche qui m'était inconnue'. *The Waste Land MS*, p.39, *The Fire Sermon* 40–1:
Odours, confected by the cunning French,
Disguise the good old hearty female stench.

37 **un suppôt de Satan**: TSE wrote to Paul Elmer More, 7 Nov. 1933 (Princeton), about *After Strange Gods*: 'or that Lawrence appears as a *suppôt de Satan*'.

43 **eunuque:** often in Corbière, for instance *Le Renégat* 10; compare *Féminin singulier* (1873) 7–8:

> nous avons la police
> Et quelque chose en nous d'eunuque et de recors.

Tristan Corbière

Donald Gallup recorded that, after the final blank leaves and stubs of the Notebook, come (on versos of unnumbered leaves and upside down in relation to the front of the volume) copies by T. S. Eliot in black ink of two of the "Rondels pour après" from *Les amours jaunes* of Tristan Corbière, the first beginning "Buona vespre! Dors: Ton bout de cierge", the second, "Il fait noir, enfant, voleur d'étincelles!" (the first has the initials "T.C." at the end, the second has "Corbière"). On separate leaves laid in at the back are pencil copies by Eliot, of two more of the "Rondels", the first entitled "Mirliton", the second "Petit Mort Pour Rire", neither with indication of authorship and the second with the name and address of (the publisher) Albert Messein in Paris added in Eliot's hand.

Edward J. H. Greene reported that TSE first read Corbière in *Poètes d'aujourd'hui*, the anthology which he acquired in 1909 or soon after; that subsequently he got hold of a copy of *Les Amours jaunes* during his stay in Paris in 1910; and that he deepened his study of Corbière 1915–1920 (*T. S. Eliot et la France*, 1951, p.62). For TSE and Corbière, see *Petit Épître*, and Appendix D (pp.402–7, 409–10). Laforgue wrote on Corbière (*Mélanges posthumes*, 1903, pp.119–28, and *Dragées*, 1920).

Epigraph: from Verlaine, *Les Poètes maudits*, quoted in the preface (p.iv) by Charles Le Goffic to Corbière's *Les Amours jaunes* (1911), the paragraph from Verlaine ending: 'Il devint Parisien un instant, mais sans le sale esprit mesquin: de la bile et de la fièvre s'exaspérant en génie et jusqu'à quelle gaieté!' Compare Corbière, *Le Poète contumace* 29–30:
> Quelque *Parisien*
> De Paris ou d'ailleurs.

1   **Marin!**: Corbière was a sailor and the son of a sea-captain. Compare Corbière, *Matelots* (1873) 97, and its exclamation: 'Matelots!' The paragraph from Verlaine quoted by Le Goffic (see the note on the epigraph) began: 'Tristan Corbière fut un Breton, un marin et le dédaigneux par excellence'.   **Marin! je te connais**: compare *The Waste Land* [I] 69–70:
> There I saw one I knew, and stopped him, crying: 'Stetson!
> 'You who were with me in the ships at Mylae! [. . .]'

je te connais: perhaps touched by the close of Baudelaire's *Au Lecteur* (which TSE quoted as the close of *The Waste Land* I):
> Tu le connais, lecteur, ce monstre délicat,
> – Hypocrite lecteur, – mon semblable, – mon frère!

2   **Qui veillait dans la nuit comme un vieil hibou**: Corbière, of himself in *Le Poète contumace* (1873) 19: 'Lui, seul hibou payant'; and again of himself in *Guitare* (1873) 7: 'Voleur de nuit, hibou d'amour'.

3   **toi qu'on nomme *an Ankou***: Le Goffic's preface to *Les Amours jaunes* (1911)

began: 'Le 1er mars 1875, dans la trentième année de son âge, s'éteignait à Morlaix un pauvre être falot, rongé de phtisie, perclus de rheumatismes et si long et si maigre et si jaune que les marins bretons, ses amis, l'avaient baptisé *an Ankou* (la Mort).' Again, p.xvii: 'la maladie en fit une pauvre caricature d'homme, l'espèce d'*Ankou*, de spectre ambulant dont se moquaient les Roscovites.' Pound wrote of Corbière in the *New Age*, 2 Oct. 1913: 'his personal appearance had earned him the nickname "an Ankou" (the corpse).' Corbière uses the word at the beginning of his prose poem *Casino des trépassés* (1874): 'Un pays, – non, ce sont des côtes brisées de la dure Bretagne: *Penmarc'h, Toul-Infern, Poul-Dahut, Stang-an-Ankou* . . . Des noms barbares hurlés par les rafales' (his ellipsis); compare TSE, 8: 'Bat sur les côtes bretonnes la mer en rafales'.

4 **barbe pointue**: compare *Do I know how I feel?* 17: 'with a pointed beard'.

8 **rafales**: Corbière rhymes on this in 'Mirliton', which TSE copied out (see the headnote above).

9–10 **Des rayons de soleil . . . après-midi . . . au Luxembourg**: compare TSE, *The Criterion*, xiii (April 1934) 452: 'I am willing to admit that my own retrospect is touched by a sentimental sunset, the memory of a friend coming across the Luxembourg Gardens in the late afternoon, waving a branch of lilac, a friend who was later (so far as I could find out) to be mixed with the mud of Gallipoli.' The friend was Jean Verdenal, to whose memory *Inventions of the March Hare* and *Prufrock and Other Observations* are dedicated; see *Letters* i 17–24, 27–36, 125, 192, 433.

11 **poudre de riz**: compare Corbière, *Déjeuner de soleil* (1873) 6: 'Kh'ol, carmin et poudre de riz'.

11–12 **la poudre de riz. / Et Lieutenant Loti**: compare Laurent Tailhade, *Odelette* (1904) 22: 'Loti, fleur des rizières'. For TSE and Tailhade, see *Afternoon* headnote, and Appendix D (pp.402, 407–8). Pierre Loti (1850–1923, naval officer, novelist and travel writer) was repeatedly Tailhade's butt in *Poèmes aristophanesques* (1904): for instance, *Mélancolie Odéonesque*, which ends 'les marrons chers à Pierre Loti'; *Ballade pour assainir la chose littéraire* 5 ('Pierre Loti, ce diamant'); *Ballade à mots couverts de l'infantile Paraguante* 11 ('Pierre Loti, par qui Zola s'afflige'); and *Ballade itérative sur la concupiscence qui nous tient du proboscide à ma tante Viaud*, each stanza of which ends with 'à Loti'.

12, 14 **Loti . . . grue**: Francis Jammes dedicated to Loti his poem *Les grues* (*De l'Angelus de l'aube à l'Angelus du soir*, 1898, listed among TSE's books in 1934).

14 **Fait le trottoirs** (variant): 'faire le trottoir', se prostituer. Compare Corbière, *Paris: I* (1873) 9–11:
Là, sa pauvre Muse pucelle

Fit le trottoir en *demoiselle*.
Ils disaient: Qu'est-ce qu'elle vend?
Fait le trottoirs . . . grue: compare Corbière, *Idylle coupée* (1873) 1–4:
C'est très parisien, dans les rues,
Quand l'Aurore fait le trottoir,
De voir sortir toutes les Grues
Du violon, ou de leur boudoir . . .
Vénerie (1873) 12: 'un pied-de-grue'. TSE, *Vers pour la Foulque*: 'une ancienne
grue', sardonically turned into translationese by TSE as 'a retired great coarse
woman' in *Noctes Binanianae*, 1939; the manuscript had rendered this 'a
superannuated prostitute' (Hayward Bequest).

The Engine I, II

The notepaper has: U.S.M.S. 'ST. LOUIS' with a flag. *The Engine*: as a child of ten, TSE had included a train-story, *Bill's Escape*, in his magazine *Fireside* (No.1, 28 Jan. 1899, and No.2, 29 Jan.; Houghton Library); ch.II: 'He heard the toot of the engine, he did not know what to do. It was sure death'; and ch.III began: 'The engine came on'.

On TSE's prose poems, see *Introspection* and note, and *Hysteria*. *The Engine* has some likeness to the prose poems of Charles Vildrac, in *Découvertes* (1912). *Le Tunnel* begins: 'Le front à la vitre du wagon, l'enfant regarde de toutes ses forces'; later, 'Or voici que le train s'engage dans le long tunnel'. Likewise the manner (especially of simile – compare TSE's 'rosebush') of *La Récréation*: 'Il règne un soleil du matin, libéral comme un coup de vin blanc'. Aiken reported on the young TSE, back from Paris: 'But what did we talk about? What to write, of course, and how to write, and what to read – Charles Louis Philippe and Vildrac, fresh from Paris – ' (*T. S. Eliot*, ed. Richard March and Tambimuttu, 1948, p.22). TSE listed Vildrac among half a dozen of the 'more important men' (as poets) in France, when writing to Scofield Thayer about *The Dial* (14 Feb. 1920, *Letters* i 362–3).

TSE is indebted to Kipling, *Bertran and Bimi* (*The Phantom 'Rickshaw*, 1891). The first paragraph of the Kipling story has 'he roused himself', and 'without ceasing' / TSE, 'I roused myself', 'ceased'. And from the one paragraph, the next page, on board ship:

Then we laid out our bedding in the bows [. . .] our forefoot [. . .] The ship [. . .] The trampling tune of the engines was very distinct, and the jarring of the ash-lift, as it was tipped into the sea, hurt the procession of hushed noise. Hans lay down by my side and lighted a good-night cigar. This was naturally the beginning of conversation. He owned a voice as soothing as the wash of the sea, and stores of experiences as vast as the sea itself; for his business in life was to wander up and down the world, collecting orchids and wild beasts and ethnological specimens for German and American dealers. I watched the glowing end of his cigar wax and wane in the gloom, as the sentences rose and fell, till I was nearly asleep.

Compare, in the order within TSE I and II: The engine . . . American business men [Kipling, American dealers] . . . cigar . . . life . . . smooth [Kipling, soothing] . . . I lay in bed [Kipling, we laid out our bedding . . . lay down] . . . the wash . . . the scuffle of feet [Kipling, forefoot . . . trampling] . . . the tune [Kipling, the trampling tune of the engines] . . . the light [Kipling, lighted] . . . the ship . . . I thought drowsily [Kipling, I was nearly asleep].

A further reason to adduce this story of Kipling's is that, two pages later, it influenced TSE in *Sweeney Erect* and *Sweeney Among the Nightingales*. *Bertran and Bimi*:

He haf found him when he was a child – der orang-outang – und he was child und brother und opera comique all round to Bertran. He had his room in dot house –

not a cage, but a room – mit a bed und sheets, and he would go to bed und get up in der morning und smoke his cigar und eat his dinner mit Bertran, und walk mit him hand in hand, which was most horrible. Herr Gott! I haf seen dot beast throw himself back in his chair und laugh when Bertran haf made fun of me. He was *not* a beast; he was a man.

(The orang-outang tears Bertran's wife to pieces.) Compare Kipling's 'orang-outang' who has his 'sheets', plus 'morning' and 'hand in hand' (the conversation being on a 'steamer'), with *Sweeney Erect* 9–12:

> Morning stirs the feet and hands
> (Nausicaa and Polypheme).
> Gesture of orang-outang
> Rises from the sheets in steam.

And Kipling's 'ape-beast', who used to 'laugh', with *Sweeney Among the Nightingales* 1–2:

> Apeneck Sweeney spreads his knees
> Letting his arms hang down to laugh,

TSE jotted down, for comparison, *Bertran and Bimi* and Conrad, in his notes for the lecture-course he taught at Harvard in 1933 (Houghton Library; bMS Am 1691 (36)).

I

Flat faces of American: TSE urged Scofield Thayer, 30 June 1918: 'pour the vials of contumely upon the fair flat face of the people' – the American people (*Letters* i 236). Compare *Murder in the Cathedral*, Part II, the third chorus: 'The white flat face of Death'.

faces of American business men: compare Henry James, *The American Scene* (1907), p.64: 'No impression so promptly assaults the arriving visitor of the United States as that of the overwhelming preponderance, wherever he turns and twists, of the unmitigated "business man" face, ranging through its various possibilities, its extraordinary actualities, of intensity.' James is contemplating disembarkation and Ellis Island.

broken only: with 'only to see' (11), inviting consideration of TSE's ways with 'only'; see Shyamal Bagchee, *T. S. Eliot: Man and Poet*, vol. 1 (ed. Laura Cowan, 1990), pp.91–104.

salient: *OED* 4: 'Of an angle: Pointing outward', 'chiefly in *Fortif*.' B 2a: 'a spur-like area of land, esp. one held by a line of offence or defence, as in trench-warfare; *spec*. (freq. with *the* and capital initial), that at Ypres in western Belgium, the scene of severe fighting in the war of 1914–18' (this last definition, from 1914).

The machine . . . having chosen with motives and ends unknown . . . The machine: given the original title for II, *Machinery*, compare TSE's paper on causality

(Houghton Library; bMS Am 1691.14 (18), p.2): 'we have direct knowledge neither of our own nor of others['] will; a single man could no more have will than could a machine. We have will by an interpretation of our own behaviour and of others.'

motives . . . unknown: compare Pope, *Epistle to Bathurst* 114: 'Must act on motives powerful, though unknown', where 109 mentions 'men of pelf' (compare TSE, 'business men'). **ends unknown**: compare *Entretien dans un parc* 30: 'ends unshaped', and *Bacchus and Ariadne* 4: 'tendencies unknown'.

certain and sufficient as a rose bush: compare Laforgue, *Dialogue avant le lever de la lune* (1886) 19–20:
– Conséquemment, comme la rose
Est nécessaire à ses besoins.
Complainte des pianos qu'on entend dans les quartiers aisés (1885) 35, 39: 'rosiers', 'suffisants'.

rose bush . . . aimless parasite: compare Shelley, *The Sensitive Plant* III 48–9:
And the leafless network of parasite bowers
Massed into ruin; and all sweet flowers.
Also *Epipsychidion* 502–3: 'Parasite flowers' and 'lampless'; eight lines earlier (by what may be mere coincidence), Shelley has 'But, as it were Titanic' ('the life of the deck'? See the note to 'if the ship goes down').

II *Machinery: Dancers*
Dancers . . . the scuffle of feet . . . the music: compare TSE's letter to Eleanor Hinkley, while crossing the Atlantic (postmark 7 July 1914, *Letters* i 37–9): 'so that we have great fun, especially when it comes to dancing to the sound of the captain's phonograph'.

taut as a drumhead: perhaps assisted by the other, nautical, sense of drumhead: OED 3, 'The circular top of a capstan'.

spider . . . he is very old: it is in a poem about the very old, *Gerontion* 65, that TSE was soon to imagine another spider. Compare the spider-Absolute of *He said: this universe is very clever* 6–7 note (including a passage from Diderot).

if the ship goes down: many a ship did (including the *Titanic* in 1912). The passenger ship *Lusitania* was sunk by a German submarine, 7 May 1915, with over a thousand dead, of whom a hundred were Americans; and the *Sussex*, 24 March 1916, with fifty lives, and three Americans injured (see the letter from TSE's mother to Bertrand Russell, 23 May 1916, *Letters* i 139 and note). So the warlike suggestions of 'salient' (1) may be salient.

I tried to assemble these nebulae into one pattern: compare *Hysteria*: 'I decided that if the shaking of her breasts could be stopped, some of the fragments of the afternoon might be collected, and I concentrated my attention with careful subtlety to this end.'

In silent corridors of death

Undated. The manuscript at one time belonged to Vivien Eliot's brother, Maurice Haigh-Wood.

1, 6 corridors of death . . . fear: compare Wilde, *The Ballad of Reading Gaol* (1898) III 246:
> That night the empty corridors
> Were full of forms of Fear,

1–2 death / Short sighs: compare *The Waste Land* [I] 63–4:
> I had not thought death had undone so many.
> Sighs, short and infrequent, were exhaled,

TSE's Note to the latter line:
> Cf. Inferno IV, 25–27:
> Quivi, secondo che per ascoltare,
> non avea pianto, ma' che di sospiri,
> che l'aura eterna facevan tremare.

Contrast *Paradise Lost* XI 146–8:
>   yet this will prayer,
> Or one short sigh of human breath, upborne
> Even to the seat of God.

3 sighing: compare Milton, *On the Morning of Christ's Nativity*, stanzas xx–xxi: 'lonely', 'sighing', 'moan', 'dying' (TSE, 5, 'alone'; 8, 'moan'; 9, 'dying').

3–4 silent sighing . . . crying: likewise rhyming with 'dying', compare *After the turning . . . 2 (The Waste Land MS*, p.109): 'the silence and the crying' (*1st reading* sighing).

4 the soul crying: compare Dante, *Purgatorio* XVI 86–8:
>   a guisa di fanciulla
>   che piangendo e ridendo pargoleggia,
>   l'anima semplicetta,

Quoted by TSE in the Clark Lectures, 1926 (*VMP*, p.56), and in *Dante* (1929, SE, pp.259–60) with the translation: 'there issues like a little child that plays, with weeping and laughter, the simple soul' (this soon issuing in *Animula*). Compare Proverbs 19:18: 'let not thy soul spare for his crying'.

4–5 the soul crying. / And I wander: compare the lines from Beaumont and Fletcher, *The Faithful Shepherdess*, II ii, quoted by TSE in 1919 (*Ben Jonson, SE*, p.156):
> Hair woven in many a curious warp,
> Able in endless error to enfold

The wandering soul; . . .

5 **And I wander alone:** in *Promenade sentimentale* 5, 11 (*Paysages tristes*, 1869; compare TSE's *Paysage Triste*), Verlaine has 'Moi, j'errais tout seul' and 'j'errais tout seul'.

7, 9, 11–12 **Without pressure . . . dying . . . warm . . . airless:** compare *Burnt Norton* I 26–7:
Moving without pressure, over the dead leaves,
In the autumn heat, through the vibrant air,
– *Burnt Norton* I 12, 'Down the passage', being linked with 'alleys', 'corridors' (13–14).

12 **Dry airless:** compare *Rhapsody on a Windy Night* 63: 'sunless dry'.

12–13 **airless sweet scent / Of the alleys of death:** compare *Hamlet*, I v 67: 'alleys of the body' (death by poison); the same speech, from the undying soul of Hamlet's father, has 'scent the morning air' (58).

12, 14 **airless sweet scent . . . corridors of death:** in *The Family Reunion* I ii, Harry speaks to Mary of 'a corridor', 'every corridor', and then asks:
What is that? do you feel it?
MARY: What, Harry?
HARRY: That apprehension deeper than all sense,
Deeper than the sense of smell, but like a smell
In that it is indescribable, a sweet and bitter smell
From another world.
In II ii, Agatha speaks of walking
down a concrete corridor
In a dead air.
And in her next speech:
Up and down, through the stone passages
Of an immense and empty hospital
Pervaded by a smell of disinfectant,
Compare also *Murder in the Cathedral*, Part I, the last chorus:
more pain than birth or death.
Sweet and cloying through the dark air
Falls the stifling scent of despair;

13 **the alleys of death:** for the cadence, compare 'the valley of death', of Tennyson, *The Charge of the Light Brigade*; but here as in a cemetery, as when nearing the climactic conclusion to Henry James's *The Beast in the Jungle* (1903): 'This face, one grey afternoon when the leaves were thick in the alleys, looked into Marcher's own, at the cemetery'. Another association of the alley with death is 'l'allée des Veuves', in Charles-Louis Philippe, *Marie Donadieu* (1904); part I

ch.III mentions this in two successive paragraphs. Contrast TSE's 'airless' (12) with Philippe: 'l'air de l'allée des Veuves se prit de finesse et de mélancolie'. For TSE on this book, see Appendix D (p.407).

APPENDIX A

Poems excised from
the Notebook

TSE to Pound, 2 Feb. 1915:

I have corresponded with Lewis, but his puritanical principles seem to bar my way to Publicity. I fear that King Bolo and his Big Black Kween will never burst into print. I understand that Priapism, Narcissism etc. are not approved of, and even so innocent a rhyme as
   . . . pulled her stockings off
  With a frightful cry of "Hauptbahnhof!!"
is considered decadent.

(Letters i 86)

Wyndham Lewis to Pound, before July 1915:

Eliot has sent me Bullshit & the Ballad for Big Louise. They are excellent bits of scholarly ribaldry. I am longing to print them in *Blast*; but stick to my naif determination to have no "Words Ending in -Uck, -Unt and -Ugger."

(*Pound/Lewis*, ed. Timothy Materer, 1985, p.8. *The Letters of Wyndham Lewis*, ed. W. K. Rose, 1963, pp.66–7, reads 'trying to print'.)

The Triumph of Bullshit

Ladies, on whom my attentions have waited
If you consider my merits are small
Etiolated, alembicated,
Orotund, tasteless, fantastical,
Monotonous, crotchety, constipated,   5
Impotent galamatias
Affected, possibly imitated,
For Christ's sake stick it up your ass.

Ladies, who find my intentions ridiculous
Awkward insipid and horridly gauche   10
Pompous, pretentious, ineptly meticulous
Dull as the heart of an unbaked *brioche*
Floundering versicles feebly versiculous
Often attenuate, frequently crass
Attempts at emotions that turn out *isiculous*,   15
For Christ's sake stick it up your ass.

Ladies who think me unduely vociferous
Amiable cabotin making a noise
That people may cry out "this stuff is too stiff for us" –
Ingenuous child with a box of new toys   20
Toy lions carnivorous, cannons fumiferous
Engines vaporous – all this will pass;
Quite innocent – "he only wants to make shiver us."
For Christ's sake stick it up your ass.

And when thyself with silver foot shalt pass   25
Among the Theories scattered on the grass
Take up my good intentions with the rest
And then for Christ's sake stick them up your ass.

Leaf excised from the Notebook, now in the Beinecke Library, Yale (Pound papers).
Manuscript in pencil. Dated either Nov. 1910 or Nov. 1916. It looks more like 1910,
and 1916 would have to be the date of revision, since TSE sent the poem to

Wyndham Lewis before July 1915; but the later date might better fit the thought that TSE had 'patiently waited' and had been at the mercy of 'Ladies', editorial and other; Pound had pressed TSE's poems upon Harriet Monroe.

1] Critics, on whom I have patiently waited *1st reading*.

2. *If you*] Those who *1st reading*. *are*] *written over illegible word* [too?].

16. *your*] my *1st reading*.

17. *me unduely*] I am merely *1st reading*.

21] Teddy bears carnivorous, engines califerous *1st reading*.

23. *only*] merely *1st reading*.

26. *Theories scattered*] guests star-scattered *1st reading*.

27. *Take . . . intentions*] Then take my good intentions *1st reading*; Take up this set of verses *2nd reading*.

28] You have the right to stick them up my ass. *1st reading*.

Title: **The Triumph of Bullshit**. Invoking such poetical triumphs as *The Triumph of Time* (Swinburne), *The Triumph of Life* (Shelley), and *The Triumph of Peace* (Shirley). **Bullshit**: the earliest instance in *OED* ('Rubbish, nonsense') is Wyndham Lewis's letter, before July 1915, about this poem of TSE's ('Eliot has sent me Bullshit'). *OED* 'bull', *slang*, orig. *U.S.*, from 1914, 'Popularly associated with "Bullshit" 1'. In his copy of Hegel's *Lectures on the Philosophy of History* (1905, p.431; Houghton Library), TSE commented on the words he underlined: 'The time-honoured and cherished *sincerity of the German people* is destined to effect this revolution out of the honest truth and simplicity of its heart.' TSE wrote in the margin: 'BULL'.

3 **alembicated**: *OED*, 'Of ideas, expression, etc.: over-refined, over-subtilized (as if passing through an alembic)'. From 1786, Mrs Piozzi, on Johnson's not being 'like the alembicated productions of artificial fire'. 1818, Lady Morgan: 'Theories of alembicated refinements'. Given TSE's opening ('Ladies . . .'), it is apt that these first two *OED* instances of 'alembicated' should be from ladies (the latter invoking 'Theories', like TSE, 26). TSE relished chemical metaphors; for instance, the notorious (and not quite right) catalyst in *Tradition and the Individual Talent* (1919).

4 **fantastical**: compare perhaps Tennyson's attack on his critics, *Hendecasyllabics* 14, 'So fantastical is the dainty metre'; Tennyson, with a similar pleasure in

'metrification', begins 'O you chorus of indolent reviewers'. (TSE's poem at first
began: 'Critics, on whom . . .'.)

6 **galamatias:** *OED* 'galimatias': 'Confused language, meaningless talk, nonsense'.
Compare TSE's 'Impotent galamatias' with Addison, *Spectator* No.275 (1712),
on 'the dissection of a Beau's head': 'Others ended in several bladders which were
filled either with wind or froth. But the large canal entered into a great cavity of
the skull, from which there went another canal into the tongue. This great cavity
was filled with a kind of spongy substance, which the French anatomists call
galimatias and the English, nonsense.'

10, 12 **gauche . . . brioche:** Laforgue liked off-rhymes on 'brioche'; *Lunes en
détresse* (1886) 6, 8: 'crèche' / 'brioche'. *Dimanches: Bref, j'allais* (1886–7) 23,
24, 26: 'dimanches' / 'blanches' / 'brioches'.

13 **versicles:** given the blasphemous refrain ('For Christ's sake . . .'), this may add to
'little verses' the sense *OED* 1, '*Liturg*. One of a series of short sentences, usually
taken from the Psalms and of a precatory nature, said or sung antiphonally in
divine service'. Also 2b: 'A verse of the Psalms or the Bible (*obs.*), now *spec.*, one
of the subdivisions of a Hebrew verse'. **versiculous:** not in *OED*.

14 **attenuate:** as participial, compare Meredith, *The Egoist* (1879): 'The idea is too
exquisitely attenuate' (*OED*).

15 **isiculous:** formed from icicle (*OED* records the obsolete form isicle).

18 **cabotin:** *OED*, 1903, 'A low class actor'; Arnold Bennett, 1903; and then Henry
James, *The Tragic Muse* (1909): 'The mountebank, the mummer and the
cabotin'. Laforgue wrote of Corbière: 'Jamais Cabotin, jamais' (*Dragées: Charles
Baudelaire, Tristan Corbière*, 1920, p.168).

25–8 Compare TSE's concluding stanza (noting his first reading 'guests') with
FitzGerald's concluding stanza to the *Rubáiyát of Omar Khayyám* (1859):
And when Thyself with shining Foot shall pass
Among the Guests Star-scatter'd on the Grass,
    And in thy joyous Errand reach the Spot
Where I made one – turn down an empty Glass!
In Valerie Eliot's Note for the 1967 publication of TSE's *Poems Written in Early
Youth*: 'At about fourteen he wrote "some very gloomy quatrains in the form of
the *Rubáiyát*" which had "captured my imagination". These he showed to no one
and presumed he destroyed.' In an interview, TSE was asked: 'Do you remember
the circumstances under which you began to write poetry in St. Louis when you
were a boy?' He replied: 'I began I think about the age of fourteen, under the
inspiration of FitzGerald's *Omar Khayyam*, to write a number of very gloomy
and atheistical and despairing quatrains in the same style, which fortunately I

suppressed completely – so completely that they don't exist. I never showed them to anybody' (*Paris Review* 21, Spring/Summer 1959, p.49). On TSE and FitzGerald's *Rubáiyát*, see Vinnie-Marie D'Ambrosio, *Eliot Possessed* (1989).

26 **Theories scattered**: compare TSE on the world, in his early Harvard essay, *The validity of artificial distinctions* (Houghton Library; bMS Am 1691.14 (27), p.3): 'It swarms with inchoate theories which ultimately perhaps mean the same thing – at the point where all meanings are lost. The vast majority of these theories never reach articulate expression, but are reabsorbed into practice.'

Ballade pour la grosse Lulu

I

The Outlook gives an interview
By Lyman Abbot kindly sent
Entitled "What it means to You
That God is in his Firmament."
The papers say "300 Boers   5
On Roosevelt have paid a call;"
But, My Lulu, "Put on your rough red drawers
And come to the Whore House Ball!"

II

The Outlook gives an interview
An interview from Booker T.   10
Entitled "Up from Possum Stew!"
Or "How I set the nigger free!"
The papers say "the learned horse
Jim Key, was murdered in his stall."
But, My Lulu, "Put on your rough red drawers   15
And come to the Whore House Ball!"

III

The Outlook gives an interview
From Rockefellar, fresh & frank,
Entitled "How my Money grew"
Or "Jesus as a Savings Bank."   20
The papers say "South Boston scores
On Roxbury at basket ball"
But, My Lulu, "Put on your Rough Red Drawers
And come to the Whore House Ball."

IV

The Outlook gives an interview   25
From Harvard's great ex-president
Called "Oh if only people knew
That Virtue doesn't cost a cent!"
The papers say "For hard wood floors
TURPTINO WAX is best of all."   30
But, My Lulu, "Put on your rough red drawers
And come to the Whore House Ball!"

Leaf excised from the Notebook, now in the Beinecke Library, Yale (Pound papers). Manuscript in ink. Dated in pencil July 1911. Stanzas I and IV cancelled. The first line of each stanza was originally 'The papers give an interview'; when TSE revised it to 'The Outlook . . .', he made the consequential change to 'gives' in I but neglected to do so in the other stanzas, as also to open the quotation marks in 7 and to close them in 11. The penultimate line of each stanza began at first 'But, I say' (I), 'But I say' (II), 'But I say' (III–IV); the present text maintains the punctuation from the first occasion when TSE revised ('But, My Lulu, . . .').

1. *Outlook gives*] papers give *1st reading*.

10. *Booker T.*] Edward Bok *1st reading*.

11–12] Called 50 kinds of Irish Stew
       And "How to fill a Christmas Sock" *1st reading*

1–2 **The Outlook . . . Lyman Abbot**: Abbott (1835–1922), American clergyman, editor of *The Outlook* (from 1893, formerly *The Christian Union*). 'He championed a modern rational outlook in American Christianity' (*The New Columbia Encyclopedia*).

4 **God is in his Firmament**: compare Browning, *Pippa Passes* I 227–8:
    God's in his heaven –
    All's right with the world!

6 **Roosevelt**: Theodore Roosevelt (1858–1919), President of the United States, 1901–9; he was Contributing Editor of *The Outlook*, and had an article in each of the five issues of July 1911.

8 **Whore House Ball**: compare *Opera* 17: 'the undertakers' ball', and one of the Columbo verses 'And the band struck up "The Whore House Ball" '.

10–11 **Booker T. . . . "Up from**: Booker T. Washington (1856–1915), black American educator, and his autobiography *Up from Slavery* (1901), which had been serialized in *The Outlook*. He had just concluded a series of six articles in *The Outlook* (6 May–1 July 1911), *The Man Farthest Down*, ending: 'in Europe the man farthest down is woman'.

10 **Edward Bok** (variant): (1863–1930), American editor; of *The Ladies' Home Journal*, 1889–1919.

18 **Rockefellar**: John D. Rockefeller (1839–1937), American industrialist. *The Outlook* (31 Dec. 1910) had recently reported (though not within an 'interview') his final gift to the University of Chicago: 'One million five hundred thousand dollars is to be set apart for the building of a great University chapel, which shall embody the architectural ideals expressed by the buildings already constructed, and so placed that these buildings shall seem to have caught their inspiration from the chapel. In this way the group of University buildings, with the chapel centrally located and dominant, will proclaim that "the University in its ideal is dominated by the spirit of religion" '.

26 **Harvard's great ex-president**: Charles W. Eliot (1834–1926), a third cousin once removed of TSE's grandfather, was President of Harvard, 1869–1909. See *Letters* i 322–3 for a letter from him to TSE, 25 July 1919.

Fragments

1. There was a jolly tinker came across the sea
   With his four and twenty inches hanging to his knee
   Chorus   With his long-pronged hongpronged
   Underhanded babyfetcher
   Hanging to his knee.   5

2. It was a sunny summer day the tinker was in heat
   With his eight and forty inches hanging to his feet –

13. O tinker dear tinker I am in love with you
    O tinker jolly tinker will half a dollar do?

24. O daughter dear daughter I think you are a fool   10
    To run against a man with a john like a mule.

25. O mother dear mother I thought that I was able
    But he ripped up my belly from my cunt to my navel.

41. With his whanger in his hand he walked through the hall
    "By God" said the cook "he's a gona fuck us all."   15

50. With his whanger in his hand he walked through the hall
    "By God" said the cook "he's a gone and fucked us all."

Leaf excised from the Notebook, now in the Beinecke Library, Yale (Pound papers).
These lines in pencil are on the verso of the leaf (following [page] 27) of which the
recto has the conclusion of *Suite Clownesque*. TSE provides the comic numbering.

[Columbo and Bolo verses]

Let a tucket be sounded on the hautboys. Enter the king and queen.

Columbo he lived over in Spain
Where doctors are not many
The only doctor in his town
Was a bastard jew named Benny
To Benny then Columbo went
With countenance so placid
And Benny filled Columbo's prick
With Muriatic Acid.

One day the king & queen of Spain
They gave a royal banquet
Columbo having passed away
Was brought in on a blanket
The queen she took an oyster fork
And pricked Columbo's navel
Columbo hoisted up his ass
And shat upon the table.

Columbo and his merry men
They set sail from Genoa
Queen Isabella was aboard
That famous Spanish whore.

Columbo and his mariners
They were a merry chorus
One Sunday evening after tea
They went to storm a whore house.
As they were scrambling up the steps
Twas then Columbo his got
Molto vivace [*musical direction*]
A great big whore from the seventh story window
She floored him with a pisspot.

Variant [*at the foot of the page*]
A great big whore with blood shot eyes
She bitched him with a pisspot.

The cabin boy they had aboard
His name was Orlandino
A child of upright character
But his language was obscene-o.
"Fuck Spiders" was his chief remark
In accents mild and dulcet.
They asked him what there was for lunch
And he simply answered "Bullshit."

[Variant above, then end of leaf]

King Bolo's swarthy bodyguard
Were called the Jersey Lilies
A wild and hardy set of blacks
Undaunted by syphilis.
They wore the national uniform
Of a garland of verbenas
And a pair of great big hairy balls
And a big black knotty penis.

King Bolo's swarthy bodyguard
They numbered three and thirty
An innocent and playful lot
But most disgusting dirty.
King Bolo lay down in the shade
His royal breast uncovering
They mounted in a banyan tree
And shat upon their sovereign.

[end of leaf]

One day Columbo and his men
They took and went ashore
Columbo sniffed around the air
And muttered "I smell whore"
And ere they'd taken twenty steps
Among the Cuban jungles
They found King Bolo & his queen
A-sitting on their bungholes.

[end of leaf]

She put the question [?] to the lad [?]
The first mate, cook, and bo'sun,
But when she saw Columbos balls
She jumped into the ocean –

One Sunday morning out at sea
The vessel passed Gibraltar
Columbo sat upon the poop
A-reading in the psalter.
The bosuns wife came up on deck
With a bucket full of cowshit
Columbo grabbed her round the neck
And raped her on the bowsprit.

Now when they were three weeks at sea
Columbo he grew rooty
He took his cock in both his hands
And swore it was a beauty.
The cabin boy appeared on deck
And scampered up the mast-o
Columbo grasped him by the balls
And buggered him in the ass-o.

One day Columbo and the queen
They fell into a quarrel
Columbo showed his disrespect
By farting in a barrel.
The queen she called him horse's ass
And "dirty Spanish loafer"
They terminated the affair
By fucking on the sofa.

Before another day had passed
Columbo he fell sick-o
He filled the pump with argyrol
And rammed it up his prick-o.
And when they touched Cadiz he cried
(And let down both his anchors):
"We'll see if there's a doctor here
Can cure the whistling chancres."

[verso of this leaf]

Columbo and his merry men
They went to storm a castle
A bullet came along the road
And up Columbo's asshole.
Columbo grew so angry then
He nearly shit his breeches.
"Come on, my merry men," he cried
"We'll kill the sons of bitches."

"Avast my men" Columbo cried
In accents mild and dulcet
"The cargo that we have aboard
Is forty tons of bullshit."
The merry men set up a cheer

On hearing this reparty.
And the band struck up "The Whore House Ball"
In accents deep and farty.

On Sunday morning after prayers
They took their recreation
The crew assembled on the deck
And practiced masturbation.
Columbo being full of rum
He fell down in a stupor
They turned his asshole S.S.W.
And he cried "I'll die a pooper!"

Now when Columbo and his ships
Regained the Spanish shores
The Spanish ladies swarmed aboard
By twos & threes & fours.
Columbo hoisted up his [?]
And then his shirt and drawers
He spun his balls around his head
And cried "Hooray for whores!"

Flourish. Skirmishes and alarums. Cries without. Exeunt the king and
queen severally.

Leaves excised from the Notebook, now in the Beinecke Library, Yale (Pound
papers). The variants may lack gravity, but here are those of wording:

The cabin boy they had aboard: this stanza cancelled.

King Bolo's swarthy bodyguard / *Were called* . . .
4. *Undaunted*] Exhausted *1st reading*.

King Bolo's swarthy bodyguard / *They numbered* . . .
2 ∧ 3] A bold and hardy set of blacks *added*.
5. *King Bolo lay*] And Bolo sat *1st reading*.

One day Columbo and the queen
5] She rammed her finger up and cried [*revised* his ass] *1st reading.*
6. *And*] "you *1st reading*; The *2nd reading.*
7] Columbo put her on her back *1st reading*; Columbo pushed her down the stairs *2nd reading.*
8. *By fucking*] And fucked her *1st reading.*

"Avast my men" Columbo cried
6] And cried right-o my hearty" *1st reading*; In accents bold and hearty *2nd reading.*
7] Columbo cried "All aft for grog" *1st reading.*
8. *deep*] mild *1st reading.*

On Sunday morning after prayers
1] One Sunday morning out at sea *1st reading.*
3] The crew were lying in their bunks *1st reading.*
4. *And practiced*] Engaged in *1st reading.*
6. *fell down*] passed out *1st reading.*
8] And he left a noble pooper. *1st reading*; And he fired off a pooper. *2nd reading.*

Now when Columbo and his ships
5] Columbo first took off his bags *1st reading.*

In TSE's letter to Aiken, 19 July 1914 (*Letters* i 40), those who deserve the injunction BLESS include Columbo and Bolo. Columbo and Bolo poems (though none of those which appear in these Notebook leaves) figure in the letters. TSE to Aiken (i 42, 19 July 1914; i 59, 30 Sept. 1914; i 125–6, 10 Jan. 1916). TSE to Pound (31 Oct. 1917, i 206):

> I have been invited by female VANDERVELDE to contribute to a reading of POETS: big wigs, OSWALD and EDITH Shitwell, Graves (query, George?) Nichols, and OTHERS. Shall I oblige them with our old friend COLUMBO? or Bolo, since famous?

(Eight lines of Columbo and Bolo follow.) TSE to Joyce, 21 May 1921 (i 455):

> I wish that Miss Beach would bring out a limited edition of my epic ballad on the life of Christopher Columbus and his friend King Bolo, but
> Bolo's big black bastard queen
> Was *so* obscene
> She shocked the folk of Golder's Green.

Pound to TSE, 27? Jan. 1922 (i 505): 'You can forward the Bolo to Joyce if you think it wont unhinge his somewhat sabbatarian mind. On the hole he might be saved the shock, shaved the sock.' TSE to Pound, 30 Aug. 1922 (i 568), has four lines of a Bolo poem; and TSE wrote to Clive Bell about the Bolo poems, 3 Jan. 1941 (Hayward Bequest).

Among the Pound papers at Yale, there are two dozen further Columbo and Bolo stanzas, one and a half on a separate leaf, and the rest on seven leaves with perforated sides from a small notebook.

With a limerick (*There was a young girl of Siberia*), there were published in *The Faber Book of Blue Verse* (ed. John Whitworth, 1990), *Columbiad: Two Stanzos* (*The Ladies of King Bolo's Court* and *King Bolo's Royal Body Guard / Were called 'The Jersey Lilies'*, this last given above), and *'Twas Christmas on the Spanish Main*, also featuring Columbo.

For TSE's subsequent elaborated development of Bolovian beliefs and customs, see TSE's long correspondence with Bonamy Dobrée (Brotherton Collection, University of Leeds). In his contribution ('A Personal Reminiscence') to *T. S. Eliot: The Man and His Work* (ed. Allen Tate, 1966), Dobrée reported:

The last two sentences [from a letter by TSE] need explaining.

They are part of an elaborated joke, nurtured through years. It is about some primitive people called the Bolovians, who wore bowler hats, and had square wheels to their chariots. This invention he apparently began to toy with when he was at Harvard, there figuring King Bolo and his Queen. He did not tell me much about those characters – though he sent me a drawing of them – but I was given portions of a Bolovian Epic (not always very decorous) and something about their religion. This latter was in part an amiable satire on the way people, anthropologists especially, talk about the religion of others.

Compare W. S. Gilbert, *The Bab Ballads*, for instance *King Burria*. For the historical figure King Shamba Bolongongo, see B. C. Southam, *A Student's Guide to the Selected Poems of T. S. Eliot* (6th edn, 1994), p.103. TSE had noted, for his Harvard course in fine art with E. W. Forbes (Feb.–May 1910): *Bolo*, 'The ground for gilding is bolo' (Houghton Library; MS Am 1691.14 (7), p.2).

APPENDIX B

The text – as it first stood in the Notebook
or the loose leaves – of *Humouresque* (published 1910)
and of the poems (here in the order of the volume)
in *Prufrock and Other Observations* (1917)

The line-numbering is of these texts; line-numbering for the published versions, when it differs, is in square brackets. Noted in the variants are differences of wording between the final state of the manuscripts and the first published texts. *1963* is noted when its wording differs from the late state of the first published texts. Not attempted is a record of intermediate stages of the text.

Humouresque

One of my marionettes is dead
  Though not yet tired of the game
But weak in body as in head:
  A jumping-jack has such a frame.

But this deceasèd marionette   5
  I rather liked – I liked his face
The kind of face that you forget,
  Locked in a comic, dull grimace;

Half-bullying, half-imploring air
  And mouth that knew the latest tune   10
His who-the-devil-are-you stare:–

  Translated, maybe, to the moon

With Limbo's other cast-off things
  Haranguing spectres, fancy him there
"The snappiest fashion, just this spring's   15
  The newest cry on earth, I swear."

"Why don't you people get some class"
  (And here contemptuous of nose)
"Your damned thin moonlight, worse than gas
  Now in New York" – and so it goes;   20

Logic – a marionette's all wrong
  Of premises – but in some star
A life! – but where would it belong?
  And after all – what masque bizarre!

Notebook, [pages] 46–7, in black ink, dated Nov. 1909. Published *Harvard Advocate* (12 Jan. 1910) with the addition to the title: (*After J. Laforgue*).

6. *I liked his*] a common *1910*.

7. *you*] we *1910*.

8. *Locked*] Pinched *1910*.

10. *And . . . knew*] Mouth twisted to *1910*.

13. *cast-off*] useless *1910*.

14. *fancy*] set *1910*.

15. *just this*] since last *1910*.

16. *cry*] style *1910*.

18. *And here*] Feebly *1910*.   *nose*] hose *1910* (*misprint, corrected in 1950, 1967*).

22. *but*] yet *1910*.

23. *life*] hero *1910*.   *but*] *1st reading*; and *revision*.   *it*] he *1910*.

24. *And after all –*] But, even at that, *1910*.   *masque*] mark *1910* (*misprint, corrected in 1950, 1967, to* mask).

[The Love Song of J. Alfred Prufrock: see page 39.]

Portrait of a Lady

I have caught an everlasting cold: – The White Devil.

Among the fog and smoke of a December afternoon
You have the scene arrange itself – as it will seem to do –
With an "I designed this afternoon for you"
And four wax candles in the darkened room
Four rings of light upon the ceiling overhead   5
An atmosphere of Juliet's tomb –
And all the disturbing things that are left unsaid.

We have been, let us say, to hear the latest Pole
Transmit the *Preludes*, through his hair and finger tips
"So intimate, this Chopin, that I think his soul   10
Should be resurrected only among friends
Some two or three, who will not touch the bloom
That is rubbed and questioned in the concert room"
And so the conversation slips
Among velleities and carefully caught regrets   15
Through attenuated tones of violins
Mingled with remote cornets
And begins –
"You do not know how much they mean to me, my friends
And how, how rare and strange it is, to find   20
In a life composed so much, so much of ways and ends
(Indeed I am not social – you knew it? ah, I knew you were not blind!
How keen you are!)
– To find a friend who has those qualities
So rare and strange and so unvalued too   25
Who has, and gives   [25]
Those qualities upon which friendship lives
How much it means that I say this to you!
Without these friendships – life, what *cauchemar*!"

Among the windings of the violins   30
And the ariettes   [30]
Of our cornets

Inside my brain a droll tom-tom begins
Hammering a prelude of its own
Capricious monotone . .   35
That is at least one definite "false note."   [35]
– Let us take the air, in a tobacco trance,
    Admire the monuments
    Discuss the late events
    Correct our watches by the public clocks   40
    Then sit for half an hour and drink our bocks   [40]
    And pay our reckoning and go home again
They are lighting up the lamps, and it begins to rain.

Part II

"Thou hast committed – "
"Fornication – but that was in another country
And besides, the wench is dead": Jew of Malta.

Now that lilacs are in bloom
She has a bowl of lilacs in her room
And twists one in her fingers while she talks.
"Ah, my friend, you do not know, you do not know
What Life is, you who hold it in your hands;"   5
Slowly twisting the lilac stalks –
"You let it flow from you, you let it flow
"And youth is cruel, and has no remorse
"And smiles at situations which it does not see" –
I smile, of course   10
And go on drinking tea.
"Yet with these April sunsets, that somehow recall
My buried life, and Paris in the spring –
I feel immeasurably at peace, and find the world
To be wonderful and youthful, after all."   15

Oh, spare these reminiscences!
How you prolong the pose!
These emotional concupiscences
Tinctured attar of rose.

(The need for self-expression   20
Will pardon this digression).

The voice returns like the insistent out-of-tune
Of a cracked violin on an August afternoon:
"I am always sure that you understand
"My feeling, always sure that you feel . . .   25
"Sure that across the gulf you reach your hand.   [20]

"You are invulnerable, you have no Achilles' heel.
"You will go on, and when you have prevailed
"You will think: at this point many a one has failed.

"But what have I, but what have I, my friend   30
"To give you, what can you receive from me?   [25]
" – Only the friendship and the sympathy
"Of one about to reach her journey's end."

"I shall sit here, serving tea to friends" –

– I take my hat. How can I make a cowardly amends   35
For what she has said to me?   [30]

You will see me any morning in the park
Reading the comics and the sporting page.
Particularly I remark
An English countess goes upon the stage.   40
A Greek was murdered at a Polish dance,   [35]
Another bank defaulter has confessed:–
I keep my countenance –
I remain self-possessed.
Except when a street piano, mechanical and tired   45
Reiterates some worn-out common song   [40]
With the smell of hyacinths across the garden –
Recalling things that other people have desired –
Are these ideas right or wrong?

III

The October night comes down, recurring as before
Except for a slight sensation of being ill at ease —
I mount the stairs and turn the handle of the door
And feel as if I had mounted on my hands and knees.

"So you are going abroad; and when do you return?   5
"But that's a useless question.
"Indeed, you hardly know when you are coming back
"You will find so much to learn."
My smile falls heavily among the bric-a-brac.

"Perhaps you can write to me."   10
My self-possession flares up for a second —
This is as I had reckoned.

"I have been wondering frequently of late
" — (And our beginnings never know our ends!) —
"Why we have not developed into friends."   15
I feel like one who smiles, and turning, shall remark
Suddenly, his expression in a glass.
My self-possession gutters. We are really in the dark.

"For everybody said so, all our friends —
"They all were sure our feelings would relate   20
"So closely! I myself can hardly understand.
        "We must leave it now to fate.
        "You will write, at any rate.
        "Perhaps it is not too late."

And I . . . must borrow every changing shape   25 [26]
For my expression — dance dance
Dance like a dancing bear,
Whistle like a parrot, chatter like an ape;
Let us take the air, in a tobacco trance —   [30]

Well! and what if she should die some afternoon,   30
Afternoon grey and smoky, evening yellow and rose;
Should die, and leave me sitting pen in hand
With the smoke coming down across the house-tops
Doubtful for quite a while   [35]
Not knowing what to feel, nor if I understand   35
Or whether wise or foolish, tardy or too soon,
– Would she not have the advantage after all?
(This music is successful with a "dying fall"
Now that we talk of dying –)   [40]
And should I have the right to smile?   40

Notebook, [pages] 22–3 (I), in pencil, title added in black ink, dated Nov. 1910; plus I 38–43 and the succeeding epigraph (Laforgue), from the excised leaf at Yale ([page] 23a) which has Bolo verses on the other side; [pages] 41–4 and [leaf] 45 (II–III), in black ink, dated respectively Feb. 1910 and Nov. 1911. Published *Others* (Sept. 1915), where the poem's epigraph from Webster was replaced by that from Marlowe which had previously been for Part II. The *1915* text does not differ in wording from *1917*.

[1]

1. *fog and smoke*] smoke and fog *1917*.

3. *With*] *rewritten or written over a word. an*] not *1917*. *designed*] *1st reading*; have saved *revision*.

7] *1st reading*; Prepared for all the things to be said, or left unsaid. *revision*.

9. *Transmit*] *written over a word* [Translate?].

14] – *added apparently at the beginning*.

16. *Through* ∧ *attenuated*] mod [?] *deleted*.

18. *And* ∧ *begins*] then *added*.

21. *ways*] *1st reading*; odds *revision*.

22] (For indeed I do not love it – you knew? you were not blind! *revision*.

23. *you*] *written over* your [?].

24. *those*] these *1917*.

25] *not 1917.*

29. *what*] *1st and final reading; quel* [underlined] *apparently 2nd reading.*

32. *our*] *1st reading;* shrill *revision in ink;* cracked *1917.   cornets*] *corrected from* cornetts.

33. *a*] an *1st reading.   droll*] [?] *1st reading;* strong *2nd reading;* rude *3rd reading;* dull *final reading.*

34. *Hammering*] *1st reading;* Absurdly hammering *revision.*

38–43] *from the excised leaf now at Yale, apparently indented so; these lines are followed by*:

III

Je ne suis qu'un viveur Lunaire
Qui fait des ronds dans les bassins
— — — — — — — — — —
Devenez un legendaire
Au seuil des siècles charlatans! . . . Pierrots.

'Devenez . . . charlatans!' then deleted. From Laforgue, *Locutions des Pierrots* XVI 1–2, 9–10.

[II]
3. *she talks*] *1st reading, 1917;* we talk *revision in pencil.*

6. *stalks*] *1st reading, 1917;* stalk *revision in pencil.*

9. *does not*] cannot *1917.*

16–21] *not 1917.*

23. *cracked*] broken *1917.*

25. *feeling*] feelings *1917.*

29. *will think*] can say *1917.*

31. *can*] have *1st reading, presumably intending* have you received.

33 ∧ 4] *space in 1917; unclear in MS because a new page at 34.*

[III]
1. *recurring*] returning *1917.*

2. –] , *perhaps.*

5. *So*] And so *1917*.

7. *Indeed, you*] You *1917*.

14. *And*] But *1917*.

24 ∧ 5] "I shall sit here, serving tea to friends." *added*.

26. *For my*] To find *1917*.

27. *Dance like*] Like *1917*.

28. *Whistle*] *1st reading*; Cry *revision*. Whistle *may not of course have intended* parrot.

29 ∧ 30] *space in MS (coinciding with page-division in this edition)*.

33. *across*] above *1917*.

34. *for quite*] *1917, Ara Vos Prec, 1920*; for *1963*.

35. *nor*] or *1917*.

[Preludes]

[I]
Prelude in Dorchester
(Houses)

The winter evening settles down
With smell of steaks in passage ways.
Six o'clock.
The burnt-out ends of smoky days.
And now a gusty shower wraps   5
The grimy scraps
Of withered leaves around your feet,
And newspapers from vacant lots.
The showers beat
On broken blinds and chimney pots   10
And at the corner of the street
A lonely cab horse steams and stamps.

And then the lighting up of lamps!

[II]
Prelude in Roxbury

The morning comes to consciousness
Of faint stale smells of beer
From the sawdust trampled street
With its muddy feet
                    that press
To early coffee stands –   5

With all other masquerades
That time resumes
One thinks of all the hands
That are raising dingy shades
In a thousand furnished rooms . . .   10

[III]
(Morgendämmerung)
Prelude in Roxbury

"Son âme
de petite putain":
Bubu.

You tossed a blanket from the bed
You lay upon your back, and waited
You flung an arm above your head
You dozed, and watched the night revealing
A thousand sordid images   5
From which your soul was constituted:
They flickered against the ceiling.

And when all the world came back
And the light crept up between the shutters
And you heard the sparrows in the gutters   10
You had such a vision of the street
As the street hardly understands;
Sitting upon the bed's edge, where
You dropped the papers from your hair
Or clasped the yellow soles of feet   15
In the palms of both soiled hands.

[IV]
Abenddämmerung

His soul stretched tight across the skies
That fade behind a city block
Trampled by the insistent feet
Of seven and of six o'clock:
– And short square fingers cramming pipes,   5
And evening newspapers – and eyes
Assured of certain certainties:
The conscience of a blackened street
Impatient to assume the world.

I am wrought by various fancies, curled   10
Around these images, which cling –
The notion of some infinitely gentle
Infinitely suffering thing.

– Wipe your hand across your mouth, and laugh.
The worlds revolve like ancient women   15
Gathering fuel in vacant lots

– And we are moved into these strange opinions
By four-o'clock-in-the-morning thoughts.

Notebook, [page] 15 (I), in black ink, dated Oct. 1910; [page] 16 (II), in pencil, dated Oct. 1910; [page] 17 (III), in black ink, dated July 1911; separate leaf laid in following [page] 17 (IV), in black ink. Published *Blast* (July 1915). The *1915* text does not differ in wording from *1917* except where noted.

[I]
Title: *Dorchester*] *1st reading*; Roxbury *in pencil*.

1, 5. *winter . . . gusty*] *ringed and linked by TSE*.

3. *o'clock*] o clock *MS*.

7. *around*] about *1917*.

13. *up of*] of the *1917*.

[II]
4. *its*] all its *1917*.

5. *stands –*] stands. *perhaps*.

6. *all*] *1st reading*; the *revision*.

9 ∧ 10 *(Such*] *written over* The *followed by a word or words apparently ending in* ades!

[III]
Epigraph: *Son âme de petite putain*. Apparently mingling phrases from *Bubu de Montparnasse*: 'un sourire de pauvre petite putain' (ch.III), 'ses histoires de pauvre petite putain' (VIII), and 'son âme' throughout, including 'où l'on vend son âme pendant que l'on vend sa chair' (VII).

3] *not 1917.*

5. *A*] *1st reading*; The *revision.*

6. *From*] Of *written above (braced) as alternative; 1917.*

8. *all the*] *1917*; the *1915.*

13. *upon*] along *1917.*

14. *dropped*] [?] *1st reading*; curled *revision.*

[IV]

3. *Trampled*] *1st reading*; And trampled *2nd reading in ink, with* And *deleted in pencil*; Or trampled *final reading with* Or *in pencil.* the] *deleted in ink.*

4. *seven and of six*] *1st reading deleted in pencil*; four and five and six *revision in pencil. TSE deleted* Of *in ink, and wrote* And *in ink above it, braced and then deleted in pencil, then* Of *in pencil.*

5. *cramming*] *1st reading*; stuffing *written above (braced) as alternative; 1917.*

7. *Assured*] *written over* S [*for* Sure?]. certain] uncertain *with* un *deleted.*

9 ∧ 10] *space in MS (coinciding with page-division in this edition).*

10. *wrought*] moved *1917.* various fancies,] *1st reading deleted in ink*; fancies that are *revision braced.*

11. *which*] *1st reading*; and *revision braced.*

17–18] *not 1917.*

Rhapsody on a Windy Night

Twelve o'clock
Along the reaches of the street
Held in a lunar synthesis
And all the lunar incantations
Dissolve the floors of the memory   5
And all its clear relations,
– Its divisions,
Definite precisions.
Every street lamp that I pass
Beats like a fatalistic drum   10
And through the spaces of the dark   [10]
The midnight shakes my memory
As a madman shakes a dead geranium.

Half past one
The street-lamp sputtered   15
The street-lamp muttered   [15]
The street-lamp said "regard that woman   [16]
"Who hesitates toward you on the corner   [17]
"You see the corner of her dress   [19]
"Is torn, and stained with sand   20
"And the corner of her eye
"Twists like a crooked pin."

The memory throws up high and dry
A crowd of twisted things;
– A twisted branch upon the beach   25
Eaten smooth, and polished
As if the world gave up
The secret of its skeleton
Hard and white
A broken spring in a factory yard   30
Rust that clings to the form which the force has left
Hard and curled and ready to snap

Half past two
A street lamp said,
"Remark the cat which flattens himself in the gutter   35
Slips out his tongue
And devours a morsel of butter."

So the hand of a child, automatic
Slipped out and pocketed a toy that was running along the quai
I could see nothing behind the eye [of t   ]   40
I have seen eyes in the street
Trying to peer through lighted shutters
And a crab one afternoon in a pool
A crab green and with a barnacle on his back
Gripped the end of the stick I held him   45

_____

Half past three
The lamps sputtered
The lamp muttered in the dark
A lamp hummed
"Regard the moon   50
"La lune ne garde aucune rancune
She winks a watery eye,
She smiles from the corners of a face   [53]
Wrinkles the hideous scars of a washed-out pox   [56]
Her hand twists a paper rose;   55
That smells of dust and old Cologne
All alone
Oblivious of the [   ] smells   [60]
That cross and cross across her face."
Always the reminiscence comes   60
Of withered dry geraniums
And dust in corners,
Smells of [chestnuts] on the streets   [65]
And female smells in darkened rooms,
And cigarette smoke of corridors   65
And cocktail smells in bars . . .

The last lamp said
Four o'clock   ·   [70]
Here is your number on the door
Memory!   70
You have the key
The lamp spreads a ring on the stair
Mount.   [75]
The bed is open, the toothbrush hangs on the wall
Put the bags in the [   ], sleep, prepare for life."   75

The last twist of the knife.

Loose leaves: published [1–3], in pencil, dated March 1911. The manuscript is very faint, especially as to punctuation. Published *Blast* (July 1915), as *Rhapsody of a Windy Night* (mis-titled, presumably, since the manuscript has *on*; *Ara Vos Prec* has 'of' on its contents page and 'on' heading the poem). The *1915* text does not differ in wording from *1917* except where noted.

4. *And all the*] *1st reading*; Whispering *revision*.

5. *of the*] *1917*, *AVP*; of *1920*.

7–8. – *Its . . . precisions*] Its divisions and precisions, *1917*, *AVP*, *1920*; . . . precisions. *1963*.

12. *The midnight*] *1st reading*; Midnight *revision.   my*] *1st reading*; the *revision*.

18. *on the corner*] *1st reading*; in the light of the door / Which opens on her like a grin. *revision*.

19. *corner*] *1st reading*; border *revision*.

21. *And*∧ *the*] you see *added*.

24. *twisted*] *brackets ( ) added, presumably for reconsideration and not as punctuation*.

29. *Hard*] *1st reading*; Stiff *revision*.

31. *which*] that *1917.   force*] *1st reading*; strength *revision above as alternative*; *1917*.

34. *A*] The *1917*.

35. *which*] *1st and final reading*; that *2nd reading.*   *himself*] *1st reading*; itself *revision.*

36. *his*] *1st reading*; its *revision.*

37. *of*∧ *butter*] rancid *added.*

38. *a*] *1917, A VP*; the *1920.*

39. *was*] *written over* he [?].   *quai*] *1915*; quay *1917.*

40. *the eye [of t   ]] 1st reading* [*of the child left incomplete presumably*].   *the*] *that 1917.   the* ∧ *eye*] child's *added.*

44. *A crab green and*] *1st reading*; An old crab *revision.*   *a barnacle*] barnacles *1917.*

45. *Gripped*] *written over* S [*for* Seized?].

47. *lamps*] lamp *1917.*

49. *A*] The *1917.*

52. *watery*] [?] *1st reading*; feeble *revision.*

53. *from the corners of a face*] *1st reading*; into corners. / She touches [*revised to* smooths] the hair of the grass. / The moon has lost her memory. *revision with* feeble *above* moon *but deleted.*

54] *1st reading, with* hideous *doubtful and with* small *written above* pox; A washed out smallpox cracks her face *revision.*

56. *old*] *1917, A VP, 1920*; eau de *1963.*

57. *All*] She is *1917.*

58] *1st reading with an illegible word and with* smells *doubtful*; With all the old nocturnal smells *revision.   Oblivious*] Unconscious *written above as alternative.*

59. *face*] *1st reading*; brain *revision.*

60. *Always the*] *1st reading*; Still the *2nd reading*; And still the *3rd reading*; The *final reading.*

61. *withered*] *1st reading*; sunless *revision.*

62. *corners*] *1st reading*; crevices *revision.*

63. *chestnuts*] *deleted with no replacement.   on*] in *1917.   streets*] street *1915.*

64. *darkened*] *1st reading*; shuttered *revision.*

65. *cigarette smoke of*] *1st reading;* cigarettes in *revision.*

66 ∧ 7] *space in MS (coinciding with page-division in this edition).*

67. *last*] *not 1917.*

68. *o'clock*] o clock *MS.*

69. *your*] *1st reading;* the *revision.*

72. *The* ∧ *lamp*] little *added.*

75. *the bags in the* [   ]] *1st reading ending with illegible word (perhaps* on the
[   ]*);* your shoes at the door *revision.*

Morning at the Window

They are rattling breakfast plates in basement kitchens
And along the trampled edges of the street
I am aware of the damp souls of housemaids
Hanging despondently at area gates.

The brown waves of fog toss up to me   5
Twisted faces from the bottom of the street
And tear from a passer-by with muddy skirts
An aimless smile that hovers in the air
And vanishes along the level of the roofs.

Notebook, [leaf] 51, in black ink. Published *Poetry* (Sept. 1916). The *1916* text does not differ in wording from *1917* except where noted.

4. *Hanging*] *1916*; Sprouting *1917*.

7. *passer-by*] *no clear hyphen but the words linked.*

8. *An*] *miswritten* And *at first.*

[Mr. Apollinax]

When M[r] Apollonax visited the United States
We thought of Fragilion, that shy figure among the birch trees
And of Priapus, terra cotta in the shrubbery
Gaping at the lady in a swing.   [5]
At the palace of M[rs] Phlaccus, again at Professor Channing-
    Cheetah's   5
He laughed like an irresponsible foetus.
His laughter was submarine and profound
Without sound
Like the old man of the seas
Under a rock in the green silence   10
Hidden under coral islands   [10]
While the desperate bodies of drowned men drift down in the green
    silence, dropping from fingers of surf.
And I looked for the head of M[r] Apollonax rolling under a chair
Or grinning inanely over a screen
With seaweed in its hair.   15

I heard the beat of centaur's hoofs over the soft turf
As his dry and passionate talk devoured the afternoon.
"He is a charming man." "But his pointed ears – he must be
    unbalanced."
"There was something he said which I might have challenged."   [20]
Of dowager M[rs] Phlaccus, and Professor and M[rs] Cheetah   20
I remember lemon in the cup, and a bitten macaroon.

Loose leaves: published [4–5]; first draft (A) in pencil (the text above); fair copy (B) in black ink (which has A's final readings except where noted). Neither has the title, or the epigraph. Published *Poetry* (Sept. 1916), which text does not differ in wording from *1917* except where noted. *1916*, *1917* and *1920* do not have the epigraph, which appears in *Ara Vos Prec* without attribution:

    Ω τῆς καινότητος. Ἡράκλεις, τῆς παραδοξολογίας.
    εὐμήχανος ἄνθρωπος.

                              LUCIAN

1, 13. *Apollonax*] Apollinax *B.*

1 ∧ 2] His laughter tinkled across the teacups. *added in A. across*] among *1917.*

2. *We*] *A 1st reading*; I *revision. trees*] trees, *B.*

3. , *terra cotta*] *deleted in A.*

4. *a*] *A 1st reading*; the *revision.*

5. *At*] In *B. again*] *deleted in A.*

6] *not 1916 (editorial censorship).*

7. *profound*] profound: *B.*

7–9] *A 1st reading*; [7] / He sometimes laughed / [8] / [9], *these four lines braced and numbered*: '2' / '1' (*both* He sometimes laughed *and* [8]) / '3' *A 2nd reading*; [7], [9] *A final reading.*

9. *seas*] *A, B 2nd reading*; sea's *B 1st reading, 1917.*

10] *deleted in A (but see 12).*

12. *While*] Where *written above in A as alternative, B. the*] *not B. desperate*] *A 1st reading*; worried *revision. down*] by *written above in A, deleted. down* ∧ *in*] under the surf *added and deleted in A.*

12 ∧ 13] You must listen under the surf *added in A and deleted.*

13. *And*] *deleted in A.*

14. *inanely*] *not B.*

16. *centaur's*] *A, 1920*; centaurs' *B, AVP, 1917. soft*] *A, B 1st reading*; hard *B revision.*

18] *A 1st reading*; What did he mean? But [*revised to* And] after all, what does he mean? *added in A following 18, with the first question then ringed with an arrow to move it before 18*;
   "He is a charming man" – "But after all what did he mean?" –
   "His pointed ears . . . . he must be unbalanced." *1917, AVP*
(He must *1920.* unbalanced", *B.* unbalanced.' – *1963*.) . *"But*] *A*; . – "But *revision*; – "but *B.*

19. *"There*] *A, B*; – "There *A revision. which*] *1916*; that *1917.*

21. *lemon in the cup*] *A 1st reading*; a slice of lemon *revision.*

Short Romance [Conversation Galante]

I observe: "our sentimental friend the moon!
Or possibly (fantastic, I confess)
It may be Prester John's balloon,
Or an old battered lantern hung aloft
To light poor travellers to their distress."   5
    She then: "How you digress!"

And I then: "someone frames upon the keys
That exquisite nocturne with which we explain
The night and moonshine: music that we seize
To body out our own vacuity."   10
    She then: "Does this refer to me?"
    "Oh no, it is I who am inane."

"You, madame, are the eternal humourist,
The eternal enemy of the absolute,
Giving our vagrant moods the slightest twist! –   15
With your air indifferent and imperious
At a stroke our mad poetics to confute – "
    And – "are we then so serious?"

Notebook, [leaf] 1, in blue ink, dated in pencil Nov. 1909. Cancelled original title (in ink): *Short Romance.* In pencil: *Conversation Galante.* Published *Poetry* (Sept. 1916). The *1916* text does not differ in wording from *1917.*

2] – *added in pencil at the beginning.*

3. *Prester*] *deleted and then rewritten; above it, in pencil* simply *deleted.* ,] *1st reading;* – *in pencil.*

9. *that*] *1st reading;* which *in pencil.*

10. *out*] forth *1917.*

APPENDIX C

The text – as it first stood in the loose leaves – of the poems
in *Poems* (1919), *Ara Vos Prec* ('completed Dec: 10th. 1919'
at the printer's, published early February 1920),
and *Poems* (late February 1920)

The line-numbering is of these texts; line-numbering for the published versions, when it differs, is in square brackets. Noted in the variants are differences of wording between the final state of the manuscripts and the first published texts. *1963* is noted when its wording differs from the late state of the first published texts. Not attempted is a record of intermediate stages of the text.

Gerousia [Gerontion]

Thou hast nor youth nor age
But as it were an after dinner sleep
Dreaming of both.
                    Come il mi corpo stea
Nel mondo su, nulla scienza porto.
          [*Inferno* XXXIII 121–2, with *mio*]

Here I am, an old man in a dry month,
Being read to by a boy, waiting for rain.
I was neither at the hot gates
Nor fought in the warm rain
Nor knee deep in the salt marsh, heaving a cutlass,   5
Bitten by flies, fought.
My house is a decayed house
And the jew squats on the window sill, the owner,
Spawned in some estaminet of Antwerp,
Blistered in Brussels, patched and peeled in London.   10
The goat coughs at night in the field overhead;
Rocks, moss, stonecrop, iron, merds.
The woman keeps the kitchen, makes tea,
Sneezes at evening, poking the peevish gutter.

                    I an old man,   15
A dull head among windy spaces.

Signs are taken for wonders. "We would see a sign":
The word within a word, unable to speak a word,
Swaddled with darkness. In the juvescence of the year
Came Christ the tiger   20
In depraved May, dogwood and chestnut, flowering judas,
To be eaten, to be divided, to be drunk
Among whispers; by Mr Silvero
With caressing hands, at Limoges
Who walked all night in the next room;   25
By Hakagawa, bowing among the Titians;
By Madame de Tornquist, in the dark room
Shifting the candles; Fraülein von Kulp

Who turned in the hall, one hand on the door. Vacant shuttles
Weave the wind. I have no ghosts,   30
An old man in a draughty house
Under a windy knob.

After such knowledge, what forgiveness? Think now
Nature has many cunning passages, contrived corridors
And issues; deceives with whispering ambitions,   35
Guides us with vanities. Think now
She gives when our attention is distracted,
And what she gives, gives with such supple confusions
That the giving famishes the craving. Gives too late
What's not believed in, or if still believed,   40
In memory only, reconsidered passion. Gives too soon
Into weak hands, what's thought can be dispensed with
Till the refusal propagates a fear. Think
Neither fear nor courage saves us. Unnatural vices
Are fathered by our heroism. Virtues   45
Are forced upon us by our impudent crimes.

These tears are shaken from the wrath-bearing tree.

The tiger springs in the new year. Us he devours. Think at last
We have not reached conclusion, when I
Stiffen in a rented house. Think at last   50
I have not made this show purposelessly
And it is not by any concitation
Of the backward devils.
I would meet you upon this honestly.
I that was in your heart was removed therefrom   55
To lose beauty in terror, terror in inquisition.
I have lost my passion: why should I need to keep it
Since what is kept must be adulterated?
I have lost my sight, smell, hearing, taste and touch:
How should I use it for your closer contact?   60

These with a thousand small deliberations
Protract the profit of their chilled delirium,
Excite the membrane, when the sense has cooled

With pungent sauces, multiply variety
In a wilderness of mirrors. What will the spider do,   65
Suspend its operations, will the weevil
Delay? De Bailhache, Fresca, Mrs Cammel, whirled
Beyond the circuit of the shuddering Bear
In fractured atoms. We have saved a shilling against oblivion
Even oblivious.   70

Tenants of an old man's house,
Thoughts of a dry brain in a dry season.   [75]

Loose leaves: published [6–7], original typescript (A). Loose leaves: published [8–9],
carbon typescript of a revised version (B), with pencil suggestions by Pound. Title
revised to *Gerontion* in A. Second epigraph, from Dante ('How my body stands in the
world above, I have no knowledge'): A; *not* B, *Ara Vos Prec*, *1920*. B comes close to
1920's punctuation, but follows A in: 14 ∧ 15 space, 20 ∧ 21 no space.

1. *Here I am, an*] *ringed by Pound and deleted.*

2. Pound ringed '*Being*', and underlined '*Being read to by a boy*'; he wrote in the
margin '? *to by*'; and he wrote above TSE's opening words, entries one below the
other: 'b – b – b / B d + b b / consonants, / & two prepositions'.

4. *rain*] A; rain, B.

8. *owner*] *ringed by Pound who wrote in the margin*: 'vs the "my" denouement of
"rented" rather delayed'.

26. *Hakagawa*] *underlined by Pound, who wrote in the margin*: '? The gentleman's
name means [*revised to* ends] in affix meaning *river* & wd. be taken for some Tiber or
Garonne by anyone knowing as much Jap as I do'. Pound also wrote, following this
and alongside 3–14: 'don't know whether / vide letter'.

30. W*eave the wind*] *Pound bracketed* the.

33. *Think now*] *ringed by Pound.*

34. *Nature*] A *1st reading*; History A, B.   *has many*] *bracketed by Pound.*

35. *deceives*] *ringed by Pound after changing it to* deceived; *Pound put a line to the
right of it as though to move it to come between* whispering *and* ambitions.

36. *with*] A *1st reading*; by A, B.   *Think now*] *deleted by Pound.*

37. *She*] *deleted by Pound.*   *gives*] comma added by Pound.   *distracted,*] A; distracted B, *a comma (which had been in A) then added by Pound.*

38. *gives with such*] *Pound bracketed* gives *and* such.

39. *Gives*] *underlined and bracketed by Pound who added* 'stet'.

44. *Neither fear nor courage*] How courage A *1st reading of the start of the line.*

53. *devils.*] *followed in A by deleted* It is commonly said

55. *in*] A *1st reading*; near A, B.

57. *need*] want A VP.

60. *it*] A, B, A VP, *1920*; them *1963.*

63. *cooled*] *comma added to A in ink*; cooled, B.

69]   Gull against the wind, in the windy straits
       Of Belle Isle, or driven by the horn,   [70]
       White feathers in the snow, the gulf claims
       And an old man driven by the trades
       To a sleepy corner. Twitching with rheumatism
On the verso of *B*, in pencil, is this draft by TSE of five penultimate lines. Pound emended 'driven by the horn' to 'running' and (his hand apparently) 'Horn'; also 'driven by the trades' to 'driven on the trades'.   *horn*] Horn A VP.   *man*] man, A VP.   *by the trades*] on the Trades A VP.

69–72]   In fractured atoms. Gull against the wind, in the windy straits
         Of Belle Isle, or running on the Horn,
         White feathers in the snow, the Gulf claims,
         And an old man driven by the Trades
         To a sleepy corner.

                     Tenants of the house,
         Thoughts of a dry brain in a dry season.   *1920*
(Horn. *1963*.) A VP has the indenting for the penultimate half-lines but not the extra line-space; for A VP's other variants, see the preceding note.

Bleistein with a Cigar

TRA la la la la la laire – nil nisi divinum stabile est Caetera fumus – the gondola stopped the old palace was there How charming it's grey and pink – Goats and monkeys! with such hair too – so the Countess passed on until she came through the little park, where Niobe presented her with a cabinet, and so departed.

Burbank crossed a little bridge
And Triton blew his wrinkled shell.
Princess Volupine arrived;
They were together, and he fell.

Defunctive music under sea   5
Passed slowly like the passing bell
Seaward: the god Hercules
Had left him, that had loved him well.

The horses, under the axletree
Beat up the dawn from Istria   10
With even feet. Her shuttered barge
Burned on the water all the day.

But this or such was Bleistein's way:
A saggy bending of the knees
And elbows, with the palms turned out, 15
Chicago Semite Viennese.

A lustreless protrusive eye
Stares from the protozoic slime
At a perspective of Canaletto.
The smoky candle end of time   20

Declines. On the Rialto once.
The rats are underneath the piles.
The jew is underneath the lot.
Money in furs. The boatman smiles,

Princess Volupine extends   25
A meagre, blue-nailed, phthisic hand
To climb the waterstair. Lights, lights;
She entertains Sir Ferdinand

Klein. Who clipped the lion's mane,
And flea'd his rump and pared his claws?   30
Thought Burbank, meditating on
Time's ruins, and the seven laws.

Loose leaves: published [10], original typescript (*A*, the variants below), with pencil comments by Pound, who wrote, at the top left, Dyptich, corrected to Diptych. Loose leaves: published [11], carbon typescript (*B*) of a later version. In *A*, lines 2–5 are indented by one typing space. *B* has the *1920* text, including the full title, *Burbank with a Baedeker: Bleistein with a Cigar*; it indents the even lines of the stanzas (though with inadvertent mis-indentation in the penultimate stanza); and it brings the epigraph almost to the punctuation as published (but with 'stopped the' and 'there how' for 'stopped, the' and 'there, how'). Published *Art and Letters* (Summer 1919), which text does not differ in wording from *1920*.

2] Descending at a small hotel; *A VP, 1920*. Pound marked the line: 'if you "hotel" this rhythm shd. be weighted a bit, I think'. (With 'think' underlined, though this may be concluding the comment.)

4. *fell.*] fell: *Pound.*

6. *slowly like*] seaward with *A VP, 1920*.

7. *Seaward*] Slowly *A VP, 1920*.

8 ∧ 9. *Pound drew a double line*: 'OK. from here anyhow'.

20. *candle end*] *hyphen added by Pound.*

21. *once.*] *Pound wrote to the right of the line*: 'punctuation?'

29. *Klein.*] *Pound marked the full stop and twice put a comma with a query.* *mane*] wings *Pound, A VP, 1920*.

29–30. *Who . . . claws?*] *Pound added quotation marks before and after, and repeated them in the margin*: 'for clarity?'

Sweeney Erect

Paint me a cavernous waste shore
Cast in the unstilled Cyclades,
Paint me the bold anfractuous rocks
Faced by the snarled and yelping seas.

Display me Aeolus above   5
Reviewing the insurgent gales
Which tangle Ariadne's hair
And swell with haste the perjured sails.

Morning stirs the feet and hands
(Nausicaa and Polypheme)   10
Gesture of Orang-outang
Rises from the sheets in steam.

This withered root of knots of hair
Slitted below and gashed with eyes
This oval O cropped out with teeth: 15
The sickle-motion from the thighs

Jackknifes upward at the knees
Then straightens down from heel to hip
Pushing the framework of the bed
And clawing at the pillow-slip.   20

Sweeney addressed full-length to shave,
Broadbottomed, pink from nape to base,
Knows the female temperament
And wipes the suds around his face.

(The lengthened shadow of a man   25
Is history, says Emerson
Who had not seen the silhouette
Of Sweeney straddled in the sun).

Tests the razor on his leg
Waiting until the shriek subsides;   30
The epileptic on the bed
Curves backward, clutching at her sides.

The ladies of the corridor
Find themselves involved, disgraced,
Call witness to their principles   35
Deprecate the lack of taste

Observing that hysteria
Might easily be misunderstood;
Mrs. Turner intimates
It does the house no sort of good.   40

But Doris towelled from the bath
Enters padding on broad feet,
Bringing sal volatile
And a glass of brandy neat.

Loose leaves: published [12–13], original typescript (*A*), and carbon typescript of another version (*B*). *A* not indented, *B* indented as *1920*. *B* has as epigraph:

> *Voici ton cierge,*
> *C'est deux livres qu'il a coûté . . .*

(Without attribution; Corbière, *La Rapsode foraine et le Pardon de Sainte-Anne* 113–4; accents added here.) Epigraph in *1920*:

> *And the trees about me,*
> *Let them be dry and leafless; let the rocks*
> *Groan with continual surges; and behind me*
> *Make all a desolation. Look, look, wenches!*

Published *Art and Letters* (Summer 1919), which text does not differ in wording from *1920* except where noted.

8. *with*] *typed over* the *A*.

11. *Orang-outang*] *A*; orang-outang *B*.

14. *eyes*] *A*; eyes, *B*.

15. *teeth:*] *A*; teeth; *B*.

16. *sickle-motion*] *A*; sickle motion *B*.

18. *down*] *A, B, AVP*; out *Art and Letters, 1920*.

20. *pillow-slip*] *A*; pillow slip *B*.

26. *says*] *A, B, Art and Letters, AVP*; said *1920*.   *Emerson*] *A*; Emerson, *B*.

34. *disgraced,*] *A*; disgraced; *B*.

36. *Deprecate*] *A, B, Art and Letters, AVP*; And deprecate *1920*.

39. *Mrs.*] *A*; Mrs *B*.

[A Cooking Egg]

Pipit sate upright in her chair
Some distance from where I was sitting;
Views of the Oxford Colleges
Lay on the table, with the knitting.

Daguerrotypes and silhouettes   5
Her grandfather and great great aunts,
Supported on the mantelpiece
An *Invitation to the Dance*.

When Pipit's slipper once fell off
It interfered with my repose;   10
My self-esteem was somewhat strained
Because her stockings had white toes.

I wanted Peace here on earth,
While I was still strong and young;
And Peace was to have been extended   15
From the tip of Pipit's tongue.

I shall not want Honour in heaven
For I shall meet Sir Philip Sidney,   [10]
And have talk with Coriolanus
And other heroes of my kidney.   20

I shall not want Capital in heaven
For I shall meet Sir Alfred Mond;
We two shall lie together, lapt   [15]
In a Five Per Cent Exchequer Bond.

I shall not want Conversation in heaven 25
Lucrezia Borgia shall be my bride:
Her anecdotes will be more amusing
Than those which Pipit could provide. [20]

I shall not want Pipit in heaven:
Madame Blavatsky will instruct me   30
In the Seven Sacred Trances:
Piccarda de'Donati will conduct me

To the communion of the Lord,
With bread and wine the tables drest;
I hope the potables will be   35
Such as my stomach can digest.

But where is the penny world I bought [25]
To eat with Pipit behind the screen?
The red-eyed scavengers are feeding
In Kentish Town and Golder's Green.   40

Where are the eagles and the trumpets?
Buried beneath some snow-deep Alps; [30]
Over buttered scones and crumpets
Weeping, weeping multitudes
Droop in a hundred A.B.C.'s.   45

Loose leaves: published [14], original typescript (A), untitled, with pencil comments by Pound. Variants below are from A except where noted. Loose leaves: published [15], carbon (B) of A (the last line has fallen off the foot, and is added to the side by TSE in pencil). No indenting in A, except for the inadvertent indenting, a single typing space, in lines 1, 2, 6, 45. Published *Coterie* (May-Day 1919), which text does not differ in wording from *1920* except where noted. Epigraph:

> *En l'an trentiesme de mon aage*
> *Que toutes mes hontes j'ay beues . . .*
>   *AVP, 1920; not Coterie*

3. *of the*] [underlined] *1st reading,* [itals.] *AVP, 1920; Of The* [underlined] *revision; of* [itals.] *1963.*

9–16] *deleted in blue crayon in B; not AVP, 1920.* (*AVP* prints here a row of asterisks, *1920* of dots.) Pound ringed the first of these two stanzas, and deleted them both, bracketing 15–16. He put X at beginning and end of 11: 'used before'. He ringed 'stockings had white toes' (12), and moved it up with an arrow as if to follow 'in her chair' (1).

11. *strained*] shaken *B pencil revision.*

13. *Peace*] *1st reading*; Pipit *revision (revision also in B).*

18. Pound wrote, beginning alongside 18 and running down beside the next stanza: 'le preux Bayard mirrour of Chivalry & Coriolanus. Cola da Rienzi'.

20. *my*] ? that *Pound (who bracketed the line)*; his *Coterie*; that *A VP, 1920.*

25. *Conversation*] Company *B blue crayon revision*; Society *A VP, 1920.*

26. *Lucrezia*] *typed over* For I

28. *those which Pipit*] Pipit's memory *Coterie*; Pipit's experience *A VP, 1920.*

30. *will*] *A VP, 1920*; shall *Coterie.*

33–6] *not A VP, 1920.*

36–8. Pound underlined 36 and 38, marking the lines with diagonal strokes at the corners.

39. *feeding*] creeping *A VP, 1920.*

40. *In*] From *A VP, 1920.*

45. *A.B.C.'s*] * [footnote] i.e. an endemic teashop, found in all parts of London. The Initials signify: Aerated Bread Company, Limited. *1920.*

44–5. Pound wrote: 'other manner intruded on the purely religious', and glossed 'other manner': 'the "modern" or joltographic'.

Mélange adultère de tout

Loose leaves: published [16], carbon typescript. No variants from *1920* other than the omission, in typing, of the French accents, and one mis-spacing ('moncénotaphe'). Published *Little Review* (July *1917*), which text does not differ in wording from *1919* and *1920*.

Lune de Miel

Ils ont vu les Pays-Bas, ils rentrent à Terre Haute;
Mais une nuit d'été, les voici à Ravenne,
Deux époux entre deux draps, chez deux centaines de poux.
La sueur aestivale, et une forte odeur de chienne.
Ils restent sur le dos écartant les genoux   5
De quatre jambes molles tout gonflées de morsures.
On relève le drap pour mieux égratigner.
Pas même une lieue d'ici est St Apollinaire
In Classe, basilique connue des amateurs
De chapitaux d'acanthe que tourbillonne le vent.   10

Ils vont prendre le train de huit heures
Prolonger leurs misères à Padoue et Milan
Où l'on trouve le Cène, et un restaurant pas cher.
Lui pense à ses pourboires, et rédige son bilan.
Ils ont vu la Suisse et traversé la France.   15
Et St Apollinaire, raide et ascétique,
Vieille usine désaffectée de Dieu, tient encore
Dans ses pierres écroulantes la forme précise de Byzance.

Loose leaves: published [17], carbon typescript. The French accents are here supplied from *1920*. Published *Little Review* (July *1917*), which text does not differ in wording from *1920*.

1. *ont*] one *mistyped 1st reading.*

3. *Deux époux*] A l'aise *1919, AVP, 1920. poux*] punaises *1919, AVP, 1920.*

8. *Pas même*] Moins d' *1919, AVP, 1920.*

9. *In*] *1919, AVP, 1920*; En *1963.*

10. *tourbillonne*] tournoie *1919, AVP, 1920.*

12. *misères*] mirères *mistyped. à . . . et*] de . . . à *1919, AVP, 1920.*

13. *l'on trouve le*] se trouvent le *1919, AVP, 1920*; se trouve la *1963. cher*] chère *1st reading.*

14. *à ses*] aux *1919, AVP, 1920.*

Dans le restaurant

Le garçon délabré qui n'a rien à faire
Que de se gratter les doigts et se pencher sur mon épaule:
  "Dans mon pays, il sera temps pluvieux,
  Du vent, du grand soleil, et de la pluie;
  C'est ce qu'on appelle le jour de lessive des gueux".   5
(Bavard, baveux, à la croupe arrondie,
Je te prie, au moins, ne pas baver dans la soupe).
  "Les saules toutes trempés, et des bourgeons sur les ronces –
  C'est là, dans une averse, qu'on s'abrite.
  J'avais sept ans, elle était plus petite.   10
  Elle était toute mouillée, je lui ai donné des primavères."
Les taches de son gilet montent au chiffre de trente-huit.
  "Je la chatouillais, pour la faire rire.
  Elle avait une odeur fraîche qui m'était inconnue,
  Et j'éprouvais un instant de puissance et de délire".   15

        Mais alors, vieux lubrique, à cet âge . . .

"Monsieur, le fait est dur.
Il est venu, nous peloter, amicalement un gros chien;
Moi j'avais peur, je l'ai quittée à mi-chemin;
C'est dommage."   20

        Mais alors, tu as ton vautur!   [20]
Va-t'en te décrotter les rides de ton visage;
Tiens, ma fourchette, décrasse-toi le crâne,
Quel droit as-tu a des expériences comme moi?
Tiens, voilà dix sous, pour la salle-de-bains.   25

Phlébas, le Phénicien, était quinze jours noyé,   [25]
Oubliant les cris des mouettes et l'écume de Cornouaille,
Et les profits et les pertes, et la cargaison d'étain:
Un courant de sous-mer l'emporta très loin,

Le repassant aux étapes de sa vie antérieure.   30
Figurez-vous donc, c'était un sort pénible,   [30]
Cependent, ce fut jadis un bel homme, de haute taille.

Loose leaves: published [18], carbon typescript, with pencil comments and changes by Pound. The indenting of lines 1–2, 6–7, 12, and 23 following, which wavered, has been regularized. Some French accents were added; others are here supplied from *1920*. Published *Little Review* (Sept. 1918), which text does not differ in wording from *1920* except where noted.

3. *sera*] fera *AVP, 1920*. Pound's change.

7. *te*] *1920*; t'en *LR, AVP*.   *ne pas baver*] ne bave pas *AVP, 1920*. Pound's change; he wrote: 'de ne pas / ne baves pas / Je t'en pris, au moins / ne bave pas'.

8. *toutes*] tout *LR, AVP; not 1920*.   *toutes trempés*] *changed in ink (apparently) to* touts trempées.

11. *primavères*] *1920*; primevères *LR, AVP, 1963*.

12. *taches*] *1963; a circumflex accent was added in error to the typescript and survives in LR, AVP, 1920.*

14] *LR, AVP; not 1920*.

15] *1920; not LR, AVP.   Et j'*] J' *1920*.

16. *lubrique, à cet âge . . .*] *1920*; lubrique – *LR, AVP*.

18. *amicalement*] *not AVP, 1920*. Pound bracketed the line.

21. *vautur*] *1920*; vautour *LR, AVP, 1963*.

22. *te*] *bracketed by Pound.   de ton*] du *AVP, 1920*. Pound's change.

24. *Quel*] De quel *AVP, 1920*. Pound's change.   *as-tu a*] paies-tu *AVP*; payes-tu *1920*. Pound wrote: 'te paye'.

26. *était*] pendant *AVP, 1920*. Pound's change (at first to 'fut').

27. *Oubliant*] Oubliait *AVP, 1920*. Pound's change, though apparently as 'Oubliat'. *les cris des mouettes*] *1920; changed in ink to* le *but without the consequential* cri; *changed in ink from* de *and* muettes; le cri des mouettes *AVP.   l'écume*] la houle *AVP, 1920*. Pound's change.

[Whispers of Immortality] [A–B]

Webster was much possessed by death;
He saw the skull beneath the skin;
And breastless creatures under ground
Leaned backward with a lipless grin.

Daffodil bulbs instead of balls   5
Stared from the sockets of the eyes!
He knew that thought clings round dead limbs
Tightening its lusts and luxuries.

I think John Donne was such another
With passions chiselled out of stone;   10
He found no substitute for death
But toothed the sweetness of the bone.

Grishkin is nice; her Russian eye   [17]
Is underlined for emphasis;
Uncorseted, her friendly bust   15
Gives promise of pneumatic bliss.   [20]

And some abstracter entities   [29]
Have not disused a certain charm.   [30]
But I must crawl between dry ribs
To keep my metaphysics warm.   20

As long as Pipit is alive
One can be mischievous and brave;
But where there is no more misbehaviour
I would like my bones flung into her grave.

Loose leaves: published [19], original typescript (*A*), with pencil comments by Pound.
[20], carbon (*B*) of this. [21–27], four further original typescripts and two additional
carbons (*C–H*), many of these with comments by Pound. Published *Little Review*
(Sept. 1918). A collation of the eight versions would be so cumbrous as to be

unserviceable, so each of the versions is given (or described) here, concluding with the *1963* text with variants of wording from *LR*, *Ara Vos Prec* and *1920*.

At the foot of *A* is typed:

Do you think this is worth doing anything to? It is very scrappy. I feel that it ought to be remodelled, if at all, entirely in the third person. Also the first two lines of the fifth verse [*A* 17–18] wont do, they are conscious, and exhibit a feeble reversion to the Laforgue manner. Minor: breastless and lipless.

(Pound's comments, written below this, pertain apparently to *C*.) For the extended reply by him, see p.371 below.

For *A*, Pound suggested titles: *Night Thoughts on immorality*, and *Night thoughts on Gautier*. On the verso, Pound listed, one below the other: 'Webster / ‖ / Don[n]e / Gautier / ‖' followed (braced and marked f / g / h, as though the previous sequence were a–e) by: 'general statement / & conclusion / no pipit' (underlining this last, probably to conclude the comment). He also jotted: 'Predelections maccabres / or the maccabre predilections'. There are further jottings by Pound, illegibly deleted.

Textual variants are from *A*. *B* is a carbon of *A* with only the two changes recorded under 4 and 11.

1. *much*] pre *written above by Pound.*

2. *He*] and *Pound.*

3. *And*] The *Pound.*

4. *backward*] *Pound wrote in the margin, and then deleted* image / backward / up ‖ [*for* upward] / Looked Toward *followed by an illegible deletion.* *lipless*] canine? *TSE in the margin;* dachshund *Pound.* (In *B*, TSE ringed 'lipless' and wrote 'canine'.)

6. *the eyes*] *Pound underlined* the.

7. *limbs*] *bracketed by Pound with* to the right of the line ?

9. *I think*] *ringed by Pound.*

10, 12] *deleted by Pound.* Pound wrote in the margin of the stanza, one below the other: 'a / b / transition'. Perhaps 'a / b' with reference to the rhyming, which was changed when 11 was moved to become 10; as to 'transition', see the next line, *He*] who.

11. *He*] *ringed by Pound, with* who. *death*] sense *revision by TSE in pencil, as also in B.*

12. *toothed*] *underlined by Pound.*

15. *Uncorseted,*] *the comma altered apparently by Pound to a semicolon and then back to a comma.*

16 ∧ 17] *In the margin a sidelong caret in ink* <.

17–20. And] *ringed by Pound.* disused] *ringed by Pound, with* ??? otherwise O.K. *Pound bracketed* 18 *and* 20 *and the whole stanza.*

21–4] *Pound ringed the first line, and the stanza, and deleted the stanza. He ringed* where *and subjoined and then deleted* ?? *Below the last line he wrote* why.

Whispers of Immortality [C]

Webster was much possessed by death;
He saw the skull beneath the skin;
And breastless creatures under ground
Leaned backward with a lipless grin.

Daffodil bulbs instead of balls   5
Stared from the sockets of the eyes!
He knew that thought clings round dead limbs
Tightening its lusts and luxuries.

I think John Donne was such another
Who cracked the marrow now and then.   10
Our sighs pursue th' elusive shade
But these w[e]re really serious men.

Grishkin is nice; her Russian eye   [17]
Is underlined for emphasis;
Uncorseted, her friendly bust   15
Gives promise of pneumatic bliss.   [20]

And some abstracter entities   [29]
Preserve a sacerdotal charm,   [30]
But I must crawl between dry ribs
To keep my metaphysics warm.   20

Our sighs pursue the vanishd shade
And breathe a sanctified amen,
And yet the Sons of God descend
To entertain the wives of men.

And when the Female Soul departs   25
The Sons of Men turn up their eyes.
The Sons of God embrace the Grave –
The Sons of God are very wise.

C: original typescript. With 11, 21–2, compare *Elegy* 1–2 (*The Waste Land* MS, p.117):
Our prayers dismiss the parting shade
And breathe a hypocrite's amen!

2. *He*] who *Pound.*

3. *And*] ? The *Pound.*

5. *balls*] eyes *typed at first, presumably in error, and then typed through.*

9. *I*] Who *typed at first, and then typed through.*

9–10] *TSE wrote in the margin in pencil* clutched? (*See D–E 11:* To seize and clutch and penetrate.) *Pound ringed 10 and wrote* who found no substitute for sense *which is A 11 as revised by TSE and Pound.*

11–12] *deleted by Pound.*

17–18] *deleted by Pound, who wrote:* 'The sons of god might [*revised to* may] feel this charm'.

20 ∧ 21] *alongside, following this line, TSE wrote:* 'I think it had better stop here'.

21. *vanishd*] *the* d *typed over* e.

23. *descend*] *Pound wrote* ? tense. *Pound further wrote* when did you last / or / what angel hath cuckwoled thee. (*Alluding to* When did you last see your father? [. . . Father?]) *Pound also interpolated within this comment* fear the converse. *Below TSE's typed inquiry (see the note to A above), are jottings by Pound, pertaining apparently to this stanza in C:* or did Jahveh / ? The Sacred Ghost / did not disdain / copulationion in carnal form / – et les anges, / le diodem / de son.

Try This on Your Piano
Whispers of Immortality [D–E]

Webster was much possessed by death,
Seeing the skull beneath the skin;
And breastless creatures under ground
Leaned backward with a lipless grin.

Daffodil bulbs instead of balls   5
Stared from the sockets of the eyes!
He knew that thought clings round dead limbs
Tightening its lusts and luxuries.

Donne, I suppose, was such another
Pursuing sense within the sense   10
To seize and clutch and penetrate.
Expert beyond experience

He knew the anguish of the marrow,
The ague of the skeleton;
No contact possible to flesh   15
Allayed the fever of the bone.

Grishkin is nice; her Russian eye
Is underlined for emphasis;
Uncorseted, her friendly bust
Gives promise of pneumatic bliss.   20

The sleek Brazilian jaguar   [25]
Does not, in his arboreal gloom,
Distil the strong rank feline smell
Of Grishkin in a drawing room.

But Donne and Webster passed beyond   25
The text-book rudiments of lust,
And crawled at last between dry ribs,
Having their Ethics of the Dust.

D: original typescript (both titles in capitals). 'I', preceding line 1, and 'II', preceding 17, were added in pencil. *E* is a carbon of *D*, without the added 'I', 'II'; variants below are from *D* except where *E* is noted. On *E*, Pound wrote the letter 'A.' beside 11–12 and 'B.' beside the last stanza, and explained these in a typed page (5. Holland Place Chambers, Kensington, W.):

"SODOMY!" said the Duchess, approaching the Ormolu clock.

If at A. you shift to "my" i.e. *your* "experience" you would conceivably reach Grishkin's Dunlap tyre boozum by the line of greatest directness.

If at B. you should then leap from the bloody, boozy and Barzeelyan Jag-U-ARRRR to the Abstracter entities who would not have resisted either the boozom or the "smell of baked meats", you could thence entauthenexelaunai to the earlier terminer

But I must crawl, etc. metaphysics warm.

having in the lines precedent used your extant rhyme in "charm", applying same to either boozum, odour, or enticement of the toutensemble

om [*hand-written*]

Omitting fourth stanza of present Nth. variant.
wash the whole with virol and leave in hypo.

At any rate, I think this would bring us nearer the desired epithalamium of force, clearness and bewtie.

EP

10] Who found no substitute for sense *Pound, adopting A 11 as revised by TSE and Pound. On E, TSE asked, of* Pursuing sense within the sense: 'Or do you prefer the original line? This one is however more coherent – in fact it is the whole idea'.

12. *experience*] my experience *Pound on E*. (See Pound's comment above: 'If at A.' etc.)

13–16] deleted in E *(not clear by whom). TSE wrote*: 'Too many possessives?'

20. *bliss.*] bliss; *Pound*.

23–4. *the . . . Of*] so . . . as *Pound*.

25–8] *Pound bracketed this last stanza and wrote* If abs ents [abstracter entities] / would fall / for this charm / Our Webster Donne [*the names ringed*] / Tribe / run [?] crawl / betw[een] ribs. *Also below this final stanza* if *and then two scrawled words. At the foot of E (see the final stanza of F), Pound wrote* Tho entities / I must to keep / metam warm.

26. *lust*] *on E, TSE asked*: 'Should I avoid using the word twice?'

[F]

Webster was much possessed by death
And saw the skull beneath the skin;
And breastless creatures under ground
Leaned backward with a lipless grin.

Daffodil bulbs instead of balls   5
Stared from the sockets of the eyes!
He knew that thought clings round dead limbs
Tightening its lusts and luxuries.

Donne, I suppose, was such another
Pursuing sense within the sense   10
To seize and clutch and penetrate:
This passes my experience.

Grishkin is nice; her Russian eye   [17]
Is underlined for emphasis;
Uncorseted, her friendly bust   15
Gives promise of pneumatic bliss.   [20]

The sleek Brazilian jaguar   [25]
Does not, in his arboreal gloom
Distil the strong rank feline smell
Of Grishkin in a drawing room.   20

There are abstracter entities
Which still maintain a certain charm.   [30]
But I must crawl between dry ribs
To keep my metaphysics warm.

F: original typescript.

Whispers of Immortality [G–H]

Webster was much possessed by death
And saw the skull beneath the skin;
And breastless creatures under ground
Leaned backward with a lipless grin.

Daffodil bulbs instead of balls   5
Stared from the sockets of the eyes!
He knew that thought clings round dead limbs
Tightening its lusts and luxuries.

Donne, I suppose, was such another
Who found no substitute for sense   10
To seize and clutch and penetrate,
Expert beyond experience

He knew the anguish of the marrow
The ague of the skeleton;
No contact possible to flesh   15
Allayed the fever of the bone.

                * * * * *

Grishkin is nice: her Russian eye
Is underlined for emphasis;
Uncorseted, her friendly bust
Gives promise of pneumatic bliss.   20

The sleek Brazilian jaguar   [25]
Does not in his arboreal gloom
Distil so rank a feline smell
As Grishkin in a drawing-room.

And even the Abstract Entities   25
Circumambulate her charm: [30]
But our lot crawl between dry ribs
To keep our metaphysics warm.

G: original typescript (variants below). *H* is a carbon of this.

2. *And*] he *Pound, with* who *deleted.*

3. *And*] or while *Pound (deleted).*

6. *the*] ? their *Pound.*

20 ∧ 21]   The couched Brazilian jaguar
            Can charm the scampering marmoset
            Distilling effluence of cat;
            And Grishkin has a maisonette.

Typed by TSE to the right of 21–4, with revisions Can charm] *typed through;*
Compels *typed below.*   marmoset] *a comma added in pencil.*   Distilling] *deleted;*
With subtle *TSE, as also in H.*   And] *typed at first, and then typed through. Above
the stanza TSE wrote* alternative *(deleted in H).*

21] but still the sleek couched *written in the margin (the first two words doubtful) by
Pound, who deleted* Brazilian. *At the foot of the page, TSE wrote* sleek & spotted /
sinuous / sleek couched sinuous / couched defensive.

22. *his] typed at first, and then typed through;* its *typed.*

25–6. And . . . the] *both bracketed by Pound, who wrote* If / *might* and, *below,*
abstracter. ('If even abstracter entities / Might circumambulate her charm'?)

27. *crawl*] crawls *Pound.*

28. *our*] its *Pound.*

Whispers of Immortality [1963]

Webster was much possessed by death
And saw the skull beneath the skin;
And breastless creatures under ground
Leaned backward with a lipless grin.

Daffodil bulbs instead of balls   5
Stared from the sockets of the eyes!
He knew that thought clings round dead limbs
Tightening its lusts and luxuries.

Donne, I suppose, was such another
Who found no substitute for sense,   10
To seize and clutch and penetrate;
Expert beyond experience,

He knew the anguish of the marrow
The ague of the skeleton;
No contact possible to flesh   15
Allayed the fever of the bone.

. . . . .

Grishkin is nice: her Russian eye
Is underlined for emphasis;
Uncorseted, her friendly bust
Gives promise of pneumatic bliss.   20

The couched Brazilian jaguar
Compels the scampering marmoset
With subtle effluence of cat;
Grishkin has a maisonnette;

The sleek Brazilian jaguar   25
Does not in its arboreal gloom
Distil so rank a feline smell
As Grishkin in a drawing-room.

And even the Abstract Entities
Circumambulate her charm;   30
But our lot crawls between dry ribs
To keep our metaphysics warm.

The text of *1963* with variants of wording from *LR, 1919, Ara Vos Prec* and *1920*.

25. *Brazilian*] and sinuous *LR, 1919, AVP.*

26. *its*] his *LR, 1919, AVP.*   *arboreal*] aboreal *1963 (error).*

29. *the Abstract Entities*] abstracter entities *LR, 1919, AVP.*

32. *our*] its *LR, AVP.*

Mr Eliot's Sunday Morning Service

Polyphiloprogenitive
The sapient sutlers of the Lord
Drift across the window-panes.
In the beginning was the Word.

In the beginning was the Word, 5
Superfetation of τὸ ἒν,
And at the menstrual turn of time
Produced the castrate Origen.

A painter of the Umbrian school
Designed upon a gesso ground 10
The nimbus of the Baptised God.
The wilderness is cracked and browned

But through the water pale and thin
Still shine the unoffending feet
And there above the painter set 15
The Father and the Paraclete.

* * *

The sable presbyters approach
The avenue of penitence,
The young are red and pustular
Clutching piaculative pence. 20

And through the gates of penitence
Sustained by staring Seraphim
To where the souls of the devout
Burn invisible and dim.*

Salmon stretched red along the wall 25
Sweet peas invite to intervene
The hairy bellies of the bees
Blest office of the epicene.

---

*Vide Henry Vaughan the Silurist, from whom the author seems to have borrowed this line.

Sweeney shifts from ham to ham
Stirring the water in his bath.   30
The masters of the subtle schools
Are controversial, polymath.

Loose leaves: published [28]; original typescript, with comments by Pound. Added by TSE in pencil above the title is a version of the epigraph, unattributed: 'Look look master here comes two of the religious caterpillars'. (So, with attribution and re-punctuated, in LR and Ara Vos Prec. 1920: 'Look, look, master, here comes two religious caterpillars. JEW OF MALTA'. [The Jew of Malta. 1963].) Published Little Review (Sept. 1918), which text does not differ in wording from 1920.

1–4] bracketed by Pound.

7. menstrual] ringed by Pound, who struck out tr to read mensual which is also written in the margin (and was adopted).

7] And after many [illegible word] months TSE, deleted.

8. castrate] deleted by Pound; enervate Pound, ringed, with before it O.K. (It was adopted; the consequential deletion of the not made in the typescript.)

9–16] marked with a brace by Pound.

21. And through] Under Pound (adopted).   gates of penitence] deleted by Pound, who drew a line connecting the ends of 18 and 21, and wrote ports of p.; penitential gates revision. Pound wrote in the margin Qy. Penetrate?

21–8] marked with a brace by Pound who wrote: 'lacking syntactic symplycyty'; he put ? beside 26 which he underlined, and deleted 25–8.

23. To] deleted by Pound (the deletion adopted).

24. *] the note is typed.

25–7]   Along the garden-wall the bees
         With hairy bellies pass between
         The staminate and pistilate, 1920
TSE had revised the lines so, at the foot of the page, though with garden-wall] garden wall; pass] revision; go 1st reading; pistilate (no comma; pistilate: 1919, AVP; pistillate, 1963).

29–30] marked with a brace by Pound.

32. *polymath*] *underlined by Pound and divided* poly|math; *below* math *he wrote (apparently)*

μαθαιος [for μάταιος?]

or

μανθανο

Sweeney Among the Nightingales

Apeneck Sweeney spreads his knees
Letting his arms hang down to laugh,
The zebra stripes along his jaw
Swelling to maculate giraffe,

The circles of the stormy moon   5
Slide westward toward the River Plate,
Death and the Raven drift above
And Sweeney guards the horned gate;

Gloomy Orion and the Dog
Are veiled; and hushed the shrunken seas;   10
The person in the Spanish cape
Tries to sit on Sweeney's knees

Slips and pulls the table cloth
Overturns a coffee-cup,
Reorganised upon the floor   15
She yawns and pulls a stocking up;

The silent man in mocha brown
Sits at the window sill and gapes;
The waiter brings in oranges
Bananas figs and hot-house grapes,   20

The individual in brown
Contracts and concentrates, withdraws,
Rachel *nee* Rabinovitch
Tears at the grapes with murderous paws;

She and the lady in the cape   25
Are suspect; thought to be in league;
Therefore the man with heavy eyes
Declines the gambit, shows fatigue,

Leaves the room and reappears
Outside the window, leaning in,   30
Branches of wisteria
Circumscribe a golden grin;

The host with someone indistinct
Converses at the door apart,
The nightingales are singing near   35
The Convent of the Sacred Heart,

And sang within the bloody wood
When Agamemnon cried aloud,
And let their liquid droppings fall
To stain the stiff dishonoured shroud.   40

Loose leaves: published [29–30]; carbon typescripts (A, B), with suggestions by Pound. The Greek epigraph (misquoted) is added to both in pencil (no space left for such, so it is not just that there was no Greek on his typewriter); *1920* epigraph: ὤμοι, πέπληγμαι καιρίαν πληγὴν ἔσω. *1919* has a further epigraph: *Why should I speak of the nightingale? The nightingale sings of adulterate wrong.* From *Edward III*, as TSE noted in pencil in a copy of *AVP* (Houghton Library). *The Raigne of K. Edward the Third* (*The Shakespeare Apocrypha*, 1908), Act II sc. ii; two lines of verse. (*AVP* has this further epigraph, with 'adulterous'.) Published *Little Review* (Sept. 1918), which text does not differ in wording from *1920* except where noted.

4. *giraffe,*] A; giraffe. B.

6. *westward toward*] ward ward *underlined and marked by Pound in A. toward*] *1920*; to LR, *1919, AVP.*

8. *horned*] hornèd *Pound in A (adopted). gate;*] A; gate. B.

12. *sit*] rest *Pound in A, deleted.* (In A, 'sit' is ringed and linked to 'Sits' in 18.)

16. *pulls*] draws *revision in A in pencil, with* pulls *written above deleted* pulls *in 13;* draws B.

18. *Sits*] *ringed in A and linked to 'sit' in 12;* Lops *Pound in A (see OED 'lop', verb 2 and 2b);* Stands *revision in pencil;* Sprawls *1919, AVP, 1920.*

20. *Bananas*] Bananas, *Pound in B.*

21. *individual*] [economic unit *comment by Pound in A*]; silent vertebrate *B, 1919, AVP, 1920.* TSE wrote in the margin of *B*: 'The animalcule in brown'. *in brown*] *1920*; contracts *B 1st revision*; exhales *B 2nd revision, LR, 1919, AVP.*

22. *Contracts*] Hovers *TSE's alternative in the margin of B, preceded by ?* tacit *Pound, deleted.*

23. *nee*] née *Pound in A, deleted (with another word scrawled over it?)*

26. *suspect;*] *A*; suspect, *B.*

27. *Therefore*] *A*; Wherefore *B, apparently, at first with T then typed over the W.*

29. *reappears*] *a comma apparently added and deleted in B.*

35. *singing*] *mistyped* singimg *in A.* (Typing errors are not generally noted here, but this one is given as an instance that might, for instance, help to identify the original typescript from which this carbon *A* derives.)

39. *droppings*] *marked '   ' by Pound in A*; siftings *Pound in B*; siftings *LR, 1919, AVP, 1963*; droppings *1920.*

Ode
on Independence Day, July 4th 1918

Tired.

Subterrene laughter synchronous
With silence from the sacred wood
And bubbling of the uninspired
Mephitic river.
          Misunderstood   5
The accents of the now retired
Profession of the calamus.

Tortured.

When the bridegroom smoothed his hair
There was blood upon the bed.   10
Morning was already late.
Children singing in the orchard
(Io Hymen, Hymenæe)
Succuba eviscerate.

Tortuous.   15

By arrangement with Perseus
The fooled resentment of the dragon
Sailing before the wind at dawn.
Golden apocalypse. Indignant
At the cheap extinction of his taking-off.   20
Now lies he there
Tip to tip washed beneath Charles' Wagon.

Loose leaves: miscellaneous [1–3]; original typescript (A, with some inadvertent single indenting), carbon of this, and carbon of a later version (no indenting, as above). Published *Ara Vos Prec*, as *Ode*, with the epigraph:
    To you particularly, and to all the Volscians
    Great hurt and mischief.

(*Coriolanus*, IV v.) In *Ara Vos Prec*, *Ode* followed *Mélange Adultère de Tout* and preceded *The Love Song of J. Alfred Prufrock*. Not in *Poems* (1920), it is the only poem published by TSE in a volume of his poems and not collected. *Ara Vos Prec* does not leave the spaces between lines 1–2, 8–9, and 15–16; Berg [leaf] 3 likewise has the title *Ode*, the epigraph and the published spacing.

14] *typed revision in* A; Sullen succuba suspired *typed deletion in* A.

APPENDIX D

Influence and influences

The 'influence' of James hardly matters: to be influenced by a writer is to have a chance inspiration from him; or to take what one wants; or to see things one has overlooked.

The Egoist (Jan. 1918)

People are only influenced in the direction in which they want to go, and influence consists largely in making them conscious of their wishes to proceed in that direction.

The Criterion, xvi (1937) 667

(i) TSE on the situation of poetry circa 1910

Letter to Virginia Woolf (22 May 1924, Berg Collection), about her talk *Character in Fiction* (later *Mr Bennett and Mrs Brown*):

It also expresses for me what I have always been very sensible of, the absence of any masters in the previous generation whose work one could carry on, and the amount of waste that goes on in one's own work in the necessity, so to speak, of building one's own house before one can start the business of living. I feel myself that everything I have done consists simply of tentative sketches and rough experiments. Will the next generation profit by our labours?

Introduction to Ezra Pound, *Selected Poems* (1928):

(p.viii) The *vers libre* of Jules Laforgue, who, if not quite the greatest French poet after Baudelaire, was certainly the most important technical innovator, is free verse in much the way that the later verse of Shakespeare, Webster, Tourneur, is free verse.

(pp.viii–ix) My own verse is, so far as I can judge, nearer to the original meaning of *vers libre* than is any of the other types; at least, the form in which I began to write, in 1908 or 1909, was directly drawn from the study of Laforgue together with the later Elizabethan drama; and I do not know anyone who started from exactly that point. I did not read Whitman until much later in life, and had to conquer an aversion to his form, as well as to much of his matter, in order to do so.

Views and Reviews, New English Weekly (12 Sept. 1935):

At different periods, of course, there may be greater or less sympathy between the older writers and the younger. What the help and encouragement of men of an older generation may be like, what it feels like, what useful stimulus or perhaps misdirection it may give, I do not know. At a time which may be symbolised by the figures 1910, there was literally no one to whom one would have dreamt of applying. One learnt something, no doubt, from Henry James, and might have learnt more. But Henry James was a novelist, and one who gave the most formidable appearance of exclusive concentration on his own kind of work.

Poetry (Sept. 1946); reprinted with a postscript, 1950, in *Ezra Pound* (ed. Peter Russell, 1950):

(p.25) Whatever may have been the literary scene in America between the beginning of the century and the year 1914, it remains in my mind a complete blank. I cannot remember the name of a single poet of that period whose work I read: it was only in 1915, after I came to England, that I heard the name of Robert Frost. Undergraduates at Harvard in my time read the English poets of the '90s who were dead: that was as near as we could get to any living tradition. Certainly I cannot remember any English poet then alive who contributed to my own education. Yeats was well-known, of course; but to me, at least, Yeats did not appear, until after 1917, to be anything but a minor survivor of the '90s.

There were, in the early years of the century, a few good poets writing in England, but I did not know of their existence until later; and it was often Pound (whose appreciation was much more comprehensive than most people realise) who directed my attention to them. But I do not think it is too sweeping to say, that there was no poet, in either country, who could have been of use to a beginner in 1908. The only recourse was to poetry of another age and to poetry of another language. Browning was more of a hindrance than a help, for he had gone some way, but not far enough, in discovering a contemporary idiom. And at that stage, Poe and Whitman had to be seen through French eyes. The question was still: where do we go from Swinburne? and the answer appeared to be, nowhere.

The Last Twenty-Five Years of English Poetry (1940), draft lecture, for a cancelled British Council Tour in Italy (Hayward Bequest)

(p.9) The kind of verse which began to be written about 1910 or so made the same break with tradition that we find in that of Wordsworth and Coleridge. But it had its origins in the sources to which the younger men of that time went for inspiration. Some of these sources are to be found in the earlier symbolist poets of France, or to be precise, in Baudelaire and his immediate followers, Laforgue, Corbière, Rimbaud and Mallarmé. Some are to be found in English poetry, both dramatic and lyric, of the sixteenth and seventeenth centuries.

(p.10) The young American poets, who came to London about that time, had left a country in which the status of poetry had fallen still lower than in

England: there was not one older poet writing in America whose writing a younger man could take seriously.

(p.11) [On T. E. Hulme, 'who left only five poems'. TSE quotes 'Once, in finesse'.] This is not a perfect poem, and the last line is definitely weak in construction. But, in the world of 1910 or so, this and a dozen poems one might choose from the work at that time of Pound, Richard Aldington, H.D., F. S. Flint, were evidence of a radical change in the whole practice of verse.

(ii) TSE on debts, including that to Dante

Preface to *Dante* (1929) [the Preface was omitted when *Dante* was included in *SE*, 1932]:

(p.11) If my task had been to produce another brief 'introduction to the study of Dante' I should have been incompetent to perform it. But in a series of essays of 'Poets on Poets' the undertaking, as I understand it, is quite a different one. A contemporary writer of verse, in writing a pamphlet of this description, is required only to give a faithful account of his acquaintance with the poet of whom he writes. This, and no more, I can do; and this is the only way in which I can treat an author of whom so much has been written, that can make any pretence to novelty. I have found no other poet than Dante to whom I could apply continually, for many purposes, and with much profit, during a familiarity of twenty years. I am not a Dante scholar; my Italian is chiefly self-taught, and learnt primarily in order to read Dante; I need still to make constant reference to translations.

(p.12) My purpose has been to persuade the reader first of the importance of Dante as a master – I may even say, *the* master – for a poet writing to-day in any language. And there ensues from that, the importance of Dante to anyone who would appreciate modern poetry, in any language. I should not trust the opinion of anyone who pretended to judge modern verse without knowing Homer, Dante, and Shakespeare. It does not in the least follow that a *poet* is negligible because he does not know these three.

What Dante Means to Me (1950, *TCTC*):

(pp.126–7) The greatest debts are not always the most evident; at least, there are different kinds of debt. The kind of debt that I owe to Dante is the kind which goes on accumulating, the kind which is not the debt of one period or another of one's life. Of some poets I can say I learned a great deal from them at a particular stage. Of Jules Laforgue, for instance, I can say that he was the first to teach me how to speak, to teach me the poetic possibilities of my own idiom of speech. Such early influences, the influences which, so to speak, first introduce one to oneself, are, I think, due to an impression which is in one aspect, the recognition of a temperament akin to one's own, and in another aspect the discovery of a form of expression which gives a clue to the discovery of one's own form. These are not two things, but two aspects of the same thing. But the poet who can do this for a young writer, is unlikely to be one of the great masters. The latter are too exalted and too remote. They are like distant ancestors who have been almost deified; whereas the smaller poet, who has directed one's first steps, is more like an admired elder brother.

Then, among influences, there are the poets from whom one has learned some one thing, perhaps of capital importance to oneself, though not necessarily the greatest contribution these poets have made. I think that from Baudelaire I learned first, a precedent for the poetical possibilities, never developed by any poet writing in my own language, of the more sordid aspects of the modern metropolis, of the possibility of fusion between the sordidly realistic and the phantasmagoric, the possibility of the juxtaposition of the matter-of-fact and the fantastic. From him, as from Laforgue, I learned that the sort of material that I had, the sort of experience that an adolescent had had, in an industrial city in America, could be the material for poetry; and that the source of new poetry might be found in what had been regarded hitherto as the impossible, the sterile, the intractably unpoetic. That, in fact, the business of the poet was to make poetry out of the unexplored resources of the unpoetical; that the poet, in fact, was committed by his profession to turn the unpoetical into poetry. A great poet can give a younger poet everything that he has to give him, in a very few lines. It may be that I am indebted to Baudelaire chiefly for half a dozen lines out of the whole of *Fleurs du Mal*; and that his significance for me is summed up in the lines:

Fourmillante Cité, cité pleine de rêves,
Où le spectre en plein jour raccroche le passant . . .

I knew what *that* meant, because I had lived it before I knew that I wanted to turn it into verse on my own account.

I may seem to you to be very far from Dante. But I cannot give you any approximation of what Dante has done for me, without speaking of what other poets have done for me. When I have written about Baudelaire, or Dante, or any other poet who has had a capital importance in my own development, I have written *because* that poet has meant so much to me, but not about myself, but *about* that poet and his poetry. That is, the first impulse to write about a great poet is one of gratitude; but the reasons for which one is grateful may play a very small part in a critical appreciation of that poet.

One has other debts, innumerable debts, to poets, of another kind. There are poets who have been at the back of one's mind, or perhaps consciously there, when one has had some particular problem to settle, for which something they have written suggests the method. There are those from whom one has consciously borrowed, adapting a line of verse to a different language or period or context. There are those who remain in one's mind as having set the standard for a particular poetic virtue, as Villon for honesty, and Sappho for having fixed a particular emotion in the right and the minimum number of words, once and for all. There are also the great masters, to whom one slowly grows up. When I was young I felt much more at ease with the lesser Elizabethan dramatists than with Shakespeare: the former were, so to speak, playmates nearer my own size. One test of the great masters, of whom Shakespeare is one, is that the appreciation of their poetry is a lifetime's task, because at every stage of maturing – and that should be one's whole life – you are able to understand them better. Among these are Shakespeare, Dante, Homer and Virgil.

To Criticize the Critic (1961, *TCTC*):

(p.23) There is one poet, however, who impressed me profoundly when I was twenty-two and with only a rudimentary acquaintance with his language started to puzzle out his lines, one poet who remains the comfort and amazement of my age, although my knowledge of his language remains rudimentary. I was never more than an inferior classical scholar: the poet I speak of is Dante. In my youth, I think that Dante's astonishing economy and directness of language – his arrow that goes unerringly to the centre of the target – provided for me a wholesome corrective to the extravagances of the Elizabethan, Jacobean and Caroline authors in whom I also delighted.

(iii) TSE on the borrowing of writers from themselves

Christopher Marlowe (1919, *SE*):

(pp.119–20) And we find that this poet [bard *1919*] of torrential imagination recognized many of his best bits (and those of one or two others), saved them, and reproduced them more than once, almost invariably improving them in the process.

(p.122) One line Marlowe remodels with triumphant success:
And set black streamers in the firmament
(Tamburlaine)
becomes
See, see, where Christ's blood streams in the firmament!
(Doctor Faustus)

TLS (26 Jan. 1928), *John Webster*, reviewing F. L. Lucas, *The Complete Works of John Webster*:

For passage after passage can be marked, in the two later plays, echoing some passage in one of the two great plays, and echoing weakly. Webster's mind was of the reservoir type. He needed to accumulate for a long time before he could transmute into original poetry. To the last Shakespeare is inexhaustible. Whatever he did was new. But Webster was not inexhaustible. His mind had to acquire a great deal before it could give out a little. And later he must have been very tired or very distracted. What the circumstances were which prevented him from doing what he might have done we shall never know. He was more blessed than most poets in having accomplished, in having put down, once and for all, that which he put down in the two great tragedies which Mr. Lucas so rightly and so fruitfully admires.

TLS (5 April 1928), *Poets' Borrowings*, reviewing Percy Allen, *Shakespeare, Jonson and Wilkins as Borrowers*:

To our mind, the most important point that Mr. Allen makes is the borrowing of writers from themselves. The debt of every poet to his predecessors and contemporaries is a scent eagerly sniffed and followed by every critic; but the debts of poets to their own earlier work are apt to be overlooked. Yet any intelligent psychologist ought to see at once that any poet, even the greatest, will tend to use his own impressions over and over again. It is by no means a matter of poverty of inspiration. Every man who writes poetry has a certain number of impressions and emotions which are particularly important to him. Every man who writes poetry will be inclined to seek endlessly for a final expression of these, and will be dissatisfied with his expressions and will want to employ the initial feeling, the original image or rhythm, once more in order to satisfy himself. It would be surprising if Shakespeare did not illustrate this tendency.

[On *Titus Andronicus* and *A Midsummer Night's Dream*] And indeed 'borrowing' is not quite the word. It would be truer to say that many things in *Titus* 'suggested' many things in the *Dream*. A single example may serve. Mr. Allen puts forward the possibility (after many other parallels, each slight in itself, but having a cumulative plausibility) that the name of Bottom and the line 'it shall be called Bottom's dream, because it hath no bottom' came to Shakespeare because of the line in *Titus*,

Is not my sorrow deep, having no bottom?

It is obvious that here we are over the frontier beyond literary scholarship. For such a parallel implies something that can neither be proved nor disproved by scholarship. Scholarship shows that Shakespeare at least had something to do with *Titus*, and there is no reason for doubting that he was the author of the *Dream*. And this is as far as scholarship goes in Mr. Allen's affair. The rest is simply a matter for psychologists to take up. But even if we are not trained psychologists, and have only some knowledge of the way in which other poets have handled and rehandled the same material, and if we weigh all of the parallel passages which Mr. Allen quotes, we are very strongly inclined to believe that Mr. Allen is right.

There is every reason to believe that Marlowe reworked some of his best lines in very different contexts and with very different meanings; and it would not be at all surprising to find that Shakespeare had done the same thing. The ordinary reader or playgoer is misled by the fact that such plays as *Titus* and the *Dream* have apparently and rationally nothing in common. But to the poet's mind such differences are superficial and unimportant. [Mr. Allen's] essential idea has no bearing on the question of attributions. Poets frequently, if not always, borrow from other poets; we need to be reminded to what extent they do, and must, borrow from themselves.

The Criterion, vii (June 1928) 155–6, on F. L. Lucas's *Webster*:

It is quite true that a poet of original genius may first distinguish himself by accomplished counterfeit of another's works; it is also true that Webster borrowed without scruple from other dramatists, as well as from such writers as Montaigne and Sidney. I only think that Mr. Lucas does not make sufficient allowance for the likelihood of a poet's borrowing from himself: or more fairly, for a poet in maturity working up into better form some image or rhythm which was an inspired flash of his youth.

I still think that the parallels are likelier the work of a man remodelling his own lines, than that of a man improving the lines of another.

(iv) TSE on the Elizabethans and Jacobeans

To Criticize the Critic (1961, *TCTC*):

(p.18) It was from these minor dramatists that I, in my own poetic formation, had learned my lessons; it was by them, and not by Shakespeare, that my imagination had been stimulated, my sense of rhythm trained, and my emotions fed. I had read them at the age at which they were best suited to my temperament and stage of development, and had read them with passionate delight long before I had any thought, or any opportunity of writing about them. At the period in which the stirrings of desire to write verse were becoming insistent, these were the men whom I took as my tutors. Just as the modern poet who influenced me was not Baudelaire but Jules Laforgue, so the dramatic poets were Marlowe and Webster and Tourneur and Middleton and Ford, not Shakespeare. A poet of the supreme greatness of Shakespeare can hardly influence, he can only be imitated: and the difference between influence and imitation is that influence can fecundate, whereas imitation – especially unconscious imitation – can only sterilize.

(v) TSE on the poets of the Nineties

Reflections on Contemporary Poetry [II], *The Egoist* (Oct. 1917):

The truth is that [John] Davidson was a violent Scotch preacher with an occasional passionate flash of exact vision.

Letter to Ezra Pound (22 Dec. 1924, Beinecke Library, Yale):

Probably the fact that Swinburne and the poets of the nineties were entirely missed out of my personal history counts for a great deal. I never read any of these people until it was too late for me to get anything out of them, and until after I had assimilated other influences which must have made it impossible for me to accept the Swinburnians at all. The only exception to the above is Rossetti. I am as blind to the merits of these people as I am to Thomas Hardy.

Baudelaire in Our Time (1927, *For Lancelot Andrewes*, 1928):

(pp.87–8) Mr. Symons is himself, we must remember, no mean poet; he is typical of the 'nineties; this influence of Baudelaire upon Mr. Symons was manifestly genuine and profound.

TLS (10 Jan. 1935), a letter:

In the interesting review of Ernest Dowson's Poems in your last issue, your reviewer suggests that I caught the phrase 'Falls the shadow' [*The Hollow Men*] from Dowson's 'Cynara.' This derivation had not occurred to my mind, but I believe it to be correct, because the lines he quotes have always run in my head, and because I regard Dowson as a poet whose technical innovations have been underestimated. But I do not think that I got the title 'The Hollow Men' from Dowson. There is a romance of William Morris called 'The Hollow Land.' There is also a poem of Mr. Kipling called 'The Broken Men.' I combined the two.

Tradition and the Practice of Poetry (1936, a lecture in Dublin; *Southern Review*, Autumn 1985; subsequently *T. S. Eliot: Essays from the Southern Review*, ed. James Olney, 1988):

(pp.13–14) I cannot help wondering how my own verse would have developed, or whether it would have been written at all, supposing that the poets of the 'nineties had survived to my own time and had gone on developing and increasing in power. Perhaps they were men who could not have developed further, but I am making that assumption. I certainly had much more in common with them than with the English poets who survived to my own day – there were no American poets at all. Had they survived, they might have spoken in an idiom sufficiently like my own to have made anything I had to say superfluous. They were in contact with those of France, and they might have exhausted the possibilities of cross-fertilisation from Symbolist Poetry (as they called it) before I had a chance. What happened was that they made it possible for me to discover these poets: Arthur Symons' book on the French Symbolists was of more importance for my development than any other book. I must be grateful to him for putting me in touch with the work of the French poets, and for not having got out of them, for his own poetry, what I was to find there myself. When one reviews one's own writing, as when one reviews one's own life, how much there is that bears the appearance of mere chance! One has been dependent upon one's predecessors for what they did not do, as much as for what they did! The one poet of that period, the youngest and the greatest, who survived, was of course Yeats; and it happened that in my own formative period Yeats was in his most superficially local phase, in which I failed to appreciate him.

The Last Twenty-Five Years of English Poetry (1940), draft lecture, for a cancelled British Council Tour in Italy (Hayward Bequest)

(p.4) Towards the end of the century, in the period we call the 'Nineties', some younger men, partly under the influence of French models, did make some significant attempt to relate their verse to living speech.

(p.5) In some of the poems of Ernest Dowson and Arthur Symons, in a verse or a line here or there of Lionel Johnson, there is a ring of the spo[k]en voice. The best known poem of Dowson's, *Non sum qualis eram bonae sub regno Cynarae*, shows a mixture of the conventions of the age of Swinburne with a new and irregular rhythm.

I cried for madder music and for stronger wine,
But when the feast is finished and the lamps expire,
Then falls thy shadow, Cynara! the night is thine;
And I am desolate and sick of an old passion,
   Yea, hungry for the lips of my desire:
I have been faithful to thee, Cynara! in my fashion.

There is in this the vague suggestive key words, as with Swinburne: 'music', 'wine', 'feast'; and also the conventional poetic diction, as with the second person singular, and the 'yea' – the Pre-Raphaelite idiom: but there is something more modern, more allied to speech, in the broken rhythm and the stanzas ending with the qualification 'in my fashion'.

American Literature and the American Language (1953, TCTC):

(p.58) In the first decade of the century the situation was unusual. I cannot think of a single living poet, in either England or America, then at the height of his powers, whose work was capable of pointing the way to a young poet conscious of the desire for a new idiom. It was the tail-end of the Victorian era. Our sympathies, I think, went out to those who are known as the English poets of the nineties, who were all, with one exception, dead. The exception was W. B. Yeats, who was younger, more robust, and of more temperate habits than the poets of the Rhymers' Club with whom he had associated in his youth. And Yeats himself had not found his personal speech; he was a late developer; when he emerged as a great modern poet, about 1917, we had already reached a point such that he appeared not as a precursor but as an elder and venerated contemporary. What the poets of the nineties had bequeathed to us besides the new tone of a few poems by Ernest Dowson, John Davidson and Arthur Symons, was the assurance that there was something to be learned from the French poets of the Symbolist Movement – and most of them were dead, too.

Saltire Review, iv (Summer 1957):

(p.57) I read John Davidson's poems first [. . .] I can't remember whether it was towards the end of my school days or in my first year or two at Harvard University. But I read them at a time when I was reading the poets of the 'nineties, who were the only poets – most of them were dead, of course – who at that period of history seemed to have anything to offer to me as a beginner. What I wanted, I think, from the poets of the 'nineties was what they did not have in common with the Pre-Raphaelites, but what was new and original in their work. And I remember three poets in particular, one of whom was John Davidson. One was Arthur Symmonds [Symons], some of his poems; another was Ernest Dowson, again one or two poems; and the third was Davidson, in his *Thirty Bob a Week*. From these men I got the idea that one could write poetry in an English such as one would speak oneself. A colloquial idiom. There was a spoken rhythm in some of their poems. Now, I admire other poems of Davidson very much indeed. I think they should be read again and again; but it is *Thirty Bob a Week* which made a terrific impact on me. I think that poem one of the great poems of the end of the nineteenth century. And with some of those by the other men I've mentioned, I think it prepared me for initiation into the work of some of the French symbolists, such as La Forgue [Laforgue], whom I came across shortly after. But *Thirty Bob a Week* has a very important place in the development of my own poetic technique.

Paris Review interview (21, Spring/Summer 1959):

(p.50) There was really nothing except the people of the 90's who had all died of drink or suicide or one thing or another.

On Teaching the Appreciation of Poetry, Critic, xviii (1960):

(p.78) At sixteen I discovered (by reading a section of our history of English literature which we were *not* required to read) Thomson's *City of Dreadful Night,* and the poems of Ernest Dowson. Each was a new and vivid experience. But *The City of Dreadful Night* or Dowson's *Impenitentia Ultima* would hardly, even today, be considered suitable for academic study at the age I have in mind.

Preface to *John Davidson: A Selection of His Poems* (1961):

I feel a peculiar reverence, and acknowledge a particular debt, towards poets whose work impressed me deeply in my formative years between the ages of sixteen and twenty. Some were of an earlier age – the late sixteenth and early seventeenth centuries – some of another language; and of these, two were Scots: the author of *The City of Dreadful Night,* and the author of *Thirty Bob a Week.*

What exactly is my debt to John Davidson I cannot tell, any more than I can describe the nature of my debt to James Thomson: I only know that the two debts differ from each other.

Certainly, *Thirty Bob a Week* seems to me the only poem in which Davidson freed himself completely from the poetic diction of English verse of his time (just as *Non Sum Qualis Eram* seems to me the one poem in which, by a slight shift of rhythm, Ernest Dowson freed himself). But I am sure that I found inspiration in the content of the poem, and in the complete fitness of content and idiom: for I also had a good many dingy urban images to reveal. Davidson had a great theme, and also found an idiom which elicited the greatness of the theme, which endowed this thirty-bob-a-week clerk with a dignity that would not have appeared if a more conventional poetic diction had been employed. The personage that Davidson created in this poem has haunted me all my life, and the poem is to me a great poem for ever.

The Runnable Stag has run in my head for a good many years now; and I have a fellow feeling with the poet who could look with a poet's eye on the Isle of Dogs and Millwall Dock.

(vi) TSE on Arthur Symons, *The Symbolist Movement in Literature*, and on France and the French Symbolists

Letter to Robert Nichols (8 Aug. 1917, *Letters* i 191):

I remember getting hold of Laforgue years ago at Harvard, purely through reading Symons, and then sending to Paris for the texts. I puzzled it out as best I could, not finding half the words in my dictionary, and it was several years later before I came across anyone who had read him or could be persuaded to read him. I do feel more grateful to him than to anyone else, and I do not think that I have come across any other writer since who has meant so much to me as he did at that particular moment, or that particular year.

Reflections on Contemporary Poetry [*IV*], *The Egoist* (July 1919) [based largely on TSE's experience of Laforgue though it does not speak of him]:

It is not true that the development of a writer is a function of his development as a man, but it is possible to say that there is a close analogy between the sort of experience which develops a man and the sort of experience which develops a writer. Experience in living may leave the literary embryo still dormant, and the progress of literary development may to a considerable extent take place in a soul left immature in living. But similar types of experience form the nourishment of both. There is a kind of stimulus for a writer which is more important than the stimulus of admiring another writer. Admiration leads most often to imitation, we can seldom remain long unconscious of our imitating another, and the awareness of our debt naturally leads us to hatred of the object imitated. If we stand toward a writer in this other relation of which I speak we do not imitate him, and though we are quite as likely to be accused of it, we are quite unperturbed by the charge. This relation is a feeling of profound kinship, or rather of a peculiar personal intimacy, with another, probably a dead author. It may overcome us suddenly, on first or after long acquaintance; it is certainly a crisis; and when a young writer is seized with his first passion of this sort he may be changed, metamorphosed almost, within a few weeks even, from a bundle of second-hand sentiments into a person. The imperative intimacy arouses for the first time a real, an unshakeable confidence. That you possess this secret knowledge, this intimacy, with the dead man, that after few or many years or centuries you should have appeared, with this indubitable claim to distinction; who can penetrate at once the thick and dusty circumlocutions about his reputation, can call yourself alone his friend: it is something more than *encouragement* to you. It is a cause of development, like personal relations in life. Like personal intimacies in life, it may and probably will pass, but it will be ineffaceable.

The usefulness of such a passion is various. For one thing it secures us against forced admiration, from attending to writers simply because they are great. We are never at ease with people who, to us, are merely great. We are not ourselves great enough for that: probably not one man in each generation is great enough to be intimate with Shakespeare. Admiration for the great is only a sort of discipline to keep us in order, a necessary snobbism to make us mind our places. We may not be great lovers; but if we had a genuine affair with a real poet of any degree we have acquired a monitor to avert us when we are not in love. Indirectly, there are other acquisitions: our friendship gives us an introduction to the society in which our friend moved; we learn its origins and its endings; we are broadened. We do not imitate, we are changed; and our work is the work of the changed man; we have not borrowed, we have been quickened, and we become bearers of a tradition.

I feel that the traces of this sort of experience are conspicuously lacking from contemporary poetry, and that contemporary poetry is deficient in tradition. We can raise no objection to 'experiments' if the experimenters are qualified; but we can object that almost none of the experimenters hold fast to anything permanent under the varied phenomena of experiment. Shakespeare was one of the slowest, if one of the most persistent, of experimenters; even Rimbaud shows process. And one never has the tremendous satisfaction of meeting a writer who is more original, more independent, than he himself knows. No dead voices speak through the living voice; no reincarnation, no re-creation. Not even the *saturation* which sometimes combusts spontaneously into originality.

> fly where men feel
> The cunning axletree: and those that suffer
> Beneath the chariot of the snowy Bear

is beautiful; and the beauty only appears the more substantial if we conjecture that Chapman may have absorbed the recurring phrase of Seneca in

signum celsi glaciale poli
septem stellis Arcados ursae
lucem verso termone vocat . . . . .
                    sub cardine
glacialis ursae . . .
a union, at a point at least, of the Tudor and the Greek through the Senecan
phrase.

The Perfect Critic (*SW*, 1920):

(p.5) But if we can recall the time when we were ignorant of the French
symbolists, and met with *The Symbolist Movement in Literature*, we
remember that book as an introduction to wholly new feelings, as a
revelation. After we have read Verlaine and Laforgue and Rimbaud and
return to Mr. Symons' book, we may find that our own impressions dissent
from his. The book has not, perhaps, a permanent value for the one reader,
but it has led to results of permanent importance for him.

(p.7) It would be rash to speculate, and is perhaps impossible to determine,
what is unfulfilled in Mr. Symons' charming verse that overflows into his
critical prose.

In the *Paris Review* interview (21, Spring/Summer 1959, p.49), TSE refers
to 'Arthur Symons's book on French poetry, which I came across in the
Harvard Union'. Among TSE's markings in his copy of Arthur Symons's
The Symbolist Movement in Literature (1908 edn, Houghton Library) is
his marking of this:

(p.104) [Symons on Laforgue] The old cadences, the old eloquence, the
ingenuous seriousness of poetry, are all banished, on a theory as self-denying
as that which permitted Degas to dispense with recognisable beauty in his
figures.

The Criterion, ix (Jan. 1930) 357, review of Peter Quennell, *Baudelaire
and the Symbolists*:

Mr. Quennell has done for his generation what Arthur Symons did many
years ago with his *Symbolist Movement in Literature*. I am not disposed to
disparage Mr. Symons's book; it was a very good book for its time; it did

make the reader want to read the poets Mr. Symons wrote about. I myself owe Mr. Symons a great debt: but for having read his book, I should not, in the year 1908, have heard of Laforgue or Rimbaud: I should probably not have begun to read Verlaine; and but for reading Verlaine, I should not have heard of Corbière. So the Symons book is one of those which have affected the course of my life.

Foreword to Joseph Chiari, *Contemporary French Poetry* (1952):

(p.viii) Symons did perform the function of bringing important poets to the attention of English readers; and for that reason his book will remain a landmark. As criticism I cannot say that Symons's book stands the test of time. He omitted one or two poets of the first importance – notably Tristan Corbière; he included one or two writers – Maeterlinck and Villiers de l'Isle Adam – whose reputation is now somewhat diminished; and even when he admired the right authors, one cannot say that it was always for the right reason.

(pp.viii–ix) Arthur Symons could treat certain poets as forming, between them, the outline of a period, so that he had no need to refer to a number of admirable poets much of whose work has permanent value (I mention in passing only the names of Verhaeren, Jammes, Samain, Tailhade, Kahn, Regnier, Vielé-Griffin).

[. . .] several significant figures of the twenties – Cocteau, André Salmon, and Max Jacob.

*   *   *

Reported by Edward J. H. Greene, *T. S. Eliot et la France* (1951):

(p.20) Eliot s'était procuré, fin 1909 ou peu après, une des éditions en deux volumes de *Poètes d'Aujourd'hui*. Il m'a dit aussi qu'il croit être le premier en Amérique à avoir possédé les oeuvres complètes de Laforgue. [A. D. Moody (*Thomas Stearns Eliot, Poet*, 1979, p.332) says that this would have been *Oeuvres Complètes*, ed. Camille Mauclair, 3 vols, Paris, 1901–3.]

Letter to Conrad Aiken (21 Aug. 1916), *Letters* i 145:

He [Pound] has just translated (with untiring energy) Laforgue's "Salome", and wants me to do the "Hamlet" to go to make up a volume between us of the *Moralités Légendaires*, and I have done a few pages of it.

Modern Tendencies in Poetry, *Shama'a* (April 1920):

(pp.12–14) The one Victorian poet whom our contemporary can study with much profit is Browning. Otherwise, almost all of the interesting developments in poetry are due to Frenchmen: Baudelaire, Gautier, Mallarmé, Laforgue, Corbière, Rimbaud.

It is curious that these men, who have so strongly influenced our contemporaries, should have impressed themselves upon us as eminently *hommes de métier*. Some of them lived as romantic or pathetic lives as any of our young men of the nineties. But as [*read* an] Ernest Bowson [*read* Dowson], like a Lionel Johnson, is at heart a conservative, putting all his romance into his life: England has been plagued with poets of this type. The Frenchmen of whom I speak were very seriously occupied with the problem of finding a sincere idiom. Baudelaire more often failed than succeeded, there is nothing permanently interesting about his diabolism; his form is often absurdly antiquated. He is a poet for the poet to study, rather than for the public to read.

The influence of Laforgue, and to a less degree of Rimbaud has been so great that it is necessary to pass some criticism upon these poets in dealing with contemporary English verse. When I discovered Jules Laforgue, ten years ago, he gave me the same revelation which I imagine he has given to other people before and since: that is, he showed how, much [*read* how much] more use poetry could make of contemporary ideas and feelings, of the emotional quality of contemporary ideas, than one had supposed. Browning, at his best, for example in 'Bishop's Blougram's Apology', had done as much: and Browning's poetry is much greater poetry. But the development of Browning had been such as to conceal from us some of the implications of his work. He had begun as a disciple of Shelley, and emerged from this into a developed mature impersonal stage: his *adolescence* had not been so important as Laforgue's. It is easier for a young poet to understand and to profit by the work of another young poet, when it is good, than from the work of a mature poet. I am no longer of the opinion that Laforgue, at the stage which he had reached at his death, was a great poet; I can see sentimentalism, absorption in himself, lack of balance. But in Laforgue there was a young man who was generally intelligent, critical, interested in art, science and philosophy, and always himself: that is, every mental occupation had its own precise emotional state, which Laforgue was quick to discover and curious to analyse. So Laforgue has been more *important*, as a laboratory study for the young poet, than either Rimbaud or Corbière. For their work, though always personal in the right sense, is either indifferent or mature. At their best, they present much more solid achievement than Laforgue. Rimbaud's *Cabaret Vert* is as solid and objective as the best of Racine; Corbière's *Rhapsode Foraine* is as substantial in its way as Villon: when he describes the procession of mendicants and cripples to the shrine of the Virgin, and says:

Là, ce tronc d'homme où croît l'ulcère,
Contre un tronc d'arbre où croît le gui

the phrase burns itself in like the *cotto aspetto* of Dante's Brunetto Latini. But on young poets, the influence of Laforgue is much stronger, and so far as it goes, a very good influence.

I think that the attention drawn to these French poets has been a very good thing for English verse. I think that the best of the younger poets to-day realise that it is impossible to ignore the discoveries of foreign poets, just as it is impossible for a good scientist to ignore what is going on abroad. So far as I can see, there is no poetry being written in France at present which is making any contribution whatever to the development of poetry; almost none of it is even readable. An infatuation with the French, therefore, would be as fatal as our natural insularity.

There is one other French influence, which, though it has not been powerful here, has been beneficial. That is Mallarmé. What Mallarmé had to say is not so important or interesting as what the poets previously mentioned had to say, but he called attention to the fact that the actual writing of poetry, the accidence and syntax, is a very difficult part of the problem. Mallarmé gets his modernity, his sincerity, simply by close attention to the actual writing. The influence of an art like Mallarmé's, upon later poetry, is comparable to the influence of abstract painting: whatever its actual value, whether it is a higher or lower form, or whether it is merely a laboratory experiment, it is bound to have a cleansing and purifying effect, to recall the attention of the intelligent to essential problems of form.

Lettre d'Angleterre, Nouvelle Revue Française (1 Nov. 1923):

Sur cette partie de ma génération dont je peux parler avec sympathie, je sais combien forte a été l'influence de Remy de Gourmont; et Gourmont est l'un des guides qui nous firent étudier Flaubert, lequel fut un maître à la fois d'art et de pensée. Et en poésie (je ne parle toujours que pour un certain groupe) Rimbaud, Corbière et Laforgue ont été pour nous des *maîtres d'art* plus qu'aucun poète anglais de leur temps.

The Clark Lectures (1926, *VMP*) and the Turnbull Lectures (1933, *VMP*): throughout for TSE on Laforgue and Corbière.

The Criterion, ix (Jan. 1930) 359, review of Peter Quennell, *Baudelaire and the Symbolists*:

When we get to Laforgue, we find a poet who seems to express more clearly even than Baudelaire the difficulties of his own age: he speaks to us, or spoke to my generation, more intimately than Baudelaire seemed to do. Only later we conclude that Laforgue's 'present' is a narrower present than Baudelaire's, and that Baudelaire's present extends to more of the past and more of the future.

Preface to Charles-Louis Philippe, *Bubu of Montparnasse* (1932):

It is a good many years ago, it was in the year 1910, that I first read *Bubu de Montparnasse*, when I came first to Paris. Read at an impressionable age, and under the impressive conditions, the book has always been for me, not merely the best of Charles-Louis Philippe's books, but a symbol of the Paris of that time. Little known even now outside of France, Philippe was then none too wellknown even within it, though he was already dead, and this book had been published ten years before. I imagine that the Paris of 1910 was more like the Paris of 1900 than like the Paris of 1932: certainly Montparnasse has changed more in these twenty-two years than it could have changed in the preceding ten. In a very much smaller way, to me *Bubu* stood for Paris as some of Dickens' novels stand for London.

The Turnbull Lectures (1933, *VMP*):

(p.287) To take the first point first, what is the relevance of this French poetry of the seventies and eighties to us and our problems?

I perhaps am of all critics the most disqualified from judging. For I know that when I first came across these French poets, some twenty-three years ago, it was a personal enlightenment such as I can hardly communicate. I felt for the first time in contact with a tradition, for the first time, that I had, so to speak, some backing by the dead, and at the same time that I had something to say that might be new and relevant. I doubt whether, without the men I have mentioned – Baudelaire, Corbière, Verlaine, Laforgue, Mallarmé, Rimbaud – I should have been able to write poetry at all. This fact alone renders me unsuitable to be a critic of them. Without them, the Elizabethan and Jacobean poets would have been too remote and quaint, and Shakespeare and Dante too remote and great, to have helped me.

On a Recent Piece of Criticism, Purpose, x (April/June 1938):

(pp.91–2) I was introduced to [Pound's] *Personae* and *Exultations* in 1910, while still an undergraduate at Harvard. The poems did not then excite me, any more than did the poetry of Yeats: I was too much engrossed in working out the implications of Laforgue.

Yeats (1940, *OPP*):

(p.252) A very young man, who is himself stirred to write, is not primarily critical or even widely appreciative. He is looking for masters who will elicit his consciousness of what he wants to say himself, of the kind of poetry that is in him to write. The taste of an adolescent writer is intense, but narrow: it is determined by personal needs. The kind of poetry that I needed, to teach me the use of my own voice, did not exist in English at all; it was only to be found in French. For this reason the poetry of the young Yeats hardly existed for me until after my enthusiasm had been won by the poetry of the older Yeats; and by that time – I mean, from 1919 on – my own course of evolution was already determined.

What France Means to You, La France Libre (15 June 1944):

Je crois que c'était une bonne fortune exceptionnelle, pour un adolescent, de découvrir Paris en l'an 1910.

Mais ce n'est pas un accident qui m'avait conduit à Paris. Depuis plusieurs années, la France représentait surtout, à mes yeux, la *poésie*. Si je n'avais découvert Baudelaire, et toute la poésie qui découle de Baudelaire – en particulier celle de Laforgue, Corbière, Rimbaud et Mallarmé – je ne crois pas que j'aurais jamais pu écrire. Cette découverte m'assura d'un fait dont la poésie anglaise de la même époque ne m'avait donné aucun signe certain; à savoir qu'il existait un langage moderne, et que la poésie anglaise conservait des possibilités inexplorées. Peut-être suis-je tenté d'exagérer l'importance que cette découverte eut pour la poésie anglaise: mais pour ce qui est de l'importance qu'elle eut dans ma vie, je crains seulement que mon témoignage ne reste en-dessous de la vérité.

Edgar Poe et la France (1948, typescript, Hayward Bequest; subsequently adapted for *From Poe to Valéry, TCTC*):

(p.5, deleted) I am an English poet of American origin, in whose formation the influence of Baudelaire and of the poets who derive from Baudelaire has been dominant.

Letter to Violet Schiff (22 Sept. 1949, British Library):

How very kind of you to write and to send me your translation of [Charles-Louis Philippe's] *Marie Donadieu*. It will be a very interesting experience to read this book again, because I have not read it since 1911, at a period when the works of Philippe made a very deep impression upon me.

Reported by Edward J. H. Greene, *T. S. Eliot et la France* (1951):

(pp.22–3) Le volume *Prufrock* ne contient que quatre poèmes qui se placent directement 'sous le signe de Laforgue'.
n. Expression employée par Eliot dans une lettre (18 octobre 1939) où il confirme l'exactitude de ce groupement. [viz. *The Love Song of J. Alfred Prufrock*, *Portrait of a Lady*, *Conversation Galante*, *La Figlia Che Piange*.]

(p.61) [on Corbière, Rimbaud, and Tailhade] Eliot a confirmé, dans une lettre [. . .] 'Any of these poets may have influenced the 1915 poems'.

(p.63) Eliot m'a confié [. . .] en signalant les premières oeuvres, que pendant quelque temps Rimbaud a exercé sur lui une influence de plus en plus importante. Il a mentionné en particulier 'Cabaret-Vert', 'un des meilleurs sonnets qui soient', et 'Vénus et Anadyomène', 'autrement intéressant que Wordsworth'.

Il avait lu Rimbaud dès 1908 [. . .] à partir de 1912 environ, Eliot relit Rimbaud plusieurs fois.

(pp.64–5) Quant à Tailhade, c'est l'âpre satirique et non l'élégiaque qui a intéressé Eliot [. . .] il est pourtant probable qu'Eliot ne connaissait guère encore que ceux des *Poèmes aristophanesques* qui se trouvaient cités dans *Poètes d'Aujourd'hui*. Ces poèmes l'avaient frappé en 1910.

(p.77) [René Taupin had corrected his saying that TSE knew André Salmon during his stay in Paris in 1910–11. Taupin proposed *Prikaz* as a source for *The Waste Land*.] Eliot n'a pas lu cette oeuvre. En 1939 Eliot se souvenait d'avoir lu de Salmon un seul des premiers recueils, et c'est à peu près tout. Ce recueil est sans doute *Le Calumet* (1910), où se trouve le poème 'Les Veufs de Rose'.

(p.80) Eliot n'a encore, à cette époque, qu'une connaissance très fragmentaire de l'oeuvre satirique de Tailhade. Au total, il connaît, soit par *Poètes d'Aujourd'hui*, soit par le *Livre des Masques* de Gourmont, soit par Aldington et Pound, une douzaine de pièces, les meilleures d'ailleurs. (Aldington a consacré au poète français une chronique dans l'*Egoist*, octobre 1915; et Pound publiera en 1918 cinq poèmes de Tailhade dans *French Poets*.)

Foreword to Joseph Chiari, *Contemporary French Poetry* (1952):

(p.x) In 1910, when I had my first introduction to literary Paris, Claudel was already a great poet in the eyes of a younger generation – my own generation. He had published *Connaissance de l'Est*, *Art poétique*, and those plays which appeared in one volume under the general title of *L'Arbre*: and I am not sure that these three books do not constitute his strongest claim to immortality. Paul Valéry, if known at all, was known only as a minor, late Symbolist poet whose work was represented in the standard anthology of Symbolist verse, *Poètes d'Aujourd'hui* of Van Bever and Léautaud. It was only in 1917, after the publication of *La Jeune Parque*, that his name was suddenly illuminated with glory; yet curiously enough, while Claudel still remained known only to few readers in England, the fame of Valéry spread as quickly as that of Proust.

Paris Review interview (21, Spring/Summer 1959):

(p.49) Then I wrote a few [poems] at Harvard, just enough to qualify for election to an editorship on *The Harvard Advocate*, which I enjoyed. Then I had an outburst during my junior and senior years. I became much more prolific, under the influence first of Baudelaire and then of Jules Laforgue, whom I discovered I think in my junior year at Harvard.

To Criticize the Critic (1961, *TCTC*):

(p.22) I have written about Baudelaire, but nothing about Jules Laforgue, to whom I owe more than to any one poet in any language, or about Tristan Corbière, to whom I owe something also.

(vii) TSE on Bergson and Bradley

HENRI BERGSON

[TSE attended some of Bergson's lectures in Paris in 1910–11. See his notes on Bergson and his draft of a paper on Bergson (both 1910–11; Houghton Library; bMS Am 1691 (130, 132)).]

In his paper on politics and metaphysics (1913?; Houghton Library; bMS Am 1691 (25)), TSE returns to Bergson throughout, including p.20:

Bergson, on the one hand, emphasises the reality of a fluid psychological world of aspect and nuance, where purposes and intentions are replaced by pure feeling. By the seduction of his style we come to believe that the Bergsonian world is the only world, and that we have been living among shadows. It is not so. Bergson is the sweet Siren of adventurous [*from wandering*] philosophers and our world of social values is at least as real as his.

[The syllabus for TSE's 1916 course on Modern French Literature included:]

LECTURE VI

The philosophy of 1910.
Henri Bergson was then the most noticed figure in Paris. The leading idea of his philosophy. Comparison with Maeterlinck: the two men have in common (1) The use of science against science. (2) Mysticism. (3) Optimism.
Influence of Bergson upon some of the men already mentioned. Is this influence good or bad? Whether it is likely to persist.
Summary of contemporary tendencies. Influence of the war.
Forecast of French thought after the war.

[The only book by Bergson on TSE's reading list for the course was *Introduction to Metaphysics*.]

The French Intelligence, in *Imperfect Critics* (1920, *SW*):

(pp.45–6) It is that the follies and stupidities of the French, no matter how base, express themselves in the form of ideas – Bergsonism itself is an intellectual construction, and the mondaines who attended lectures at the College de France were in a sense using their minds.

Lettre d'Angleterre, *Nouvelle Revue Française* (1 Nov. 1923):

Sur cette partie de ma génération dont je peux parler avec sympathie, je sais combien forte a été l'influence de Remy de Gourmont; et Gourmont est l'un des guides qui nous firent étudier Flaubert, lequel fut un maître à la fois d'art et de pensée. Et en poésie (je ne parle toujours que pour un certain groupe) Rimbaud, Corbière et Laforgue ont été pour nous des *maîtres d'art* plus qu'aucun poète anglais de leur temps. D'ailleurs, je ne trouve pas qu'il soit toujours possible, qu'il s'agisse des Anglais ou des Français, de séparer maîtrise de pensée et maîtrise d'art. Sauf quelques exceptions: je peux témoigner de l'importante influence qu'ont eue sur mon développement intellectuel *L'avenir de l'intelligence* et *Belphégor* (non que je veuille classer ensemble MM. Mauras [Maurras] et Benda), et de même, sans doute, à une certaine époque, *Matière et Mémoire*: livres qui à coup sûr impliquaient à mes yeux la maîtrise de pensée, mais non pas (je dis: à mes yeux) la maîtrise d'art.

TLS (23 Feb. 1928), reviewing Julien Benda, *La Trahison des Clercs*:

[Benda] is the author of [. . .] two books which constitute the most formidable attack upon Bergson that has yet been made.

The most brilliant modern example of the former [indirect influence] is Bergson. Apart from one little pamphlet issued in 1914, Bergson has always abstained from direct influence upon human passions; yet his influence in practical directions, in France at least, has been immense, and has profoundly affected *clercs* so different and so opposed as M. Le Roy and M. Maritain. And Bergson is a philosopher whom M. Benda has several times attacked, and with the greatest cogency. But is Bergson responsible for his own influence on persons who are not pure philosophers, but partly men of action?

What France Means to You, La France Libre (15 June 1944):

Je suppose qu'il y a encore des bergsoniens: mais pour avoir vraiment connu la ferveur bergsonienne, il faut être allé, regulièrement, chaque semaine, dans cette salle pleine à craquer où il faisait ses cours, au Collège de France.

Letter to Eudo C. Mason (19 April 1945; Humanities Research Center, Austin):

It seems to me so far as I am competent to judge that you are justified in your interpretation of *The Waste Land* but I am surprised to think that any indications of Christian tradition were present in *Prufrock*. I was certainly quite ignorant and unconscious of them myself, and at the time, or at least before the poem was finished, was entirely a Bergsonian; but as I always say, an author's knowledge of certain facts has value, whereas his interpretation or understanding of his own poem, and especially many years after writing it, may be no more authoritative and may for special reasons be less reliable than that of anyone else.

A Sermon preached in Magdalene College Chapel (1948):

(p.5) My only conversion, by the deliberate influence of any individual, was a temporary conversion to Bergsonism.

Introduction to Josef Pieper, *Leisure the Basis of Culture* (1952):

(p.11) Certainly, 'Where are the great philosophers?' is a rhetorical question often asked by those who pursued their philosophical studies forty or fifty years ago. Allowing for the possibility that the great figures of our youth have become magnified by the passage of time, and for the probability that most of those who ask the question have not followed modern philosophical developments very closely, there remains some justification of the lament. It may be merely a longing for the appearance of a philosopher whose writings, lectures and personality will arouse the imagination as Bergson, for instance, aroused it forty years ago [. . .]

Letter to Shiv K. Kumar (21 Jan. 1953), quoted in Kumar's *Bergson and the Stream of Consciousness Novel* (1962), p.154:

I was certainly very much under his (Bergson's) influence during the year 1910–11, when I both attended his lectures and gave close study to the books he had then written.

F. H. BRADLEY

[TSE's Harvard doctoral dissertation bore the title *Experience and the Objects of Knowledge in the Philosophy of F. H. Bradley*. In his Preface to the published edition (*Knowledge and Experience in the Philosophy of F. H. Bradley*, 1964), TSE recorded: 'From October 1911 until June 1914 I was a student in the Harvard Graduate School as a candidate for the degree of Doctor of Philosophy.' He completed the dissertation in 1916, but did not return to Harvard for the formal defence of it, choosing not to make the Atlantic crossing during the Great War. (See TSE's correspondence with J. H. Woods in 1916, *Letters* i 132, 134, 136–7, 142–3, 152–3.)]

Letter to J. H. Woods (28 Jan. 1915), *Letters* i 84:

I find that I take so much keener enjoyment in criticism than in construction that I propose making a virtue of a vice and recasting my thesis with a mind to this limitation; as I find satisfaction only in the historical aspect of philosophy. I had great difficulty, even agony, with the first draft, owing to my attempt to reach a positive conclusion; and so I should like to turn it into a criticism and valuation of the Bradleian metaphysic – for it seems to me that those best qualified for such tasks are those who have held a doctrine and no longer hold it.

Knowledge and Experience in the Philosophy of F. H. Bradley reprints as Appendix II TSE's essay from *The Monist* (Oct. 1916) on *Leibniz' Monadism and Bradley's Finite Centres*.

A Prediction in Regard to Three English Authors, Vanity Fair (Feb. 1924):

My purpose is not to attempt any exposition of his [Bradley's] philosophy, but to suggest the total effect of this philosophy upon a sensibility. This effect is all the more remarkable, because the philosophy is a *pure* philosophy: it borrows none of the persuasiveness of science, and none of the persuasiveness of literature. It is, for example, a *purer* philosophy than that of either of his most distinguished (but younger) contemporaries: Bergson and Bertrand Russell. For Bergson makes use of science – biology and psychology – and this use sometimes conceals the incoherence of a multiplicity of points of view, not all philosophic. Has not his exciting promise of immortality a somewhat meretricious captivation?

But the question is, for philosophy, says Bradley somewhat drily, not whether the soul is immortal, but whether, and in what sense, it may be said to exist here and now.

Philosophy may be futile or profitable, he seems to say, but if you are to pursue it at all, you must work with such and such data – which are neither literature nor science. All we can do is to accept these data and follow our argument to the end. If it ends, as it may well end, in zero, well, we have at least the satisfaction of having pursued something to the end, and of having ascertained that certain questions which occur to men to ask, are unanswerable or are meaningless. Once you accept his theory of the nature of the judgment, and it is as plausible a theory as any, you are led by his arid and highly sensitive eloquence (no English philosopher has ever written finer English) to something which, according to your temperament, will be resignation or despair – the bewildered despair of wondering why you ever wanted anything, and what it was that you wanted, since this philosophy seems to give you everything that you ask and yet to render it not worth wanting.

The Criterion, iii (Oct. 1924) 1–2, *A Commentary*:

Francis Herbert Bradley is dead: our contemporaries will no doubt record the fact respectfully, as the death of the last survivor of the academic race of metaphysicians, and will hurry on to the discussion of the latest scientific novelty. It is not for his achievements in his time that I wish to honour Bradley; not even as the man who broke the authority of Mill, or as the man who restored the rank of Britain amongst philosophers. I am engaged with the future. The reserved power of Bradley's philosophy resides perhaps herein: that, with all his apparent debt to Hegel, his philosophy is quite unaffected by the emotional obliquities which render German metaphysics monstrous.

Few will ever take the pains to study the consummate art of Bradley's style, the finest philosophic style in our language, in which acute intellect and passionate feeling preserve a classic balance: only those who will surrender patient years to the understanding of his meaning. But upon these few, both living and unborn, his writings perform that mysterious and complete operation which transmutes not one department of thought only, but the whole intellectual and emotional tone of their being. To them, in the living generation, the news of his death has brought an intimate and private grief.

See also *Francis Herbert Bradley* (1927, *SE*).

Index to the Editorial Material

See also the Index of Titles and First Lines. Not indexed are cross-references within the notes from one poem here first published to another such, and references to the *OED*.

I GENERAL

Abbott, Lyman 312
Ackroyd, Peter 119
Acts of the Apostles 290
Adams, Henry 5, 169, 185–6, 169–70, 185–6, 218, 230
Adams, J. Donald 239
Addison, Joseph 309
Aeschylus 171
Aiken, Conrad xl, 5, 8, 79, 110, 112, 121–2, 141, 154, 169, 176, 179, 184, 203, 208–9, 215–16, 218, 234, 248–9, 254, 256, 262, 267–8, 270–2, 276, 283, 297, 320, 402–3
Aldington, Richard 203–4, 217, 389, 408
Allen, Percy xxviii, 392–3
Altdorfer, Albrecht 267
Amos 272
Andrewes, Lancelot 144
Antonello of Messina 268
Apollinaire, Guillaume xxx, 111, 116, 143, 152, 159, 269
Aquinas, St Thomas 229
Aristophanes 204–5
Aristotle 189, 209, 229, 281
Arnold, Edwin 201, 224, 257
Arnold, Matthew 213, 226, 237, 285
Augustine, St 194

Babbitt, Irving 134
Baedeker, *London and Its Environs* 199–201, 203–4, 238, 268, 285
Bagchee, Shyamal 180–1, 264, 270, 298
Baillie, Joanna 285
Baillie, John 214, 253
Bakewell, Charles 229
Bakst, Léon 269
Banville, Théodore de 107, 130, 165

Barnett, Lionel 220, 273
Barrie, J. M. 5
Baudelaire, Charles 111, 124, 138, 146, 151, 156, 158, 179, 186, 208, 288, 294, 387–8, 390, 394–5, 403, 405–7, 409
Beach, Sylvia 321
Beaumont, Francis, and Fletcher, John 273, 301
Beinecke Rare Book and Manuscript Library, Yale University xv, 6–7, 61, 307, 312, 314, 320, 331, 394
Bell, Clive 321
Benda, Julien 254, 410
Bennett, Arnold 309
Bentley, Nicolas xix
Berg Collection of the New York Public Library ix, xiii, 172, 201, 244, 387
Bergson, Henri xxix, xxxii, 107, 125, 135–6, 141, 155, 158, 189, 194, 207, 231, 233, 241, 244, 248, 253, 409–13
Berkeley, George 253
Bertrand, Louis 233
Bhagavad-Gita, The 220, 273
Blake, William xxvii, 141, 190, 195, 221, 258
Blast 208, 305
Blood, B. P. 278
Bodleian Library, University of Oxford xxxi
Bok, Edward 313
Bonnefis, P. 179
Bosanquet, Bernard 207, 274
Boswell, James 124
Bradley, F. H. xxix, 105, 185, 207, 209, 217, 235, 248, 258–62, 412–14
Bradshaw, David xxviii
Braybrooke, Neville 8

Exodus 144, 284–5
Ezekiel 205, 285

Faber, Geoffrey 292
Faust 171–2
Ferry, Anne 6
FitzGerald, Edward xxxvii–xxxviii, 244,
    309–10
Flanagan, Hallie 113
Flaubert, Gustave 187, 217, 222, 232, 404,
    410
Fletcher, Ian 267
Fletcher, J. Gould 6
Flint, F. S. 389
Forbes, E. W. 321
Ford, John 394
Fort, Paul 147
Francatelli, C. E. 151
Francis, St, of Assisi 144
Frazer, J. G. 118, 209, 223, 239
Freud, Sigmund 208
Frost, Robert 388

Gallup, Donald xiii–xviii, xxviii, xxxvii, 59,
    199, 203, 208, 211, 215, 294
Gardner, Helen 155, 180, 215, 221, 226,
    230, 289
Garnett, Constance 188
Gauguin, Paul 249
Gautier, Judith 212
Gautier, Théophile 149, 158, 211, 283,
    291, 366, 403
Genesis 280
Gilbert, W. S. 104, 151–2, 165–6, 168,
    173–4, 247, 252, 254–5, 287, 321
Goethe 171–2
Golden Treasury, The 121, 134, 196, 234
Gordon, Lyndall xviii, 124, 176–7, 269
Gourmont, Remy de 8–9, 104, 139, 196,
    232, 248, 269, 404, 408, 410
Grant, Raymond 120
Gray, John 107, 109, 141, 163, 167, 266–
    9, 287–9
Gray, Thomas 132, 134, 275
Green, T. H. 7, 105, 114, 166, 185–6, 235,
    244, 260
Greene, Edward J. H. 120, 294, 402, 407–
    8
Griffiths, Eric 121, 158–9
Gross, Harvey 269, 272
Guiney, Louise Imogen 204

H.D. 389
Haggard, Rider 280
Haigh-Wood, Maurice 301
Hall, Donald xiii

Hanscom, Beatrice 153
Hardy, Thomas 107, 119, 252, 395
Hare, Augustus and Julius 155
Harris, Bernard 120
Harris, Wilson 284
Harry Ransom Humanities Research Center,
    Austin xv, xxv, 149, 176, 411
Hartmann, Eduard von 120, 139, 207
Harvard Advocate 105, 108, 116, 127,
    144, 147–8, 165, 211, 245, 277, 408
Haussmann, W. A. 119, 122, 125, 161,
    260
Hawker, Robert Stephen 209–10
Hawthorne, Nathaniel 116, 130, 145, 163,
    231
Hayward Bequest, King's College,
    Cambridge 105, 126, 199, 203, 229,
    248, 285, 296, 321, 388, 396, 407
Hayward, John 6, 180, 221, 230, 248, 289,
    292
Hebrews 263
Hegel, G. W. F. 173, 308, 413
Heine, Heinrich 204
Herbert, George 144–5, 160
Hermes, Gertrude xix
Hinkley, Eleanor 116, 149, 191, 219, 299
Hinton, C. H. 160
Hirsch, David H. xiii
Hobbes, Thomas 214
Hollander, John 206, 283
Holmes, Anne 120, 229
Homer 159, 237, 287–8, 389, 391
Hood, Thomas 138, 160
Hook, Theodore 254
Horace 105
Hosea 263
Houghton Library, Harvard University
    xxiv, 4, 105, 134, 141, 150, 152, 164,
    173, 185–7, 194, 199, 207–8, 212, 217,
    220, 222, 229, 233, 235, 238, 242, 244,
    249, 252, 259–62, 268, 271, 273–4, 278,
    297–8, 308, 310, 321, 381, 401, 409
Housman, A. E. 144
Howatson, M. C. 171
Howells, W. D. 107, 266
Hulme, T. E. 389
Hunt, Leigh 151
Huntington Library 208, 256, 267
Hutchinson, Mary xxv, 9
Huxley, Aldous 217
Huysmans, J.-K. 199

Isaiah 181, 189, 194, 263

Jacob, Max 402
Jain, Manju xviii

James, Henry xxiv, xxx, 9, 113, 145, 147, 164, 169–70, 181, 183, 191, 193, 205, 211, 234–5, 249, 268, 298, 302, 309, 385, 387
James, William 112, 208, 239, 247–8, 278
Jammes, Francis 147, 295, 402
Jarry, Alfred 103
Jeans, James 126
Jeffery, Violet M. xxviii
Jerome, Jerome K. 8
Job 114, 183, 189, 272, 279–80
Joel 243
John, St, gospel 181, 258, 263; epistles 195
John, St, of the Cross 152, 249
John, St, the Baptist 268
Johnson, Lionel 396, 403
Johnson, Samuel xxxiii, 124, 175, 308
Jones, David xix
Jonson, Ben xxxviii, 104, 146, 273
Joyce, James 174, 230, 291, 321

Kahn, Gustave 127, 402
Kant, Immanuel 105, 259
Kauffer, E. McKnight xix
Kaye, Richard 268
Keats, John 129, 138, 144, 147, 182, 188, 190, 200, 206, 209, 226, 231–2, 234, 244, 263
Killorin, Joseph 249
Kings 226
Kipling, Rudyard xxviii, 6, 123, 141, 149, 158, 160–1, 169, 171, 187, 223, 227, 239–40, 243, 270, 275–7, 288–9, 297–8, 395
Kissane, James 114, 141
Kleist, Heinrich von 103
Knight, G. Wilson 136, 259
Kreymborg, Alfred 103
Kumar, Shiv K. 412

Laforgue, Jules xii, xvi, xxx–xxxii, 103–8, 110–13, 116, 120–1, 124, 126–7, 130–2, 134–9, 141–3, 146–8, 151, 153, 156, 158–9, 162–3, 168, 174–6, 179, 189, 192, 206–7, 217, 228–9, 232, 236, 240–1, 243–4, 251–2, 283, 294, 299, 309, 331, 366, 387–8, 390, 394, 397, 399–410
Landor, W. S. 201
Lawrence, D. H. 292
Le Goffic, Charles 294–5
Lear, Edward 122, 167
Léautaud, Paul 104, 127, 153, 158, 204, 294, 402, 408
Lehar, Franz 148
Leland, Charles Godfrey 206

Lemprière, John 238
Leonardo da Vinci 268, 292
Lewis, Wyndham 123, 208, 305, 307
Leyris, Pierre xxxvii, xl–xli
Lippmann, Walter 194
Longfellow, Henry Wadsworth 110, 211
Lorrain, Jean 153
Loti, Pierre 295
Lovelace, Richard 175
Lowry, Robert 288–9
Lucas, F. L. 392–4
Lucian 344
Luke, St, gospel 144, 226
Lusitania, the 299

Mackail, J. W. 177
Madden, Edward 171
Maeterlinck, Maurice 103, 124, 256, 402, 409
Magdalene College, Cambridge xix, xxvi, 218
Mairet, Philip xxv
Mallarmé, Stéphane xxv, 108, 289, 388, 403–4, 406
Mantegna, Andrea 268–9
March, Richard 249, 297
Marchand, Leslie A. 234
Marino, G. B. 235
Maritain, Jacques 410
Marlowe, Christopher 331, 391–2, 394
Marston, John 195
Marston, Philip Bourke 236
Martin, Graham 207
Martin, Hugh 214, 253
Martin, Stoddard 120
Marvell, Andrew 133, 139, 189, 228–9, 239, 242
Mason, Eudo C. xv, 176, 411
Massinger, Thomas 164
Masterman, C. F. G. 114, 141
Masters, Edgar Lee 196
Materer, Timothy 123, 208, 305
Matthew, St, gospel 281
Mauclair, Camille 402
Maurras, Charles 410
Mayer, John T. xviii, 9, 124, 160, 251, 262
McKeldin Library, University of Maryland xviii, 76–7, 79, 92–3, 256, 267
Melville, Herman 206
Memling, Hans 268
Meredith, George xix, xxiv, 111, 153, 156, 196, 201, 242, 309
Merrill, Stuart 162, 165, 208, 212, 217, 233, 291
Merry Widow, The 148
Merz, J. T. 121, 250

II T. S. ELIOT'S WORKS

(i) poetry; (ii) plays; (iii) prose; (iv) letters; (v) interviews

(i) poetry:

(ii) plays:

(iii) prose:

(iv) letters:

(v) interviews

Index of Titles and First Lines